"What's a theologian, whose speciality it the nature of humanity? Isn't Reformed il depravity, itself a crime against humanit e and other contemporary questions, argui - swer the big questions about meaning, id s they can position themselves in relation tʊ ᴜʊᴅ ᴀɴᴅ ᴛᴏ ᴛнᴇ story of God's relationship to humanity attested in Scripture. To an age poised between modern confidence in science that reduces humanity to its materiality and postmodern suspicion of fixed forms that throws open the Pandora's box of human plasticity, Farris calls for a reconsideration of the biblical narrative and a retrieval of the way the church has traditionally interpreted it. While not shirking the contemporary challenges—their name is Legion—Farris here lets Jesus Christ, the God-man and light of the world, illumine what it means to be human."

—**Kevin J. Vanhoozer**, Trinity Evangelical Divinity School

"Farris offers an eminently analytical account of theological anthropology that will appeal to readers from a variety of Christian denominational backgrounds. Don't be fooled by the textbook appearance: this volume contains plenty of incisive engagements with both historic and contemporary perspectives that both esteem and plague the human condition. This is a kaleidoscopic theology and philosophy in ten jam-packed chapters."

—**Paul Allen**, Corpus Christi College

"Joshua Farris has written a very helpful book on a timely topic. Contemporary discussions of the nature of humans are fraught with confusion and opacity. Yet theology has much to offer to alleviate these plights. With clarity and charity, Farris treats a myriad of pertinent topics in this principled introductory text. Scripturally grounded, historically informed, philosophically savvy, and scientifically engaged, this book offers a provocative and compelling theological vision for humanity's place in God's cosmos."

—**James M. Arcadi**, Trinity Evangelical Divinity School

"Joshua Farris is a leading figure in the resurgent field of theological anthropology. In this excellent volume, he distills years of first-rate research into a lively and informative introduction to the subject. This introduction is philosophically savvy as well as theologically substantive in its content and argument. Farris begins every chapter with scriptural and cultural material to prompt initial questions, which he then brings into conversation with the catholic or holy tradition. Along the way, he expounds the body-soul relationship, creaturely and divine purpose, beatific vision, and deification, boldly pointing the way for Protestants committed to a robust account of theological anthropology."

—**Jerry L. Walls**, Houston Baptist University

An
Introduction
to Theological
Anthropology

An Introduction to Theological Anthropology

HUMANS,
BOTH CREATURELY AND DIVINE

JOSHUA R. FARRIS

Baker Academic
a division of Baker Publishing Group
Grand Rapids, Michigan

Published by Baker Academic
a division of Baker Publishing Group
PO Box 6287, Grand Rapids, MI 49516-6287
www.bakeracademic.com

Printed in the United States of America

Library of Congress Cataloging-in-Publication Data
Names: Farris, Joshua R., author.
Title: An introduction to theological anthropology : humans, both creaturely and divine /
    Joshua R. Farris.
Description: Grand Rapids : Baker Academic, a division of Baker Publishing Group, 2020. |
    Includes bibliographical references and index.
Identifiers: LCCN 2018059471 | ISBN 9780801096884 (pbk.)
Subjects: LCSH: Theological anthropology—Christianity.
Classification: LCC BT701.3 .F367 2020 | DDC 233—dc23
LC record available at https://lccn.loc.gov/2018059471

ISBN 978-1-5409-6216-4 (casebound)

20   21   22   23   24   25   26   7 6 5 4 3 2 1

To my grandparents James R. Brown and Dorthene Brown,
for your examples of how to live and die

Contents

Foreword

MARC CORTEZ

Humanity is a hot topic in today's world. You don't have to look far to find discussions about what it means to be human—occasionally identified as such but often approached through conversations that on the surface are more about ethics, politics, and other social issues. However, debates about sexuality, race, medical technologies, parenting, education, and other similar discussions ultimately express various visions of what it means to be human and how that should shape our visions of human flourishing in the world today. Once people see this, they usually come to appreciate rather quickly the vital importance of thinking about anthropology today.

Yet if you ask people about specifically *Christian* perspectives on what it means to be human, it will not take long to hear about three problematic ideas, each of which seems to render many Christian anthropologies suspect, if not downright harmful. In one corner, we have substance dualism, which many view as sundering the spiritual from the physical, creating a hierarchy in which the true meaning of humanity is found in the higher, spiritual realities of the immortal soul that ultimately trump mundane things like eating, drinking, and having sex. Such a view seems inevitably to denigrate created realities in general and the human body in particular. In another corner, we have Reformed theology with its doctrine of total depravity, in which not only are all human persons guilty of sin (Christ excepted) but also every aspect of human existence has been thoroughly corrupted by sin. For many, such a view seems to make sin such a prominent focus of a Christian anthropology that we lose the ability to appreciate the goodness and beauty of the human person, viewing ourselves only as objects of wrath and condemnation. Finally, in the corner that completes our unholy anthropological triangle, we have traditional ideas about the creation of the human person, whereby God immediately creates each and every human soul. As comforting as it might have been in earlier eras to emphasize God's direct role in the creation of each unique human person, such a quaint idea seems to many to be utterly untenable in the light of what we now know about the evolutionary history of humanity and the inseparable relationship between the mind/soul and the body, which requires a more complicated, messier, and less immediate way of understanding God's role in the creation of humanity.

On this account, holding any one of these views is probably sufficient to render your anthropology troubling; unwisely adding a second would move your anthropology into the dangerous category; and if you were foolish enough to include all three in a single anthropology, you should probably just go sit in the corner and not talk to anyone until you've changed your mind.

Yet that is precisely what Joshua Farris has done with *An Introduction to Theological Anthropology*. More than merely summarizing various key issues and debates—though the book certainly does this well—Farris offers us a constructive account of an anthropological world that has become foreign territory to many, inviting us to consider the power and the coherence of a vision of humanity that has shaped much of Christian theology from the beginning and that continues to represent the views of many Christians around the world today. Farris not only is well aware of the kinds of worries so quickly summarized above but also takes us on a whirlwind tour of a broad range of arguments that suggest this view has the resources to address each: a substance dualism that embraces the material, a Reformed anthropology that celebrates the human person, and a creationist view of the soul that understands the complexity of modern science. In addition, this book not only seeks to address those classic worries but also demonstrates ways in which such an anthropology has unique resources for engaging contemporary discussions about the significance of the body, gender and sexuality, human freedom, race, disability, and others.

I would thus like to take this as an opportunity to extend an invitation to two different kinds of readers. If you just need a book that raises a host of fundamental questions about Christian perspectives on what it means to be human, surveys some of the key positions taken, and helps you understand why those discussions matter for life and ministry today, you will find much of value in what follows. However, I want to extend a special invitation to those most likely to disagree with this book's conclusions, those already convinced that things like substance dualism and a Reformed emphasis on original sin are simply untenable in modern conceptions of the human person. Even if you remain unconvinced by the various arguments offered here—and I would certainly choose different paths in several key places—this book will provide a journey worth making, an opportunity to see afresh a classic view of humanity, though one that has been "updated" by being brought into dialogue with contemporary questions and concerns. At the very least, you may find yourself coming to see that this view has a kind of power and coherence you had not previously appreciated.

As the psalmist asks, "What are mere mortals that you should think about them, human beings that you should care for them?" (Ps. 8:4 NLT). That question has pursued God's people throughout the ages, with each answer inevitably shaping our identities and ways of living in the world. In this book, Joshua Farris has given us a tremendous resource for exploring together one answer to that question along with its various implications across a range of issues. Take this as an opportunity to see old answers in new ways, maybe gaining as well a greater sense of why so many Christians over the years have found this approach to the psalmist's question so compelling.

Preface

Humans—Creaturely and Divine

You made them a little lower than the angels.

Hebrews 2:7

... That you may be filled to the measure of all the fullness of God.

Ephesians 3:19

With all the noise of contemporary culture, it might seem rather ambitious to advance a theological vision of the human. In the present climate, passionate discussions on the nature and purpose of the human are at the center of social, political, and cultural understandings. With discussions on the appropriate vision of sex or race relations, it is apparent that we are living in a time deeply divided in our understanding of the human. Some suggest that humans are biological accidents with a unique autonomy in the world. Others argue that humans are the central objects for God's creative and redemptive purposes. The central and driving question behind all these complicated issues has to do with what we mean by the term *human*. What is the human being?

The contemporary social and theological anthropology literature in several cases (e.g., Kathryn Tanner, Ingolf Dalferth) paints a picture of humanity merely as changeable, feeble, and contingent. Contemporary science often portrays the human as wholly physical in nature without an immaterial part, and it is not uncommon for contemporary philosophy and theology to follow the lead of the sciences.[1] Among those who are theistically inclined, some carve out space for the transcendent (i.e., an attribute often ascribed to God for his externality from the world and his not being limited by creaturely contingencies, such that even when God is active in the natural world, it is his transcendent and other-world nature that is manifest) and immaterial (i.e., nonmaterial; typically intended to convey that immaterial substances are nonspatially extended) nature of human beings, while others firmly reject the transcendent and immaterial nature of human beings, seeking to find meaning and significance in the immanent processes of human life, albeit grounded in divine action. All of these approaches to the human represent humanity in its creaturely and deeply embodied life.

Other theologians, driven by ancient and traditional readings of the Bible, seek another kind of vision. They see the enduring and transcendent values embedded in human practice and customs as pointing to and requiring a transcendent immaterial reality that grounds and propels us forward to the divine. Some of these enduring values emerge in the context of human interaction and include justice, love, goodness, and beauty. The inevitable confrontation with these values in our conscious states of awareness presses us to imagine reality as something higher and deeper than the physical reality in which we embroil ourselves.[2] We necessarily require some higher transcendent being to ground and make sense of a reality that reflects these transcendent and enduring values. In this spirit, I offer some reasons to think that this requires that we, too, are immaterial and bear some transcendence as immaterial beings.

A theology of God and humans who are immaterial (otherwise called "souls" or "spirits") overlaps with an important topic in the history of philosophy and theology: the meaning of life. Historically, the debate has been over atheism (e.g., the belief that God does not exist and that this is central to one's worldview; instead nature supplies an explanation for all that occurs) and theism (e.g., the belief that God, or a supernatural being, exists and is central to one's worldview and that this being makes sense of the world's origins, morality, meaning, and purpose). There is a long-standing belief in the history of the Christian tradition, along with the other major monotheistic

1. One useful resource in the "science and religion" literature is Murphy and Knight, *Human Identity*. For a collection of essays on human identity that is informed by the scientific findings and is also sympathetic to the view that humans have or are souls, see Swinburne, *Free Will and Modern Science*.

2. This understanding of humans and the world is, arguably, common to the patristic theologians in early Christianity. The fact of transcendence is found uniquely in Scripture, tradition, and the sacraments as aspects of Christian revelation through the Spirit, which corresponds to the soul/spirit of human beings. For a helpful treatment, see Boersma, *Scripture as Real Presence*, esp. 131–58.

religions, that God and the soul are necessary conditions for life to be meaningful or, alternatively, necessary for the most meaningful life or the achievement of eternal meaning. And we are now seeing a revival of interest in this discussion in recent years with greater nuance than previously established. Thaddeus Metz has recently summarized the contemporary discussion by carving out not two positions but four positions.[3] He calls the four positions "extreme supernaturalism," "moderate naturalism," "moderate supernaturalism," and "extreme naturalism." "Naturalism" is a term that describes reality as predominantly explicable in terms of natural and physical processes alone, and, generally, these are atheistic in outlook. In other words, on these views both God and the soul are not necessary for life to be meaningful, and, according to extreme versions, the belief is that God and soul would undermine the meaningfulness of life.[4] Given that theism is the outlook of the present work, I am most interested in offering reasons for supernaturalism either in its "extreme" or "moderate" forms. For the achievement of life's meaning, internal to the Christian tradition is that God is the ultimate meaning for all of creation and that the soul is necessary to experience the fullness of life eternal in the age to come. We will look at some of these reasons in chapters 1, 2, and, especially, chapters 9 and 10.

Other reasons we might suggest for why God and the soul are important have to do with the relational connection that a soul has to God and the fulfillment of the soul's desire for God; these topics we will touch on in every chapter that follows.[5] Central to *An Introduction to Theological Anthropology* is that humans are both creaturely (e.g., in short, the view that all things that are not God are created by God and depend on God for their existence) and divine (e.g., the view that humans are not literally God [or gods] but that human purpose is fulfilled in union with God and that humans become partakers of God, as Peter states in 2 Pet. 1:4), and this is made sense of in light of ancient belief that humans are essentially souls (or spirits) that have

---

3. Metz, *God, Soul and the Meaning of Life*.

4. One reason that might be suggested for why belief in God and soul would undermine the meaningfulness of life is that it would hinder or undermine personal autonomy, and the belief in God and soul would seem to yield the reality of the afterlife where souls are met with just rewards and punishments for their obedience to or violations of God's commands.

5. One reason for assuming the stronger version of supernaturalism—"extreme supernaturalism"—is that meaning is an all-or-nothing state of affairs based on a particular metaphysic that the meaningfulness of human life is predicated on our participation in God's life. While this position is common to the Christian tradition, I do not argue for it here, although it may be assumed in my notion of deification, which we will look at in chaps. 6 and 10. The more modest reasons for thinking that supernaturalism is important to the meaning of life come from the possibility of achieving one's purpose in the afterlife, acquiring eternal good in the afterlife through God, and other related reasons. See Metz, *God, Soul and the Meaning of Life*, 27–34.

a unique connection to their Creator in creation and in redemption. While there are other views of human constitution and purpose on offer in evangelical thought, I will lay out these other views and argue in favor of humans as ensouled beings with a unique connection to God that is fulfilled in union with God. We will touch on these options as well as other details of the God-human relationship in what follows.

It is true that the volume you have in your hands is a brief introduction to theological anthropology, so you may be expecting a mere survey of topics and some of the prominent views. To be sure, I intend to make good on that expectation. However, I also intend to advance an overarching vision of humanity that is consistent with ancient and biblically driven views of the human and that, at the same time, is commensurate with and informed by contemporary reflections from the sciences. In other words, don't let the word *introduction* throw you. The present volume is traditionally disposed, given my intention to portray the human as both creaturely and divine (i.e., divine in purpose but not as if we are demigods as in ancient Greek religions). Many theological anthropologies are concerned with the creaturely or fallen nature of humanity, but such a vision, by itself, is myopic and limited. When a broader swath of data facilitates our understanding and reception of biblical revelation, it yields an integrated vision of humanity as heavenly as well as earthly. By "heavenly" I am not necessarily communicating the notion that souls are made out of heavenly stuff—assuming there is such a thing—although souls may have properties in common with heavenly beings. At a minimum, I mean to convey that souls, particularly human souls, have a destiny—heaven.

How to Use This Book

This book is a critical survey of theological anthropology from a broadly Reformed perspective. I have not attempted to cover all the positions within theological anthropology. It is impossible to be encyclopedic in an introduction. Some may find the approach taken here too beholden to the analytic literature on personal ontology and not sympathetic enough to phenomenology or the cognitive sciences. Others will undoubtedly find it unsatisfying that I have not covered this or that topic. Some may wish that I delved deeper into biology and offered up some more detailed narrative on how it is that evolution and Christianity are compatible. Instead, what I have attempted to do well is threefold.

First, I offer a set of readings on a wide set of issues that intersect with traditional theological anthropology. In other words, I survey what I find to be the most important topics in the theology of human nature. While this is a systematic presentation of these topics, the reader can easily turn to the individual chapters and read them as self-contained units that provide summaries of many of the positions and questions often raised in the various loci within theological anthropology. This provides a starting point for additional research and reflection. My goal has been to cover topics typically treated in traditional systematic theologies in the section on theological anthropology, which brings me to the second highlight and how the reader will find it useful.

Second, I have arranged the theological topics in an arguably standard way of arranging theological loci. I have arranged these topics in such a way as to move fluidly through the biblical-theological narrative from creation to redemption to the eschaton. However, within this framework I discuss topics in a much more systematic and philosophical manner than what one typically finds in biblical theology. I do this by raising the broader philosophical questions of what, who, and why I am. I also address the topics that emerge within Christian dogmatics. Some examples include the *imago Dei* (image of God), the origin of the soul, original sin, and deification. While all of these have some grounding in the scriptural narrative (i.e., materially), they are not, properly speaking, topics (in their developed and robust form) that emerge immediately (i.e., formally) out of the text of Scripture. They require the information from the biblical material as well as the material from tradition (e.g., Reformed theology), history (ancient, medieval, and modern), philosophy, and the phenomenal data found in experience. This makes for an integrated approach in keeping with this book's systematic nature. With that in mind, though, there are plenty of resources for the biblical theologian, the systematician, and the philosopher of religion to draw from in their own projects on anthropology.

Third, while I would not claim to have supplied a comprehensive and thoroughly integrated vision of the human, I am confident that the present volume moves in that direction. What you have in your hands is more than a mere survey or academic introduction of the present issues on offer for the theologian. I offer the reader an introduction that is shaped by concerns theologians have had throughout the history of the Christian church. What this means is that some of the conclusions I offer are hardly controversial, but others are. They were not controversial throughout most of church history, but we have experienced and are presently experiencing some radical shifts away from traditionally accepted conclusions to radical revisions of the stance of the catholic church (in the common use of the term and not to be narrowly defined as Roman Catholic) on a number of issues. I attempt to present some of the relevant dogmatic material in a readable and contemporary fashion.

So while many topics are often considered outdated, I seek to remotivate the discussion and offer some reason for thinking that these discussions are still important for us today.

An Invitation

The story of humanity laid out in divine revelation begins in Genesis 1–2 with the creation of Adam and Eve, the first human pair. It shifts in Genesis 3:6 with their partaking of fruit from the tree of the knowledge of good and evil, which God commanded Adam and Eve not to eat from. In this act, on my view, the author intentionally conveys that Adam and Eve die and will die, spreading a curse to the rest of humanity, which affects the whole of creation (and will later be restored according to Rom. 8).[6] God's story of redemption begins in Genesis 3, where he clothes them and provides for their needs by prohibiting them from the tree of life. Through the establishing of covenants, God enters into relationship with Adam and those divinely chosen to represent God to humans. By establishing covenants, God gives life and blesses that life in the way described in Genesis 1. The life that Adam and Eve lost is the life of God's presence, which he restores in Jesus Christ.

Yet, there is another dimension, one that directs the human story. Human destiny is found in the vision of God. The richness of the scriptural imagery is the primary means in which God reveals himself. In the Old Testament, God reveals his glory by way of an image through the visual sense of sight. God reveals himself to Moses in Exodus 33, where Moses sees the back of God. Isaiah sees God's glory as he sits on the throne in Isaiah 6:1. Jacob sees the Lord in heaven through a dream by way of a ladder that leads to heaven in Genesis 28:12–13. Daniel has a similar vision of God on the throne in his glory in Daniel 7:9. All of this points to and anticipates the divine-human, Christ, who reveals God. As Christ states in the Sermon on the Mount, "Blessed are

---

6. The concept of death is undoubtedly a complex one that overlaps with other traditional concepts such as mortality and immortality. There is an important sense in the catholic tradition that the first humans were immortal in their relationship to God, a reality that was intended to be sustained but was lost after the first sin (i.e., primal sin). However, I take it that death has multiple complex yet related meanings that are intended in Scripture. In keeping with much of the tradition, it seems that death is a just punishment for humans, but exploring this concept in more detail deserves the attention of philosophers and theologians. For a famous debate, see Taylor, *The Scripture-Doctrine of Original Sin*; J. Edwards, "The Great Christian Doctrine of Original Sin Defended." For a contemporary view that sees humans as created mortal, pre-fall, but sees the fall as a loss of blessing found in the tree of life, see Middleton, "Death, Immortality, and the Curse."

the pure in heart, for they will see God" (Matt. 5:8). And the means by which humans see God is via Christ. In John 14:9b Christ states, "Anyone who has seen me has seen the Father." The final end of the journey for humanity is not the vision of some aspect of Christ as with his humanity or his body but to see the fullness of God in Christ. As Hans Boersma has so helpfully put it, "The only reality worthy of being called the sacramental truth (res) of our lives is the end-point of our lives: God in Christ."[7] By "sacramental" Boersma means to convey that all of created reality (i.e., natural creation and the Old Testament) is teleological in nature and points us to the triune God revealed ultimately in the person and work of Christ. Our goal is God in Christ through a vision that sums up or comprehends all of history. The last book of Scripture, Revelation, describes the final state of humans, the new heavens and the new earth, in richly visual ways. John in Revelation describes the purpose of humanity in ways that give credence to this notion of *visio Dei* (the vision of God). For in Revelation 22:4–5, "They will see his face, and his name will be on their foreheads. And night will be no more. They will need no light of lamp or sun, for the Lord God will be their light, and they will reign forever and ever" (ESV). Playing on the themes of light, it is by seeing God in Christ that humans are able to see all else, and this is the end for which humanity is created.

Christ is the light that illuminates the prominent theme of this introduction, thus the subtitle *Humans, Both Creaturely and Divine*. Christ unites the creaturely nature of humanity with divinity. While this unity is concretely defined in Christ, several Reformed theologians understand the vision of Christ as the means by which humans see God and are united to God. Unlike some ancient understandings where deification subverts our creaturely design, in Christian thought, and particularly Reformed developments of it, the vision of Christ (and, specifically, God in Christ) is the means by which humanity is affirmed and elevated through the humiliation of God the Son in the incarnation, which culminated in death.

This is the story of the Bible in a nutshell, but the story contains many other details. Tracing the details of what the Bible says isn't the end of the theological task. Instead, the theologian's task requires the hard work of organizing the categories of the Bible into a coherent system for a contemporary audience. The task of the theologian is one of faith seeking understanding in which the theologian works from the premises of faith, found in revelation and tradition, while seeking to understand those premises in light of their larger Christian framework. The task requires the hard work of engagement

7. Boersma, *Seeing God*, 11.

with other relevant anthropological disciplines such as philosophy of mind, biology, and neuroscience.

Think of *An Introduction to Theological Anthropology* as a guide. As with all guides, you will at times hike well-trodden paths. Other times, if you are lucky, the guide will take you off the beaten path, maybe even into uncharted terrain. That is what I intend to do in what follows. Undoubtedly, you, the reader, will not agree with all the details, and you may not even agree with the overarching vision. But as one of my professors stated, sometimes you need to try on a pair of boots, walk around, and see how they fit. You can always try on another pair. Or, in our age of innovation, you can always modify the boots to meet the demands of the territory at hand. Come along with me to think hard about one of the most complicated but fulfilling areas in contemporary Christian theology. Try on this vision of what it means to be human. See if it fits.

Acknowledgments

Warm thanks to Ryan Brandt for his help on the Christology material and the material on freedom of the will; even more, a special thank-you to him for his help in coauthoring an earlier published article on the beatific vision, which has come to constitute a significant portion of the last chapter in the present volume. Thanks to S. Mark Hamilton, J. T. Turner, Jerry L. Walls, Matthew Damore, Marc Cortez, Zach Stallings, and Kevin Wong for reading portions of the book or a couple of chapters and for offering several helpful suggestions and criticisms. I also thank Ryan Peterson and Matthew Levering for reading and for giving feedback on the preface and introduction, along with Ben Arbour and Tyler McNabb for general conversations about the structure of the book.

A special thanks goes to David Nelson and James Korsmo for their care, patience, and thoughtful suggestions on improving the manuscript. Many thanks to Robert Maccini, Ryan Davis, Jeffrey Reimer, and Sara Strauss for copyediting and proofing the whole manuscript. I am also appreciative of an anonymous reader who made comments on the whole manuscript. Thank you to the Carl F. H. Henry Center, The Creation Project, for granting me some time and space to finalize and make some of the last touches on the manuscript. The views represented here are my own and do not necessarily represent the views of The Creation Project or those of the John Templeton Foundation.

Introduction

Where Do We Begin?

Humans, Prolegomena, and Method

For I know the plans I have for you.
Jeremiah 29:11

This is a journey. Consider the present chapter a map or a compass. It is a map in that it lays out the various directions that will follow in what is to come. It is a compass in that it provides the basic principles for theology and a way of approaching the human. I will lay out the broad parameters for thinking about theological anthropology and situate what is to follow in the broader theological categories concerning anthropology. What we have here, then, is an opportunity to gather some of the tools necessary for the journey of exploring theological anthropology.

Human Identity as Narrative Identity

In an attempt to answer the human identity question (What does it mean to be human?), I work through three interrelated subquestions: (1) What are we by nature? (2) Who are we in relation to one another? (3) Why do we exist? I take it that all three questions are central to the question of human identity. Commonly these are dealt with in isolated fashion, as if one question is more important than the others. However, if we are to obtain a full and

1

well-rounded theological understanding of the human, then we must discuss questions of human constitution as well as questions about who we are in relation to others and why we exist.

Analytic philosophical conversations on human nature are concerned with the constitution question of what it means to be human. By "constitution" I mean to convey that humans have parts that factor in their makeup, including essential and nonessential parts. Most contemporary explorations begin with the question of whether humans are material or immaterial or both. Often found in the province of philosophy of mind, these topics have been of renewed interest to Christian philosophers and theologians as they apply the data from the philosophy of mind to a wider set of anthropological concerns. Even biblical scholars are taking note of the human constitution question in their investigations of the biblical material on what it means to be human (see Joel B. Green, N. T. Wright, and John Cooper).[1]

Materialism is the view that humans are composed essentially of material parts and that there are no immaterial parts. Dualists, on the other hand, endorse the notion that humans are composed of both material and immaterial parts. Traditionally, some sort of dualism has been the default position of the church. Many of the divines in catholic Christianity (e.g., Augustine, Anselm, Aquinas, Calvin) endorse not mere dualism but substance dualism of some variety.[2] Substance dualism is the view that humans are composed of two substances (i.e., property bearers): soul (or mind) and body. On the other end of the spectrum, from materialism are those who hold that humans are not material at all but are immaterial beings through and through (this would fit under the categories of immaterialism or person-body dualism). There are a variety of positions on what it means to be an immaterial being through and through. I will offer up just one promising example: Berkeleyan idealism, a view named after the great philosopher Bishop Berkeley. An idealist of the Berkeleyan sort believes that there are souls (or minds) and bodies but that persons, and their bodies, are only immaterial in nature. Bodies are not material substances as with the materialist above; rather, they are dependent on minds, or one mind (i.e., the divine mind), and are experiential qualities. Only

---

1. Some may be perplexed by my inclusion of the philosophical theologian John Cooper, but I include him only because he has engaged substantially with the material in Scripture on this subject.

2. There are those from both camps who wish to claim Aquinas as support for their position. In fact, many interpret Aquinas's personal ontology as fitting within monism, but, as is often pointed out, Aquinas in fact speaks of the soul as having powers distinct from other material substances and as persisting during the intermediate state after physical death. Many theologians and philosophers see this as evidence that Aquinas was a substance dualist—or something near it.

minds and their ideas exist. There is another monistic view (i.e., ontologically, or what philosophers call the structure of being and existence, humans are one kind of thing) that is neither materialism nor immaterialism, called neutral monism.[3] Defenders of neutral monism argue that reality is neither mental nor physical, fundamentally, but something else. What that something else is remains to be seen, but what defenders can say is that at rock bottom there is not mental stuff and physical stuff but rather a discrete kind of substance or stuff that gives rise to the physical and the mental. It is a negative claim that distinguishes it from materialism and dualism, but given the fact that we have satisfying positive theories of mind and reality, we will set this view aside in the present context. There are sufficiently robust theories that are sensible enough for our consideration here. I will concern myself, however, with a closer examination of the first three—materialism, dualism, and immaterialism—when I take up the nature of human identity in chapter 1.

Narrative identity has to do with both our relations and our purpose. Our story, as humans, also has something to contribute to how we understand the nature of humanity. There are two questions (or sets of questions) that are distinct. First is the question of narrative for all humans. In this way, we are interested in questions of humanity in relation to God's creation of the world. What is our vocation on earth? How do we fit into God's plan of creation? How do we fit into God's plan of redemption? What is it that distinguishes humans from the rest of creation? Second, just as the question of human constitution has a universal answer, there is also a more particular or individual answer to the question of narrative identity. What is the narrative of individual human identity? In other words, who am I in relation to other human beings? Who am I in relation to God and the order of creation? More specific questions will certainly come up when reflecting on the narrative of individual humans—for example, What is my narrative in this life? I have a distinctive contribution to make in this life in virtue of my particular background as a male or female, as a Middle Easterner or Brazilian. I am what I am in virtue of my being a barber, a teacher, a police officer, a social worker, or some other specific vocation. These questions about our narrative are fascinating, but in the present context we are interested in the broader questions that situate and make sense of these roles in society. For example, I address particular identity questions as they pertain to God's intentions for us in creation and redemption. These questions provide the broader categories in which to synthesize one's sense of ownership

---

3. *Russellian monism* is another term for the view, named after the philosopher Bertrand Russell. See Stubenberg, "Neutral Monism."

of one's life. Narrative identity is incomplete without consideration of the who and the why questions.

The second question we will look at (after the constitution question) in striving to understand human identity is, Who are we in relation to others (other human beings or our environment)? The question of who I am in relation to God's creation has something to do with the way God has made me to participate in the environment. I am a human individual who finds some meaning and significance in relation to my environment and in relation to others. I am causally dependent on my parents for my coming into the world. I am causally dependent on other humans for governing society well. I am causally dependent on other humans for flourishing. I am causally dependent on other humans for understanding parts of the world that I do not have access to because of space limitations or a lack of skill.

Human purpose shapes human identity. Why in the world are we here? Why does it matter? Why did God create us, assuming there is a God? One of the assumptions of the present book is that we have a distinct purpose as God's image bearers on the earth and that this ought to shape how we perceive all the particularities of our situation and story in the modern world. The narrative of humans from Genesis to Revelation provides for us the framework for thinking about human purpose.

How Should We Approach the Study of Human Nature?

Answering the questions above requires stepping back to answer a broader question in Christian theology: What are we studying when we study Christian theology? The short answer is this: we are studying the trinitarian God of Christian monotheism.[4] God is foundational and central to the study of Christian theology. More specifically, Christian systematic theology considers the question of God in relation to his acts (e.g., creative and redemptive acts). The whole of Christian theology can be categorized accordingly.[5] Humans are products of God's highest acts in creation and redemption. It is important to note that the study of creation and redemption is a study of God and his acts because they serve as the macrocategories for thinking about the world, and more specifically humans, in one unified vision. Guided by this

4. For an introductory work on the basics of the Christian faith as codified in the Nicene creedal tradition, see Heine, *Classical Christian Doctrine*. For a more thorough treatment of the Nicene tradition as the background, context, and boundaries for theological reflection, see Young, *From Nicaea to Chalcedon*.

5. See Webster, *Confessing God*. Also see a distinct version of theism called "theistic personalism" in Morris, *Our Idea of God*.

macrosystematic understanding, I will recommend several guiding principles for our study of the human.

I am working specifically within what might broadly be referred to as the evangelical Reformed tradition. By "evangelical" I intend to convey the idea that the Bible is the norming norm—that is, the norm that norms all other norms. The Bible is the highest authority for theological development. However, we must understand that the Bible is the church's book; hence, Scripture (divine revelation given to Christ's redemptive community) is intended to be read and appropriated in the community of faith. Following from this, there are other theological authorities involved in the appropriate placement of the building blocks that constitute Christian theology. These include creedal statements (e.g., the Apostles' Creed, the Nicene Creed, the Athanasian Creed), conciliar statements recognized by the universal church (e.g., the First and Second Ecumenical Councils), confessional statements (e.g., the Thirty-Nine Articles of Religion, the Westminster Confession), and the great theologians within one's tradition, reason, and experience. At this point, it might help to introduce a term that, as used here, may be new to some readers. The present book advances a theological anthropology that is also *catholic*. By "catholic" I basically mean to convey that theology is the product of the church's (i.e., the universal church's) ongoing reflections on doctrine conveyed to contemporary society yet not divorced from its historical development within this broad tradition, or Tradition. By "Reformed," in the phrase "evangelical Reformed tradition," I am roughly describing the tradition that renovated the church by steering it away from the doctrinal excesses found in the Roman Catholic Church concerning the relationship between Scripture and Tradition, justification, sanctification, ecclesiological excesses in papal teachings, and, potentially, soteriological excesses concerning Mary.

Some may call the tradition "catholic Reformed." By placing "catholic" first, one is highlighting the priority of the catholic church over all the major subtraditions (Roman Catholicism, Eastern Orthodoxy, and Protestant Christianity).[6] One is giving not only logical priority to being catholic but also significance to one's identity as a catholic. Otherwise, one might refer to the present tradition as "Reformed catholic" so as to place an emphasis on "Reformed" as a descriptor of the catholic church.[7] The concern with using

---

6. For one helpful recent attempt to publicly advance a statement of unity, see "A Reforming Catholic Confession," https://reformingcatholicconfession.com. The present statement casts a broad net that is quite evangelical. The framers are operating with a view of "Reformed" or "Reforming" as nearly synonymous with Protestant.

7. In this context I am not attempting to specify the name "Reformed catholic" merely to Presbyterians or Anglicans, although some use it in that refined sense. Nor am I attempting to

this language is that the Reformed tradition is conceived of as one part of the larger church. One might prefer "Reformed Catholic" so as to highlight the church catholic while not subjugating the term *Reformed* to one description of catholic among many. The influential sixteenth-century English theologian William Perkins uses this term *Reformed Catholic* to describe the Reformed tradition in his Puritan context. He describes it in the following way: "By a Reformed Catholic, I understand anyone that holds the same necessary heads of religion with the Roman Church: yet so as he pares off and rejects all errors in doctrine (i.e., the parameters of which one theologizes), whereby the said religion is corrupted."[8]

I might add to this that a church is catholic if that church falls within a certain confessional stance and practice. Herein, the semitechnical term *rule of faith* (i.e., the standard by which we judge the interpretation of specific doctrines; carried along in the first four ecumenical councils, though some accept the first seven ecumenical conciliar statements) becomes important for describing churches as "catholic."[9] It seems to me that there are two necessary conditions for a church to be catholic. First, the church must confess the first four to seven ecumenical creeds within the Nicene tradition. By "confess" I mean to convey the idea that the creedal truths function as a guide to one's reading of the Scriptures and are the rubric for organizing theology (e.g., that God is creator of all things; we are creatures; Christ's incarnation, death, and ascension are the central events in creation and redemption; the church is unified and is the sphere of God's redemptive activity).[10] Second,

---

exclude Baptists from the fold of catholicity—that is, as noncatholic. There may be a sense in which Baptists could call themselves catholic, but this is an open discussion and an issue that deserves additional attention. This is relevant to the human story. For a useful contemporary exposition of an infant baptism perspective within the Reformed tradition that understands baptism in terms of external regeneration, see Sutton, *Signed, Sealed and Delivered*. For a sacramental believer's baptism perspective that assumes some version of regeneration, see Hicks and Taylor, *Down in the River to Pray*. The questions about how baptism is related to one's understanding of church and the individual not only bear on the human story but also tell us something about human nature. For example, an infant baptism perspective, of the kind advanced by Sutton, arguably presumes that humans are regenerate in terms of a status change (not in terms of internal regeneration), legally recognized as part of the covenant family at baptism, and granted a unique blessing. Human identity is necessarily (maybe essentially) covenantal and communal. There is a small but growing body of literature on baptism in relation to theological anthropology, but there is a need for additional research and reflection on this topic and the implications for other doctrinal topics.

8. Perkins, *Reformed Catholicke*, 555. Also see Warfield, *Westminster Standards*, 4.

9. For information on the first seven ecumenical councils, see "The 21 Ecumenical Councils," New Advent, http://www.newadvent.org/library/almanac_14388a.htm.

10. There are several other themes that should function as organizing concepts for how we think about humans. For example, in the Nicene Creed and the Chalcedonian statement, Christ's end implies human purpose.

this confessional stance has an impact on the reception and the practice of the church service (i.e., the "rule of practice").[11] In other words, the practice of the church has a sacramental order that is passed down from generation to generation. For example, the practice of the church concerning baptism understands baptism as one baptism for the forgiveness of sins (i.e., some understanding of regeneration is in order).[12]

It is in this broader context that we should understand and work out our theology. This applies to Christian theology generally and to anthropology specifically. With that in mind, in order to develop an appropriate understanding of the human, we must not just take up and read the Bible; we must also read it in light of what the church catholic has said in response to it. In this way, the readings, appropriations, and goals of the church have a role to play in the present dogmatic exercise concerning anthropology. So long as the church does not contradict a clear teaching of Scripture, we ought to understand the *anthropos* (the Greek word used for the human) not only as a product for philosophical speculation but also as a product that is ultimately understood in light of God's revelation to his church.

First, the study of the anthropos is properly directed to God as the final purpose of humanity and the proper object of worship. While this guiding principle is about God, it also communicates something important about humanity. Humans are created and redeemed by God. Humans are fully revealed by God in the Christian Scriptures. Given that the Scriptures yield the idea that humans are created by God as his unique creation and are central to his redemptive purposes, humans are intended for some kind of relationship to God.

Second, the study of the anthropos requires not mere analytic dissection of parts but rather attention to the whole macrostructure within Christian dogmatics (i.e., the doctrinal and theological essentials or central truths that constitute the one true faith passed down from the apostles and embodied in

11. Arguably, there is a catholic tradition, or Tradition, that is united on essential Christian truth following Ephesians 4:5. I have suggested that the unity of the church comes in two forms, doctrinal unity and practical unity. How we think about that unity also depends on other ecclesiological assumptions. The Roman Catholic Church has a centralized government that terminates in the Roman bishop—that is, the pope. The Reformed church often emphasizes a "confessionalism" as a form of unity. There is also a conciliar form of unity reflected in authoritative doctrinal statements as the culmination of received wisdom, which is characteristic of the Anglican Communion and, arguably, the Reformed tradition.

12. Allen and Swain, *Reformed Catholicity*, 1–17. The notion that catholicity is characterized by the "rule of faith" in the church's doctrine and practice seems to reflect the basic idea in Allen and Swain's helpful work. Allen and Swain are developing this notion from their tradition as Presbyterians, but much of what they develop applies more broadly to the Reformed tradition. For an Anglican perspective on what it means to be Reformed Catholic, see Fenwick, *Anglican Ecclesiology*, 414–28.

the life of the one universal church), reflecting the narrative of Scripture. In this way, an appropriate understanding of the human takes into account not only divine acts but also the logical relationship that the individual *imago* has to creation, to sin, to redemption, and to the eschaton.[13]

Third, the study of the anthropos requires situation in traditional sources of theological knowledge. By "traditional sources of theological knowledge" I mean to convey that there are normative sources that ought and commonly do inform our theological reflections, which include Scripture, tradition (or "Holy Tradition"), reason, and experience. In the present volume, I am interested in how the wider study of Christian dogmatics impinges on and informs our understanding of the nature of human beings in relation to God. Christian dogmatics is the study of theology in light of the conceptual topics that are central to a Christian understanding about a particular subject.[14] I like to think about the subject as theo-conceptual architecture because the dogmatician (i.e., systematic theologian) is seeking to put all the pieces together to make up one larger edifice.[15] Contemporary Christian dogmatics is similar to a jigsaw puzzle. As with a jigsaw puzzle, the pieces of systematic theology are shaped, affected, and colored by the other parts that compose the whole. In other words, the study of human nature is not reducible to the study of scriptural passages or the siphoning out of the doctrine of the *imago Dei* from the other categories. Rather, it is a study of the pieces in light of the whole. In studying a magnificent piece of art, you might focus your attention on one facet of the piece, but that aspect can be properly appreciated only in light of the whole. In photography, for example, a master photographer often focuses the lens in such a way as to highlight one feature of the whole picture. The focus may be on a bride with her bridesmaids in the background or on a rose in a field of green. By isolating, we are not severing but rather focusing. The traditional sources help us to read the biblical narrative on humans in this way.

At the center of the biblical narrative about humans is the notion of covenantal representation. In Genesis, God makes a covenant at creation. Humans are God's covenantal representatives in the world. Functionally and relationally, humans represent God to the world and the world to God. And

13. For one helpful model for approaching the task of systematic theology from an analytic perspective, see McCall, *Analytic Christian Theology*.

14. For one fine example in the Reformation tradition, see Bavinck, *Reformed Dogmatics*. The section on the image of God in *Synopsis of a Purer Theology* provides clear parameters for a Reformed theological anthropology; Velde, *Synopsis*, 1:314–38.

15. For a discussion about theological method, see Farris and Arcadi, "Introduction to the Topical Issue." For a variety of different perspectives, see the entire special issue of *Open Theology* that this piece introduces.

God carries along the redemptive story, based on the blueprint from creation, through the covenants of the Old Testament into the New Testament. In the New Testament all of the Old Testament promises to humans are not replaced, undermined, or subverted but rather fulfilled and, arguably, transfigured in the person and work of Christ.[16]

Fourth, the study of the anthropos ought to be situated in the habits of the wider church, such as prayer, the study of and meditation on Scripture, and fasting. As the object shapes and informs our understanding of the human, so our modes of thinking and practices—reflecting those of the saints and theologians who precede us—affect the study of theological anthropology.[17] Traditionally, systematic theology was seen as a discipline that has God as the focus of study, but God is not simply a focus of intellectual study but also the focus of one's dispositions rightly ordered. The purpose, then, is not simply to organize doctrinal topics but to simultaneously perceive, experience, and see God and his actions in creation and redemption.

Fifth, the study of the anthropos should be informed by other disciplines relevant to the physical and social aspects of humans. Reflecting theologically on the physical and social sciences has shaped and continues to shape our thinking about the human and the contingent questions it raises for a vision of the human.[18] Throughout the course of this book, I draw from disciplines beyond theology as they impinge on the study of human nature.

All that said, the present method is concerned with truth—truth about the human—rather than merely facts, such as the biological data suggesting that humans have been around several million years or what the Bible says about human beings. The present method is motivated by the desire to acquire knowledge of what the Bible means and not just what it says.

16. For a helpful treatment, see Maston and Reynolds, *Anthropology and New Testament Theology*.

17. Ryan Peterson has rightly highlighted this important aspect of theology when commenting on the movement of analytic theology. While he is somewhat sympathetic to the movement and consequentially the fruit it has and will bear, he is concerned that the practitioners of the movement have drunk more deeply from analytic philosophy of religion than from traditional catholic Christian sources as well as the practices characterizing the life of the church. He develops his argument in the broad context of thinking about theology in light of the beatific vision. The whole process of theology should, according to Peterson, point us to the divine and help us gain a clearer vision of God. See R. Peterson, "Theological Predication."

18. This is reflected in a host of contemporary theological works. Several organizations are devoted to this kind of exploration (e.g., the John Templeton Foundation; BioLogos; the Center for Science and Culture at the Discovery Institute). It is also reflected heavily in several journals (e.g., the *Journal of Theology and Science*; *Zygon*; *European Journal of Science and Theology*; *Perspectives on Science and Christian Belief*).

Necessarily, the search for truth does not settle for what one discipline says but rather seeks after coherent meaning informed by all the disciplines. Without situating all the facts about the human in a wider theological framework, the study of the human is cut short. Theological knowledge situates and gives meaning to all the facts of human existence. The study of the human, then, is a meaningful interdisciplinary exercise guided by theology and directed to theology.

Biology has a place in our theological anthropology. If we take it that humans are evolutionarily generated beings, at least with respect to their physical parts, then biology will have a role in shaping the story that we put forward concerning humans. I will touch on these issues (e.g., Adam, the origin of souls, original sin) to some degree in several chapters. Undoubtedly, some will see biology as having a more fundamental role in shaping our understanding of the human.[19]

Cognitive science or the brain sciences also inform our anthropology. Particularly, cognitive science plays an important role in raising questions about human constitution and the mind-body relation.[20] That relation is one of the key themes of this volume, and I will touch on some of the findings in the brain sciences as we consider that key facet of what it means to be human.

The social sciences, too, have a meaningful role to play when interrogating the human story. What we are in the larger human story has something to do with what we create. Despite what Jürgen Moltmann has argued, we are not solely historical products or products of a narrative waiting to be revealed.[21] Neither are we products of the social class controversies, as is often advanced by Marxists. Instead, I am assuming that we are substantial beings (i.e., substances), with essences, created by God, who has granted us capacities (at creation) that affect the social and historical processes of human history. Understanding the human has to do not only with inquiring about human ontology and reviewing the findings of biblical studies but also with accounting for the creation of culture. I will draw from the social sciences, specifically anthropological studies, where appropriate, but, once again, a detailed study is beyond the scope of the present work.

19. See Lilley and Pedersen, *Human Origins and the Image of God*.
20. A well-regarded example is Graves, *Mind, Brain and the Elusive Soul*.
21. Moltmann raises these sorts of questions by using the social sciences in several places. See Moltmann, *Man*, x. See Moltmann's monumentally important work *Theology of Hope*; also Moltmann, "Man and the Son of Man." Moltmann's anthropology is influenced by literary critical theory, socialism, and Christian Marxism. Hegelian dialectical philosophy is crucial to an understanding of Moltmann's theological anthropology. For a useful exposition of Moltmann's theological anthropology, see G. Chapman, "On Being Human."

Reformed Emphases in Anthropology

As the present volume approaches the anthropos from a catholic Christian perspective (i.e., the Nicene tradition), it also leans heavily on the Reformed divines and distinctives. These will season the discussion here. As I read and digest Reformed divines (e.g., Calvin, Turretin, Owen, Edwards, Hodge, Arminius),[22] five emphases or distinctives of theological anthropology are worth noting. Some of these are shared with the broader catholic church but have, arguably, received more attention or greater emphasis in the Reformed tradition.

The first emphasis is that the whole human narrative is characterized by divine gift giving.[23] This is in contrast to what we find in the ancient world, where the emphasis is on transaction. You give me what I deserve. If I do something for you, then the natural response is that you will repay the favor; and so it goes in a constant exchange. The New Testament advances a vision that is in stark contrast. The world is set up with a divine gift-giver giving to his creatures. God is described as the one who gives life and blesses that life, and this is characteristic of God's actions toward his covenantal children in the Old Testament.

Another distinctive that is broadly shared in the catholic church but may receive more attention in the Reformed tradition is that God and humans are described according to the distinction between Creator and creature. God is the Creator of the world and all that is in it. As such, God sets the laws. God is not a creature and thus is not subject to anything but his own nature. We, along with the rest of the created animal kingdom, are creatures, dependent on our Creator and subject to him and what he commands. Though we are free creatures, we are not permitted to do whatever we wish to do. Instead, we are created with boundaries that serve to govern and help us achieve our potential according to divine design. We are created with obligations. We have not achieved the full potential of God's design; instead, we have violated those obligations.

Original sin is also emphasized in the Reformed tradition. This is not to say that Roman and Eastern traditions do not have a place for original sin, or sin more generally. With much of the broader catholicity, the Reformed tradition sees original sin, and sin more generally, as emphatically a violation

22. Jacob Arminius is a Reformed theologian despite the fact that his soteriological commitments were not Calvinistic in the modernist sense. I take it that Reformed theology is a reference to a sociological and ecclesiological tradition that is broader than Calvinistic soteriology.

23. Divine gift giving is a feature of both Eastern Orthodoxy and Roman Catholicism. See Hart, *The Beauty of the Infinite*; Marion, *The Reason of the Gift*.

of divine law. Finally, we have some of the strongest versions of original sin carried along in the Reformed tradition, particularly following Augustine's lead on sin (i.e., original guilt). This is an emphasis certainly distinct from the East following the patristic writers (e.g., Gregory of Nazianzus) but also, to a lesser extent, distinct from the Roman Catholic tradition following Aquinas.[24]

In keeping with divine gift giving and a strong version of original sin, the Reformed tradition highlights the human response of faith to the call from God's word. The response of faith is important because, rather than a works righteousness, the Reformed tradition highlights a response to God's ultimate gift of salvation. The condition for receiving and retaining salvation is not a repayment to God or obedience to laws but rather a response of faith. By this, I am not suggesting that the Latin and Eastern traditions do not have a place for gift giving, nor that they understand salvation as including works righteousness or merit, but I am suggesting that the emphasis on a response to God's call is highlighted in the Reformed tradition, which is an emphasis common to evangelicalism. This is closely related to another theme or metaphor common to the Reformed tradition.

The sense of hearing takes logical priority in the Reformed tradition. Logically preceding a response of faith to the divine call to receive divine grace is the matter of human hearing—hearing the call of the Holy Spirit's instigation and internal work in human beings. Upon hearing, humans respond in faith. The metaphor of hearing is not in contrast to the metaphor of seeing (common to the catholic tradition, broadly speaking) but could be construed as a kind of seeing.[25]

Souls, Bodies, Seeing, and Hearing

Traditionally, the final end of humanity has been the vision of God. Thus, the study of God serves this end, as by it we seek to see God and to see our world in light of God.[26]

24. I do not want to simplify the distinct options available in the Latin tradition (or in Roman Catholicism). There are many on offer. I also must say that, in large measure, Aquinas follows Augustine, and Augustine's commitment to one version over another is not clear, but still the strongest versions of original sin (i.e., original guilt) originally found in Augustine are often adhered to in the Reformed tradition—but there are finer distinctions that I will address in chap. 4.

25. For a model of Reformed or Reformational theological reading of Scripture that highlights many of the aspects listed here, see Allen and Swain, *Reformed Catholicity*.

26. For a helpful exposition of this classical understanding of theological prolegomena, which presumes the actualization of human capacities, see Oden, *Classic Christianity*, 55, 780–85, 794–95. For Oden, in keeping with ancient understandings of theological prolegomena in relation to theological anthropology, not only is knowing God important as an intellectual

Embodied souls live and move because God gives life. Embodied souls are creaturely beings not to be confused with the divine being. However, as we will see, embodied souls have a divine purpose. But because of the stain of (original) sin that extends to every human being, all humans are incapable of achieving their divinely intended goal, let alone relative human goals, hence our creaturely reality is plain to our experience. Thankfully, God does not leave humans in this predicament; instead, he sends his Son. In sending his Son, God gives himself in an act through which he invades human life, and it is here that all humans find blessing in life in the fullest measure. Christ, no doubt with the application of the Holy Spirit, enables our hearing God, our seeing God, and our union with God.

We have capacities for seeing God in creation and redemption. Undoubtedly, we see God in creation in that his attributes are clearly perceived, as Paul declares in Romans 1. For it is in creation that we, as humans, enter into a covenantal relationship with God and that the basic parameters for relating to God and to the rest of his creation are laid out. Our redeemed souls enable us to see the world aright, according to God's perspective. In the context of discussing pain and suffering, Kelly Kapic hints at an understanding of beatific vision with the use of the metaphor of lenses. With our redemptive eyes, properly adjusted, we are able to see rightly the nature of our creaturely existence, particularly our sin-affected existence (both in body and in soul). He says, "When our responses to people are informed more by marketing images than theological reflection, we see ourselves and others through distorting lenses and mistreat each other. We give undue preference to youth and strength, and we ignore those who do not fit the culture's ideals."[27]

Important to personal and narrative identity, seeing and hearing are not only prominent themes in the biblical story line regarding humans but also prominent metaphors and themes in catholic Reformed constructions of what it means to be a human in reference to capacities and powers. Personal identity (which we will explore more deeply in chapter 1) touches on what we are as human beings. Identity is a relation that a thing has to itself. Ancillary to this question are the questions of what kind of thing we as humans are, what capacities we have, and for what purpose those capacities are designed. The metaphors of seeing and hearing correspond to specific faculties of embodied souls. Narrative identity (which we will also explore more deeply later, starting in chapter 1) builds on personal identity and is

---

discipline but also knowing the character and attributes of God corresponds to a sufficiently developed interior life. Oden places the beatific vision in the context of the resurrected body of the saints, but this is a debated position in the Reformed tradition.

27. Kapic, *Embodied Hope*, 49.

not, strictly speaking, identical (no pun intended) to it. Narrative identity is the second-order or contingent identity. Think of it like an added layer of clothes. Better still, you might think of it like the clothes or the masks we put on in the various roles we play in life as parents, teachers, police officers, and so on. However, our narrative identity touches us more deeply than do individual roles we play in life. It touches the heart of what matters to us most and often is integrated more deeply with our personalities, character traits, and behaviors.

Seeing is an activity that occurs as a result of a faculty that we humans have by virtue of the kind of beings we are. As a capacity (i.e., a power like thinking and volition) of the soul, vision or sight can function by way of achieving an end, or it can fail to achieve that end. Those who are unable to see and are blind (or largely so), we would say, are disabled in terms of their vision. More than that, there is a sense in which vision can be optimal or functioning to the highest degree possible. Beatific vision is like this. It is a capacity not of the eyes but of the immaterial soul. It is a capacity for perceiving and experiencing the divine goal of human beings.

Hearing is similar and might be construed as a capacity that falls under beatific vision. When we hear the divine, we do so as human beings who respond to the gospel story (hence it is logically prior in some sense to the beatific vision in the redemptive economy or it is simultaneous with it), where the divine displays life and blessing in their fullest extent.

These two aspects are part and parcel of the narrative identity that shapes and forms human beings in their respective redemptive identities and gives us some idea of what it means to be human. Soul/body considerations also fit with our narrative identity. As human beings, we are, arguably, souls that endure through time. We are also embodied beings that function normally and properly with our bodies. Our souls and bodies function as the metaphysical ground for seeing and hearing, and when they are functioning properly in union, we call this *theosis* (union with the divine, sharing in the divine life, or, as the East states it, we participate in God's energies but not his essence).

Unfortunately, contemporary Reformed theologians are often critical of the doctrine of beatific vision (with its intimate doctrinal relationship to theosis), along with the doctrine of the soul. Michael Horton, in his recent useful introduction to systematic theology, represents a common tendency in contemporary (particularly Reformed) theology to regard anything related to or associated with Platonism with contempt. He is quite critical of Platonic variations of the beatific vision, believing that they exalt humanity to a status that is never intended by God. By understanding beatific vision in this context,

Horton is concerned that they violate the Reformed impulse that the knowledge of God is dependent on God's revelation of himself to us.[28] However, it is precisely here that I think Horton would be right to point out the necessity of hearing and responding to God's revelation as undergirding our vision of God. In one important passage, Horton expresses his displeasure for some understandings of beatific vision:

> In continuity more with the East, Reformed theology identifies theosis-glorification with our sharing in Christ's bodily resurrection on the last day rather than with the ascent of mind. In other words, the focus is on our being united to Christ's historical and eschatological career rather than on returning to a supposedly primordial union with God prior to embodiment. Reformed theology is even willing to speak of glorification in terms of beatific vision, but here again it is closer to an Eastern (Irenaean) emphasis on the resurrection of the body than it is to the preoccupation of much of Western reflection on beholding and ascending into the divine essence. In fact, Reformed theology can be said to affirm the beatific vision only in a form radically revised from its pedigree in Christian Platonism.[29]

As the reader can see, Horton is quite critical of Platonism and the Western tradition concerning anthropology and the beatific vision. There is something bequeathed from Plato through Augustine and others that is important in the development of ancient and medieval theology and as well influences Reformed theology, and that is participatory realist ontology. This is the view that all of reality somehow participates in the life of God, his energies (not to be confused with his essence, according to theologians in Eastern Orthodoxy), or his accidents (as seen in the Western tradition) through divinely created ideas. And God has structured the world in such a way where humans are "microcosms" that mediate this reality to the rest of creation,

28. Horton, *Pilgrim Theology*, 30–50. See esp. his comment on p. 30.
29. Horton, *Pilgrim Theology*, 333. Horton's comments seem to miss the importance of vision in the Reformed tradition not as something separate from other eschatological categories but as distinct in an important sense. It also seems odd to me when he states that the Reformed theological tradition follows the East more than the West, when the Reformed theological tradition is largely Western. As with many of the philosophical categories relevant to anthropology and soteriology, the Reformed theological tradition is influenced by Thomas Aquinas. This is also true of the beatific vision. Many of the most recognized Reformed theologians follow Aquinas in their understanding of the beatific vision. In fact, as I will show in a later chapter, Francis Turretin follows nearly verbatim what Aquinas states. In chap. 10 I will show that Aquinas's view of anthropology and personal eschatology has influenced the Reformed theological tradition quite significantly. This is not to say that the Reformed theologians don't also follow Irenaeus, but neither does Irenaeus represent the diversity of views in the Eastern tradition. In fact, many Eastern theologians are Christian Platonists.

and they themselves have a parallel structure to that reality that makes them fitting participants in it.[30]

While it seems accurate to say that the emphasis of the Reformed tradition in personal eschatology is not on a disembodied mental ascent or the return to a primordial union with God, the Reformed tradition does give some weight to the capacities of the soul, including the mind, as primary for the beatific vision.[31] As we will see below, the Reformed tradition carries along what is often considered the "catholic" soteriology of human "transformation" in the doctrines of beatific vision and deification in addition to the Reformed distinctives of faith and justification.[32] In fact, as I show below, the Reformed theological tradition has a place for the vision where the disembodied mind has an intellectual vision of God. This emphasis, if nothing else, has some affinity to aspects of Platonism. In other words, the Reformed theological tradition on the beatific vision is more nuanced and complicated than what we find stated in the quotation from Horton above. Yet it seems important to state that the Reformed theological tradition places a premium on the immaterial nature of humanity and the intellectual nature of the vision. Thankfully, some contemporary theologians have reignited the discussion about the beatific vision as an important theological item to retrieve from the past. The importance of the beatific vision is felt when we consider the theocentric focus of it in contrast to the contemporary model that highlights the physical resurrection alone apart from the vision.[33] Having a theocentric focus is important for our anthropology because our anthropology is teleologically directed to God and made sense of in light of divine action. Contrastively, a model of physical resurrection (i.e., new creation) apart from the vision

30. There are other metaphors used that fit with this participatory realist ontology. See Balthasar, "Eschatology in Outline," 441. Balthasar sees "vision" as implying distance between our reality and God's reality shared. Balthasar's concerns with beatific vision are debatable takes on the vision as it was developed throughout the tradition. Vision, closely connected with a participatory ontology and deification, is the means by which union with God obtains. This participatory notion of humans in divine reality appears to be in line with many Reformed theologians, including Calvin. See Vorster, *The Brightest Mirror of God's Works*, 59–99; Canlis, *Calvin's Ladder*, 164.

31. For what one important symbol of the Reformed theological tradition has to say, see the Westminster Confession of Faith, chap. 32.

32. A significant article defending that both beatific vision and deification were central to the development of soteriology exemplified in several important Reformed theological divines is Mosser, "Recovering the Reformation's Ecumenical Vision of Redemption." Mosser argues, quite persuasively in my opinion, that both the beatific vision and deification are essential to the dogmatic core of catholic soteriology, which the Reformed tradition does not, arguably, give up.

33. Three resources deserve a mention: Boersma, *Heavenly Participation*; Boersma, *Seeing God*; Levering, *Jesus and the Demise of Death*, 109–26. Boersma is working within the Reformed tradition. Levering is not, but his work has relevance to the Reformed tradition.

has shaped contemporary evangelical discussions and is, arguably, characterized by an excessive anthropocentrism.[34] In other words, the former model is focused not solely on the most obvious immanent activity of humans but rather on the transcendent activities of the divine as that which grounds human activity and points humans beyond the earthy processes to God's life as a trinitarian being.[35]

With all introductions, there is a need for ground clearing. We have accomplished that by looking at some of the basic terms for theological anthropology, canvassing some of the basic categories, laying out some of the distinctives to the approach taken throughout the book, and, finally, touching on some of the highlights and themes that will surface as we progress. What I offer in *An Introduction to Theological Anthropology* is a way forward by looking back in order that we may look forward. As evangelicals continue to wrestle with the historical contingencies of their own time, taking a look back with present considerations in mind so that we might move forward is, I suggest, necessary. Evangelicalism as a movement or a tradition is downstream from the Reformed tradition, as I see it, and as a movement it cannot afford to neglect its heritage and the categories that have shaped it and will continue to do so.[36]

34. See, for example, Wright, *Surprised by Hope*.

35. Michael Allen helpfully connects this notion of God's invisibility and transcendence to the beatific vision in a recently published article. See M. Allen, "Visibility of the Invisible God"; also M. Allen, *Grounded in Heaven*.

36. The Reformed tradition is not the only tradition that has richly informed evangelicalism. Evangelicalism has also been informed by the pietistic tradition, the fundamentalist tradition, and variations of the social justice traditions. See Bebbington, *Evangelicalism in Modern Britain*. He describes four distinctives of evangelicalism: conversionism, biblicism, activism, and cruciformity. Each one of these distinctives finds some footing in the richness of the Reformed theological tradition and is aided by the metaphors of "seeing" and "hearing" that shape and form a theology of the human being, as "seeing" and "hearing" are the orienting metaphors for what it means to be human and the ground for human behavior.

1

What Am I?

Creaturely and Redemptive Identity

What is mankind that you are mindful of them,
human beings that you care for them?

Psalm 8:4

We can't conceive of half a soul.

René Descartes,
Discourse on Method and
Meditations on First Philosophy

Humans live and die by stories. This much we seem to know from experience. As we have seen in the introductory chapter, humans exist within a narrative structure. Humans identify with some narrative that gives them an explanation of origins, meaning, morality, and destiny. However, narrative identity requires some metaphysical or ontological commitments. Narratives themselves are not reducible to biology and not capturable in biological terms. In fact, human language, rationality, and consciousness presuppose an immaterial being—or so I will argue in the present chapter.

Scriptural Starting Point

In Psalm 8 David reflects on human nature. Set in the broader context of God's glory in the creation of the world, the psalm summarizes in poetic form the nature of humans as the centerpiece of God's creation. David's reflection reveals something about God through his human creation. David raises the profound question, "What is mankind that you are mindful of them?" (Ps. 8:4). His answer is not intended to be a complete and satisfying answer to the question, but it stirs the imagination. David answers by defining several attributes and characteristics of the human. Most immediate, he claims that God made humans a little lower than the heavenly beings. Humans are the crowning achievement of God's glory, signified in David's statement that God "crowned them with glory and honor" (Ps. 8:5). Humans are rulers over all creation (Ps. 8:6). In all of this, humans are created with dignity and with the purpose of taking dominion over the earth.

It is true that David fails to give a direct answer to the question he poses, but his view seems to presuppose some answer to what humans are by nature. In other places of Scripture, that presupposition does seem to be of an immaterial substance. Solomon's reflection on human purpose in relation to the creation story of humans in Genesis 2, arguably, presupposes this understanding that humans are soul-body compounds. Solomon says in Ecclesiastes 12:7, "And the dust returns to the ground it came from, and the spirit [*ruah*] returns to God who gave it." The notion that one's body returns to the ground and one's soul goes to be with God seems to restate what we find in Genesis 2:7. The author of Genesis 2 describes humans as composed in some way of the dust of the ground and indicates that the life that is given is given to the body to make it alive. This "breath" spoken of can be naturally read in light of the larger canon of Scripture as the soul that God creates and is uniquely highlighted in contrast to the rest of God's creation, signifying the fact that God is adding something new. Gregory of Nazianzus, in the fourth century, reflecting a common theological appropriation of Genesis 2:7, comments on this passage, "The soul is the breath of God, a substance of heaven mixed with the lowest earth."[1] In fact, according to some Old Testament scholarship, what is naturally read here as referring to the soul or spirit of the person can be legitimately translated as "soul" or "spirit." In this context, the important words used are *ruah* and *nephesh*, where *neshamah* is the divine action of breathing and *ruah* and *nephesh* are the results that highlight different aspects (in a merism), but both refer to the "soul." A parallel passage bears out this appropriate usage: "Thus says God, the LORD, who created [*bara'*] the heavens and stretched them out, who spread out the earth and what comes from it, who gives breath [*neshamah*] to the people on it and spirit [*ruah*] to those who

---

1. Louth, *Genesis 1–11*, 51.

walk in it" (Isa. 42:5). The distinction made between breath as mere breath and spirit is present in this passage.[2]

A commonsense understanding of humans buttresses this understanding of humans as souls. By "commonsense" I intend to convey the idea that certain beliefs are natural to believe and become knowledge when our cognitive faculties are functioning properly, where souls (or immaterial spirits) seem to be the common belief not just in theistic traditions but also among the ancients.[3]

There is good reason to begin with common sense, and that is because we already begin there in our daily lives. When I wake up in the morning, I take it for granted that I exist and that I have several options before me: I can go for a jog first or drink coffee first. Implicit therein, I take it for granted that I am thinking and that I can deliberate and have a choice between two options. My experience suggests to me that I am free. When I begin, I do so with natural intuition and conscious experience, because there are givens in our experience that are basic to all the operations we confront in life. We begin there because it grants us knowledge of the actual world around us and because the possibilities before us are somehow rooted in what is actual. Naturally, we are inclined to believe that we are distinct from our bodies, which is buttressed by the fact that we are inclined to believe in something like a soul prior to any *tutoring*, and this has been the case throughout most of history for most people in most parts of the world.[4]

2. For a concise theological anthropology from an Old Testament perspective, see Hoffmeier and Siefert, "What Are Human Beings?" Old Testament scholar James K. Hoffmeier is convinced that Gen. 2:7 yields a distinction between the dust referencing the body and *ruah* referring to the distinct part of human beings, namely, a soul or a spirit. For Hoffmeier, the commonly assumed thesis that Old Testament conception rules out a soul or dualism is not substantiated from these and many other texts. The traditional reading of the Old Testament, particularly with *ruah* and *nepesh*, actually make some latitude for translating and interpreting them, in some cases, for the soul or spirit.

3. See Bloom, *Descartes' Baby*. Bloom argues for the naturalness, intuitiveness, and commonsense belief that we are dualist. He is certainly not the only psychologist or scientist who defends the natural belief in a soul, and there are others who defend a robust dualism of soul and body. For a treatment of Reformed or commonsense epistemology, see also Plantinga, *Knowledge and Christian Belief*. My arguments for a soul, and specific versions of the soul, are not merely dependent on "intuition," but intuition and common sense are the starting points. They are further buttressed by deeper reflections on our experience of the first-person, and the soul becomes necessary for grounding some empirical data. Plantinga's epistemology begins with the eighteenth-century Scottish philosopher Thomas Reid. And while there are complicated ways of taking Reid or establishing his commonsense epistemology, there is a shared understanding among commonsense "foundationalist" (i.e., the foundations of knowledge) epistemologies that we begin in common sense and in that which is actual for developing knowledge about what is possible. See Nichols and Yaffe, "Thomas Reid."

4. While some would eschew starting with common sense and natural beliefs that we are disposed toward, there is no good reason, in principle, for not adopting this philosophical

Let's take an example that will serve to motivate this claim. When a person reflects on his or her hands or feet, the person naturally distinguishes the self from his or her hands and feet. Hands and feet are distinct objects of consciousness that are nonidentifiable with me, nor do they essentially constitute who I am. Who I am is made up of something else fundamentally and essentially. I am a mind or a soul, for I could lose my feet and hands and still I would remain the same person. In fact, I could lose several parts of my body and remain the selfsame person. Taking this in mind with the fact that there is no physical object with which I identify, I have reason to consider the possibility that I am something other than my body. And, through repeated attention given to the question, I either come to form the belief that I am distinct from my body as attested to by the feature of "frequency" that my mind is inclined to think that I am not my body or I come to develop a deeper appreciation for the intuitiveness of the belief based on the fact that I learn more through conscious attention given to the features of my body in contrast to my personhood.[5]

Other Scripture passages reflect this same understanding that we *seem* to have of ourselves. When Mary in the New Testament says, "My soul [*psychē*] doth magnify the Lord" (Luke 1:46 KJV), she is referring to the whole self (in the sense of a merism: by referring to the whole self through its parts), yet she seems to be referring to the subject of her own actions not reducible

---

starting point. Some object that such a starting point is philosophically naïve, but we all begin here. And there is good reason to begin here because all of knowledge, as it is rooted in experience, begins with the initial deliverances of experience. Our question is, What is it that we learn from our shared experiences? And this requires careful, clear articulation and attention to the details of the basicality of our experience. The only time that we should doubt or reject the deliverances of our basic experience is when we have an overriding reason to deny some item within our conscious experience.

5. See McNabb, *Religious Epistemology*, esp. 25–37. McNabb advances a criterion for determining the warrant of a belief using "frequency." His development of a commonsense account for arriving at beliefs about persons as minds is called "proper functionalism" Reformed epistemology, which is consistent with the deliverances of cognitive science. There are other forms of Reformed epistemology that give more credence to greater or deeper forms of justification for a belief based on attentiveness to one's own internal items of the mind through a comparison and contrast of features or properties that "seem" to be present. This is called an internalist approach to epistemology that gives greater credence to the internal contents of the mind that individuals have access to in contrast to the "proper functionalism" as reliabilism above. Frequency, as a criterion, functions then in different ways on both systems. On reliabilism it functions to show that beliefs are more likely warranted beliefs in light of the frequency criterion, and on internalism it provides additional justification and surety that certain beliefs are accessed and representations of the world. Both ways are viable approaches to arriving at the belief that I am my soul or mind and not, strictly speaking, my body. For an approachable work that uses a similar rational framework as McNabb and that spells out some of the conclusions of cognitive science, see Clark, *God and the Brain*.

to the parts therein and not captured by the whole of the parts that she has. Instead, she is referring to some subject that has desires, emotions, thoughts, inclinations, volitional states, and the like. She is neither her body nor the parts of her body. She is, arguably, something other than her body, or at least something higher than the body she inhabits.

In Psalm 42:11 the psalmist presupposes this commonsense dualism when he enters into a conversation with his soul. He raises the question, "Why, my soul, are you downcast? Why so disturbed within me? Put your hope in God, for I will yet praise him, my Savior and my God." The psalmist is assuming some distinction between self or soul and body. The psalmist does not reflect on or speak directly to the body or the parts of the body, as if they can respond. Rather, he communicates with his soul or self in an attempt to bring about some causal change in the emotional states he is experiencing.

The New Testament picks up on the Old Testament theme of our soul or spirit going back to God once we die somatically. Consider the example of Luke 23:46, Christ's death on the cross, where he exclaims, "Father, into your hands I commit my spirit [*pneuma*]." Similarly, Stephen in Acts 7:59 says, "Lord Jesus, receive my spirit [*pneuma*]." Conceptually, these and other New Testament passages point us in the direction of personal persistence after somatic death. *Pneuma* and *psychē* are common parallel terms to the Old Testament words *ruah* and *nepesh*, and while these may be translated as "wind," "breath," or "life" more generally, there are, arguably, cases where they can be translated as "soul" or "spirit" and should be interpreted as such.

Beyond the reasons given above, there is a growing consensus in much of the contemporary theological literature that humans are not souls or composed of souls. In fact, there is a tendency among many recent theologians to think that the Old Testament yields a conception of the human person that is quite at odds with a belief in the soul as an immaterial substance, because, in their view, the Old Testament authors present a picture of human beings that is necessarily holistic, even monistic (i.e., individual human beings are one kind of thing). Alister McGrath represents this opinion when he states,

> Yet it is widely agreed that this is not how the writers of the Bible understood these ideas. The notion of an immaterial soul was a secular Greek concept, not a biblical notion. The Old Testament conceives of humanity "as an animated body and not as an incarnate soul." The biblical vision of humanity was that of a single entity, an inseparable psychosomatic unit with many facets or aspects. "Soul" is an Anglo-Saxon term used to translate a variety

of biblical terms, often having the general sense of "life." Thus the Hebrew word *nephesh*, translated as "soul" in some older English Bibles, really means a "living being."[6]

McGrath is certainly not the only theologian who has made these claims. In fact, this is fairly common in much of the contemporary theological anthropology literature, and while it sounds like sophisticated biblical scholarship, it is actually a debatable thesis.[7] To suggest that there is an Old Testament consensus regarding the nature and constitution of persons is debatable.

While the thesis that holism is at odds with the view that persons have or are souls can and has been challenged primarily based on the Scripture's teaching of a temporary disembodied intermediate state found in New Testament eschatology, it can also be challenged from the perspective of the Old Testament. Challenging the "holism as monism" thesis of anthropology as the consensus of Old Testament scholarship, Richard Steiner has recently argued that there are several cases in the Old Testament that presume that humans are composed of souls or are souls that can, potentially, exist disembodied. In fact, he even challenges the view that *nepesh* and *ruah* exclusively mean "breath" or "wind." He argues that there is at least one definitive case where *nepesh* means "soul" as an immaterial substance that can exist disembodied, as found in Ezekiel 13:18, 20, and there are several other cases where it either could

6. McGrath, *The Big Question*, 137–38. McGrath quotes the Old Testament scholar H. Wheeler Robinson.

7. For a representative sampling, see Jeeves and Brown, *Neuroscience, Psychology, and Religion*; Murphy, *Bodies and Souls*; Brown, Murphy, and Malony, *Whatever Happened to the Soul?*; Cooper, *Body, Soul, and Life Everlasting*; Murphy and Knight, *Human Identity*; Corcoran, *Rethinking Human Nature*; Jeeves, *The Emergence of Personhood*; Jeeves, *Rethinking Human Nature*. For theologians proper, see Vorster, *The Brightest Mirror of God's Works*, 28–32; van der Kooi and van den Brink, *Christian Dogmatics*, 267–68. Van der Kooi and van den Brink suggest that the "immortal soul" doctrine is indebted to Greek philosophical thinking rather than the holism of Scripture. Here, as in much of contemporary theology, there is a tendency to read the Old Testament, as well as the New Testament, as entailing holism and not substance dualism. The authors in these works often assume holism as monism, and they assume that dualism is either explicitly or implicitly given over to Greek philosophy, but these charges neither reflect accurately on the doctrines entailed by various combined scriptural passages, nor do they give sufficient credence to the wider catholic tradition as an authority, nor do they often give credence to sophisticated philosophical arguments. John Cooper, in *Body, Soul, and Life Everlasting*, has challenged the view that "holism" as a thesis is inconsistent with substance dualism. James Hoffmeier and Richard Averbeck have also stated to me in conversation that they are unsure how monism has become a "consensus" view within contemporary theology and why theologians suppose that there is such a consensus report in Old Testament scholarship. In fact, this sort of claim made by Murphy, among others, is similar to another claim that "monism" is the consensus view among neuroscientists.

be translated as soul or it is likely referring to a soul and not mere "breath," "life," or "wind." He further shows that this is common to the ancient Near Eastern understanding of human beings rather than its being a "Greek" idea that was imposed by early Christianity on the passages of Scripture.[8] The reason why the Ezekiel 13 passage can and must be translated and interpreted as presenting a soul or spirit follows from a common cultural ancient Near Eastern understanding that witches could cast a spell on clothes that were then able to capture the disembodied souls. This understanding that there is a distinction between the person, as soul, and the person's body is reflected in another Old Testament passage, 1 Samuel 28, where, at the request of Saul, the witch of Endor conjures the dead soul of Samuel, who is actually present and communicating with Saul.

These and other examples motivate the claim that we are not simply our bodies. We are not reducible to our bodies or captured by the bodies we inhabit and through which we experience the world. We are commonsensically distinct from our bodies. We are something else or something higher than our bodies. However, another view of the world is distinct from the biblical view of the world and understands humans in a different way.

Secular Naturalism as a Starting Point

Secular naturalism is the view that nature is a self-contained system that explains itself without any interference from the outside. Nonphysical entities are often dismissed with the wave of a hand by those defending secular naturalism. Angels and deities are considered spooky entities that are out of place in an intellectually sophisticated view of the world that is explained solely by natural processes. The physical world is explained physically, not nonphysically. Spirits, souls, minds, angels, and gods are left out of the metaphysical explanation of the world's history. Human persons, too, are explained by the physical events within the world. They are not souls, spirits, or minds that derive some explanation from beyond the physical domain but rather are situated securely within a physical explanation of causes and effects.

In my view, the evidence shows that secular naturalism is a nonstarter when it comes to human beings, especially for Christians, who affirm that beings like God and angels exist and are largely unaffected by the natural order of physical causes and effects or, at a minimum, exist prior to the natural world and are not causally determined in their natures or actions

---

8. Steiner, *Disembodied Souls.*

by natural causes and effects. Human beings, as well, arguably, are not the kinds of beings that can be explained solely by the history of the physical world, which the reader will see as the chapters unfold here (especially chapter 2). Both physics and biology are inadequate to explain all that we know about human beings. Particularly, when we seek to describe values, purposes, and intentions, we are left bereft of resources from the natural physical world, assuming values, purposes, and intentions are taken as real (i.e., mind-independent realities), because these aspects of reality depend on beings with consciousness and the properties that follow from consciousness (e.g., free will, moral conscience, rationality).[9] The fact of humans existing as morally dignified beings in the world, too, lacks support from secular naturalism. In fact, if we assume that human persons are real and that the ideas they have in and about the world are real, then we have at least one fundamental fact from every single human being that contributes to the history and nature of the world, and these are left unexplained in secular naturalism, where all that is found in humans is brains and blood and guts.

Secular naturalism is closely related with, even presumed in, two other common views of humanity: evolutionary humanism and secular humanism. Evolutionary humanism is the view that humans are the most complex products of biological evolution through a long history of genetic mutation and adaptation of species versus the belief in a soul created by some deity that places us in a unique relation to the rest of the world. On secular humanism, humans are metaphysically, ethically, and axiologically central to the naturalistic evolutionary story and are the most important arbiters of value, given that they are the latest and most developed products in evolution.

It is this story of secular naturalism and evolutionary and secular humanism that continues to hold the imagination of many people throughout the world today. And it departs from traditional theistic imaginations of the world in that it denies the transcendent nature of reality as found in a personal being and creator of the world, divine intervention, the role of miracles, the soul, and the afterlife. And it rejects various sources of knowledge as ways

9. Several thought experiments from philosophy help bring out this intuition. We could, for example, look at a dissected brain and see the various physical parts that go into making that brain, but even cutting up the brain into little pieces will not deliver these desires, concepts; instead, it shows us neurons. The point is that we can look at all the various parts of the brain and find that there is no garden-variety object that satisfies what it means to be me. There is no fact that adequately, and certainly not sufficiently, satisfies who I am. There is something other than the brain and its parts that I seem to be identified with. For a useful work that develops an argument against secular naturalism as a viable ontological frame for explaining consciousness, see Moreland, *Consciousness and the Existence of God*.

of arriving at truth recognized throughout much of human history, including religious experiences, the priority of first-person conscious experience, tradition, and revelation.[10] As the competing anthropological narrative to theistic, even Christian anthropology, secular humanism will come up in every chapter as an alternative way of explaining some datum central to the anthropological story, and it begins with the kinds of beings humans are by nature; hence, the question of human constitution is relevant to both a Christian anthropology and a secular anthropology.

Strict Identity and Personal Identity[11]

What is identity? Identity is that relation a thing or substance has to itself, and this is fundamental to yet distinct from one's narrative identity (i.e., the story of an individual) and one's self-concept (which includes how I see myself in relation to other people). Personal identity is more specific in that it is the relation that one has to oneself. In other words, I am identical to self. I, as a person, am no one else, and I have this unique relationship to myself that is shared with no one other than myself. The same is true for others. They, too, have this relationship to themselves in such a way that they do not share the same relationship with any other.

Having established that we, human beings, are primarily individual persons (even if we are persons of a particular biological kind), we can press on to argue for the metaphysical conditions and characteristics of personhood. Persons are characterized as beings that have consciousness, experience the world in a first-person manner, contribute something to the world by way of their own subjectivity, bear dignity, and are moral in nature. When we consider the characteristics of persons, what are those characteristics, and are they compatible with the products generated in the natural world? Further, are they explicable in terms of underlying physical causes and effects in a closed system? This order opens the door to alternative ontologies. I will briefly lay out some common personal ontologies for consideration.

10. See "Humanism and Its Aspirations: Humanist Manifesto III, a Successor to the Humanist Manifesto of 1933," American Humanist Association, https://americanhumanist.org/what-is-humanism/manifesto3/. For a fascinating contemporary exploration of secular humanism, see Harari, *Homo Deus*. Yuval Noah Harari builds his narrative for how we address the questions of the future in his secular humanistic frame, and it shows how it is that humanistic philosophy gave rise to Western individualism, pragmatism, Marxism, feminism, transhumanism, and futurism.

11. For the most important collection that includes historical and more recent readings, see Martin and Barresi, *Personal Identity*.

Reductive physicalism: the view that all of the world can be reduced to its component fundamental physical parts; that is, physics explains everything. Human persons are identified with their physical parts and are explained by those physical parts. This seems to amount to the elimination of persons as psychological beings that experience value and life as real entities.[12]

Nonreductive physicalism: the view that the world is made up of physical parts, so physics provides some explanation for the goings on in the world. However, physics does not explain all of the world in its entirety, and there are other facts that persons, particularly, contribute to the world. Human persons are nonreducible to their component parts. They are psychological beings that bear properties that are nonreducible to the physical parts, but they are composed of physical parts that give rise to these properties. The properties themselves contribute something to the body of the person.[13]

Constitution physicalism: a view that is similar to nonreductive physicalism in maintaining that "humans" are nonreducible to their component parts or the parts interacting together but further holds that humans are composed of higher-order emergent properties of the material parts interacting together. Consider, for example, a wooden desk: the desk is not the wood, but it is constituted by the wood and is more than the wood that constitutes it. Emergent psychological properties are constituted by the body but not reducible to the body.

Hylomorphism/Thomism: a view common to the medieval period and much of the Reformed tradition that holds that humans are composed of two features or ingredients: matter and form. These component parts are nonreducible to their respective parts and are somehow fitted to each other in a matter-form arrangement, which produces something distinct: a new substance. This view can be worked out as a version of monism or a version of dualism, where there are two discrete and modally distinct parts: matter and soul. Recent ways of working out hylomorphism give credence not to a classic Aristotelian and Thomist framework of matter and form but rather to a powers ontology that is nonreducible to the underlying parts.[14]

12. For a clear treatment of reductive physicalism (or some position close to it), see Kim, *Physicalism*.

13. O'Connor, *Persons and Causes*.

14. For one of the clearest expositions of the varieties of Thomism, see Brower, *Aquinas's Ontology*, esp. 273.

Substance dualism: the view that persons are identical not to the material body but to the immaterial part (e.g., the soul, the spirit, the mind) or some compound configuration of both body and soul. On most versions of substance dualism the carrier of personal identity is the soul.[15]

In what follows, I address some of the philosophical evidence corresponding to the scriptural and theological data.[16] I do this for two reasons. First, coming from the epistemic standpoint of phenomenal conservatism, I take it that we have prima facie evidence for human beings being a particular kind of thing. In such a view, there are specified conditions that make sense of our conscious experience and are necessary if we are to experience possibility and contingency in life. Furthermore, these actualities provide us with the tools for considering "possibilities" in our world and, potentially, outside of our world. And such a view cannot be easily dismissed at the wave of a hand because of science or some predetermined grid that is brought to the experiential table, for even these begin in experience.[17] Second, I take it that

15. See Farris, *The Soul of Theological Anthropology*; Swinburne, *Mind, Brain, and Free Will*.

16. A large portion of what follows on the philosophical literature on personal identity relating to theology is drawn from Farris, "The Soul-Concept." See also my distinct theological argument in Farris, "Substance Dualism."

17. For a treatment of "conceivability" or "imagination" as the starting point for thinking about the world, see Taliaferro and Evans, *The Image in Mind*, 11–37. This approach has its critics, but it is impossible not to begin here in one's philosophical reflections. Within such a philosophical method, it is not as if a mere appeal to intuition is satisfactory but that an appeal to an actual intuition where some mental item is intuited as "clear" and "coherent" given one's experience of the world. It is a place to start for determining what is actual and what is possible. Hence, it is appropriate to begin here, which I do, but there are deeper kinds of justification. There is an interesting alternative approach in modernity that takes it that our basic experiences of the human should recognize that common sense, rationalism, experience, and most of the philosophical approaches throughout history have led to despair in our personal existential point of view and that this is the starting point of all humans (see Hegel and Heidegger). Instead of beginning with our common experiences and what they tell us about humanity, the argument is that that leads to despair and that despair must be subverted through another process that comes from the outside—this is a philosophical vantage point called "idealist existentialism" for Hegel and "topology" for Heidegger. For a sophisticated treatment of philosophical humanity that begins here and points us in the direction of a theology of humanity, see Lacoste, *Experience and the Absolute*. On this view, not only did the ancients, like Plato and Aristotle, get it wrong, but so too did the medievals (Augustine, Aquinas), in addition to the early moderns like Descartes, Locke, Hobbes, Leibniz, and Reid. All of the latter thinkers give some role to common conscious experience as a starting point for knowledge of humans. The notion of common sense, itself, flowers when we come to Thomas Reid in the history of modern philosophy. Since his time, it has been developed and refined in complicated ways, which we will not explore here. For Lacoste, commonsense knowledge or knowledge arrived at through some other human means (e.g., through the rational a priori or through empiricism) gives us only contingent truth (i.e., the givens or "facticity") but not definitive knowledge, which is only given to human creatures in

a natural reading of Scripture's teachings on the self (assuming that God has revealed truth that corresponds to naturally revealed truth) will either yield the same conclusions or be made sense of in light of this foundational material. I work through the literature on personal identity arguing in favor of a "simple" view, which probably entails a soul view (however, one could affirm an absolutely simple material particle). Third, I work through the theological literature on human persons and argue in favor of a simple-substance view as satisfying the theological data. In this way, relational and functional views, arguably, presuppose simple substance. I suggest that there is a good deal of overlap between the theological and the philosophical literature.

Personal Identity

I begin the approach to theological anthropology by considering some of the philosophical foundations. It seems to me that a particular conception of personal identity undergirds and grounds a scriptural and theological understanding of persons. In the following, I address the philosophical literature on personal identity, and I argue in favor of the simple view by, first, raising some concerns with physicalist ontologies and complex views of personal identity. In the second part of this section, I lay out some significant reasons for thinking that the simple view of personal identity, which entails a substantial soul of the person, is necessarily true.

It is common within the literature to read of four views on personal identity: the body view, the brain view, the memory or character view, and the simple view.[18] The views other than the simple view are not sufficient for personal identity but have their place in both philosophical and theological developments of persons. Later in the discussion, I suggest that each view

---

liturgy. Other than beginning with a pure third-person scientific perspective, another epistemic approach to arrive at the truth about humans is through pragmatism that is up for discussion. See Rorty, *Philosophy and the Mirror of Nature*. In a famous definition, Rorty states, "One is justified in believing that P [some proposition] if and only if one has engaged in the social practice of showing that one's belief that P sustains appropriate relations to the other beliefs supported by the 'epistemic authority' of one's social community" (186). Such an epistemic standard is rooted in one's own social community and it lacks the grounding of other means of justification for knowledge. Further, it is not clear why one's immediate community is to be preferred over some other community, especially if that community is free sailing without the anchoring of the past. For an example of pragmatism in philosophical anthropology that impinges on the theological, see Pihlström, *Pragmatism and Philosophical Anthropology*.

18. Apart from the simple view, the others seem to presuppose a relational ontology, generally speaking. Consider a few resources in the literature on personal identity: Perry, *A Dialogue on Personal Identity and Immortality*; Baillie, *Problems in Personal Identity*; Perry, *Personal Identity*; Shoemaker, *Personal Identity and Ethics*.

helpfully relates to the simple view in two ways but that a simple-soul view (as I describe it) provides the preconditions for theological anthropology. First, each view helps fill out a more comprehensive picture of persons. Second, each view provides evidential support for identifying one soul over another soul. I will look at each view in turn and offer reasons why I do not accept it as sufficient for personal identity.

The first position, the body view, is often associated with Aristotle.[19] The bodily criterion for personal identity is the view that persons are identified with their bodies. Broadly speaking, the view does not say that I identify with one aspect of my body or one physical part connected with my body. In fact, the "I" is a linguistic reference for the body or biological organism. Alternatively, and related to this, one could say that the body constitutes and makes me *me*.[20] Thus, I am my body. This is one popular view held by philosophical and theological physicalists, respectively.[21]

A helpful illustration of the intuitive problems found with the body view or some similar view is seen in the Harry Potter books. In book two, *The Chamber of Secrets*, and book seven, *The Deathly Hallows*, J. K. Rowling introduces the reader to the Polyjuice Potion. A person can turn one's body into the body of another by simply dropping into a potion a hair of the organism into which the person wants to transform. I can conceive of a similar state of affairs. Let us say that my friend of several years had massive cosmetic surgery in order to take on the tone of voice, the face, and the body of Tom Cruise. Would this then make that person Tom Cruise? Not at all. You might press the conceivability of the state of affairs further, wherein scientists could change the DNA of a person—in this case, my wife's DNA. Would she then cease to be the person I once married? I do not believe so. We know from the intuitive reasons given above, and the arguments from the previous section, that a person is not strictly identical with his or her body, bodily constitution, or biological organism. This is not to say that the physicalist has no resources at hand, but it does point in the direction of there being something other than the body that is sufficient for personal identity. What might that be for the physicalist? There are two options. One option is to claim that there is

---

19. Another distinct view is called "animalism." The thesis of animalism is simply that I am a human animal, and on many versions I am only contingently a person. See Olson, *The Human Animal*; Merricks, *Objects and Persons*.

20. See Shoemaker, *Personal Identity and Ethics*, chap. 2; also DeGrazia, *Human Identity and Bioethics*.

21. A monist of a sort who is not a materialist could hold this if he or she held that there is something more fundamental to matter and nonmatter. The body might be of this sort of thing. This is beyond what we normally think of as a body, though. On this kind of view, physical matter would be more than gunk, physical stuff, and chemicals.

some fact of the matter beyond that of the body and the physical parts that constitute that body. The second option is to say that there is no fact of the matter, but this seems wrong for the simple fact that something seems to individuate me that I come to believe in my phenomenal experience. If the latter, then it seems that we have reached a stalemate and there is no further question to be explored. If the former, then there are some additional problems worth considering on physicalism. First, it is not clear at all what that fact might be. Second, if there is a fact of the matter that makes one person that person, then either it is potentially inaccessible to us because there is no conceivable physical fact that sufficiently distinguishes one person from another person or it is simply a brute fact of the matter with no sufficient explanatory fact from the physical world in sight. But, let us consider some other related problems.

I wish to mention one problem, that of the persistence of identity. It is difficult to see how persistence in and through time works on a bodily or bodily-constitution view. The body changes every day and takes on new cells; it seems that it is, in fact, not the same body after a phase of time. The idea of personal identity with the body rubs against some basic intuitions about personal identity. Intuitively, from my basic experience of the self, I am something distinct from my body by virtue of the persistent conditions of the self. I realize that materialists affirming something like a body view have responses to this sort of problem, but it appears that the materialist must trade in what is an obvious *given* for what is a confused and complex notion of personhood. Why should one be inclined to reject what is given for what is confused and complex? There is no prephilosophical or intuitive reason for doing so even if materialists can offer a coherent explanation for the above-mentioned intuitions.[22]

A second common materialist view of personal identity is the brain view. The brain view is similar to the bodily-criterion view, because in both views persons are identical to a material object. It seems very natural indeed for proponents of materialism to link the self or the linguistic "I" with the brain on the basis that the brain is responsible for much of the goings on in the biological organism (i.e., body).[23] The brain view is the view that the person identifies with the brain in a holistic sense or identifies with some aspect of the brain, say, the cerebral cortex, wherein the brain controls the functioning of

---

22. This is not a sufficient refutation for denouncing these versions of the bodily view, but I have given some initial reasons for rejecting the view. It is not my intention to offer a foolproof case against these positions here.

23. Van Inwagen, *Material Beings*, chap. 15. Van Inwagen represents one of the earlier animalist views.

the rest of the body—call this the "control center." Here again philosophers seem to assume a linguistic reference "I" as identical with the brain controlling the body. This, as well, seems to have problems. Let me ask a couple of questions and explicitly draw out the implicit answers to those questions. Am I a brain? Do brains think? At first glance, these two questions seem very odd. The question "Am I a brain?" seems to immediately imply a response of no, but I do have a brain. The second question, "Do brains think?" seems odd, because it seems that a brain does not think. Usually, when speaking of thinking, we refer to a person doing the thinking. We could say it this way: "I use my brain to think." This seems much more natural. I can hardly imagine what it means for a brain to think. It is similar to someone saying, "Hand picks up the cup." A hand may pick up a cup, but it is someone's hand picking up the cup. I use my hand to pick up the cup. As a result, the brain view is not a satisfactory view of personal identity either.[24] There are additional considerations that further buttress these intuitions that we will explore below, but, for now, I am raising some of the initial concerns with physicalism as a way of making sense of personal identity. While these concerns are not decisive, they do give us a place to start in our reflections on the nature of our conscious states of awareness. The problem is that these concerns remain upon deeper reflection.

A third and prominent view is the memory or character view of personal identity. This view associates the person with his or her memories or character. The idea is that the person cannot be strictly identified with a physical thing or a physical part. Personhood itself must be more than a physical kind of thing; it must be something of a nonphysical kind: thoughts and memories. Arguably, then, mental items constitute personhood, and these are continuous with one another.[25]

Historically, the memory or character view is associated with John Locke.[26] Although the memory view and the character view can be distinguished, I think that ultimately they are one view, and philosophers often associate them with each other. Proponents of these theories may come from the camp of materialism/physicalism or from the position that persons are immaterial kinds of things. A noticeable difference between this view and the previous two views is that personal identity, according to the memory or character

24. See Foster, *The Immaterial Self.*
25. This possibly assumes a kind of event ontology preceding a substantial ontology. This view requires a causal/relational link between memories. It is also arguable whether this view really is a materialist view of persons at all. There is no relation made to the body/brain but to mental items.
26. Locke, *An Essay Concerning Human Understanding.*

view, is not and cannot be reducible to some physical thing. This requires a materialism of a nonreductive sort.

The character view states that personal identity is found in the connection between the mental states/properties that make up the character (i.e., as in internal virtue and value structure) in question and the present mental states/ properties. On the memory view, I am who I am in virtue of the memories I have in continuous succession. In other words, the memories that are related in continuous fashion constitute who I am. The similarity between the memory and the character views is that there is a continuous link of memory and character states that compose the person. On the character view of personal identity, a person identifies with his or her character states. These are states of being the person has. For example, Johnny exists as a person with the state of being irresponsible, because by not paying his bills, Johnny conditions habits of irresponsibility. Another example: Sammy has the character state of developing a weak will with respect to alcohol. This is so because Sammy has in the past given in one too many times to having an excess of drinks.

Now let's examine the memory view using a thought experiment. Consider person A, who lives a long life full of memories of himself with family, in school, and at work. Person A is fully aware of his past life and experiences day after day. He believes that his daily existence is somehow connected to the past events that he recalls in his memory. Consider person B, who wakes up one day after having surgery on her brain. When she awakens, she has the exact thoughts and memories of person A. This is verifiable because the memories and thoughts of both persons A and B are identical in historical recall. Person B has no recollection of having thoughts or memories of a previous person or historical accounting of another person; she thinks only as if she has been person A. Hence, there is a problem with the memory view, because on appearance, if there is a person A, that person A is not person B. The manner of one's thinking does not necessitate the reality of the situation. My belief that I have climbed Mount Everest does not mean that I have done so. My memory is not sufficient for personhood, although it might be helpful for evidentiary reasons. Memory plays a large role in the formation of personhood, and thus it offers a great deal of evidential support for the reality that this person is this person and not that other person.[27] One could consider various sci-fi examples to bring out this understanding. William Riker, in *Star Trek: The Next Generation*'s 150th episode (season 6, episode 24), splits into two, and both have identical memories and character

27. Remember Thomas Reid's classic thought experiment about a boy who was flogged. See Reid, "Of Mr. Locke's Account of Our Personal Identity."

states, yet we can see that there must be some other fundamental fact that makes Riker *Riker*.

The character view does not, at least immediately, run into the same problems as the memory view. The character view avoids the subjective criterion found in the memory view by requiring states of affairs to constitute personhood. Character states constitute the person and cannot be as easily altered or manipulated as can memories.[28] That said, both views seem to run into the problem of fully satisfying our commonsense ideas and intuitions about human persons. Intuitively, it is wrong to identify persons as a bundle of memories or a set of character states. Instead, when we think and speak of human persons owning memory and developing character states, we speak as if there is a person or a thing *owning* the memories and *having* the character states; thus, it seems that both views are unsatisfying.[29]

Although these views are insufficient for personal identity, they still have a place in the discussion of personal identity. For example, the bodily continuity view might count as empirical evidence for the reality of the same person/soul. Also, theologically, it has a role in accounting for the resurrected body. The memory or character view also has a place in theological discussion. Like bodily continuity, it has a place in supporting the belief in a person as a particular person.[30] It also has a role in the development of souls/persons. The memories we have from our past shape and form the quality of life we have. Character states have a positive role in human flourishing. If an individual substance is obeying God, he or she will have a more enjoyable and flourishing life, as promised in Scripture, in contrast to those who continue in patterns of unrighteousness.[31]

The fourth position, the simple or soul view, identifies persons with souls or some fundamental item found in the brain that is metaphysically indivisible.[32] The simple view is distinguishable from various materialist constructions of human persons and the memory or character view of human persons. On the variation of the simple view that I advance for theological purposes, I take it

---

28. Consider Perry, *Personal Identity*; Perry, *A Dialogue on Personal Identity and Immortality*; Baillie, *Problems in Personal Identity*.

29. Swinburne, *The Evolution of the Soul*, chaps. 8–9. Also, a useful argument is found in Swinburne, "Personal Identity."

30. Swinburne, *The Evolution of the Soul*, chap. 9. Swinburne develops a similar argument.

31. Walls, *Heaven*, 111. Walls makes this argument when speaking of personal identity in the afterlife within the context of trinitarian identity and relational ontology.

32. A person may hold to a proper physical part or something of the sort and does not have to hold to the soul view as synonymous with the simple view. See Swinburne, *The Evolution of the Soul*, chaps. 8–9; also Swinburne, "Personal Identity"; Lowe, "Identity, Composition, and the Simplicity of the Self."

that persons are identical with a soul or an immaterial mental thing.[33] In this case, I am distinct from my body, my brain, and my memory or character. In keeping with the arguments given earlier, I as a person must exist for memories and states of character to exist. This simple view of persons says that persons are not reducible to a material object and are not a bundle of properties (as in the memory or character view). Persons are irreducibly simple, as argued above from phenomenology, introspection (the simple argument), and conceivability and replacement (the replacement argument).[34] Some of the benefits that follow from the simple view include the features of independence and endurance, which presume absolute identity (we will see more on "absolute identity" below). The philosophical benefits overlap with and parallel what we find in theological literature on persons. To this we turn.[35]

The distinct features of the simple view of personhood include independence and the endurance of the substantial soul. The soul, as I see it, is independent in that its identity is not dependent on anything else. The soul has a kind of identity not dependent on or reducible to other properties or substances. The soul precedes its properties in some sense, thus having a kind of independence from them. Next, the soul is an enduring kind of thing. It endures through time. If the soul were a bundle of properties that fluctuate, then identity would fluctuate, or so it seems. On a simple view, predicating properties and identity of the *thing*, or *substance* (i.e., property bearer), is possible. A metaphysical simple has a stable kind of identity that does not fluctuate according to the various sortal phases it encounters. Sortal (i.e., a feature of a thing, substance, in change) phases are nonessential properties wherein a substance exists in and through various moments of existence.[36] Theologically, this is important in accounting for human persons in general and individual persons in particular. A simple substance exists in and through the various stages of time as substantially the same thing. On this view, the person is still the same person even when going through various phases of existence. Predicating properties of a person at two different phases of existence

33. A materialist could develop a simple view by saying that "I" exist somewhere in my brain as a simple self that is not divisible. For reasons I have already mentioned, I do not accept a materialist view of persons because it requires rejecting what is most apparent or what is an experiential given.

34. The fact that I am not my body or a material object can be brought out by distinguishing essential properties and relational properties. Relational properties are nonessential properties.

35. With the simple view, one is able to say that persons as souls can be numerically identical through change yet can change qualitatively.

36. I have written a similar section surveying personal identity with some distinctions in application as part of a completely different argument in a purely philosophical context elsewhere. See Farris, "The Soul-Concept."

is possible. For example, John may exist with a full head of hair at one phase yet persists as the same person while losing his hair. As a metaphysical simple, John is able to exist at different phases.

The simple view seems to make sense of one's reading of Scripture for theological development. It is not my brain or even my eyes that read the Scriptures, but it is "I" that persists absolutely through the stages of my reading various aspects of Scripture. This, then, is presupposed in our reading of Scripture and provides other theological benefits.

Turning to the feature of independence, we find one theological benefit following the assumption of a simple view. If there is an absolute self that has independence, then there is the possibility of predicating properties of the substance/person. Theologically, one can predicate properties of goodness or badness of the individual substance in question. Paul says in Romans 6:17–18, "Thanks be to God that, though *you* used to be slaves to sin, *you* have come to obey from your heart the pattern of teaching that has now claimed *your* allegiance. *You* have been set free from sin and have become slaves to righteousness" (emphasis mine). Paul in effect is ascribing two properties to the person. Once the person was a slave to sin, wrongdoing or badness, and presently the person is a slave to righteousness. One is a property of badness, and the other is a property of righteousness. Other properties—for instance, having wisdom and the freedom to actualize one's latent capacities—naturally presuppose the distinction of an independent substance and its properties. It seems to me that a person is still the same person even if there is some significant accidental change (i.e., change relating to properties). It is not clear, given the initial considerations above, how a physical object could persist as an enduring object, because physical objects are composed of parts and those parts are lost through time and the object (if in fact it is the same object) gains new parts. But what it is that makes a physical object *that* specific physical object is unclear. Again, specifying one particular feature or property that distinguishes not simply the general or common nature of the thing in question but rather what makes one physical object that specific physical object is difficult and, arguably, impossible to discern. This is just one of the unique challenges for a physicalist view of persons that is not uniquely problematic on a simple-soul view. However, on the simple-soul view, what makes the person *that* specific person is not the physical object that it has or is embodied in but rather the soul itself, which is distinct from the physical object in question. On this view, the person is substantially the same person yet accidentally different.

The criterion of endurance—that is, an entity persists substantially the same through change—has theological significance as well and is a unique benefit to the simple-soul view. Substances, at least on this construal, have the theological advantage of identifying a substance/person in and through the stages of time, but this is not the case for a physical object that is constantly changing with cells that are dying and regenerating. The physicalist/ materialist would need to establish that there is an actual thing present that is distinctly that person in order to claim endurance as a unique benefit, but, again, this is a significant challenge for the physicalist. Persons, again, are not reducible to properties, events, or relations. In fact, we can make sense of the reality that persons in redemptive history exist through sortal phases.[37] This means that human persons can identify themselves as enduring in and through the experience of time and change. So, for example, Chris is a thief and a swindler, but upon hearing the gospel of Jesus Christ through his friend Jerry, he comes to know Jesus and is no longer a thief and a swindler. There is a real and important sense in which this person Chris is the same person, yet there is also an important sense in which Chris is different.[38]

The simple-soul view is commensurate with most forms of substance dualism, because it posits a simple substantial "I" that has a body. My intent here is to demonstrate the philosophical truthfulness of the simple-soul view; the soul as a metaphysical substance accounts for personal identity. Additionally, the philosophical literature here seems to find many parallels with the theological literature. I believe that this view coheres with the nature of the theological literature on personhood and the *imago Dei*.

The simple view of persons outlined above seems to account for the commonsense understanding of personal identity. Furthermore, it provides a natural accounting of the scriptural narrative of human beings. Such a view is compatible with a variety of personal ontologies and is, arguably, compatible with variations of substance dualism. Both compound and pure variations of substance dualism affirm that persons are fundamentally immaterial pure substances. It is possible that variants of hylomorphism are compatible with the simple view of personal identity. Thomism, mentioned earlier, is the view that persons are composed of soul and body and that the soul is the form of the body or the principle of life activating the body. While the body and the soul are connected, it is difficult to discern whether the soul really is a metaphysical simple in the way described above because of its existence spatially in the body. The difficulty of how it is simple is a question deserving additional reflection among philosophers. If we have reason to take it that persons just

---

37. Swinburne, *The Christian God*, 13–14.
38. I do not think that the other views of personal identity ground this important distinction allowing for change and sameness.

are their metaphysically simple souls, then this creates a challenge for hylomorphism. For on hylomorphism, persons are composed of a physical nature and a nonphysical form or soul.

There are views other than substance dualism on the table for discussion. It is not clear that they are compatible with the simple view of persons, but one might circumvent the problem and argue for what has been called a not-so-simple simple view of personal identity as advanced by Lynne Rudder Baker, which is worked out with her constitution view (i.e., where persons are higher-order properties/capacities that are constituted by their bodies but are not identical to those bodies). On the not-so-simple view, it is not that we are metaphysically simple but that I am identified with the first-person perspective I have that is constituted by my body, yet my perspective is non-reducible to the parts of my body or even the parts of my body interacting together.[39] Rather, it is a novel higher-order property that makes me *me*. One might be inclined to call this the "software" view of humanity because the first-person perspective (i.e., software) depends on hardware but is not identical to that hardware.[40] Taking into account the bodily-constitution theory and the fact that minds/persons are dependent on the hardware does raise concerns about the stability of the view, which is one reason in favor of some version of substance dualism.

Now let's look at some additional reasons for thinking that substance dualism of some variety, in which the mind or soul is a pure immaterial substance, is superior and more likely true than hylomorphism or some other sophisticated version of physicalism.

Why Accept Substance Dualism as a Theological Position?

I offer three reasons for accepting substance dualism that correspond to the idea in the arguments given above that the human person is a metaphysical simple. I give a reason from my experience, otherwise called knowledge by acquaintance (i.e., knowledge from first-personal conscious experience or,

39. Other personal ontologies might be able to garner the not-so-simple simple view in their court, which is the view that humans are composed (i.e., they comprise complex parts) but persons are identical to the first-person consciousness rather than a proper or actual substance (i.e., a thing; instead it is an impure substance). The relation to the actual substantial parts is not identical to the first-person perspective. On this view, I am identical not to the animal part(s), but rather to my first-person perspective, and, yet, this is circular because there is not a substance to point to. Certainly, other versions of complex/composite substance dualism that affirm that personal identity is found not strictly in the soul but also in the body could endorse something like this view. Variations of hylomorphism are included in that view.

40. Thanks to Kevin Wong for reminding me of this.

stated simply, a reason from experience), in the philosophical literature, along with two other arguments. The first argument is from the simplicity of the self; the second is an argument for my being simple and not identifiable with the material aggregate I call my body.

I suggest that I have a basic and direct experience of myself.[41] I am simple and absolute because I cannot be broken down into parts. I cannot be reduced to my essential constituents or properties. I am the kind of thing that exists in and through my thinking and the stages of my bodily existence. I am fully present at each stage of my existence. I know this through introspection. I know when something is crawling on my arm as I am thinking about myself. I know that if I were to lose one limb, I would still be me. Even if I were to lose part of my brain, I would still exist. If I were to lose my memory of past events, this would in no way nullify my existence. I know that I would still exist because distinct memories are not essential to my being who I am. We can imagine a situation in which a criminal is guilty of a crime committed but has since hit his head in such a way as to alter his state of awareness. We would still, presumably, claim that this person is guilty and deserving of whatever punishment was originally given. I know that I am not an inference of my thinking but rather a precondition of my thinking. When I think about anything, it presupposes a thing thinking. If I am thinking about eating a burrito or a pizza, then I have knowledge by acquaintance—with myself and my thinking. According to my phenomenal seemings, I exist at every point through change and there is a property of self-presentation that bears itself at every moment of my conscious existence. The point is that I have a kind of existence that is absolute and simple. The nature that I have undergirds thinking and bodily existence.[42] While self-evident properties could be articulated on other views of personhood, it is not clear that the feature that individuates the selfsame properties that present themselves in and through one's thinking is explained on all the views of personhood. What is required is some fundamental fact that makes one person that person and not another person. It seems, once again, that a metaphysically simple view of personhood is necessary if we want to supply a sufficient view of personhood where some fundamental fact makes this person that person. In this way, a soul supplies us with an advantage.

41. See Chisholm, "The Problem of the Criterion." Chisholm develops this notion of "seeming" more fully. Also see Tucker, "Phenomenal Conservatism."

42. Chisholm, *Person and Object*, chap. 1. Chisholm has famously developed the notion of self-presenting properties. He offers a very convincing argument in favor of our being directly acquainted with our self through having an individual proposition that uniquely identifies the person. From this basis we are able to individuate. I am able to individuate myself and others. What I have done here is asserted that I have direct acquaintance with my self, which seems to be a natural perception. Furthermore, it seems that this is the commonsense view of self.

Stewart Goetz and E. J. Lowe have each individually put forth a similar argument, in keeping with the intuitions above, in favor of a simple self not dependent on the material body or nonessential properties.[43] This is an argument from intuition. Goetz goes on to argue that one's consciousness of actual states of affairs grounds the intuitive logic of possibility.[44] His argument is essentially this: (1) I am essentially a simple entity (having no parts that can be separated). (2) A physical body is essentially complex and thus has parts able to be separated. (3) The principle of the indiscernibility of identicals says that for identity to take place, x must have every property had by y at a time, and the same goes that y must have every property had by x. It would not be the case that at different times the same person, x, would be essentially bodily, for there are times that x might lose her legs in the act of battle, but presumably she would remain the same person. (4) Therefore, on the basis of these premises, I am not identical with my (or any) physical body. It is still possible that I am a proper part of my body or depend on some minimal bodily composition or something of the sort.[45] But if there is a distinct kind of thing thinking, and thinking is not material, it is more likely that I am a nonmaterial thing over against a proper physical part of my body.[46]

A more modest argument, which might be accepted as promising by a wider audience, is an argument from replacement, indicating that I am a distinct kind of thing that has a simple nature not dependent on the material body. The replacement argument is given by Alvin Plantinga.[47] Plantinga argues along these lines: I am a substance, but if I am a physical substance, I would be a proper part of my physical body, composed of my body or collocated with my body. I am not my body or a proper physical part of my body. I am not composed of my body or collocated with my body. Therefore, I must be an immaterial kind of thing. Plantinga offers some thought experiments to bring out this argument. He begins by asking the question, "If I am a physical thing, what kind of physical thing am I?" The argument begins with an

---

43. Goetz, "Modal Dualism"; Lowe, "In Defence of the Simplicity Argument."

44. Goetz, "Modal Dualism."

45. Lowe, "Identity, Composition, and the Simplicity of the Self." Lowe gives an argument for my being a simple self that leaves open the possibility that I am minimally dependent on part of my body. The problem with Lowe's ontology of human persons is that it leaves no place for near-death experiences or the intermediate state wherein the self can exist apart from the body. This is problematic.

46. Goetz, "Modal Dualism," 102. Goetz, in discussing the possible conclusions of the argument, mentions this possibility that I could be a physical proper part. Being aware of one's simplicity is a strong intuition.

47. Plantinga, "Against Materialism."

intuition conceiving possibility: I have the property possibly to exist when my body does not.[48] We know from experience that surgeons can replace organs with new organs. We know of people who have had liver, heart, knee, hip, ankle, and lung replacements. What about my brain? Would I exist if I had a brain replacement? It seems at least conceivable that I am distinct from my brain and possibly could exist apart from my brain.[49] It seems possible that I could still exist with all my bodily parts destroyed.[50] If this is possible, I cannot be identical with the whole of my body that I presently have or with the composition of my body.

Then Plantinga asks the question of speeding up the process of replacing each part of my body down to the cellular level at a rapid pace. (Think of the transporter in *Star Trek*, which transfers the particles of the person from one time and place to another time and place.) Would the rate of speed for replacement undermine the fact that I am modally distinct from my body and all the body's parts? It seems not. If replacement is possible at a much slower pace, why should it matter if the rate is much faster? Plantinga's point is that it is likely that we are not identical to our bodies, nor do parts of our bodies compose or collocate with our selves.[51] At the end of the day, it seems plausible that we would remain the selfsame person through replacement, and the speed for which this occurs would have no bearing on the possibility of its occurring.

If these arguments work, we have reason to reject various forms of materialism in favor of the view that human persons are a soul with a body.[52] The arguments listed above give some grounds for thinking that persons are not material things, identified with a physical part, or composed of material things but are a different kind of thing. This kind of thing has different persistence conditions than do material kinds of things, and they are distinct from material things. It is important for my purposes to establish a prima facie case in favor of substance dualism. Any philosophical or theological anthropology ought to accept the notion that the human substance or soul as substance is a simple immaterial thing.[53] I believe that this is not only philosophically

48. Plantinga, "Against Materialism," 388.

49. Swinburne, *Evolution of the Soul*, chap. 8 and new appendix C. This is one version of the argument for substance dualism from modality. It fits very well with the argument from replacement with respect to conceivability and modality.

50. Plantinga, "Against Materialism," 388–89.

51. Plantinga, "Against Materialism," 390–91.

52. For a useful cataloging of these arguments and others like these, see Moreland, *The Recalcitrant* Imago Dei.

53. Again, this is the most common view throughout history, including ecclesiastical history. It is very common among the patristics and the medievals. For one very thoughtful example, see Gregory of Nyssa, *On the Soul and the Resurrection*, 40–44.

true but also assumed in the scriptural portrayal of humanity. Hence, this provides a basis for approaching the Scriptures. Additionally, if my basic experiences interface with the text of Scripture and accord with the traditional understanding, then we have additional justification for affirming a theological notion of persons as simple souls.

An Ethical Argument for Dualism, Not Materialism

Materialist philosopher David Shoemaker has argued that the normal means of determining the criterion of identity in specific moral actions is irrelevant to substance dualism.

> Holding people responsible, compensating them, determining the moral relation between fetuses and the adult humans into which they develop, determining the moral relation between early- and late-stage Alzheimer's patients, and . . . rationally anticipating some future experience(s)—all of these practical concerns and commitments presuppose our ability to identify and track whatever criterion of identity turns out to ground them; they presuppose a tight connection, that is, between the metaphysical and epistemological senses of "criterion of personal identity." Consequently, any theory of personal identity to which we lack this kind of epistemological access is just going to be *practically* irrelevant.[54]

In other words, the normal means of detection is a separate issue from the fact of the soul's existence. However, this line of reasoning misses something important about the soul doctrine that is necessary for determining personal identity as the ground for moral actions.

Jonathan Loose carefully articulates why the soul is not irrelevant to moral matters:

> The "soul criterion" cannot be dismissed on the grounds that it entails an understanding of personal identity that is irrelevant to practical concerns. Nor is this criterion less able to reveal the facts about identity in a given situation as compared with a complex criterion based on empirical (typically physical or psychological) continuity. In either case there are conceivable situations in which we could be deceived or uncertain about the identities of persons. The reasonableness of the claim that empirical continuities provide evidence of identity establishes that the soul criterion is not at a disadvantage in this respect.[55]

54. Shoemaker, *Personal Identity and Ethics*, 32–33.
55. Loose, "Christian Materialism and Christian Ethics." See also, in the same volume of essays, some similar points made by Menuge, "Christian Physicalism and Our Knowledge of God."

According to Loose, the soul has no disadvantage in this way. In fact, a complex, empirically based criterion for personal identity (e.g., the memory or character view) is compatible with a view of personal identity that includes a doctrine of the soul. Loose is right, then, to point out that the soul brings no impediment to determining moral identity.

In fact, one could argue that the soul doctrine has at least one advantage. Souls, on most views, lack the feeble changeable properties characteristic of bodies. Thus, souls, arguably, are simple in themselves and can endure through time as the selfsame individuals that exist absolutely. If this is true, then souls can ground the persistence of the same individual in and through various moral actions.

I have argued elsewhere for one variation of the soul doctrine: persons are not only identical to souls but also have a unique property or feature that makes each person identical to his or her self. On this view, souls have a subjective or personal essence feature/property (i.e., a feature or a property that sufficiently describes a subjective consciousness or a person). In keeping with what I argued earlier, if we are able to provide a sufficient explanation of persons, then we need a thing that carries a fundamental fact that distinguishes it from the body, its parts, and uniquely describes the person. We need what some philosophers have called a primitive feature that sufficiently describes the person and distinguishes one person from another. This grounds moral action across time.[56] How, then, does the body factor into personal identity? Defenders of the personal ontologies listed above answer this question in different ways.

The Body and Narrative Identity

If persons are substances—immaterial substances—and persons are identical to the immaterial part of the human being, this seems to leave little room for the body. The body, it would seem, has no direct role in strict personal identity. Rather, the body is, on the surface, not part of personal identity. It is not that the body is unimportant to personal identity but, more radically, that it is nonessential to personal identity. Such a state of affairs does raise an important question.

Does the body have no role to play in who we are? In other words, is there any reason to think that bodies are relevant to who we are as persons? It would seem that at one level the body is simply irrelevant but that at another level

---

56. I have developed a similar argument elsewhere in a theological context where I criticize Lynne Rudder Baker's view. See Farris, "Bodily-Constituted Persons."

this cannot be. As in other facets of our lives, some contingent features are significant, we assume, to who we are. They are not essential to our personal identity, but they are important nonetheless. Like our vocations (as firefighters, chaplains, professors, etc.) or the choices we have made in our past, our bodies are important. Our bodies are even more important in that they are fundamental to so much that we participate in in this life. Our bodies are a fundamental part of our narrative identity.

Narrative identity is the identity that is contingent on the relationships we enter into. Narrative identity is fundamentally second-personal (i.e., narratives that use "you" in a way that brings the reader into the story and that helps the reader imaginatively assume the identity of the character in the story) in that our narrative depends on the relationships we have with other people and our environment. When I say, "I am a professor," I am making a statement about my story. I am saying something about what it is that I am in the context of the relationships that I have and the functions that I fill in my sphere of influence. When I say, "I grew up in St. Louis, Missouri," I am once again making a statement about my story and some of the facts contained therein. It is here that I believe the body plays a fundamental role in one's narrative identity.

The creaturely nature of my existence comprises, in part, my narrative identity. The creational story bears this out when discussing the human being as born of God's breath and of dust (Gen. 2). In fact, the whole of my identity is wrapped up in the fact of my being a body-soul unit capable of reflecting the divine in the context of my creaturely nature. In contrast to any denigration of the body, the Scriptures presume that the bodily nature, in addition to the soul, is necessary to my story—that story I share with others. Kelly Kapic has made this clear:

> There is nothing in the biblical account of creation to hint that earthiness or human physicality is bad or problematic. Finite? Yes. All remain creatures and will never become the self-existent and self-sustaining Creator. That is and always remains reserved for God alone. Yet this finite creatureliness is not shameful or immoral but purposeful and good. The psalmist happily connects creation with God's wisdom:
>
>> O Lord, how manifold are your works!
>> In wisdom you have made them all;
>> the earth is full of your creatures. (Ps. 104:24)[57]

57. Kapic, *Embodied Hope*, 46.

The scriptural narrative describes our creaturely existence as being formed by our generation. Consider Job 14:1–2:

> Man who is born of a woman
>> is few of days and full of trouble.
> He comes out like a flower and withers;
>> he flees like a shadow and continues not. (ESV)

This does raise some questions about how it is that the body functions in our personal identity. One could take up several lines of thought in developing the role of the body in one's narrative identity. I will mention three reasons why the body factors prominently in one's narrative identity.

First, the body plays a role in one's gender identification. If we take it that gender is related to biological sex, chromosomal sex, and the like, then the body has an important role to play in gender identity, arguably. The body is a way for the soul to act, and acting apart from the body would be difficult in some cases to conceive.[58]

Second, the body plays a role in our physical activity. Consider the fact that our everyday life is embodied. We eat with our bodies. We hear with our bodies. We see with our bodies. This leads to another important aspect of our bodies.

Third, the body plays a role in our social interactions. We use our bodies to communicate verbally and with touch and nonverbal bodily expressions. It is also important to point out that our bodies provide ways for interacting with God through prayer, praise, liturgy, and, really, all actions rightly governed and done in faith. The Christian story supports the fact that our bodies are important for interacting with God. As exemplified in the creation story and the redemption story, we are embodied beings. In our final state of existence in the future, we will also be embodied with new bodies.

Narrative Identity and Contingent Identities

We have several identities in some important sense. We are not simply the constitutional makeup of body and soul, as described above. Yet while all our activities refer to the soul and/or body, the most interesting aspects of our lives include our conditioning, our choices, and the contingencies of our lives.

---

58. J. Peterson, "Three Forms of Meaning." Peterson raises concerns about artificial intelligence being able to act because of the disembodied problem. Thanks to Kevin Wong for pointing this out to me.

While contingent, our narrative identities are also causally influential on our outlook. We are bodily beings that are nurtured by our parents, who live and behave according to ethnic and national boundaries. We, too, come into being in the context of ethnic and national boundaries. We are bred, to some extent, within a nation that has practices, customs, laws, and artifacts, and we carry many of these with us through life. They sustain our existence and give us meaning. To suggest that these are unimportant to how we think and understand our human identity would be silly. The whole history of the world is marked by ethnic and national distinctions that play some role in the shaping and sustaining of human identity. In fact, ancient Israel's kingdom was marked by its ethnic and national distinctions, which played a role at every level of Israelite life. The eschatological kingdom of God that is to come will be marked not by one ethnicity but rather by national diversity that will characterize the whole life of individuals who participate in the newly formed kingdom.

Within our ethnic and national identities there is what some might consider a culture. Culture is socially constructed by large groups of people (ethnicities, nations) and groups of people within those larger groups of people.[59] These groups shape perspectives, tastes, and sensibilities. Examples of groups within the United States include various Asian communities and Hispanic communities as well as Caucasian communities. Common to all nations are the cultural distinctions between the working class and the rich, and many nations also have a middle (and upper-middle) class. Other examples of cultural difference that play into our narrative identity include the distinctions between regions of the United States, from West Coast to East Coast and North to South. For upper-middle-class families living in the South as well as the Midwest and presumably other parts of the United States, it is commonly expected that children will receive a college education, even higher forms of education (from graduate to doctoral education). Another cultural feature is that people of the middle to upper-middle class tend to look more highly on those who bring children into the world than those who do not bring children into the world. In other words, it is, arguably, an issue of status. It is also not uncommon for different parts of the United States to be dominated by loyalties to a particular sports team for which friends and families arrange their schedules accordingly. In small towns this loyalty often applies to high school sports teams and extends across generational gaps. It is common for small towns to rally around their high school football team as a

59. Acts 17:26 seems to give credence to the legitimacy of nations as God's design by recognizing different nations in God's providential care and as a reflection of creational diversity.

collective activity that carries with it all sorts of ritualistic practices: singing chants, saying prayers, and hitting up the local diner after the game. Culture is important in theological anthropology for understanding human identity individually and also for grasping an understanding of our communal and societal identities. It is also important for understanding the contingencies of how it is that Christian theology has shaped the foundations of a particular society/community and how it functions to maintain the very practices that cause the society/community to persist.

Another important facet of narrative identity includes gender and sexuality. I mention this here because gender and sexuality are shaped and molded in the context of cultural perceptions on what it means to be male and female. Furthermore, our culture shapes how we practice our gender in our daily living. Certainly, symbols and artifacts that are often perceived as gendered are social developments within a particular culture, but I am in no way suggesting that this is not already preceded by the ontological constitution of human beings. We will take up this topic in more detail in chapter 8.

Narrative Identity and Metathemes of Creation and Redemption

I have laid out some of the pertinent data regarding the creational identity of human beings. God designs human beings as covenantal beings intended for relationship with him. God fashions humans in a particular way so that they have the capacity to enter into relationship with others as covenantal representatives in the world.

Relatedly, some important features of our narrative identity are continuous with both creation and redemption. God elects a people with whom to enter into a covenant. First, he chose the original created human beings, and after the fall of humankind, God chose a covenantal people to carry out his plan of salvation. Second, God gives humans capacities to respond to his communication, and as we respond appropriately, our capacities for seeing and knowing God grow. Third, as Brian S. Rosner has carefully noted in more than one place, one important feature of our identity is the fact that God knows us.[60] Not only does God know all the facts about us, such as how many hairs we have on our heads (Matt. 10:30), but also he knows us as his covenantal representatives who are called with a purpose and a task—something that David finds comfort in (2 Sam. 7:20). For those of

60. See Rosner, *Known by God*.

us who are saved and united to Christ, God knows us in a more intimate relational and familial sense (1 Cor. 8:3). Even more, it is not simply God generally but Christ, the Son of God, who knows us. The whole of the triune God knows us. God the Father knows us as his children, the Son knows us as our brother, and the Spirit seals us in love to the Father and the Son (see Rom. 8, especially v. 29, and Rev. 2). Building on the themes of God's knowing us and our responding appropriately to God's knowing us, we grow in our capacity to both hear and see God.

Consider one of the most important biblical passages about hearing: "The gatekeeper opens the gate for him, and the sheep listen to his voice. He calls his own sheep by name and leads them out. When he has brought out all his own, he goes on ahead of them, and his sheep follow him because they know his voice" (John 10:3–4). This broader theme of Christ's calling and our response brings together several other themes within John's Gospel that echo the theme of God's choosing and knowing his covenantal people in the Old Testament, which is also tied to another theme in John, that of vision or seeing God. For example, when Christ calls Mary Magdalene by name after his resurrection (John 20:16), she not only hears him but also, responding to his voice, later says, "I have seen the Lord!" (John 20:18). All of this is made sense of by the purpose statement in John's Gospel, which is that readers may believe that Jesus Christ is the Son of God (John 20:30–31). This theme of believing in and coming to know Christ is exemplified in Christ's call and then in our response (as seen in Mary Magdalene and also Nathanael and the Samaritan woman). Similar to the way we see God knowing us in the Old Testament and Christ knowing us in the New Testament, we see a stepping-up process from both Testaments in terms of our capacity to imagine God in Christ as we *image* Christ. Yet this process, as I understand it, does not mitigate or expunge the creational image and capacity for hearing, responding to, and seeing God. Rather, it builds on and enhances it.

This theme of personal identity in Scripture not only ties to God's knowing us as his covenantal people but also includes our hearing and seeing. Hearing and seeing are often overlapping themes that contribute to our understanding of personal identity, or narrative identity, as seen above in John's Gospel. Jesus bears out this important theme in John when he says, "Anyone who has seen me has seen the Father" (John 14:9). Upon hearing the gospel call, humans perceive the identity of Christ in a novel way— where Christ is God the Father's beloved Son and the one who reveals God the Father. In this way, something occurs to the capacities of the one responding.

Conclusion

As I laid out above, the Reformed theological tradition highlights "hearing" as a metaphor for the internal response of the soul by the Holy Spirit's work. Hearing and responding to the true revelation of God—Christ, "who is the image of God" (2 Cor. 4:4)—is a theme that plays itself out in the whole of the New Testament, where the people of God (the church) identify as God's sheep (John 10:3–4) and children (Rom. 8:29). Yet our new status in the new covenant is predicated on or evidenced by our hearing, responding to, and seeing God in the revelation of the Son of God—Jesus Christ. I have argued, briefly, that an important part of narrative identity, spelled out in the Scriptures, includes the notion of hearing and seeing. In the previous chapter I discussed how seeing was an important and dominating theological theme of medieval theology that described human destiny. This theme did not conclude in the Middle Ages but rather was carried along and refashioned in important ways in the Reformed tradition. One of the dominant topics of the Reformation is its emphasis on "hearing," and "hearing" as it is related to "seeing" God and seeing all of reality in view of the triune God at work.

All of this has an important role to play in how we develop a conception of personal identity. Personal identity is an area of concern that touches on the what and the who of individual agents. The what and the who are related, which is why I started this discussion by giving an answer to the first part of the question. In that section I considered the various metaphysical options of personal identity. These include the body view, the brain view, the memory or character view, and the simple view. I concluded with the suggestion that we are probably souls (i.e., immaterial substances). I also argued that we have good biblical and theological reasons, not only philosophical reasons, for accepting the simple view of personal identity as the metaphysical accounting for the biblical and theological data. Building on these metaphysical options, I worked through some other themes in personal identity, a kind of thickening up of how we understand personal identity. I suggested that we think about personal identity as narrative identity. In this way, I gave some answer to the who question of personal identity. Moreover, I argued that our personal identity is composed of the content from the movement and the purpose found in the biblical story as it has been received and understood by Christians through the ages. These ideas point to a more robust understanding of personal identity and require that we consider persons in light of their bodies and in light of their relations with God and others.

2

What Am I and Where Did I Originate?

Are We Apes, Humans, or Gods?

Don't be afraid; you are worth more than many sparrows.

Matthew 10:31

God is said to have rested from all his work (Gen. 2:2), not by retiring from the administration of things, but by ceasing from the creation of new species or individuals (which might be the principles of new species). Thus he works even now (Jn. 5:17) by administering the instituted nature and multiplying whatever was; not, however, by instituting what was not. Now the souls which he creates every day are new individuals of species already created.

Francis Turretin, Institutes of Elenctic Theology, *question 13*

Mary Shelley's *Frankenstein* paints a picture of human creation, but not from traditional conceptualities of the divine imparting life to a body or the creation of souls in bodies. Rather, Shelley relates a story of human origins (although it is not entirely clear that the creature is in fact human, even if the parts composing the daemon previously composed other humans) from the hands of another human. Contemporary stirrings reflect this move toward a reconceiving of humans in fresh new ways. In recent discussions on the nature and uniqueness of humans, the conceptual options for conceiving human origins have expanded. In a theistic context, while humans are often construed as biologically generated organisms, the identity of humans is already situated in a broader story of divine creation along with the view that humans are somehow unique among organisms.[1]

As with other facets of the human story, human origins yield content on our creaturely status as well as our divine status. Human origins point to our creaturely status before God, and the fact that humans come into existence necessitates that human existence is somehow dependent on something else or some*one* else. It dictates that our existence is neither causally necessary nor independent of other conditions. We are not eternal, immutable, or essentially immortal in nature. In fact, our creaturely origins seem to point us to the divine cause in whom we live and have our being—as stated in the book of Acts (17:28). From another perspective, our origins might point to our divine end as human beings.[2] The fact of our existence is mysterious,

---

1. It is important to point out that the soul of humanity is central to much of the dogmatic developments of human uniqueness throughout church history. In fact, the Roman Catholic Catechism bears this out when it says, "The divine image is present in every man" (§1702), and "Endowed with 'a spiritual and immortal' soul, the human person is 'the only creature that God has willed for its own sake'" (§1703). The Reformed theological tradition did not depart from the general contours of human uniqueness as spelled out in the Roman Catholic Catechism. In fact, almost every Reformed symbol describes or presumes the uniqueness of humanity from the rest of God's creation in virtue of an "immortal soul" that is able to know God and is able to grow in virtue. The *Large Emden Catechism* (1551) reflects this understanding of humanity: "This image of God was in Adam in the beginning, by virtue of which he was immortal, holy, wise, and lord of the entire world, and thus was endowed with the freedom and ability to completely execute or disregard the commandment of God." The Westminster Confession of Faith offers even more detail to the Reformed heritage: "After God had made all other creatures, He created man, male and female, with reasonable and immortal souls, endued with knowledge, righteousness, and true holiness, after His own image" (chap. 4, art. 2).

2. Several possible theological implications follow from the creation of souls. For one, if there is a necessity that God (or a supernatural being) create the soul directly, then it could serve as an important argument from nature for the existence of God. As a source of theological reflection, the human and, particularly, the soul have provided fertile foundations for thinking about God and his relation to the rest of creation. One implication is that the soul is heavenly in origin like the angels. The difference, at least initially, is that humans have bodies, but how this differs in the eschatological state is a matter of important discussion. Another implication is that the created soul is necessary for the knowledge of the eternal reality and of God's nature, which is the primary distinction between humans and other animals. Another possible implication is that human origins imply human purpose—namely, heavenly occupation. The present discussion also overlaps with an important discussion about the relationship between nature and grace (i.e., the relation between humanity in creation and humanity in redemption). Human origins could yield the fact that humans are designed for union with the divine even if humans had not fallen into sin, which tells us something about human nature and the story of humans that requires the intended end of the elevation of human nature. Whether human

even mysteriously divine in origin. Our existence is not just mysterious in the way that all of creation is mysterious; there are distinct facts about the story of human origins for which some special divine action seems necessary. The physical network of causes and effects is uniquely unsuited to account for the origins of individual humans. While the physical network of causes and effects is, arguably, necessary, it is insufficient and unable to bring about the transcendent nature of human beings. If in fact there is some unique transcendent feature or property of humans, then this might give us a glimpse into human purpose.

Before we address the topic of human origins, we must consider the nature of what it means to be human in the scientific literature and the science-and-theology literature. There is often a complicated assumption that the same humans we interact with are genetically connected to a wider biological species, often called *Homo sapiens* or, more recently, *Homo sapiens sapiens*.[3] This raises additional questions about the nature of humans or what set of humans we are describing when we bring the biological data in conversation with the theological data. Kenneth Kemp has recently parsed out distinctions in a way that helps facilitate discussion.[4] We might think of humans from a biological, philosophical, or theological standpoint. Biological humans are genetic humans. This of course raises the question of where to draw the line on the nature of humans. Do we draw the line at *Homo sapiens*, or Neanderthal, or some other species that is in proximity in the evolutionary line? Philosophical humans are described as those creatures that are self-aware, rational, and have a set of abilities that are dependent on first-person consciousness. Yet this raises the possibility that there could be other individuals that have first-person consciousness along with the abilities to self-reflect and deliberate who would not normally be categorized historically as human. We could conceive of other persons with these abilities on other planets, or potentially on earth, who lack the genetic

ends are accidental human nature or essential is a subject of much discussion. Also, the fact that humans have a natural end raises the question about how the supernatural end is related (as something only added by God in and through the church or as something that is simply a fulfillment of what is natural). Finally, human origins have implications for the beatific vision. As Douglas Farrow helpfully states, "Now it may be that the immediate creation of the soul implies no more than that the soul is the kind of thing that can recognize that God is and what God is, the kind of thing that can articulate the honor owed to God as first principle" (Farrow, *Theological Negotiations*, 43).

3. A reference to a slightly more advanced subgroup within *Homo sapiens*, which includes Neanderthal. See Fran Dorey, "*Homo Sapiens*—Modern Humans," Australian Museum, https://australianmuseum.net.au/learn/science/human-evolution/homo-sapiens-modern-humans/.

4. Kemp, "Science, Theology, and Monogenesis."

connection to us now. But then what about theological humans? Theological humans, according to the Bible and the Christian tradition, are those who are recipients of God's saving grace in and through the covenants that God revealed to us in Scripture.

With these important distinctions laid out, it is not my intention to separate or divide them when talking about human beings, for there are ways to reconcile the terms. I see these as helpful conceptual distinctions instead of actual distinctions. However, with additional data from science (e.g., paleontology, biology, cognitive science), we may need to spell out these distinctions of the theological human from human communities that may be understood as philosophical humans or from other sets of humans in the biological sense. These distinctions are particularly helpful when trying to articulate the relationship that humans have to Adam in the Christian story. The story presumes that humans are related to Adam, but the question is how and who is it that is being referred to in the biblical text. But these matters are complicated by both evolutionary theory and by the discussion on the age of the earth. On a young-earth view, where the earth has existed for somewhere between four thousand and twenty thousand years, it is easier to make sense of the fact that all humans, biological, theological, and philosophical, are related to Adam. On this account, there is not a challenge for thinking about Adam as biologically or genetically related to all of humanity. However, when we consider that the earth is old, we are confronted with a set of complicated interrelated questions about Adam and humanity: Is Adam historical? When did he come on the scene? Is all of humanity related to Adam? If they are related, then how so? What set of humans presently in the species classification is related biologically or genetically to Adam? For now, I take it that while these conceptual distinctions are helpful for clarifying the discussion, there is not an actual distinction that amounts to a separation between the biological, the philosophical, and the theological. Theological humans described in Scripture do not appear to be actually distinct from a biological categorization of the same species somewhere in the distant evolutionary past. Furthermore, I take it as a common working assumption that philosophical humans are described in Scripture and are not somehow sets of human communities that are excluded from the scriptural class of people designated as covenantal participants.[5] However, we need to

5. I further take it that all humans on earth are united as one set of people. Are humans human by virtue of being in the image of God? Or do all humans on earth just bear the image of God as a common property? On either account, one can take it that all references to humans in Scripture are references to humans on Earth. We will look at these issues in a bit more detail in a later chapter.

provide some narrative explanation that accounts for some of the details of the biblical story line as they relate to the evolutionary data and an old earth where "humans" (at least biologically construed) have been around for several hundred thousand years, and possibly millions, because presumably all biological humans would not be genetically related to the historical Adam directly referenced in the biblical story line. For these reasons, there have been recent attempts to think about human origins in fresh ways that include the broader evolutionary framework. I see this generally as a positive development within the literature on constructive and systematic theological anthropology. To this we turn.

In his extensive and thoughtful interdisciplinary theological engagement with human origins, J. Wentzel van Huyssteen argues that we must understand humans as concrete embodied wholes that are situated in a wider biological evolutionary framework with kinship similarities to higher-order animals. Humans, he suggests, are products of biological evolution rather than direct divine creations that are somehow externally and causally, and tenuously, related to biological evolution. Van Huyssteen thoughtfully shows that humans are unique not in that we are soul creatures but because of our history, sophisticated language, self-awareness, moral awareness, consciousness, and imaginative capacity. This view finds support in paleontology and cognitive science.[6]

Van Huyssteen, following Edward Farley, and others are convinced that Christians need to reconceive the story of human origins: we ought to conceive of humans in this wider biological-evolutionary story. Van Huyssteen offers three options for understanding humans. The first states that the "real" human is found in the sciences, with little more than a nod to theological disciplines. The second states that the "real" human is found in the theological disciplines, with a head tilt to the sciences. The third option is what he calls the dualistic option. According to this option, humans are somehow composed of a spiritual substance and a bodily substance. He writes,

> Any theologian wishing to choose this dualist option would find it almost impossible not to fall back into the second option, giving only lip service to the biological and embodied aspects of what it means to be human. This kind of theological view acknowledges our biological and evolutionary dimensions, but what is argued further is that we have developed so far beyond our animal and instinctual natures toward something spiritually unique, that we have virtually no biological nature to take into account at all when talking about humanness. On this view human agency is interpreted as whatever transcends

6. Van Huyssteen, *Alone in the World?*, 278.

the biological, and therefore focuses almost exclusively on the "spiritual," or on culture, language, freedom, history, and the personal.[7]

Van Huyssteen has laid out three options for conceiving of humans in the context of the data received from the sciences and the data received from theological disciplines. It is precisely this third option, or something near it, that I wish to defend by surveying the various options of human origin stories. In fact, I contend that in our perceptual vision of human nature, something is missing. That something is a capacity for spiritual vision and an explanation for the soul's coming into existence. These two features are insufficiently accounted for when a human being is said to emerge solely from the material stuff that precedes it. It is difficult to see how material stuff could produce a human that includes a fundamental immaterial part—a soul. In no way is this an attempt to mitigate the uniqueness of human history or custom, as emphasized by van Huyssteen and others, but it is to suggest that such an approach is not inconsistent with the claim that humans are souls with a richer transcendent story of origins. Upon entering into the discussion of the contemporary story of human origins, I will argue that such a story lacks a sufficient condition for human origins. The result is that we must reenter an old debate on the origin of the soul. I will come to this in a moment, but first I discuss humans as evolutionary products.

The Evolutionary Story

A question about the compatibility of human evolution with Christian thought has prompted and continues to prompt the thinking Christian. The general story is as follows. All physical organisms are adaptive and encounter gradual change, sometimes radical change. Concerning physical organisms, one common assumption is that all physical organisms are connected continuously all the way back to a common ancestor. The mechanisms for the evolutionary development between species are adaptation to the environment and natural selection (i.e., intrinsic variation between species, differential reproduction, and traits inherited that bring about survival and reproduction or the demise of a species). There is much debate about the essential features of evolutionary theory. Biologists themselves disagree on what is entailed by the evolutionary story, and those within the Christian community disagree substantially on what factors are compatible with the Christian story. I will parse out some of these distinctions below as we consider the human evolutionary story in light of Christian anthropology.

7. Van Huyssteen, *Alone in the World?*, 277–78. See also Farley, *Good and Evil*, 82.

The growing consensus seems to be that some variant of evolutionary theory is in fact compatible with the Christian story of human origins.[8] However, that depends on what we mean when are talking about evolutionary theory. Mere evolutionary theory that amounts to minor adaptive changes within species has unanimous support within the Christian community, even among those who support a strictly literal interpretation of the Bible and hold to young-earth creationism. Those who depart from a strict literalism of parts of the Bible and deny young-earth creationism, instead affirming old-earth creationism, are able to affirm some sort of "continuity" of species between animals and humans. It also seems plausible that a common ancestry between humans and lower-level animals is compatible with the biblical story, at least as it is construed physically and biologically.

At least one variation of the evolutionary theory is clearly out of bounds in traditional Christianity. I call this view "evolutionary humanism" (i.e., the view that humans are on an upward incline, becoming more developed as a species in biological evolution, and this without the mediation of some supernatural agent guiding or intervening in the process) because of its affinities to secular humanism, which denies theism or theistic activity in the world.[9] Evolutionary humanism, in short, is the theory that humans are the apex of evolutionary development and that morals, values, and purpose are human constructs or by-products of the evolutionary story. In other words, humans are the arbiters of morals, values, and purpose. Humans in this narrative have developed from higher-level animals all the way back through the history of the world. On this theory, God has no unique or special role in the evolutionary production of humans; instead, humans are solely products of physical causes and effects. Humans find their cause for existence in the causal nexus of the physical world.

There are two ideas here that are specifically out of bounds in Christian anthropology. First, as stated in the Nicene Creed and the Apostles' Creed, God is the maker of heaven and earth, of all things, visible and invisible. Those variations of evolutionary humanism that give no credence to the world as a creation of a Creator, let alone a personal Creator, miss the mark

8. This is not always the case. In fact, there is a controversial discussion still going on about the age of the earth. "Evolutionary theory," to be fair, is a rather imprecise term and depends on a variety of ideas and what one considers to be essential to evolution. For some examples of various perspectives, see Nelson and Reynolds, *A Case for Young-Earth Creationism*; Dembski, *Intelligent Design*, 122–49; Keathley, Stump, and Aguirre, *Old-Earth or Evolutionary Creation?*; Moreland et al., *Theistic Evolution*.

9. A classic example is Huxley, *Evolutionary Humanism*. See also Madigan, "Evolutionary Humanism Revisited"; de Waal, *The Bonobo and the Atheist*; Harari, *Homo Deus*; Pinker, *The Blank Slate*. For a useful critique, see Tallis, *Aping Mankind*.

of Christian orthodoxy. Second, these two creeds describe God as the explanation for all individual things in the world and as the director of the world's events toward a particular goal. Given the emphasis on God's creation of all things, visible and invisible, there is a strong sense in which Christians agree that God is the Creator and that this provides an explanation for all physical organisms in biological evolution. Furthermore, the creeds tell us that all of creation is directed by the trinitarian activity of God toward the life to come, which concerns God's kingdom of life and blessing. Within these boundaries there is a great deal of conceptual space for conceiving the compatibility of evolutionary human origins with the Christian story of origins. This raises another question often raised in the Christian story of origins.

Adamic Origins in Creation

Recent theological discussions on evolutionary origins have raised a question about the nature of Adam. It is not uncommonly assumed that biological evolution precludes the surface-level reading of the Bible in which Adam and Eve are portrayed as direct creations of God and as the progenitors of humanity.[10] This is because biological evolution, or so it is argued, presents a messy origins story in which humans emerge from their animal predecessors rather than in a single-file origination directly linked to the first human pair. This raises a set of interrelated questions. Are we the progeny of Adam and Eve? Was there no Adam and Eve? Do we originate from an aboriginal community for which Adam and Eve are the representative pair? Were there other humans (i.e., *Homo sapiens* or *Homo sapiens sapiens*) around during the time of Adam and Eve who are not genetically linked to Adam and Eve? Supposing that there was not a direct original descent from a human pair but rather a messy descent from the first group of hominids that so happened to emerge from their animal kin, we would still have one option left that provides a coherent explanation of the biblical story line. One could assume that Adam and Eve were the first humans selected by God to represent humanity, and on this story, God would view all of humanity through the lens of Adam. With that said, the debate on this issue is not decisively in favor of a no-Adam view.[11]

10. This is often called the "de novo" creation view of Adam and Eve's origins. They are simply created by God out of nothing. There is not any obvious scientific evidence against the view, nor is it inconsistent with, at least, some versions of evolutionary theory.

11. For a conservative set of views that presuppose some version of creationism (e.g., young-earth creationism or old-earth creationism), see Madueme and Reeves, *Adam, the Fall, and Original Sin.*

There are some biblical and theological reasons for endorsing a historical Adam (i.e., a historical pair). Two New Testament passages seem to presuppose the legitimacy of the literal Adam in light of his relationship to humanity and to Christ. Romans 5 sets up a parallel between Adam and Christ that is central to the narrative of redemption through the covenants. For humanity, Adam brings death and curse (5:14). For humanity, Christ is set up as the second Adam, and as the greater covenantal representative of humanity, who brings life and blessing (5:15–18).[12] First Corinthians 15 also presupposes some sort of link between Adam as the first representative of humanity and Christ as the second. Several questions emerge from the relationship between Adam and Christ that are pertinent to how one understands humanity. Is Adam the natural and creational head of humanity? Is natural humanity (through Adam) necessarily prior to the supernatural head of humanity (through Christ)? Does Adam bring about death to humanity in his created life or through sin or, in some way, through both his creation and sin? Is a historical Adam necessary, in some way, if we have a historical Christ? Would we have a Christ without an Adam? All of these questions are relevant to one's theological anthropology. It does seem that there is an important parallel between Adam and Christ that presupposes a literal historical Adam. At a minimum, Adam (or some human for which "Adam" is the literary stand-in) is a representative of humanity who has been divinely selected among an aboriginal humanity as a necessary piece of the scriptural story line. The broader theological tradition calls this first representative "Adam," but whether this was actually his name seems insignificant to the factuality of an actual first human representative. But why think there was a historical Adam?

The first reason one might give for there being a historical Adam is that it accounts for the integrity of the scriptural narrative, which purports to give us an unbroken chain between Adam and the succeeding covenantal representatives throughout the Old Testament. And if we take it that the creation story has some historical elements, it would make sense to read Adam in light of the broader historical facts that present themselves later on in the Old Testament.

Second, theological tradition seems to support the fact of Adam or some historical figure that precedes Christ as humanity's head. Paul himself seems to presuppose a theological tradition that considers Adam a historical

---

12. Douglas J. Moo makes a strong exegetical case that Paul's theology includes the necessity of Adam as a historical figure to make sense of the scriptural story line, with specific attention given to Rom. 5. See Moo, "'The Type of the One to Come.'"

predecessor.[13] One might take this simply to mean that this was the historical and cultural milieu in which Paul found himself, but this does not establish the truthfulness of a historical Adam. While the present sort of argument is not decisive in favor of a historical Adam, the belief in a historical Adam seems to be a deeply entrenched belief in Paul's mind and in the communities from which he is working, and it is these sources that make up the final texts of the canon.

Third, the dominant view of the tradition that proceeds from the canon of Scripture seems to assume a historical Adam. It is arguable that all three major periods of Christian history (patristic, medieval, and Reformed theology) affirmed the belief in a historical Adam.[14] Donald Macleod argues that the historical Adam is necessary for the dominant belief in the Reformation that Adam's federal headship is related to his being biologically first in the emergence of humanity, which provides the basis for the transmission of human sin.[15]

Fourth, there is, arguably, a metaphysical necessity for a historical Adam. Some have recently argued that a literal Adam, consistent with the scriptural story, is necessary for the emergence of original sin. In fact, "originating sin" presupposes an originator. It seems that sin is a result of human agency that is somehow passed down to all humanity through the first sin (i.e., what theologians call the "primal sin"). If sin has an origin that is not from God, then it does seem to follow that it finds its origination in a human author.[16]

These and other arguments present themselves as lines on which future theologians will need to do additional work, research, and thinking, but, as seen above, there has already been a significant amount of reflection given to these topics. That said, there is still a need for additional reflection on the challenges presented from an old-earth view of how it is that humans, or some set of humans, are related to Adam. While they are not decisive, treating them dismissively is hardly acceptable. Along with the question of the historical reality of Adam and Eve, the evolutionary story of human origins raises an additional question about the creation of humans, to which we will now turn.

13. For a set of literature on Paul and his understanding of Adam, see Scroggs, *The Last Adam*; Thiselton, *First Epistle to the Corinthians*. For a popular yet sophisticated defense of the historical Adam and Eve, see C. Collins, *Did Adam and Eve Really Exist?* See also John H. Walton's important work on the subject, *The Lost World of Adam and Eve.* See also a long yet helpful review of Walton's *The Lost World of Adam and Eve* with additional important Old Testament literature that impinges on these questions: Averbeck, "The Lost World of Adam and Eve."

14. Madueme and Reeves, *Adam, the Fall, and Original Sin*, esp. chaps. 4–6.

15. Macleod, "Original Sin in Reformed Theology," 137–39.

16. See Reeves and Madueme, "Threads in a Seamless Garment."

Evolutionary Humanism, Theism, and Emergentism

Peter Enns sums up the evolutionary view (along with a no-historical-Adam view) quite well. He is convinced that the findings of biology, as it impinges on the human story, necessitate a reconceiving of human origins, and he is convinced that an evolutionary story can be consistent with both contemporary science and essential Christian teaching on God and humans. The basic idea is that the evolutionary chain of development from lower-level physical organisms is an unbroken chain leading to higher-level organisms all the way to humans. Rather than being a direct and immediate creation of God, humans are emergent products within the evolutionary chain of being. At some point in evolutionary history, humans emerge as the most complicated physical organisms. Enns says the following:

> Evolution, however, is a game changer. The general science-and-faith rapprochement is not adequate because evolution uniquely strikes at central issues of the Christian faith. Evolution tells us that human beings are not the product of a special creative act by God as the Bible says but are the end product of a process of trial-and-error adaptation and natural selection. This process began billions of years ago, with the simplest of one-cell life forms, and developed into the vast array of life on this planet—plants, reptiles, fish, mammals, and so forth—and humanity. These humans also happen to share a close common ancestry with primates. Some Christians reconcile their faith with evolution by saying that God initiated and guides this process, which is fine (and which I believe), but that is not the point here. The tensions that evolution creates with the Bible remain, and they are far more significant than whether the earth is at the center of the cosmos, how old it is, and whether it is round or flat.
>
> If evolution is correct, one can no longer accept, in any true sense of the word "historical," the instantaneous and special creation of humanity described in Genesis, specifically 1:26–31 and 2:7, 22. To reconcile evolution and Christianity, some assert that there was a point in the evolutionary chain where God elevated two hominids (or a group of hominids) to the status of image-bearer of God (Gen. 1:26–27). According to this scheme, "image" is understood as the soul, God-consciousness, or other qualities that make us human.[17]

Enns offers a helpful summary for us to consider as we look at the broader evolutionary story in relation to Christian anthropology. To be clear, Enns revises a traditional view of human origins. He states that humans are the end product of the evolutionary process, which he contends is inconsistent with what the Bible states in the creation story. He proceeds to offer an alternative

17. Enns, *The Evolution of Adam*, xiv.

attempt to reconcile the biblical text and modern evolutionary theory rather than the view that God simply adds the soul to the body. To Enns, this is simply a revision of a literal or superficial reading of the biblical text. In the end, he disagrees with the traditional account given in the quotation above, and he is convinced that we will need to alter some of the ways we read the details in the biblical text in order to tell a coherent story of humans that integrates Christian teaching and modern evolutionary theory.[18]

In response, if we are to give any credence to the findings of biological evolution (through archaeology, carbon dating, etc.), then we must advance some modest articulation of a story that includes Enns's prescribed story of evolution. Minimally, humans are related to lower-level biological organisms through biological evolution. Furthermore, human minds are, somehow, functionally (in a strong sense) dependent on their brains. To the former claim, some evidence shows that in our human anatomy, we are related to higher-level physical organisms. To the latter, the fact that our souls are intimately united to our bodies both locally (in terms of the development of the broader compound of body and soul) and broadly through evolution makes sense of other commonsense facts about mental experience. In fact, our mental experience is severely affected by our bodies and brains. When we imbibe a sufficient amount of caffeine, we notice a significant change regarding the state of our conscious experience. We are more awake and alive to whatever is rumbling around up there in the mind. Furthermore, when we experience a blow to the head, there is an obvious effect on our state of awareness.[19]

This creates an apparent challenge for views that contend that humans are souls that are modally (i.e., possibly) and actually distinct from their bodies. Regardless, it seems clear to me that views that affirm that souls necessarily and essentially depend, in some functional sense, on their bodies are not subject to the challenge of evolution.[20] This is because these souls are already tied to the evolutionary process and are products of that same process, even if one contends that same process is insufficient. The same logic seems to

18. Enns, *The Evolution of Adam*, xv. He proceeds to argue that the bigger problem for the Christian is that of reconciling Pauline texts in the New Testament on Adam and humanity. Rather than reconfiguring accidental features of the texts that bear very little on the logic of human redemption, Enns is convinced that Paul's clear analogy between Adam as fallen humanity and Christ as new humanity forces us to reconceive of the basic logic of the redemptive story as spelled out in the Bible. This is a steep price to pay and a move that Christians should be careful to tread.

19. See Hasker, *The Emergent Self*.

20. See Swinburne, *The Evolution of the Soul*. Swinburne provides us with the most sophisticated substance-dualist defense of human beings in light of science and biological evolution to date.

apply to views that understand the soul to be conceptually distinct, yet not modally or actually distinct, from the body. If the soul is already embedded in some way within the causal web of evolution, is the product of evolution, and is dependent on biological evolution for both its origins (at a minimum for the soul's determinable structure and the general conditions for the soul) and its development, then there is no apparent problem.

Substance dualism seems to encounter a problem when we consider it as a version of creationism. In this form of substance dualism, the soul has some distinct ontology and causal origin story from other physical organisms. If this is the case, then creationist souls could exist apart from the biologically emergent product (i.e., the body) and would have no obvious ontological or causal connection to it. Creationism, on the surface, appears to be an implausible option because it rubs against our basic intuitions about embodiment in which our souls have a more tightly fine-grained relationship to our bodies and brains. While not incoherent or inconceivable, the creationist soul seems difficult to accept. One can tell a story, however, that while the human body is a biological product of evolution, the soul is not. It could be that the soul is affected by certain bodily behaviors as well as actions done to the body through causal interaction, but, once again, some fine-grained relationship seems amiss on this view. That said, there is some reason to think that humans are souls and that the souls are uniquely different from other physical organisms (either by degree or by kind), which points us to the divine. Let us consider some of the reasons for thinking about souls in a broadly creational context.

The Origin of the Soul

John Calvin describes the creation of humanity as "the noblest and most remarkable example of [God's] justice, wisdom, and goodness." For Calvin, the origins of the human soul highlight the distinct characteristics of God: his justice, wisdom, and goodness. Humans are the most exalted of all God's creatures. Furthermore, Calvin is clear that "we cannot have a clear and complete knowledge of God unless it is accompanied by a corresponding knowledge of ourselves."[21] While Calvin would say that the rest of God's creation fits or shares, in some measure, these glorious aspects of God, it is the human that points to the Creator in the clearest and most precise way possible. For Calvin, our knowledge of self is wrapped up in knowledge of

21. See Calvin, *Institutes* 1.15.1.

God and points us more profoundly to our Creator. The two are interwoven, and this is borne out in the origin story. Humans are not only higher than other created objects but also unique in kind, according to Calvin, and this provides the ground for our having higher-order capacities for thinking about God because of the distinction in nature that humans have in relation to other animals. As our faculties are higher than those of other creatures, they are also substantively different.

How, then, should we conceive of human origins? If we reject the naturalist (i.e., the view that all that exists does so within the causal network of physical causes and effects and that there is no outside agent or causal framework that affects the closed system of physical causes and effects) story of human emergence, which is a tenet of evolutionary and secular humanism, then what views are on the table for discussion? Apart from some finely grained versions of materialism, it would seem that some variant of substance dualism or Thomism (of a dualist variety or a monist variety) is worthy of consideration.

Earlier I discussed the notion of the soul and some ways in which to conceive of the soul in relation to the body. It seems to me that there are three ways to conceive of the soul in the contemporary literature and various ways to work out those conceptions. The soul can be conceived of as a pure soul, a kind soul, or a hybrid soul.[22]

A pure soul is also called a relational soul. As a relational soul, it has the ability to embody distinct physical objects. It is not bound to one kind of body over another kind of body. In fact, pure souls seem to lack a biological-kind relationship to a body. There is no apparent essential or necessary relationship between a pure soul and a body. At a minimum, pure souls can causally interact with the body of which they happen to take ownership; they are not bound necessarily or essentially, nor are they biologically propertied. Pure souls could inhabit human bodies or feline bodies. Furthermore, pure souls that have once inhabited a human body could inhabit a higher-order body (whatever that might be), say, in the next life, or a lower-order body, as with a canine or feline body. In this case, and fitting with the picture of creationism above, these souls have no obvious ontological or causal relationship to evolution or to the physical product of evolution. There are other kinds of souls that might be more promising routes for the Thomist or the substance dualist with respect to the integrity of the soul and body relationship.

22. I began developing these distinctions in Farris, "Pure or Compound Dualism?" See also Farris, *The Soul of Theological Anthropology*, esp. chap. 2.

A kind soul is different. A kind soul is the sort of soul that has a biological-kind relationship to its body.[23] Kind souls are not pure or relational souls. On this understanding, souls have a natural propertied relationship to a larger compound or structure and fall under a particular biological kind. Such a view could be articulated as a naturally fitting view with biological evolution. And such a view would not allow, at least not intuitively or immediately, the transfer of souls from one body to a totally distinct kind of body. So, as in the earlier case, a specifically human soul could not naturally transfer from a human body to a feline body or to some lesser body (like a cockroach). This opens the door to two distinct possibilities. One possibility says that souls have a necessary and essential relationship to their bodies as kinds, which together constitute a larger whole. On this view, the soul is conjoined to the body from its inception and in an ongoing sense, and it is not conceivable that it could persist without its body.

Another possibility is what one could call a hybrid-soul view or a kind-soul view 2.0. According to a hybrid-soul view, the soul bears a kind property and falls under a kind in biology. The soul fits within the causal evolutionary framework. Thus, minimally, it has an aptness or propensity to be embodied in a particular kind of body, but it can be decoupled from that body and exist disembodied. This is not to confuse it with other views in which souls are simply unembodied; rather, it is to understand the soul as contingently disembodied, albeit in an unnatural sense.

These variants of souls correspond to different views on substance dualism. Let me parse out some versions of substance dualism. I have laid out three versions of substance dualism in another place.[24] First, corresponding to a pure or relational soul that has the ability to relate to different kinds of bodies in the same way (dependent on the powers accessible through the body) is a view often called "pure-substance dualism." Pure-substance dualism is a strong version of substance dualism that maintains a strict distinction between soul and body. Both a soul and a body are substances (i.e., property bearers) in their own right. They are distinct, and the properties that they come to bear are distinct. They have no essential relationship to each other and conceivably could exist just fine without each other. They just so happen to relate causally to the other accidentally, in an ad hoc way. They are like that married couple that consists of two very independent people who

23. There is a colloquial use of the term *kind* in reference to the soul that I do not intend here. For example, someone might say, "Do you know Uncle Tommy? He is a kind soul." In other words, he is a gentle soul.

24. Farris, *The Soul of Theological Anthropology*, 39–46.

happen to get along in some harmonious relationship.[25] On this view, it is not clear whether there is a mere causal interaction relationship or a kind of parallelism in which the two causal histories happen to parallel each other in what appears to be a harmonious relationship. It is not entirely clear that the body and the soul have a harmonious relationship, unfortunately.

A second way of construing the relationship of soul and body is similar to the first one but affirms a tighter, more fine-grained relationship between a soul and a body. I will call this "compound-substance dualism." This view affirms that a body and a soul are distinct but that the two substances compose a larger compound, one that is whole by virtue of the fact that they are naturally and, for some properties, necessarily joined together.[26] In this way, they more closely reflect the married couple whose persons are mutually dependent on each other and have built an integrative relationship such that each person works in harmony with the other with specific tasks and functions that fulfill a shared set of goals. If the persons were somehow to separate, there would be significant harm to the functioning of the individuals to such an extent that the powers of each would be diminished. In a similar way, on compound-substance dualism, souls disconnected from their bodies will experience a significant breakdown in functionality and a diminishing of powers.

Third, and similar to the previous view, is an alternative "compound-substance dualism." On this view, souls and bodies can enter into a relationship whereby they exist as parts of a larger compound structure (e.g., like the parts that constitute a house). On a compound view, we can offer an account of the soul-body relationship that maintains a Cartesian distinctive, that the soul is actually distinct and independent from the body, of their causal external connection, yet still allows for a tight relationship by virtue of the powers achieved in the union. The Cartesian distinctive of the soul is that the soul is externally related to the body as it is both modally and actually distinct from the body as having an intrinsic nature distinction and that it can persist without the body. On a composite view, a soul actually enters into an internal relationship with a body in such a way that the two become one aggregate,

25. Leibniz used an illustration of two watches that fits well here. The two parts, body and soul, happen to be synchronized: one appears to have some causal efficacy on the other, but in reality they are moving in tandem. Leibniz presses this illustration further than I intend by showing that the relationship is merely correlational and that there is never a causal relationship. See G. W. Leibniz, *Monadology* 7 and 56, in *Discourse on Metaphysics and the Monadology*.

26. It is possible to understand the dualism of substances in one of two ways. The first is to conceive of them as one bodily substance and one soulish substance. The second is to conceive of the soul as the only true substance in itself, but when it is embodied, we have a distinct substance in the sense that the soul-body compound is, strictly speaking, not identical to the soul itself. The body might not be a substance in its own right; instead, it could be stuff.

yet there is still a modal and conceptual distinction between body and soul, rather than on the compound view where the soul and body relate externally to constitute a compound in the way that the wooden logs come together to constitute a log cabin. Such a view finds more compatibility with Thomism (if the distinction were only conceptual, then it would be a Thomism or Aristotelianism construed as monism, where the matter-form relationship constitutes one substance, namely, a human being as a body; or as dualism, where the soul and the body compose a human being). A marital relationship of one-flesh union more naturally reflects this articulation of substance dualism.

The distinctions made above affect our understanding of the various options on the origin of the soul.[27] In several ways, these options are not mere philosophical idiosyncrasies but rather impinge on theological issues concerning the genesis of the soul, the person, and the soul or person in relation to the body. The relationships between the soul, the person, and the body also have implications on the nature of what it means to be human as a creature in its fallen state and, in some respects, impinge upon the purpose of human nature. To the various options for the soul's origin we turn.

Origen's Preexistence of the Soul

Origen is famous for the view that souls not only are immortal in nature upon coming into existence but also preexist their bodies. On such a view, the person or soul exists prior to its existence in time and space or prior to embodied mortality. In fact, it exists in a kind of heavenly state of existence. Such a view assumes a radical form of Platonism in which the highest form of existence is immaterial in the Platonic heaven, for both divine being and human being. While the view coheres quite well with the notion that humans are creaturely (in the sense that they have mortality as embodied beings) and divine (by virtue of the purpose or end of souls), this view has very slim support from contemporary theologians. In Latin medieval theology, preexistence of the soul is largely eclipsed in favor of soul creationism, in which souls come to exist as embodied in time and space. Furthermore, as far as I know, not one theologian in Protestant or Reformed theology endorses it.

Traducianism

Traducianism is the view that souls are somehow generated via the parental progenitors through an immaterial mechanism or a psychosomatic

27. I develop these distinctions in Farris, "Considering Souls." A modified version of this has been published in Farris, *The Soul of Theological Anthropology.*

mechanism. On this view, at least one human soul, if not a pair of souls (i.e., Adam and Eve), is created by God. God creates one soul, or a pair of souls, directly or immediately, as we will find in creationism below and distinct from Origen's preexistence view above. By creating one soul or soul pair, God sets up the mechanisms and the conditions for the generation of succeeding souls that will follow in time and space. Souls, then, are created and come to exist (after the first soul or pair of souls) through a process of generation across time (i.e., diachronically).

Pure, compound, and composite versions of substance dualism cohere with traducianism, depending on how it is that the soul and body relate and how the "material" functions in the generation of souls. Another traducian possibility is that human souls are generated by the intentions of parents as those intentions coincide with the biological process. As parents supply the biological material, so they supply the soulish potentiality, which contributes to the generation of an individual person. It is also conceivable that a soul is integrated with the powers of a body and therefore a body functions in the emergence of the soul. If in fact souls always form prime matter (e.g., Aristotle, Aquinas), then it would make sense that souls emerge by virtue of the psychosomatic act of the parents bringing about the production of the human being.

Traducian souls can come into being from an act of fission, connecting through a process of fusion. Parental souls split off and form one new soul. On a fissile view of souls, souls actually split off from previous souls. Souls are like lumps of clay that can divide into other lumps of clay. So a soul can split in half and become a new soul. In the same way, the process can repeat itself. On a fissile view, souls have a built-in mechanism to split off time and time again. Souls have the potential through some medium (say, in procreation) to bring about a new soul. So, on this view, souls are not created all at once, actually or literally, nor do souls split off directly from Adam and/or Eve.[28]

Lumps of clay illustrate not only fissile souls but also parturient souls. On a parturient view of souls, souls have the capacity, under appropriate circumstances, to disseminate new parts. These new parts come to form and constitute a new soul (or soul-body arrangement). In the same way that one could pinch off several parts of a lump of clay, so it is with souls. Souls have parts and can give parts of themselves in and through procreation to compose a new soul or set of souls (as in cases of twins or triplets). The difference between a fissile view and a parturient view is clear. Fissile souls split off

---

28. Although, the present view might more naturally illustrate a parturient variation of traducianism.

and become new souls, immediately. Parturient souls have parts and give off some of their nonessential parts that can set up the conditions or establish the powers for producing new souls. Parturient souls are similar to material things in the sense that both have parts that can be manipulated.

Traducianism has a long history of support in the history of Christian thought. It has wide support in Lutheranism (except for Philip Melanchthon). It also has some support in Reformed theology (e.g., William Shedd, Augustus Strong). While creationism was the dominant view throughout the history of Reformed theology, traducianism is gaining considerable support among contemporary Reformed evangelical theologians.[29] Like other options, it has a unique place for conceiving of humans as divine (i.e., having a divine end or purpose) and creaturely.

Creationism

Creationism is the most widely supported view throughout Christian history. It finds significant and overwhelming support in Roman Catholicism and in Reformed Christianity. Creationism is the view that souls are created immediately and/or directly by God. Souls are the types of substances that require a higher-order transcendent cause and could not come into existence by a material process. Souls also are the types of entities that require a direct cause, not mediated by other causes, in divine action, unable to come into existence by the direct production of some other material entity or immaterial entity. Souls must have some explanation that is higher and more powerful than other entities. The most obvious type of soul that would cohere with a creationist view is a simple or pure soul that has no intrinsic relationship to a body. On the pure version of creationism, souls and bodies are so radically different that God must create the soul. The picture is something like God creating the soul immediately and/or directly and then attaching it to the body (i.e., establishing an interactive relationship between *this* soul and *this* body). On the surface, it appears that in this case parents do not have a direct causal role in the origination of the soul. Parents have direct causal control only with respect to the body that happens to interact with the soul that comes into existence. However, there is no reason to think that variations of compound substance dualism could not also be creationist. On compound variants, the soul could still be a soul that requires a transcendent causal explanation (i.e.,

---

29. This for two reasons. First, many think that traducianism supplies a more intuitive explanation for the transmission of sin (see this discussion below). Second, many think that traducianism supplies a more natural union between body and soul to such an extent that the soul is a product of the biology.

a cause that is not personal in the commonsense understanding of personal but rather divine in a way that is not accessible to humans) for coming into existence. It could be that the soul simply has some properties that make it appropriate for embodiment, in a particular kind of body.

Composite substance dualism could also be a form of creationism. Recall that on composite substance dualism, the soul and the body are not individually substantial but rather compose one substance (possibly a form-matter arrangement). In this way, the soul informs the matter in question. However, while there is this internal relationship between body and soul, on some accounts the soul is ontologically higher than the body in its relationship to God; that is, souls are ontologically closer than bodies to God's being, although they are part of the body and must be brought into existence by some higher transcendent cause.

Emergent Dualism

There is a new view of the substantial soul available to Christian theologians, and it gives us a different overarching picture of how persons come into existence. It is called "emergent dualism." Arguably, there are multiple variations of this view, but the most popular and sophisticated articulation of it—which is also radically different from other views on offer—is William Hasker's version.[30] For Hasker, the soul is the product of physical processes. Granted, on his view, the soul is already situated in a broader theistic explanation, but divine agency plays no direct or immediate role in the production of souls, including the original pair of souls (i.e., Adam and Eve). Souls are directly and immediately produced by complex physical processes from biological evolution and the causal chain of procreation brought about by parents of those souls. Thus, matter already has a built-in propensity and power to produce souls. Rather than giving direct power to God in the production of souls, Hasker posits that matter, configured in complex ways, fills the role of the Creator.

Souls, for Hasker, are products of biological evolution. In this way, Hasker reconceives the nature of souls as they are traditionally understood. Souls are more intimately tied to their brains and bodies without becoming the forms of bodies (as in hylomorphism or Thomism). Human souls are also naturally related to previously produced animal souls, assuming that animals in fact have souls.

It is clear that Hasker highlights the creaturely nature of human beings. Human beings, both materially and immaterially, are causally embedded in the

---

30. William Hasker has developed his view in several places, most notably in *The Emergent Self*. He distinguishes his view from both creationism and physicalism in "Why Emergence?"

physical framework of causes and effects. Human beings, it seems then, are more closely related to other physical organisms. Interestingly, human souls are subject to similar conditions, disabilities, corruptions, and weaknesses that other biological organisms are subject to. Embodiment is the normal condition of human existence.

Humans have some potential for disembodied existence, but it is not clear at all that humans will in fact persist beyond their embodied existence. Given the nature of the soul as emergent from the body and the brain, it naturally follows that souls will dissolve upon the death of the body. Minimally, souls will cease to function in any meaningful way without their bodies. This becomes problematic, as we will see below, if Scripture and the Christian tradition yield a belief in disembodied soulish persistence, in which souls (at least some souls) will exist in God's presence and see God in a fuller, richer, and intimate way (i.e., the beatific vision). To be fair to Hasker, he does leave open some room for the possibility that God sustains denuded souls in existence apart from the original sustaining brain, but this still leaves open the question about how it is that souls can function properly. Does God simply supply unique powers to the soul during the disembodied interim state? Alternatively, maybe God supplies a distinct brain (i.e., an intermediate body) to sustain the soul during the interim state after somatic death and prior to somatic resurrection.

I am convinced that we can have our cake and eat it too by merging elements from emergent dualism and creationism. The benefit of creationism, apart from its support from the Christian tradition, is that it motivates the intuitive belief in the simplicity and the uniqueness of the soul in a way that other views of human origins cannot. Also, it grounds the soul more directly in divine agency and not in the contingencies of material existence.

Creationism and Emergence[31]

There is an alternative set of views available when thinking about human origins. If one wishes to stay deeply connected to the Christian tradition and has sympathies with creationism but would also like to see a tighter, more fine-grained relationship between body and soul as situated in biological evolution, then some variant of creationism with emergentist elements is a viable route to thinking about humans. What if we could blend the benefits of Hasker's emergent dualism with the benefits of creationism? With the former, the advantage is that humans are truly creaturely because they have the kind of existence that is functionally beholden to biological determinables, and

31. Farris, "Emergent Creationism" (modified and republished in Farris, *The Soul of Theological Anthropology*).

they are products of biological evolution. With the latter, the benefit is being able to account for human transcendence.

Variations of creationism that are also emergentist could be parsed out by a Thomist or a Cartesian. One essential distinction between these approaches is that the soul is related to the body internally or externally, respectively. On Cartesianism, the soul is related externally in that the soul and the body are causally related but not somehow subsumed in the other. On Thomism, the soul is related internally in that the soul is literally in the matter or the matter is composed as a certain kind of substance. Yet on both views, it is possible that the soul could be decoupled from the body.

On either Thomism or Cartesianism, the soul can both emerge and be created in two senses. If we assume a view of divine causation that transcends nature, in which the divine is present at all times and there are discrete events within biological evolution, then there is a sense in which one can understand objects as coming into being by an immediate cause yet also by an ultimate divine cause (namely, divine agency). This is one way of parsing out an emergentist version of creationism. We can parse out the view in a different way if we construe the soul as a part of one larger substance or species nature. On this model, one could understand the soul as having some direct relationship to God's action of bringing it about, but the soul's existence is somehow dependent on the whole of the human body/brain. Thus, the soul is a part of the body/brain and actualizes its normal or common properties respective of a naturally functioning human nature. One could say, then, that there are jointly necessary and sufficient conditions for the soul's coming into existence: (1) God acts, sufficiently, by way of bringing about the particular soul; and (2) the body/brain, at some sufficient complexity, is a necessary condition for the soul's origination.

When and from Where Does the Soul Come?

The origin of human persons is central to both philosophical and theological discussions. The question of when the soul, mind, or person comes into being has direct implications for bioethical discussions (e.g., abortion, cloning, fetal-tissue experimentation, assisted suicide). When is a person present? And from where does the soul or person come? Determining the answers to these questions as substance dualists depends on the presence of a soul. When a soul is present with the body, it is often assumed that the person is also present. But when, in fact, the soul is present will be unclear if the soul is not able to be empirically verified apart from one's testimony. The fact of a bodily substance's presence might provide some evidence for the fact that the soul is present. Some might take this to entail a weakness of substance dualism and rather affirm some variant of physicalism or hylomorphism.

On physicalism, you might take it that a human person is simply a rational animal—that is, an individual substance of a rational nature. On a variant of physicalism (or hylomorphism) called animalism, the person is present whenever a rational animal is present. The body itself, with its detectable toto-potentiality (i.e., where the properties of personhood are present in potential in the material substance), yields the fact that a person is present. The challenge, undoubtedly, as we saw in chapter 1, on personal identity, is that it is unclear that a person is identical with his or her body or brain.

As to the question, From where does the soul and/or person come? all theists take it as basic that the world, including humanity, is created by God and comes into existence as a result of divine action. However, as we have seen, how one understands this to occur depends on one's view of personal ontology. We have creationist variations of personhood, which take it that God brings about the existence of the person directly and immediately. Normally, creationism is some version of substance dualism, immaterialism, or hylomorphism (i.e., where the matter and the form constitute a human). In other words, something other than the physical itself brings about personhood. Physicalist accounts of persons are motivated by a number of things: the success of the sciences, the causal autonomy of biological evolution, and some variation of physical causal closure. Physicalists are often not motivated to endorse some variation of direct or immediate divine creationism.

The idea of the material generation of souls or persons is becoming ever more popular among theologians, philosophers, and scientists. With the recognition that consciousness is a unique property of organisms and nonreducible to the component parts that compose the bodily organism, many affirm some variant of emergentism that is causally (i.e., where the brain is the proximate cause) brought about from purely physical processes. This could be a version of creationism, albeit a remote version, in which God is removed from the process as the direct and proximate cause yet acts as the remote cause for the persons coming to be. Both dualists (at least some) and materialists have affirmed something like a material emergentist generation of persons.

The problem with physicalist versions is quite plainly an underlying concern with respect to personal identity, as discussed earlier. Material objects generally lack the persistence conditions to identify as the selfsame object across time. Furthermore, and more importantly, there is not a garden-variety feature or set of features in a body that one can point to and say, "There we have the person." Rather, as with all material objects, the boundaries for determining where persons might be present are rather vague. So it is with the origination of personhood. The vagueness of personhood is exemplified when we consider the embryo in the womb of the mother. As with all empiricist theories of persons, the identity of the embryo does not characteristically display those common features of persons that we normally associate with persons (e.g., rationality, consciousness, moral conscience, free will). In fact, it is unlikely that the embryo exhibits anything like consciousness in the womb. In this specific case, the physicalist cannot resort to psychology, memory, or character as a way to determine personhood. Added to this, both the brain and the body are sufficiently vague so as to have no demarcating criteria for determining personhood. There are alternative options worth considering.[32]

Many Christian theologians affirm a version of Thomist anthropology. Central to an understanding of Thomism is the soul, when construing it as hylomorphic monism or hylomorphic dualism. Let me briefly explain these terms. Monism is the view that a human being is only one kind of thing: a body. Monism says that persons are composed of one kind of stuff that is sufficiently integrated as a substance. The soul functions as the informing principle that works with mechanistic material to make the material the kind of thing it is. There are other variants of Thomism that make some distinction between the soul and the body such that the soul is modally if not actually distinct from the body.[33] The advantage of (at least some variations of) Thomism is that the soul and the body share in a genus-species relation, which amounts to the view that when a human body is present, the soul is also present. On Thomism, the kind nature is dependent on the soul as a form of the matter.[34]

What about Cartesianism? It has been argued that Cartesianism runs into some challenges, especially for those with particular religious convictions, regarding the problematic implication that if the body is contingent to personhood, then, for example, it might be morally permissible to commit abortion if a person is not present. Stewart Goetz and Charles Taliaferro discuss this problem as they interact with Patrick Lee and Robert George:

> Consider the ethics of abortion and the Patrick Lee and Robert George view
> of sexual ethics. Lee and George hold that the dualist tradition makes abortion
> more permissible than, say, their preferred more materialistic Thomistic stance,

32. For a thorough critique of materialist views in the context of bioethics, see Moreland and Rae, *Body and Soul*.

33. For a useful exposition of Thomism and its variations, see Brower, *Aquinas's Ontology*, 273, esp. table 12.1. I am not suggesting that all of these variants are acceptable or coherent options. I am inclined to say that they are not.

34. Moreland and Rae, *Body and Soul*.

because it is unlikely that fetal life has any consciousness until eight to twelve weeks. As such, a dualist might well claim that there is no person present until at least there is consciousness, and thus a prohibition against killing persons would not rule out an early abortion. Without committing ourselves one way or the other on the permissibility of abortion, we note that dualists who believe in the impermissibility of abortion can defend their views on multiple grounds. We do not think there are compelling grounds for claiming that souls must always be conscious, or for accepting Descartes' view that consciousness is an essential property of the self. If that is the case, one may claim that the soul is present (as Lee and George hold) from conception, but not conscious. On such a view, the fate of the fetus may be the same as that of the soul. Alternatively, one may argue against abortion on the basis of a sanctity of life principle, or on the grounds that the fetus will become ensouled or an embodied person.[35]

The worry seems to be that the contingency of the body allows for the possibility of the absence of the person (i.e., soul). However, one could tell a story about the soul-body arrangement that would incline one to think that the soul is present at the body's origination. Taking our cues from Thomism, the Cartesian might hold that souls are kind souls and not simply generic or relational souls. Kind souls have properties that find natural expression when interactively relating to a body. In normal and natural circumstances, the belief in a kind soul would motivate a view of the soul's origination that parallels the origination of the body.

On first appearances, it is not entirely clear whether the person or soul is present at the moment of conception on a Cartesian view. For if the body is a contingent part of human persons, it is possible that when the body is present, the soul is not. On this basis, it has been argued that abortion is morally permissible. However, the situation is not quite so clear. Wisdom would dictate an alternative approach to the embryo in the womb. Given that there is an interactive relation between the soul and the body, and the two respective parts, presumably, actualize the properties and powers of the other, it would seem that we have reason to assume that the soul is present when there is an embryo present. With the presence of a new human organism, it is safe to assume that a soul is present. In the worst-case scenario, the person is not present, but this in itself does not justify abortion.

35. Goetz and Taliaferro, *A Brief History of the Soul*, 214. Goetz and Taliaferro are interacting with Patrick Lee and Robert George in their excellent defense of a variation of Thomist hylomorphism in *Body-Self Dualism in Contemporary Ethics and Politics*. Lee and George are drawing from another work, Haldane and Lee, "Aquinas on Human Ensoulment." For an alternative Thomistic option to that of Lee and George, see Niederbacher, "Anthropological Hylomorphism," 119–20.

Instead, the act is impermissible on the grounds that abortion prevents a good to the soul.[36]

The objection raised by Lee and George, representing a long tradition of criticism, is that the dualistic tendency to separate the soul and the body yields a denigrated view of the body. The objection is that the body bears instrumental value to the soul, but not intrinsic value. Goetz and Taliaferro offer a thoughtful response by way of highlighting the integrative and functional unity of the soul and the body. On an integrative view, the soul and the body function as a unity. In other words, when I am embodied, it is this body that is my body. The body contributes good value to the flourishing soul, and therefore how we use the body and how we treat it will affect how we treat the soul. Thus, the conclusion that dualism denigrates the body does not necessarily follow.[37]

We began this chapter talking about the daemon in the Frankenstein story, which has become a common symbol for revisionist understandings of human nature. Contemporary reflections signal a paradigm shift in how we understand human nature. Human uniqueness has become central to the scientific, philosophical, and theological discussions. But with the move toward a purely natural and physical understanding of human nature, doubts about the connection between human nature and uniqueness have become commonplace. Yet, representing much of the wider Christian (even catholic) tradition, I argued that the soul (particularly a kind-natured soul) remains a viable option for determining the uniqueness of human nature. Through a consideration of some of the challenges with an old earth and evolution, I argued that human nature points us to human uniqueness *via* human origins, which creates space for fresh reflections on human purpose. Overlapping with the topic of human nature, human origins, and humanity's relation to Adam, the nature and content of the *imago Dei* (the image of God) in humankind is another traditional topic in a theological anthropology. By considering the

---

36. There is an additional objection to the Cartesian view, a view that some have referred to as a collection of views in the Plato-Augustine-Calvin-Descartes tradition, where there is a distinction between person and body, wherein the person is strictly identical to the soul, or the soul is the core of the person, and the body is contingent. It is not uncommon to include Plato, Augustine, and Descartes in this tradition of substance dualism. Elsewhere I have consciously and explicitly included the theologian John Calvin as an important figure in this tradition who ties the dualist tradition to the Reformed tradition. While it is true that some in the Reformed tradition might affirm something like the more materialistic hylomorphism of Lee and George, it is arguably the case that the tradition is more dualistically heavy. See Farris, *The Soul of Theological Anthropology*, esp. chap. 1, where I explore the position within the broader Christian tradition.

37. Goetz and Taliaferro, *A Brief History of the Soul*, 214.

various options on the *imago Dei*, I lay out a novel view that is consistent with traditional reflections on the "image" in humanity, but also one that avoids some of the modern and contemporary challenges often raised against it. Humans are image bearers of the divine, and it is here that we find a central theme in the biblical story line that highlights both the creaturely and the divine aspects of human nature.

3

What Am I in Relation to God?

The Image as Creaturely and Divine

Let us make mankind in our image.

Genesis 1:26

Q. 17. How did God create man?
A. After God had made all other creatures, he created man male and female; formed the body of the man out of the dust of the ground, and the woman of the rib of the man, endued them with living, reasonable and immortal souls; made them after his own image, in knowledge, righteousness and holiness.

Westminster Large Catechism (1647)

Apart from human eschatology, no Christian doctrine evokes questions about humanity as creaturely and divine more than that of the *imago Dei*. Images of the Greek gods and idols of the ancient Near East come to mind when one thinks about the *imago Dei*.[1] The spectrum

---

1. Think of the Greek gods and their humanlike ways. While inaccurate, discussion around the "image" concept does raise questions about the extent to which humans are like God and God is like humans. The idol concept comes closer to an accurate portrayal of the "image" concept in the Christian Scriptures, as has been persuasively argued by G. K. Beale. See Beale, *We Become What We Worship*. See also Harari, *Homo Deus*, 43–49. Harari, reflecting on humanist philosophy, actually encourages a frame of mind that humans are divine beings and that we

of views on the image is quite diverse, ranging from aspects or properties of the body to the spirit, and some thinkers eschew substantial matters in favor of relational or functional views. In the present chapter I advance a modestly constructive case for one substantial view through a survey of the various options for evangelical Christians. I argue that the *imago Dei* has primarily to do with human identity reflected in creaturely and divine ways, and that this can be captured in the Reformed emphasis on a holistic immaterial substantial ontology. In this way, I take it that the *imago Dei* is a formal concept that shapes the whole of the scriptural portrayal on human identity. It is also a central concept in the story of humans. My approach is not accepted by all. Some hold that the biblical data provides only a small fraction of information on humans, according to a few texts.[2] However, I argue that the *imago Dei* is foundational to and crucial to one's understanding of the creation story, and is important to the redemptive story where the image is elucidated and brought out in new ways. While it is a formal and central concept to the biblical story, it also conveys some specific information about humans.

The doctrine of the *imago Dei*, though not fully developed there, occurs in the very first chapter of the first book of the Christian Scriptures. Later pieces of revelation develop the Christian conception of the image in thoughtful and layered ways, but the divine and creaturely nature of humans emerges from the creation of the first pair of humans in Genesis 1:26–28. The first occurrence of "image of God" language is in Genesis 1:26 and of both male and female in Genesis 1:27, where humans, both Adam and Eve, are created in the image of God. The second passage that makes reference to the image, Genesis 5:1–3, reiterates the fact that Adam and Eve, and for that matter humans in general, are created in the image and likeness of God. But what in fact does it mean to say that humans are created as images of God or in the image of God? Given the state of the present literature and the historical literature on the subject, it would seem that there is either not a clear teaching founded on the passage or that the meaning of the image is in seed form with the need for additional development.

What do we know about the "image" in Genesis 1:26–28? From the context, we know that God is in the process of completing his creation of the world and that humans are the penultimate climax of that creative activity, with

---

should improve the human situation through the power of technology. Harari likens humans to the Greek gods and the quest for becoming gods through medicine and technology as we enter into a new phase of the human story—posthumanism. Hence, the image of humans as it relates to god(s) has an important relationship to the why, the purpose, of the human story, which we will consider toward the end.

2. See David Kelsey's influential and important book *Eccentric Existence*.

the ultimate climax being God's rest from his creation. Like the animals, the humans are created according to their kind. That kind is unique among the created order in the course of God's world project through the covenants (where covenants provide the primary contexts for divine action toward God's chosen or elect people; therein God blesses and gives life to his people and holds them to a set of standards). Humankind is unique because God created humans last, prior to his resting from that creative work, and God calls his creation not only "good" (as he states with the plant and animal creation) but "very good." In addition, humans are unique in that they alone are described as God's images in the world. Some unique status is granted to humans in God's created order. Therefore, the *imago*, in its creational covenantal context, has something to do with human identity.[3]

If we take it that words only have meaning as they are related to other words in a grammatical structure in a wider context, then we must try to understand the meaning of "image" in relation to other words in a grammatical structure in a wider context.[4] That wider context in which to situate "image" is its covenantal context. Within the covenantal context, images serve as functional representations, as seen in the ancient Near East.[5] As noted and exegetically laid out by Stephen G. Dempster, the "image" was a common notion in the ancient Near East for the kings as representatives of God, which is grounded in a proper understanding of Genesis 1:26–28 and Genesis 5:1–3 especially.[6] Where God, as Creator, has created and designed the world, he seeks to take dominion, but he does so through his covenantal representatives (his image bearers).[7] Hence, for Dempster, both "dominion" and "dynasty" serve as controlling motifs in Old Testament theology patterned throughout the Scriptures, yet originating in the creational covenant. Dynasty refers to the genealogy that is tied to the covenant where God acts toward his people. It is an important concept that bears on the Old Testament narrative development of

---

3. For a development of this notion, see R. S. Peterson, *The* Imago Dei *as Human Identity*.

4. See Barr, *The Semantics of Biblical Language*.

5. See John Walton's important work, *Genesis 1 as Ancient Cosmology*.

6. See Dempster, *Dominion and Dynasty*. Other theological treatments of the image of God also see the concept of image in light of its Hebrew, ancient Near Eastern, and Old Testament contexts. For a sampling, see Middleton, *The Liberating Image*; Levenson, *Creation and the Persistence of Evil*; Dumbrell, *Covenant and Creation*, 33–34.

7. Divine agency as dominion is clearly brought out in the creational narrative where God creates and takes dominion over his sanctuary setting in the garden as the royal agent in the narrative. God shows his agency in dominion by naming and speaking things into existence. This theme is brought out especially in the prophetic literature and is made explicit in John 1:1, where the Word brings the world into existence, or God brings the world into existence by the Word. This speaking and naming function is represented in the first human agent, Adam, who reflects his Creator in naming the animals (Gen. 2:19–20a).

the covenants, and it serves as the means for carrying forward God's blessing of human life to the rest of the world. Dynasty, also, is the means by which humans carry out the creational vocation of becoming the stewards of the whole earth, which mediates God's blessing to the whole earth.

Genesis 1 is the most natural place to begin in a study of the image and its meaning. After the creation of the rest of the world, God creates human beings. When he creates them, he has in mind the image for which they are created and fashioned accordingly. In Genesis 1:26 God says, "Let us make mankind in our image." Arguably, God has in mind the "image" all along but his previous creations have not met up to the standard, so humans are created as God's images on the earth in contrast to other creatures.

The most apparent features or characteristics of the image are seen in Genesis 1:26 and 1:28, read in the wider context. In both verses humans are given *commands*, or they are given *blessings*, for the purpose of carrying out God's dominion in the earth. Humans, you and I and we, are told to procreate and multiply in order to establish a dynasty in the world, which is confirmed in conjunction with Genesis 5:1–3—the Genesis lineage. The notion of humans as images of their fathers comes out in the lineages, consistent with the ancient Near Eastern understanding of the image who transfers the image in a royal dynasty, and parallels what we find in Scripture as it portrays the relationship between God and humans. Here in Genesis 5 the royal dynasty is laid out for the reader.[8] In the ancient Near East, it is not uncommon to read of kings as the "images" or "representatives" of god(s), and that same image is carried along in the royal genealogy where the image is transmitted. What we have in Genesis is a royal lineage of God's elect people who are carrying along the creational vocation through the royal lineage that, as it were, extends the blessings from the covenant by carrying along the "image" that God has chosen. Humans, you and I and we, are told to take "dominion," and this not apart from our procreative function. Thus, on the surface, we are given functions, and these functions are tightly conjoined with the nature of the image.

Another aspect of the creational image is clear when we read the passage in light of later passages in Genesis. Humans have a unique kind of *dignity* in the world in virtue of their representative function in the covenants. Genesis 9:6, still continuous with the creational covenantal context of the image, is one explicit instance that bears out this notion that humans are dignified beings.[9] It

8. See Blocher, *In the Beginning*, 89–90.
9. For a thoughtful and detailed exegesis and biblical-theological development of this concept from Gen. 9:6, see Kilner, *Dignity and Destiny*. Kilner develops a case that the image has some special character of dignity. He also develops the notion that humans have a unique destiny

states, "Whoever sheds human blood, by humans shall their blood be shed; for in the image of God has God made mankind." The nature of human shedding of blood incurs a debt of punishment, which is telling with regard to human identity. An alternative interpretation understands this passage to mean that humans are uniquely suited as the ones to carry out the punishment on other humans.[10] I am inclined to think that both concepts are present, implicitly or explicitly, but even if they are not both present and only one is highlighted, the notion of humankind being dignified is upheld as something intrinsic to the creational covenantal understanding of the *imago Dei*. This has led to much reflection on the nature of the image as the basis for ethics.[11]

A Canonical and Biblical-Theological Reading of the *Imago Dei*

Before we move on to a systematic analysis, it is important to try to tie together the big themes found in Scripture to offer a coherent interpretation of the biblical material. I take it that Scripture, as codified in the Protestant canon, has a unified and clear message that God intends for his church. This is divine revelation to his church. However, when we look at the data in the rest of the Old Testament and the New Testament, we have some challenges. The first challenge is that there just is not that much there. The second challenge is that when we arrive at the New Testament, we seem to have a different meaning of the *imago*. Is there some continuity among the various texts?

Some are surprised that the "image of God" language is only used early on in the Old Testament revelation, later to be picked up in the New Testament. Yet the Wisdom literature takes up and expounds materially on the *imago Dei* concept because of its focus on creational wisdom, which can be understood only in light of the fact that humans are covenantal representatives who are called to live out their lives before God and the rest of creation as stewards of that creation. Psalm 8, with its emphasis on the glory of creation,

---

as those created in God's image. Christ is, properly speaking, the image of God, as stated in the New Testament, for which we are destined. Kilner is quite critical of a structural model, arguing that it has been the impetus for a great deal of harm throughout history, but the fact is that this argument can be inverted in favor of the structural view. The image, with its universal character, has been the motivation for many goods throughout history in social and political debates. The fact that all humans are created in God's image, if this is in fact tied to an essential or stable property or nature (i.e., kind-nature; common essence), actually furnishes a ground for the dignity or honor deserved to all human beings.

10. See Garr, *In His Own Image and Likeness*, 163.

11. For a stimulating defense of natural-law theory within the Reformed tradition that takes this passage as significant exegetical support for a natural view of the image as containing ethical content, see VanDrunen, *Divine Covenants and Moral Order*.

specifically humans, and the dignity of humans seems to allude to the creation of the *imago Dei*. The echoes and allusions to the image concept serve as paradigmatic to how one should read and appropriate the *imago Dei* in light of Wisdom literature. All that has been said thus far requires that we think about how to organize the scriptural material on the *imago Dei*. I will describe several ways that theologians have organized the material and offer one suggestion as a way forward for thinking systematically about the image concept.

Systematically Working through the *Imago Dei*

There is a larger systematic question when we take into account all the biblical data listed above. How should we order and arrange the data? This is precisely where models become necessary and have commonly found their way into the discussion. There are at least three models for understanding the *imago Dei* (structural, relational, functional), and possibly four (substantive).

Let's step back for a moment and discuss the broader systematic contours of how we ought to situate these models. I have been working from a broadly Reformed view of the "anthropos." On such a view, it is not inconsistent to think of human nature in the context of God's glorious redemption of the world through his covenantal partners (i.e., humans). Also, for Calvin, our understanding of humans is necessarily tied to our understanding of God: to know self is to know God. It is in this confessional context that we treat the human being as a reflection of the divine, on which we long to gaze. Hence, our confessing the anthropos is always a pointer to seeing, knowing, and confessing the one true God of Christianity as he has revealed himself in redemptive history through the covenants and most perfectly in God the Son enfleshed. The various models below have the resources to integrate the biblical, historical, and philosophical data in differing ways.

Models of the *Imago Dei*

Structural Model

The structural model is the view that the image is identified with specific features or properties or capacities (e.g., consciousness, freedom of the will, the soul). On this model, humans uniquely reflect God in virtue of some feature or set of features, and they act as representatives of creation in virtue of these distinctive characteristics that set humans apart from the rest of creation.

Recently, it has fallen on hard times. It is, arguably, the most prominent model throughout church history and remains a popular view that associates the "image" with some unique feature or capacity of being human. Often when people seek to understand the *imago Dei*, they look for some unique or defining feature of the human that sets them apart from the rest of the animal kingdom. Others will look for that defining faculty or capacity that overlaps not with the rest of the created order but with the divine nature. Several options have been advanced. Two common features that are attributed to the human include rationality, corresponding to the faculty of the mind, and volition, corresponding to the faculty of the will. In Reformed circles these are often seen as essential features of the *imago Dei*, for they pertain to two communicable attributes of God: knowledge and righteousness. It is clear that the mind (construed either as a part of a substance or a power of the soul) and the will (a part or power of the soul) are faculties that distinguish us from animals and overlap with the divine. In virtue of the mind, we are able to see, grasp, and make sense of reality. Additionally, the will enables us to obey God's commands and live out God's purpose for our lives. One might include conscience in this list because humans depend on their consciences for daily living. Conscience is a basic source of moral knowledge, something setting us apart from the animal kingdom and giving us a glimpse into the divine mind.

There is one obvious benefit with a structural model that gives precedent to human capacities. Traditional anthropology highlights two prominent faculties of humans: the intellect and the will. And, on a vision of humanity that highlights the "beatific vision" (*visio Dei*) with an attending confession of God, capacities of intellect and will ground the relationship between one's knowledge of God and God's being and character. As we grow in the attributes relevant to human flourishing, our capacities to know and will the true, the good, and the beautiful are experienced with greater degree.

Some have suggested that isolated capacities are insufficient to capture what it means to be creatures created as bearers of the divine image. From this perspective, we should think of humans not just individuals with isolated capacities but rather as a collective group in the context of God's relationship to his covenantal representatives.[12] No doubt, we have focused primarily on the individual, but it is a concrete individual that is tied to a common nature that is revealed in a covenantal community, so it is not entirely clear how or that we could sharply distinguish the individual from the community or the community from the individual. If we conceive of the human as a composite

12. See Cortez, *Theological Anthropology*, 20–21.

of body and soul, then we might ask which part of the human more closely resembles the divine. In catholic Christianity, as spelled out in the Nicene tradition, God is an immaterial being, not a material being that can be divided.[13] If this is the case, and the image has something to do with the ontology of human beings, then the intuitive answer to this question is the mind or the soul of the human. As we will see with Calvin, many would agree that the image finds a proper seat in the mind or soul of the human, not in the body; however, Calvin is quite clear that the body does have a place or a role in the image, so it is not discarded.

There are other objections to the structural model in its various forms. One objection is that the image is concrete and historical in nature rather than abstract in nature. Some have argued quite passionately that structural views are abstract in nature and divert from concrete, lived realities of human existence.[14] The potential has been to segregate and denigrate certain categories of human beings because they fail to exhibit what the "strong" perceive as most admirable or most attractive in humans. Historical examples include certain races (e.g., black people in the 1800s in the Southern slave states), the unborn, and the handicapped.[15]

It is arguable that this common objection to the structural model overstates its case. No doubt it is true that humans have mistreated certain groups throughout history on the basis of some feature that the group in power sees as inferior, but there is nothing intrinsic to the structural model per se (depending on the variation that one is working with) that entails the denigration of one people group or culture. Instead, on the structural model, one could argue that all humans, by the very fact of being human, are dignified beings,

---

13. For a distinct view, William Lane Craig endorses a pseudo-Apollinarian view of the image, which is the view that Christ is the eternal archetypical image of humans. See Moreland and Craig, *Philosophical Foundations*, chap. 32.4.

14. Kelsey, *Eccentric Existence*; McConville, *Being Human in God's World*, 16–29; Grenz, *The Social God and the Relational Self*, 186–201; McFadyen, *The Call to Personhood*, 18; Cortez, *Theological Anthropology*, 37–40. Cortez makes an important point: "Thus, the functional/relational approach does not completely reject the insights of the structural approach, but it does serve to place the structural considerations within a broader framework. Structural capacities do not define the image, but they are certainly involved in how we express the image" (Cortez, *Theological Anthropology*, 145). This point is worth considering because one might argue that the "image" is dependent on a substance or structural capacities, yet not identical to them. However, in the present book I have sought to invert the metaphysical relationship of the structural/substantive as the "broader framework" that is present in all relations and functions wherein something is intrinsic and essential (or common) to humanity and present at all times of human existence. This makes the image stable rather than beholden to the shifting sands of human choice and human contingency.

15. See Kilner, *Dignity and Destiny*, chap. 1. Cortez, too, raises the present concern in *Theological Anthropology*, 20.

regardless of having any mental or physical characteristic that a group in power might see as inferior. More important, one should note that natural law takes it that humans are fundamental bearers of basic rights inherent to every human creature regardless of the ability to reason well, which is coherently accounted for in some versions of the structural model as a kind-nature (i.e., common nature of being human). It is precisely on this basis that Martin Luther King Jr., rightly in my opinion, appealed to the inherent dignity and worth of black Americans. He described this dignity as "inalienable" and not dependent on "gradations"; all humans are dignified because they are created by God as image bearers of God.[16] In other words, the contingencies of human existence and functioning are dependent on a stable image furnishing the worth of each individual human being.

While many contemporary theologians are not inclined to accept the structural model as the one and only true model of the image, it also appears to me to be underappreciated in the recent literature. However, one recent and important systematician, Paul K. Jewett, highlights the significance of structural capacities (e.g., reason, will, memory) and properties (humor), not so much arguing but suggesting that the predominant feature that emerges is self-transcendence. He is clear that these capacities pop up in almost every context regarding the human and must be held in high regard.[17]

Relational Model

Relational accounts often highlight the setting apart of humans from the rest of the created order, rather than capacities, powers, or some isolated capacity (as in the structural model), on the basis of their relationship to God as set apart from the created order to steward it. Dissatisfied with the structural model because of its demarcation between fully developed humans and animals or less developed humans, defenders of the relational model find some promise in human relationality to God and to other humans. Robert Jenson offers one thoughtful relational account. Jenson describes his view as follows: "Our specificity in comparison with the other animals is that we are the ones addressed by God's moral word and so enabled to respond—that we

16. See King, "The American Dream." For a development of the problem with grounding the image on the degree to which an individual human or group of humans are capable to perform specified actions or to have the potential to do something, see Kilner, *Dignity and Destiny*, 22–35.

17. Jewett, *Who We Are*, 384–94. Another recent defender of this view is Levering, *Engaging the Doctrine of Creation*, 145. There are other famous variations of the structural model, although it is not clear that they fall neatly under it. See Balthasar, *Theo-drama*, 397; Tanner, *Christ the Key*. These variants of the model may fit more naturally with a christological model of the image.

are called to pray." He adds to the description: "The final specification of 'the image of God' is love."[18]

However, the present account suffers from the same sorts of criticisms that are often brought against structural accounts. How is it that underdeveloped humans, such as a person with severe intellectual disabilities or a fetus, can pray or engage in a loving relationship with God? It is not entirely clear that they can, which raises the concern as to whether the present view is satisfying as an account that dignifies the individual.

That said, there is an important modal insight when we reflect on the nature of the *imago* in the creation story. When the creation story says we are created in the image so that we might have dominion on the earth, we realize that there is at least some possibility that we are not bearing the image or could potentially not bear the image (as is common in the Lutheran tradition) if we fail to carry out the dominion justly and faithfully.

On a relational model, the human purpose is to participate with God in certain relational contexts. These relational contexts provide the conditions for humans to experience God more fully. On such a model, we have a vision of the human that highlights its confessional and visual nature; relating to God through prayer enhances one's ability to know, experience, and confess the one true God of Christianity.

It is not uncommon in the contemporary literature to combine the structural model with a relational model of the image. The fittingness of a relational model is made sense of by the capacities that humans have to function properly.[19] However, what is highlighted is not the degree to which one's capacities are strengthened but rather the situatedness of the human in relation to God and his design for his creatures.

Functional Model

The functional model highlights the fact of human tasks as accurately describing the *imago*. Old Testament theologians appear to predominantly affirm a functional model of the *imago Dei*, but there is not one specific way of parsing out the functional image that is consistent among them. Taking their cues from Genesis 1:28, they see a close and intimate relationship between the image and the call to take dominion through dynasty, but whether the image is, strictly speaking, identical with the task of dominion is open for discussion.[20]

18. Jenson, *Systematic Theology*, 2:58–59, 72.
19. One example of this move is found in Hoekema, *Created in God's Image*, esp. 66–102.
20. See Middleton, *The Liberating Image*. Middleton advances what is possibly the most sophisticated constructive development of the functional view on offer in the contemporary literature.

Unless there is a dominant feature or property to which we can refer that sums up human identity, or a feature or property to which all other human properties reduce, it is not clear that the views above are sufficient in themselves. Instead, all of them require and depend on a particular kind of substance, a substance that sums up what it means to be human. In other words, capacities, relations, and functional relations are dependent on a substance. J. P. Moreland expresses this quite well:

> There are two ways to accomplish such functionalization. First, the image of God can be taken in the representative sense according to which humankind was made to represent God in his activity of ruling on the earth on God's behalf. Second, the image can be taken in the relational sense according to which it is constituted by certain interpersonal relationships with God and other persons. It should be obvious that either approach presupposes the ontological understanding. Something can represent God in the way just specified only if it has certain powers and attributes apt for carrying out the appropriate representational activities. And an entity can stand in certain relations and not others depending on the kind of thing the entity is, and an entity flourishes in certain relations and not others depending on the sort of thing it is.[21]

Moreland makes the point that all attributes (i.e., functions and relations) are contingent on a substance or properties that compose part of a property-thing. As such, these attributes require some ontological description of the *thing* in question. They do not somehow simply stand alone, but rather are tied to some *thing*. Substances are fundamentally countable entities within the ontology of the world. This is not to make the stronger claim that one must affirm that the *imago* is strictly identical to the substance, but, at a minimum, the *imago* requires a substance and will have some reference and recourse to the substance in all human activities. Substances are necessary when attempting to articulate the nature and content of the *imago*.

Body and Soul in the *Imago Dei*

My thesis has been that the *imago Dei* displays human identity in creaturely and divine ways. The Creator-creature distinction is present in the creation story in Genesis and is expressed in several other passages of Scripture (e.g., Ps. 8). There is no doubt that humans are creatures who by their very nature are not the divine. It is also important to highlight humanity in its divine

---

21. Moreland, *The Recalcitrant* Imago Dei, 4.

ways, as expressed in the creation story. For it is only humans that have a unique status in relation to God and to the world as distinct from the rest of creation; this then points to something that is higher than humanity. Added to this, as we will see in a later chapter, humans have an end that is higher than their creaturely nature. This discussion comes into play when we think about humans as body-soul arrangements. Basic intuitions throughout Christian reflections on the anthropos lend themselves to the notion that the body represents more clearly our connectedness to the creaturely realm and the soul has some clear reference to the divine.

Some have argued that the *imago Dei* is or has primary reference to the body. There is a common view in a body of Old Testament scholarship that in the ancient Near East kings were physical representations of the gods. And, furthermore, the notion of the image has a strong similarity with the notion of idol in the ancient world, so it is easy to see why the body would be picked out as the item for God's chosen representative that is called to take dominion on the earth through dynasty.[22] There may be some exegetical motivation for identifying the body with the image. In the creation story humans are created according to their kind (which is implied by their contrast with other "kinds"), as animals and plants are created "according to their kinds." There is an apparent link between individual animals and their interrelatedness in virtue of the generation that ensues within physical kinds. This generative pattern within physical kinds is present with humans. Furthermore, it is not lost on the careful reader that "images" in the ancient Near East were physical representations of the gods, and, so it is argued, humans are physical representations of the God of Israel.[23]

It should be unsurprising that the identification of the image with the human body is a minority position in the Reformed tradition, if it is a position at all until modernity. We could survey several noted theological authorities (e.g., Calvin, Turretin, Edwards, Owen), and we would find overwhelming support for the belief that the image has to do either with the holistic unity of the body and soul (possibly with some unique reference to the soul) or with nearly an exclusive reference to the soul alone. Part of the motivation for such a view is that God, in the wider Christian tradition, is conceived as solely immaterial without a body. For the greatest conceivable being—God (following Augustine, Anselm, and Aquinas in addition to Reformed divines)—is not subject to any deterioration but is an immutable and independent being. God is not, directly, the subject of empirical study.

22. Turner, "Temple Theology, Holistic Eschatology, and the Imago Dei."
23. Robert Culver discusses this family of views in his *Systematic Theology*, 250–52.

In other words, we cannot see him with the physical eyes. Rather, he is a subject that we come to know primarily through ideas, through spiritual discernment, and as the metaphysical cause of the world. If this is the case, then, if something is to image *this* God in any meaningful sense, then that image would likely be immaterial, or so the argument might go. If we are to have the capacity to see God, then we must be not essentially or solely physical in nature but rather nonphysical in nature because God is non-physical in nature. And if God lacks a body, then what is there of God to see for purely, or even primarily, physical creatures? We will see later that the body is important to seeing God because of the incarnation, but the point stands that we are not essentially physical and we see God who is not essentially physical and only has a body contingently in the incarnation. More on that later.

The Reformed tradition generally bears this intuition out. Australian theologian Charles Sherlock reflects this sentiment:

> To regard our physicality as fundamental is inadequate and dangerous. . . . The basic problem of the human condition is not our finitude, but our rebellion against God, with the consequent tyranny of the finite that it brings. Many people, from Confucian Chinese to modern westerners, have a strong tendency toward materialism, both in the consumer sense and also in terms of defining humanity. Australians like to think of themselves in strongly physical terms, stressing the importance of suntans, sport and physical appearance. While much of this sort of materialism needs to be challenged, the importance of physical health and well-being, and of the senses, cannot be excluded from what it means to be human.[24]

Sherlock gives a healthy, well-balanced picture of humanity that highlights the priority of the immaterial, yet without excluding the significance of the physical. The ingrained disposition to see humans as material beings, Sherlock rightly suggests, has to do with our infatuation with the creaturely nature (i.e., the "human condition" as "finite" creatures) and another kind of materialism: physical gratification otherwise called consumerism. According to Sherlock, we have cultivated a sense of humanity that is consumed with the material, and we have done so to the detriment of how we perceive human nature and purpose.

Let me make one argument to suggest that the physical description of the human substance is insufficient for yielding an adequate picture of human beings by considering the *imago Dei* in its wider biblical-theological context.

24. Sherlock, *The Doctrine of Humanity*, 77.

Capturing the Biblical-Theological Data on the *Imago Dei*

It is important to take note of the wider scriptural description of humans as God's covenantal representatives. The teaching on the *imago Dei* is not limited to the creational covenant, even if the creational covenant is an important starting point in one's development of *imago* doctrine. In fact, the *imago Dei* comes up in every phase of the biblical-theological narrative. I take it that there are three ways to capture all of the scriptural data on the *imago*: the strict human identity view (i.e., the "image" is identical to humanity in general, highlighting the creational humanity), the continuity human identity view (i.e., the "image" is grounded in creational humans and pregnant, as it were, but matures and develops over the course of covenantal history), and the christological view (i.e., the view that Christ is, strictly speaking, the "image" or the archetypal image and all other individual humans are ectypes; further, this view can be worked out along the lines of Augustinian realism, where individual humans are parts of Christ's substance).

From Creation to Fall

Throughout historical discussions of the image, the development from creation to the fall of humanity has been seen as a significant shift in the story of humans. If humans were created to function as God's covenantal representatives, then it is natural to raise the question as to whether humans lose the image during or sometime after the fall. No doubt the Reformed tradition has given several distinct answers to this very question. Some have argued that there is no distinction in the image before and after the fall, some have maintained that there is a formal and material distinction such that one is lost but the other remains (Karl Barth), and others have suggested the complete loss of the image altogether (Luther). There is a significant change in human nature upon the fall; this much seems plainly borne out by the scriptural narrative when God describes his disappointment with Adam in Genesis 3 and with humanity in general in Genesis 6. However, it is clear that even after the fall, all of humanity is described as image bearers according to Genesis 5:1–3 and Genesis 9:6, along with a host of passages later in the Old Testament and in the New Testament. To say that the image was completely lost would be out of sync with the scriptural portrait of humans.

Depending on which view one subscribes to, it might make more or less sense to describe humans as having lost the image altogether (e.g., functional and relational views). On a structural view and a substantive view, one can make a case that the image is sustained in and through change, even significant change. For on a substantive view, so long as individual humans actually persist from one stage of redemptive history to the next as the selfsame substance, it would remain that the image stays intact. No doubt on a substantive view there is a place for the loss of certain specified properties or functional capacities, but this is not to be confused with the loss of the image itself.

From Fall to Redemption

Humans experience another significant change from fall to redemption (or, in other words, *through* redemption). By virtue of union with Christ, some significant changes occur: those who have fallen out of God's grace (see Rom. 3:23) after sinning are reconciled with God and restored to a place of peace with God in redemption (Rom. 5:1). In the redemptive portrayal of humans, humans are described as "images" (Col. 3:10; James 3:9), and, furthermore, humans are called to imitate Christ, grow in the renewal of their minds, and grow in holiness.

From Redemption to Glory

Finally, humans experience additional significant change, all the while enduring as the selfsame substance.[25] Humans move through redemption into glory. Several biblical passages (Rom. 8; 1 Cor. 15; 2 Cor. 5) describe this state as the highest and most flourishing state for human beings, something akin to God's glory displayed in the temple. I will take up this theme in more detail toward the end of the book, where I discuss the beatific vision and deification.

It is important to realize that biblical texts require the theologian not only to unite the texts into a coherent narrative but also to systematize the data into a coherent whole that is relevant to our contemporary situation, guided by the church's reflections throughout the ages. Additionally, specific doctrinal concepts and terms develop in their meaning over time as the tradition clarifies, refines, and teases out their significance. This is the case with the doctrine of the *imago Dei*. To this point, I have tied together several texts into a meaningful narrative as I explicated the meaning of the *imago Dei*. Added to this, I have offered some thoughts on how to systematize the data. It is important not to stop here but rather to continue developing and refining the concept in light of other theological authorities. I put forward John Calvin as

---

25. Augustine's fourfold distinction fits here: (1) able to sin and able not to sin in creation; (2) not able not to sin after the fall of humanity; (3) able not to sin upon redemption; (4) unable to sin in glory.

one thoughtful theological lens through which to think about the doctrine in a way that is consistent with what I have laid out above.

Calvin as a Model for Understanding the *Imago Dei*

Very little is written on Calvin's anthropology, but it is clear that Calvin was a substance dualist who had similarities to both Plato and Augustine (and, in some cases, he uses language reminiscent of Aristotle). Although some aspects of his anthropological thought are difficult to pin down, Calvin seemed to hold to a view that human persons are essentially souls naturally connected to a body wherein the *imago Dei* is essentially an expression of the soul.[26] I will explore six aspects of Calvin's anthropology as he develops it in the *Institutes*, book 1, chapter 15.

First, Calvin's anthropology is clearly in the Plato-Augustine-Descartes tradition[27] in that there is an emphasis on immaterial ontology in contrast to what was popular among many medieval theologians, hylomorphism.[28] In the Plato-Augustine-Descartes tradition, as I have explained, human persons are souls essentially or at their core. In one place Calvin says that the mind is not a faculty of the body but must be a faculty of the soul (185). Calvin

26. Depending on one's version of anthropology, other theologians could endorse the idea that the image of God is specifically grounded in the soul. If one endorses Thomistic dualism, where human persons are soul-body composites wherein the soul can survive the demise of the body, then one could say that the image is found in the soul. If one is a hylomorphist, then the picture might be different. On some versions of hylomorphism, the soul is just the form of the material, but it is the material object that is a particular. If a hylomorphist takes the image to be a property (e.g., rationality), then it could be a property of the soul. If a hylomorphist construes the image to be a concrete particular, then he or she could endorse the view that the image is specific to each person.

27. I realize that Descartes was not existent yet, but Calvin would fall in line with this tradition and contributes to this tradition, or at least what some would later consider or construe as this tradition. See Kehr, "The Doctrine of the Self," which develops the philosophy and theology of Augustine and Descartes. This is similar to Calvin's overall theology as developed in the *Institutes*. The difference is that Calvin is much more explicitly practical and is generally not interested in philosophical speculation and scholastic dissection. More importantly, Calvin saw his overall theological project as having the aim of the person being conscious of God or having knowledge of God, which is, arguably, predicated on the metaphysical foundations of the self—although with Calvin knowledge of self entails knowledge of God and vice versa. For an excellent and more up-to-date exploration of Descartes and Augustine, see Menn, *Descartes and Augustine*.

28. See Calvin, *Institutes* 1.15 ("Discussion of Human Nature as Created, of the Faculties of the Soul, of the Image of God, of Free Will, and of the Original Integrity of Man's Nature"), sect. 1–6, 1:183–94. Calvin explicitly says that Plato was closer to the truth than other philosophers and speaks of Plato in the affirmative. Subsequent page references to this chapter of the *Institutes* in this section appear in the main text.

believes that the soul is essential to the human person and separate from the body in some sense. It is not clear precisely how the two are separate, just that the soul is essential and that the body, by implication, is contingent. While contemporary theologians may have difficulty with how he arrives at this conclusion, it is simply my point that he does arrive at this conclusion. His use of Scripture to support this at times is suspect, yet his conclusion is clear. He says this: "Now, unless the soul were something essential, separate from the body, Scripture would not teach that we dwell in houses of clay (Job 4:19)" (185). He proceeds to offer further support for this notion as it is found in Scripture. The Scriptures, he says, refer to the tabernacle of the flesh and say that judgment depends on what we have done in the body. "For surely these passages and similar ones that occur repeatedly not only clearly distinguish the soul from the body, but by transferring to it the name 'man' indicate it to be the principal part" (185). This is a very important point supporting the idea that Calvin affirmed a broadly Augustinian view of persons and is within the Plato-Augustine-Descartes tradition. As Calvin referred to the soul as the essential part of man, it seems that he still held that the body was a part at least contingently.

Calvin implies that some sort of immaterial substance ontology is logically prior in the order of beings, causally necessary, and fundamental in terms of value attribution. He bears this out in numerous places, including in his explication of anthropology.[29] One passage is explicit: "Now, I understand by the term 'soul' an immortal yet created essence, which is his nobler part" (190–91). He later uses Ecclesiastes 12:7 as support for the claim that humans are essentially souls that survive their deaths and experience God in heaven (184). It is important to keep in mind that Calvin was a creationist who affirmed the creation of the immaterial part or the soul as substance and held that God creates the soul directly on the basis that it is higher than physicality. Elsewhere in the *Institutes*, Calvin clearly rejects the soul's emanation from God and traducianism in favor of creationism (190–91). The human is not the same nature as God; thus Calvin is refuting Manichaeism. In contrast, God creates the soul directly wherein the soul is not confused with physical matter, thus distinguishing humans from the rest of the created order and making them likened to God. This leads to a second point concerning Calvin's anthropology.

---

29. This is apparent in Calvin's view of ecclesiology, which is really a reflection of his anthropology. In his ecclesiology he stresses the importance of the immaterial and that which corresponds to the soul. Thus, all things that are essential to Calvin's ecclesiology include that which is soulish in nature. Bodies are important, but souls are profoundly significant in Calvin's anthropology because they grant us intimate access to God.

Furthermore, in keeping with his emphasis on the immaterial soul, Calvin employs the language of faculty psychology and develops his anthropology on the basis of it. Calvin is committed to the notion that humans, as image bearers, are spiritual and that their faculties are primarily spiritual in nature. In other words, actions are rooted in the intellect and the will—both good and bad. As the immaterial substance is present at creation and continuous in the redemptive story, Calvin relates wisdom to the intellectual faculty and righteousness to the volition.[30]

Second, Calvin holds that God created humans to be immortal. "But since God not only designed to give life to an earthen vessel, but also willed it to be the abode of an immortal spirit, Adam could rightly glory in the great liberality of his Maker" (184). The logic that immaterial substance is higher than and transcends physicality is latent in the notion of a direct creation by God of the human soul, something that Calvin shares with Aquinas implicitly. Herein Calvin affirms both the value of the soul as higher than physicality and the value of the physical body as the "abode" or life for the soul to exist in and function.[31]

Third, Calvin holds that the soul is higher than the body both ontologically and in terms of redemption, but this does not undermine the importance of the body. Calvin does not sharply divorce ontology and redemptive matters but rather sees his ontology as intricately related to the doctrine of redemption. "For the body is not affected by the fear of spiritual punishment, which falls upon the soul only; from this it follows that the soul is endowed with essence. Now the very knowledge of God sufficiently proves that souls, which transcend the world, are immortal, for no transient energy could penetrate to the fountain of life" (184). "In short, the many pre-eminent gifts with which the human mind is endowed proclaim that something divine has been engraved upon it; all these are testimonies of an immortal essence" (184–85). It is interesting that, in the mind of Calvin, the created nature of the human soul or mind in action seems to reveal something transcendent. God is revealed in the human being's whole nature, not in some isolated faculty, as many would

30. There is a common debate in medieval theology over the emphasis or priority of the will or the intellect. This debate continues in Reformed theology, where with the scholastic Reformed theologians the priority is typically on the intellect following Thomas Aquinas and with the magisterial Reformed theologians it is the will. See the discussion in Vorster, *The Brightest Mirror of God's Works*, 20–23.

31. This logic can be applied to other aspects of Christian theology and has been used to affirm the intrinsic value of the body or physicality in general. The very fact that God dwelt among us in the temple, according to the Old Testament, bears this out. The fact that the Logos, the Second Person of the Trinity, became incarnate and assumed not only a human soul but also a human body affirms the value of the body.

like to say by way of critique concerning structuralist/substance views of the image.[32] This nature directs us to the divine and supports human immortality. Calvin proceeds to provide evidence for this. "For the sense perception inhering in brute animals does not go beyond the body, or at least extends no farther than to material things presented to it. But the nimbleness of the human mind in searching out heaven and earth and the secrets of nature, and when all ages have been compassed by its understanding and memory, in arranging each thing in its proper order, and in inferring future events from past, clearly shows that there lies hidden in man something separate from the body" (185).[33] Calvin cites several scriptural passages in support not only of the ontological priority of the soul but also of the redemptive priority of the soul. He also cites numerous passages in support of the notion of the soul as essential to the human person. Many of these passages refer to the essential nature of the soul concerning salvation. He cites the following: 2 Corinthians 7:1; 1 Peter 2:25; 1 Peter 1:9; 1 Peter 2:11; Hebrews 13:17; 2 Corinthians 1:23 Vulgate; Matthew 10:28 and Luke 12:5; Hebrews 12:9; Luke 16:22–23; 2 Corinthians 5:6–8; and Acts 23:8 in reference to the Sadducees, who did not believe in spirits or angels (185–86).

Fourth, Calvin speaks of the redemptive value of the body to the person and the *imago Dei* even though the soul takes priority. This is borne out in a couple of ways. One way is in terms of physical death as punishment and physical resurrection as reward. Calvin agrees with Augustine that there are two kinds of death and that the soul does not become extinct or go out of existence in virtue of the fact that it is immaterial.

> For, while the whole man is called mortal, the soul is not thereby subjected to death; nor does reason or intelligence belong to the body merely because man is called a "rational animal." Therefore, although the soul is not man, yet it is not absurd for man, in respect to his soul, to be called God's image; even though God extends to the whole excellence by which man's nature towers over all the kinds of living creatures. Accordingly, the integrity with which Adam was endowed is expressed by this word, when he had full possession of right understanding, when he had his affections kept within in the bounds of reason, all his senses tempered in right order, and he truly referred his excellence to exceptional gifts bestowed upon him by his Maker. And although the primary seat of the divine

32. See Cortez, *Theological Anthropology*, 20. He calls this an "individualist" problem and says that we cannot isolate a capacity of the individual person but rather must emphasize the collective unity concerning the image. He also cites Stanley Grenz (*The Social God and the Relational Self*) on the matter.

33. Calvin is drawing from or is influenced by others. See Tertullian, *Against Marcion* 2.9; Augustine, *Retractations* 1.10.3.

image was in the mind and heart, or in the soul and its powers, yet there was no part of man, not even the body itself, in which some sparks did not glow. (188)

Calvin says that to some degree all aspects of the world shine forth God's glory (188). It is important to point out that Calvin affirms Moses's commending of God's grace toward humans on the basis that humans are souls who image God, and this image of God or representation of God is holistic, encompassing all facets of the human—albeit with a priority for the soul.

Fifth, Calvin has a teleological dimension with respect to human persons and the *imago Dei*. This point overlaps with the next point in that there is a christological dimension to the human soul / *imago Dei*. In numerous places Calvin refers to the person and the *imago Dei* as finding some sort of completion or fullness in relationship to Christ. In one place Calvin refers to the human as the image, yet he expounds on that by saying that humans are not the full definition of the image of God—although Christ is the full definition of the image. He says this: "Nevertheless, it seems that we do not have a full definition of 'image' if we do not see more plainly those faculties in which man excels, and in which he ought to be thought the reflection of God's glory" (189). This means that even though Calvin has a view that the soul / *imago Dei* is reflective of the divine from the beginning of creation, it is not complete in some sense. There is a sense in which humans better reflect or more fully reflect God's nature in redemption. This leads to Calvin's christological anthropology.

Sixth, Calvin has a christological dimension with respect to human persons and the *imago Dei*. In section 4 of chapter 15 Calvin develops this explicitly. He takes this up elsewhere when he develops his understanding of salvation, but here he links the image of God directly to Christ. This raises interesting questions about his particular anthropology. There are a couple ways in which one could interpret Calvin on this issue.

1. One could interpret Calvin along teleological/eschatological lines in that the soul is the image of God in the soul's final state or relationship to Christ.
2. Alternatively, one could interpret Calvin in terms of the image always being present in humans, yet fully or completely in humans in some accidental sense when they are finally redeemed in union with Christ, in that man more fully reflects or represents God.

I take the second interpretation or something akin to it to be what Calvin would affirm, and it fits with what I have developed in this chapter. In fact,

Calvin has affirmed that humanity is the image of God. In contrast to other commentators (whom Calvin cites) who privilege Christ as the starting point for our reflections on the image, Calvin begins with the creation narrative as supplying us with sufficient, yet not comprehensive, information about humans as image bearers.[34] The support for this is twofold. First, Calvin clearly speaks of the human soul as unique and representing God from creation— even prior to redemption. Second, Calvin, in the quotation in the fifth point above, says that humans do not fully define the image, and then he proceeds to explain what "fully" means. He seems to indicate that this means that it is where the faculties in humans "excel," and in this way humans are a reflection of God's glory. Thus, for Calvin it is in humans' faculties functioning properly to their full extent and in terms of glory. The notion of degree seems apt here. Here again is the quotation, with the sentences that follow:

> Nevertheless, it seems that we do not have a full definition of "image" if we do not see more plainly those faculties in which man excels, and in which he ought to be thought the reflection of God's glory. That, indeed, can be nowhere better recognized than from the restoration of his corrupted nature. There is no doubt that Adam, when he fell from his state, was by his defection alienated from God. Therefore, even though we grant that God's image was not totally annihilated and destroyed in him, yet it was so corrupted that whatever remains is frightful deformity. (189)

Calvin proceeds to discuss the restoration of humans by citing Scripture supporting the notion that Christ restores humans to their original condition (189). It is important to note, in favor of the second interpretation above, what Calvin says in relationship to the image of God and Christ as the image of God: "Now we see how Christ is the most perfect image of God; if we are conformed to it, we are so restored that with true piety, righteousness, purity, and intelligence we bear God's image" (190). Arguably, Calvin is saying here that there are degrees of perfection concerning the image of God, and this would fit with his teachings elsewhere on the beatific vision, union with Christ, and deification. He does say that humans are the image of God in terms of their soul, but also he compares humans to the Christ-man, who is the perfect image by which we become the image of Christ. Thus, there is a stable reality with degreed properties attributed to or predicable of the stable reality.

Alternatively, one could develop Calvin's anthropology accordingly. Calvin comments on the restoration of the image of God concerning those who are in relationship to Christ: "Therefore in some part it now is manifest in

34. See Calvin's commentary on Col. 1:15.

the elect, in so far as they have been reborn in the spirit; but it will attain its full splendor in heaven" (190). It is important to note here that Calvin leaves himself open to something that is greater and grander than simply restoration of what was lost with respect to the image of God; there will not only be restoration but something higher than that in heaven or, in biblical categories, in "glory." This theme would certainly fit with Calvin's notion that heaven is higher than earth and that the soul is higher than the body. The idea that the human soul as an image bearer will gradually attain glory or the perfection of the image of God according to the image of Christ seems to open the door to humans stepping up ontologically. Connected to this, the notion of an ontological ladder to a higher reality supports the fact that Calvin has a robust notion of teleology and Christology concerning the human soul and the image of God.[35]

Much of Calvin's anthropology is not sufficiently retrieved and developed in the contemporary literature, but it is clear that his view of human persons and the image of God are securely in the tradition of Augustine and in the spirit of Plato concerning the immaterial nature of man as the core.

Revisiting the *Imago Dei*?

In keeping with the data described thus far, there remain some options on the table for our consideration. An articulation of the image itself must have the resources to provide an accounting for the creational and redemptive data. As I suggested earlier, the biblical data, as found in the creation narrative and affirmed, if modified, in the New Testament, asserts that the image of God has something to do with our human identity in that it is a descriptive term for human beings. As humans, we are designed by God as his image bearers. Such a view that has a robust place for the compound substance of body and soul is fully consistent with the insights and main features of Calvin's view. There are alternative theories on offer worthy of our consideration, but in the end it seems that some sort of substantive-holistic view concerning the

35. This notion of teleology and man's degreed growth in glory, or becoming an image bearer more fully, is an underdeveloped aspect of Calvin's anthropology. While the interpretation of Calvin as endorsing an ancient ontology that uses the ladder imagery has met with some resistance with its association to participatory models of redemption that some perceive to be out of sync with Reformed theology, it has seen a considerable interest among contemporary theological interpreters. For one important example, see Canlis, *Calvin's Ladder*. Canlis argues that Calvin should be understood in the Augustinian tradition of deification, which highlights the fact that humans "participate" or "share" in God's attributes analogously. Here again we see the influences of Plato (see esp. *Symposium* 210a–212c) via Augustine.

kind-nature of human beings is the right approach when making sense of all the data. Let us consider the alternative views before looking more seriously at the sort of substantial view that I will suggest.

The Patristic Christological View

We have already examined views in the family of the patristic model. I wish to suggest that there might be a way to bring together Augustine with the patristic view by tying together all redeemed substances as parts of one larger substance: Christ. On this view, Adam is the substance of all fallen humanity and Christ is the substance of all redeemed humanity. It is not uncommon to associate the "freedom" capacity view of the image with the christological view because humans are described as being sufficiently porous until they are united to and grafted into the substance of Christ himself.[36] The obvious challenge with associating the image with "freedom" alone is that this is one isolated capacity, and if there is one individual (e.g., a person who is cognitively disabled) that fails to display or manifest this capacity, then it would raise doubts about that individual's image-bearing capacity. However, if the exponents of this view intend something more akin to a passive openness to the divine-human relationship, then there is a distinct challenge. How is it that all humans are image bearers? It seems that the creation narrative describes all human creation, specifically, as bearing the image of God (and particularly God the Creator, not one person of the Godhead). There are, arguably, two challenges here. First, it does not appear that all humans are image bearers on the christological model, because not all humans are redeemed and united to Christ in the new covenant, only the elect. Second, the creation narrative fails to specify or suggest that the image is Christ alone; rather, the image seems tied to the whole of humanity in God's creation. There is no doubt some unique relation to Christ as the image bearer, specified in the New Testament (see 2 Cor. 4:4), but how it is that redeemed humans are related to Christ in imaging God is an open question and not clearly spelled out in the passages of Scripture.

The Personal View

Gerald Bray has recently advanced what some call the "person" or "personal" view of the *imago Dei*. He argues that the *imago Dei* is identified

---

36. This is the case with Tanner's view in *Christ the Key*, 1–58. Tanner takes it that humans are properly subjects that deserve our reflection of them in relation to Christ alone. For Tanner, this whole discussion about "natures," "created substance," "faculties," "capacities," and other related notions is largely not within our realm of reflection.

with the person rather than some isolated property, relation, or function. This view holds that personal relationships make us image bearers of God. Bray says, "Relationships are only possible between persons, and it is this elusive concept, the thing which defines man as a 'who,' and not a 'what,' which gives the image its meaning."[37] Kant's view might fall along these lines because of his emphasis on the kind of substance we are (note also Bray's tendency to affirm that "humans" as images describe the image as a "who" and not a "what"): persons in a similar way that God is a person. It is the transcendence that we have in virtue of our being persons that makes us like God. It is easy to see why this is an attractive view. Ryan Peterson has recently criticized this view and supported what he has called the "human identity" view, arguing that we should not confuse identity, as personhood, with human identity. As it is similar to the structural, relational, and functional theories, the personal theory is insufficient in that it fails to capture the meaning of the image as it is spelled out in the Genesis narrative. In Genesis the emphasis of the image is placed on the whole of humanity, which finds its ultimate identity and purpose in relation to God; this does not, however, exclude the individual parts that make up the collective whole.[38] Peterson, in agreement with this general line of reasoning, argues that the property (or properties) of personhood provides the conditions for the image but is (or are) not the image itself.[39] Rather, it is humanity as a whole that bears the image from creation, and it is this image that has a purpose or telos found or realized in the New Testament teaching on the saints in relation to Jesus.

The Election View

The preceding reflections exclude one important contemporary view of the *imago*: the election theory. Motivated by the recent successes of the biological and brain sciences, defenders of the election view argue that there is one strong motivation for revising our understanding of humans to focus not on our distinction from animals but on our similarity to animals. Rather than highlight some trait, faculty, or power distinctive of the human and setting apart the human from the animal creation, we should reenvision

37. Bray, "God's Image in Man," 222.
38. R. S. Peterson, *The* Imago Dei *as Human Identity*, 79–83.
39. R. S. Peterson, *The* Imago Dei *as Human Identity*, 81. See also I. McFarland, *Difference and Identity*, 147–48; however, in more than one place McFarland is critical of the dominion function of humanity. See also Horton, *Lord and Servant*, 103–4. As seen above, a similar argument has been used by Christian philosophers with respect to the structural capacities and properties of humans (e.g., Richard Mouw, Jerry L. Walls).

our understanding of the human in light of humanity's close and intimate relationship to the animal world. Several evolutionary biologists argue for the justified denial of species essentialism—that is, the notion that individual organisms are parts of a biological grouping in virtue of essential properties. Rather, individual organisms are grouped in that way precisely because they are causally generated within a "genealogical nexus."[40] Several attempts have been advanced to reconcile the notion of *uniqueness* with the findings of biological evolution (e.g., Rahner's transcendental orientation, Pannenberg's disposition to new experiences, van Huyssteen's anatomical distinctions), but they have, arguably, failed. In an attempt to summarize the findings, Joshua Moritz argues that the concern is twofold. First, as with the challenge to demarcate human species, there is not a clear demarcation of what human uniqueness is and where it is found. Second, and further supporting the first claim, there is substantial evidence that nonhuman hominins have similar traits, albeit in a much weaker sense, to humans in terms of their capacity for symbolic reasoning and technological innovation.[41] If we are to assume that humans are biological organisms (not necessarily kinds because of the denial of species), then we should opt for some other ground and conception of the *imago*.

In light of the evidence, there are several theological solutions on offer. One could include the animal kingdom in the image-bearing activity of humans.[42] However, the question would simply be pushed back further. Where does one then draw the line? There is no obvious answer. Others have suggested dispensing with talk about the *imago Dei* as a central or essential doctrine within Christian theology.[43] However, this seems a rather bleak proposal given the centrality of the *imago* in biblical revelation and in the church's reflections through the ages. There is a third option.

Joshua Moritz argues, assuming that the biological evolutionary findings are reliable, that an "election" view is preferable. Image bearing is situated in divine election rather than in specific traits, faculties, or properties. In this way, the election view avoids all the problems associated with the structural, relational, or functional views developed with some reference to capacities—as seen above. While this is one interesting option for our consideration, I am convinced that another route may be more promising.

First, the biological evolutionary findings are inconclusive. There are still some scholarly voices in the biological community that support the ontology

40. Moritz, "Evolutionary Biology," 49.
41. Moritz, "Evolutionary Biology," 52–54.
42. Deane-Drummond, "Are Animals Moral?," 209.
43. Putz, "Moral Apes."

of the human species.[44] Second, these findings tend to be rather anemic because they are generally formulated in a vacuum apart from other findings in the social sciences as well as in philosophy. Finally, as I argued above, there is at least one property that distinguishes human creatures from other creatures and provides the ground for transcendental features, which enable us to fulfill our representative function.[45] Lynne Rudder Baker calls it the property of robust first-person consciousness.[46] The first-person-consciousness criterion provides some evidence for a distinct human substance, minimally, and for a human soul as substance, maximally.

A Biblical-Theological Summary of the Imago Dei

In keeping with a broad theme of vision, there is something apparent in the nature of human beings that is echoed in the scriptural narrative regarding the vision of God. As I have noted previously, vision is a capacity of perception and a kind of knowledge that gains us access into the divine nature. Thus, there is something significant about the properties and capacities of humans that allows for this perception of the divine. Common within catholic reflections, human nature (particularly Christ's human nature) becomes a means by which humans gain access to the divine nature. For as Paul clearly articulates in several passages, humans have knowledge of God's attributes (see Rom. 1:19) and have the capacity for moral knowledge (see Rom. 2:15).

Additionally, the creation narrative seems to capture something about the image as relevant to human identity. Concrete human nature itself points us to the divine Creator. As shown above, the *imago* is not, strictly speaking, identical to capacities or properties, nor is it merely a functional reality (à la Middleton) or a relational reality (e.g., Barth, Jenson). It is something that captures the nature of humanity. The point is that it seems to have some recourse to the actual properties of human nature. Election theories that construe the *imago* as extrinsic or external to human beings fail to capture what is present at creation: human beings themselves in their holistic reality (including properties, relations, functions). Furthermore, if one takes seriously the unfolding progressive revelation via the covenants, then the christological view fails to capture what is in fact present at creation: the human being.

The fall reflects this understanding of the *imago* as having something to do with the very properties of humans. The divine author of Scripture conveys

---

44. Ereshefsky, "Species." The discussion on species essentialism is a conceptual mess and requires a good bit of work clarifying various positions.

45. I have argued this point elsewhere. See Farris, "Bodily-Constituted Persons."

46. Baker, *Naturalism and the First-Person Perspective.*

that the *imago Dei* is present after the fall, thus pointing to the fact of the *imago* as, somehow, persisting despite corruption and sin. It is not as if the image is extinguished after the fall; it persists. Although humans are not functioning in the way that God has commanded, at least after the fall, the presumption in Scripture is that they are still God's image bearers, however corrupted they may be. Two passages explicitly point this out. In Genesis 5:1–3 God still recognizes fallen humanity as his image—"When God created mankind, he made them in the likeness of God" (v. 1)—because the image appears to be transferred in the royal dynasty from the parental covenantal representatives. And Genesis 9:6 says, "Whoever sheds human blood, by humans shall their blood be shed; for in the image of God has God made mankind." Both passages presuppose the fact that humans are created in the image of God and that this persists after the fall.

Some think that "dignity" is necessarily tied to or wrapped up in the *imago Dei*, but it is not clearly identical with it, even if the image grounds human dignity. The notion of dignity seems tied to our personal nature as those capable of entering into deep, meaningful relationships as conscious individuals with freedom of the will, morality, and conscience. If the "personal" view is not, strictly speaking, what we are intending by the *imago Dei*, then it would seem that "dignity" is something distinct as a category or property of image bearers. This is not to say that *imago Dei* has nothing to do with dignified beings but that the two are, at a minimum, conceptually distinct, even though dignity is not identical to or the primary attribute of the image. Some beings have dignity that are not image bearers, like higher-order animals. They, too, deserve our respect and just behavior. It seems right, however, to say with Kant that humans, as transcendental agents, bear the property of dignity. But why think that the property of the *imago Dei* is something more than an external, accidental property? As shown earlier, the property has some tie to human capacities and normative functioning that will culminate in higher-order functioning for humans. So there seems to be something that is internal to the nature of being human concerning the *imago Dei*. These reflections raise a more fundamental concern about the *imago Dei* and its relationship to the human soul. Is the *imago Dei* an essential property of the soul or a common property of the soul?

Image as an Essential or Common Property of Human Nature

While the *imago Dei* is not merely an external property but rather an internal property of the soul, it is not clear whether it is essential or accidental in nature. It may be that the property is accidental in that human souls are not essentially *imago* bearers, but only contingently so. It is conceivable that humans could be created without the *imago* property (unless we take that property as strictly identical to some essential property like rationality or personhood—as is common within catholic developments). There might be some conceivable world in which God decided to create humans without creating them as images of himself. This would not be so if the property were strictly identified with personhood, but the collective covenantal nature of humans seems to be the highlight of the scriptural pattern. That said, it is hard to conceive of when in fact we humans, individually construed, would not instantiate the *imago Dei* property. The nature of the scriptural pattern describes our human nature, in a multiplicity of ways, as signifying and pointing to God's nature and glory. In fact, the Scriptures presume that humans are always *imago* bearers in creation and in redemption. Even when humans have sinned, they are still marked with divine glory as image bearers (e.g., Gen. 5; 9; Ps. 8; 1 Cor. 11). What in fact the mark of divine glory is is not entirely clear. We will know the full extent of God's plan for human identity only in the eschaton, when humans have directly encountered the presence of God and experienced the physical resurrection.

The question that remains is whether the *imago Dei* is an essential property. What would that property be? As I stated earlier, it is not one isolated property, capacity, or function. So what might it be? It may be a property of human nature that is primarily and essentially attributable to the soul. Could the human have been created without the *imago Dei*? It seems so. For God could have created other beings that are like human beings but are not *human* beings and are not themselves in the image of God. In which case the *imago Dei* would not be an essential property, but it could be a common property. Given our context in the covenants, the image is present throughout the story of Scripture as seen in the passages listed above. In this way, it might be a common property rather than an essential property. It is true that if it is not an essential property, then it is an accidental property, but this should not take away from the significance or permanence of the image for humans in their covenantal contexts. A common property is a normal property of a human substance. Like the body, which is generally a part of a human nature, so is the image. While the soul is naturally embodied and functions properly with the body, so the human substance is naturally inclined to fulfill its purpose of that which it is not yet.

Conclusion

This chapter began by talking about pictures evoked by the *imago Dei* doctrine. The doctrine raises all sorts of questions about who we are as human beings, what our destiny is, and how we relate to God. Undoubtedly, the scriptural portrait of humans as images overlaps with the "idol" concept developed in the Old Testament reflecting the ancient Near Eastern understanding of kings as images of God and also the central biblical theme of humans as covenantal representatives who carry out God's creative purposes of "dominion" and "dynasty" in the world (i.e., our vocation). Traditionally, humans were reflections of God similar to the face seen in a mirror. On many traditional accounts, human beings are ensouled beings who have some similarity relationship to God that sets them apart from the rest of the created order. Working within these patterned ways of thinking, the present chapter expanded some of these categories to argue that the *imago Dei* is identical to or closely related to human identity, but human identity as it is tied to a substance, particularly a soul as substance, that has the powers of rationality, free will, moral conscience, and first-person consciousness.

As the reader can see, there are many challenges with developing a doctrine of the *imago Dei*. One of those challenges has to do with the unsystematic way in which the "image" concept is dealt with in Scripture and the sparing use of the term throughout both Testaments of the Bible. One might be tempted to think it is not all that important in Scripture, but this, it seems to me, would be a mistake. The concept finds its anchor in the creation story as a central and guiding theme through the rest of Genesis, particularly in Genesis 5, with its themes of dominion through dynasty, and Genesis 9, with its emphasis on the image as honored or dignified in a unique way in the context of the divine law. The New Testament, too, picks up the theme of the image, but in surprisingly different ways. With that, it appears, as argued in the present chapter, that there is a continuity of meaning regarding the *imago Dei* as a leitmotif that links humanity in the Old Testament from creation, to fall, and to the New Testament, with its emphasis on redemption and glory. Our final destination is new life through the resurrection, where we will experience the presence of God and come to see his glorious presence through the person and work of the divine-human (Christ) upon hearing the gospel (i.e., good news) proclaimed. It is here that we will see God, and by him we will see his splendid creation. As John states, "The city does not need the sun or the moon to shine on it, for the glory of God gives it light, and the Lamb is its lamp" (Rev. 21:23). God's image bearers are the primary recipients of that glory.

I suggested three ways to organize the Old Testament and New Testament data on the image that seem to give credence to the creational image of humans, the redeemed image of humans, and the christological view of image. I suggested that something like a strict human identity view highlights the creational image expressed by humans and that the redeemed image is God's extrinsic work of highlighting the reality of the creational image. Consider this view like the spotlight theory, where God's redemption shines a light on the creational image. Distinctively, humans are images at creation in seed form, but that seed is only developed by the redemptive water found in Christ. Consider the view as similar to the seed in relation to the full-grown tree, which has an inner potency that requires God's impartation of grace to grow into a mature fruit-bearing tree. Finally, another theory is the christological theory, which says that only the particular Christ is the image, and those who are united to Christ are ectypes of the archetype.

4

What Does It Mean to Be Free?

Freedom as Creaturely and Divine

Now the Lord is the Spirit, and where the Spirit of the Lord is, there is freedom.

2 Corinthians 3:17

This image of God was in Adam in the beginning, by virtue of which he was immortal, holy, wise, and lord of the entire world, and thus was endowed with the freedom and ability to completely execute or disregard the commandment of God.

Large Emden Catechism (1559)

After an exploration of various personal ontologies, I concluded that persons are, strictly speaking, identical to their souls or their souls plus bodies, but that persons are likely more than their bodies and brains. The previous chapter explored the nature of the *imago Dei*, an appropriate term for all human beings. Upon working through the various views on offer, I argued that something like a "human identity" view is probably the way we ought to think about the *imago Dei*. The image is not simply one structural capacity or function or even the relationship we find ourselves in, yet all of these are important descriptive attributes of the nature of humans and are informed by the broader scriptural narrative. That said, neither is the personal view (i.e., the view that the image is identical to personhood or some of the particular facts about persons or the diversity of individual humans) adequate to account for all the descriptive features (e.g., the covenantal communal structure, the fact that it is both individual and communal, that it is uniquely expressed in Christ) of the image that Scripture gives us.

Keeping with an understanding of the *imago Dei* as a reference to the whole of human identity, in the present chapter I will explore the nature of agency, specifically human agency. Human agency is one important aspect of our identity as God's image bearers. The human story presumes human agency in creation and in redemption.

The present subject has been of interest to philosophers, which has direct bearing on the theological concerns surrounding free agency. Philosophers are interested in several interrelated questions about the nature of moral agency. Their preoccupation often centers on the nature of human freedom. In what sense am I free to do what I choose? A common answer is that all human agents are free to do as they choose without constraints or with some constraints. The factors shaping and forming one's will include external or internal constraints or both. More on this below.

Science, as well, has an interest in agency. In recent years, the biological sciences have started to provide material on the nature of agency. Even more than the biological sciences, the neurological sciences have entered the dialogue by providing important data that, depending on one's understanding of the mind-brain relationship, will affect how one understands agency.

This is also true of the queen of the sciences, theology. Human freedom has a long and venerable tradition of discussion in systematic theology. Human freedom pops up in nearly every discussion concerning human identity. If not foregrounded, it makes up part of the background to human creation, the fall, redemption, and the eschaton.[1]

Situating Agency in the Anthropological Story

An important theological discussion that has received insufficient treatment in contemporary theology is that of agency in relation to the stages of

---

1. For a survey of Reformed anthropology, see Helm, *Human Nature from Calvin to Edwards*. Helm shows that much of the Reformed theological tradition is committed to the essentiality of the soul as a part of an individual human nature and that most of the tradition is committed to an understanding of human nature according to faculty psychology (i.e., the intellect and the volition are distinct parts of the human soul) regarding issues of agency and freedom. This changes when we get to Edwards, whose anthropology, in many ways continuous with the Reformed tradition, is also an idealist immaterialist with respect to the body and reconceives the faculties not so much as substantial parts but as affective powers of the soul or spirit.

theological anthropology—stages that humans, particularly graced humans, move through in the scriptural story line. Humans are characterized by what they can and cannot do in these stages. Without fail, this discussion necessarily dives into other theological loci (e.g., the image of God, theology proper, salvation) with an explicit emphasis on human capacities. There is, then, an unavoidable overlap here with relevant philosophical discussions. Kevin Timpe and Audra Jenson bear this out in their important article on free will when they say, "We will focus primarily on modal facts about persons in the various stages, even though there will also be non-modal facts which differ as well." They proceed to describe the various stages:

> The pattern in understanding the stages of theological anthropology that we follow is one which parallels the *exitus reditus* pattern. Speaking of this pattern, Rudi Te Velde says that it is "a double—in fact a circular—movement: the coming forth (*exitus*) of all things from God, and the return (*reditus*) of all things, particularly man, to God as the ultimate goal. . . . It is, so to speak, a metaphysical scheme, derived from the order of reality itself (*ordo rerum*), providing the Christian theologian with a conceptual framework which allows for a systematic treatment." This pattern traces the overarching relationship of humankind with God from its initial state of creation, through sin and the fall, then returning to God in the eschaton. We think that this pattern, with respect to human freedom, is no accident, but is instead woven into the Christian narrative regarding human nature and its relationship to God. It is, in other words, an attempt to illustrate the contour of the Christian theology that it assumes.[2]

This pattern is, arguably, the pattern found in Scripture as we move from the fall to redemption. The pattern is characterized not only as what humans do but also, even more (depending on some theologies), as what God does toward his creatures. The stages that Timpe and Jenson follow include *status integritatis* (the pre-fall state; humans are free to sin and free to not sin), *status corruptionis* (a post-fall state; humans have fallen from a state of grace or from a state of innocence and are freely able to sin, but humans are not able to not sin), and *status gloriae* (the post-glorification state; humans are redeemed to a perfect extent and are able to not sin, but humans are not able to sin). In Reformed circles, sometimes an additional stage is included after justification, yet prior to glorification, and this is the stage where humans are able to not sin, even if they still do sin at times.[3]

2. Timpe and Jenson, "Free Will," 235.

3. Berkhof, *Systematic Theology*, 277. Berkhof explains that the benefits of redemption are made available after justification. Some Reformed theologians make a distinction between

Theological Anthropology and Freedom in Philosophical Perspective

The preceding anthropological story presupposes some framework for thinking about freedom. To explore this, let us take a brief look at the various philosophical conceptions of freedom in light of a theological reading of various passages of Scripture.

Again, how we philosophically conceive of humans as free and responsible agents will shape and color how we read the Scriptures and, more than that, will affect how we systematically tie together all the data that informs a wider conception of creaturely and divine freedom.

Broadly speaking, there are two ways of philosophically developing a conception of human freedom. The first is the view called *compatibilism*. The second is called *libertarianism*. On the first view, human actions are determined by preceding causes. However, this determinism is compatible with human responsibility, or so it is argued. Humans are responsible for their actions. The ways of making sense of (i.e., making compatible) these two claims will be explored below. On the second view, human actions are not determined, but instead humans are able to do otherwise. Often this is considered the commonsense view of human freedom and is thought to provide a robust foundation for thinking about human responsibility. The old expression "Responsibility implies ability" applies here. The idea is that responsibility begins in the agent as the source; but more than that, the agent or the agent's volition is unconditioned by factors external and internal to the self, such that responsibility is causally found in the agent and not elsewhere.

Compatibilism

Once again, compatibilism is the view that human actions are determined and humans are morally culpable for those same actions. Defenders of this view are convinced that the preceding causes or states are not incompatible with but rather make sense of human choices.

Theologically, many in the Reformed tradition have appropriated passages of Scripture in light of compatibilism as the best or most natural way to understand God's revelation of human freedom. Several passages in the Old Testament Wisdom literature naturally yield a reading that makes sense along compatibilist lines.[4] Proverbs 16:9 reminds us, "The mind of man plans

---

the start of *ordo salutis* as the moral (i.e., regeneration), then the legal (i.e., justification), as Berkhof explains (418). Nonetheless, there is this important state in the Reformed *ordo salutis*.

4. I use the NASB translation in this paragraph.

his way, But the LORD directs his steps." In Genesis 50:20 Joseph says to his brothers, "As for you, you meant evil against me, but God meant it for good in order to bring about this present result, to preserve many people alive." The psalmist in several places describes God as the one who directs and providentially orchestrates our lives. For example, Psalm 90:17 says, "Let the favor of the Lord our God be upon us; And confirm for us the work of our hands." Other passages describe God as determining who to favor and who not to favor. Psalm 84:11 says, "For the LORD God is a sun and shield; The LORD gives grace and glory; No good thing does He withhold from those who walk uprightly." Other psalms describe God's favor as something that God does for us, not predicated on something we do. Psalm 89:17 is one example: "By your favor our horn is exalted."

In an Old Testament covenantal context, God is described as the one who elects, blesses whom he chooses, and makes his elect great. See, for example, Genesis 12:2: "I will make of you into a great nation, and I will bless you; I will make your name great, and you will be a blessing." See also Numbers 6:24–26: "The LORD bless you and keep you; the LORD make his face shine on you and be gracious to you; the LORD turn his face toward you and give you peace." All that is done of a redemptive sort (i.e., God's action of new creation) is brought about by God, or so it has been argued, noncausally necessitated by human actions.

In one important place God is described as the one who providentially brings about all that humans do prior to their birth. God providentially orchestrates one's being in the covenant, being redeemed, and doing good works. Psalm 139:16 says, "Your eyes saw my unformed body; all the days ordained for me were written in your book before one of them came to be." Accordingly, the psalmist understands it that God has ordained his days and they have been written down before they have come to pass. While this verse might suggest some form of determinism, it also does not exclude compatibilism. In fact, one could read this as God's knowledge of the future.

One of the most important New Testament passages that compatibilists have appropriated in support of their position is Acts 2:23, which says that Jesus Christ, when he was given to authorities, was "delivered up according to the definite plan and foreknowledge of God" (ESV). This suggests that God has a determined plan that humans are a part of, but it lacks a determinative meaning that favors compatibilism or determinism more generally. For if it is possible to understand this "definite plan" as a part of God's knowledge that God is working out in time via human agents, then, once again, the present passage could be read in light of several metaphysical positions concerning human freedom, divine sovereignty, and divine knowledge of future events.[5]

Some will argue that these passages can be read and made sense of in other ways, but it is worth noting that they can be and have been read as favoring some form of determinism or compatibilism. No doubt reading these passages in this way presupposes a prescribed framework and is underdetermined by the data we are given. Nevertheless, there is a long and sophisticated history of theological interpreters who have appropriated these passages in this way.

Biblical theologian D. A. Carson has argued that the Scriptures do not simply suggest or yield a doctrine of compatibilism but necessitate it. In one place he claims, "Compatibilism is a necessary component to any mature and orthodox view of God and the world."[6] Carson in several places offers his defense of the doctrine, which he takes to include the view that God is sovereign and that humans are responsible.[7] Thomas McCall succinctly summarizes Carson's position as follows: first, "God is utterly sovereign, but his sovereignty never functions to mitigate human responsibility," and second, "human beings are morally responsible creatures, but their moral responsibility never functions to make God absolutely contingent."[8] While many classical Christian theists would endorse these claims, it is not clear at all that these are sufficient conditions for a doctrine of compatibilism.[9] As we will see

---

5. It is clear that these passages taken together rule out what is often called "open theism," the view that the future is neither determined nor known, because it doesn't exist or God has self-limitations. On some versions of open theism, future contingent events cannot exist, nor could they be determined, because they are by their nature dependent on contingencies that have yet to be explained or caused. For a clear layout of the variations of the view, see Arbour, *Philosophical Essays against Open Theism*. While it does seem that open theism is not compatible with classical theism (assuming a broader definition and not the narrow definition often assumed when describing God as metaphysically simple, immutable, impassible, and atemporal, but a perfect-being theism that is compatible with theistic personalism), classical theism has been articulated in more than one way. Most obviously apart from a compatibilist view, many classical theists would endorse a Thomist view as antinomy or a mysterian view of God's relationship to human freedom. Other acceptable traditional or classical views include simple foreknowledge and Molinism (middle knowledge, where God knows contingent free choices of humans through the choices of individual humans in a given possible world that God has chosen as the actual world).

6. Carson, *The Love of God*, 54.

7. See Carson, *Divine Sovereignty and Human Responsibility*; Carson, *How Long, O Lord?* Carson attempts to dispel the consequent that God is the author of evil by allowing for human responsibility. Several theologians cite Carson's *Divine Sovereignty and Human Responsibility* as an authority on the topic. See Peterson and Williams, *Why I Am Not an Arminian*, 137, 149; Groothuis, *Christian Apologetics*, 636.

8. McCall, *Analytic Christian Theology*, 60.

9. For a thoughtful evaluation of Carson's exposition and defense of compatibilism, once again see McCall, *Analytic Christian Theology*, 56–81.

below, they are not, and in fact there are versions of libertarianism that are easily conformable with these claims—possibly all forms of libertarianism. Insofar as libertarians can make sense of God sovereignly orchestrating all events toward his determined ends, according to his will or according to his knowledge, a libertarian could claim that God is "utterly sovereign" and that humans are "morally responsible." But it is important to note that moral responsibility is grounded differently, depending on which variation of compatibilism one affirms or the variation of libertarianism one affirms.

There are certainly philosophical reasons favoring compatibilism, especially if one affirms a physicalist anthropology. It is worth noting that many Reformed theologians are compatibilists, but they are not physicalists; rather, more often than not, they are immaterialists or dualists. That said, physicalism seems to favor compatibilism. Philosophically drawing on some of the findings from the scientific community, it suggests that humans are physical in nature. There is some support for it in the wider Christian tradition (e.g., Jonathan Edwards, Augustine), but if we are unsatisfied with absolute determinism and find support for responsible freedom, then we are left with compatibilism. Those defending a physicalist view of human persons, particularly a reductive version of physicalism, will argue that humans are causally determined. The argument is something like the following: All physical object actions are causally determined by physical laws; human objects are physical objects; therefore, actions caused by human objects, given that they are physical, are determined by physical laws. However, many philosophers and theologians are convinced that the scientific data is not determinative on this score and that there is more to human freedom requiring, at a minimum, nonreductive physicalism, where humans have higher-order emergent properties and powers that are not reducible to the physical parts that constitute them or to the physical parts interacting. With that in mind, most theologians with affinities for determinism will opt, at a minimum, for compatibilism, where they understand human actions not as causally determined by external factors but as causally determined by internal factors. Let us turn now to consider some of the compatibilist options.

Classical Compatibilism

Defenders of classical compatibilism define free actions as freedom to do what one desires. For example, if I am confronted with the option of going to the theater to watch a movie or going to the mall to shop, then because I desire to go to the theater more, I would choose the theater over the mall, assuming there were no other overriding considerations (e.g., I need to find a pair of dress pants for work). While this is a simple example, it illustrates the present view that my choices will follow my desires. This is popular among many in the Reformed tradition who affirm some sort of Calvinistic soteriology. God providentially orchestrates the end of humans and the fulfillment of that end through their choices, which are governed by one's affections. This applies, as well, to the *ordo salutis*, where God works through created causes. Jonathan Edwards famously takes this basic line when he describes the freedom of created minds. He understands created minds to act according to their desires. Whatever a mind's greatest or highest desire, that causally brings about what that agent will choose to do.[10]

There are obvious challenges to this understanding of compatibilism. One in particular is the problem of compulsive behavior. This is a well-documented problem in the literature. Marc Cortez summarizes the problem in this way in the context of talking about compulsive desires as psychological disorders: "Classic compatibilism would seem to portray this as a free decision because it stems from my own desires, but most would reject the notion that a compulsive behavior should be viewed as a free action."[11] No doubt this objection has met some responses in the literature. I simply note it here as one consideration in the agency discussion.

Hierarchical Compatibilism

Hierarchical compatibilism is the view that humans are free when they act according to their true selves. When a person acts according to his or her truest desires, convictions, habits, dispositions, and character states, then that person is said to have acted freely. In other words, I act most freely when I act according to my true inner self, whatever that may be. It might be the combination of all the internal factors that give rise to a higher-order desire for which I act. However, it is not clear that this view can adequately account for the problem of various psychological disorders like compulsive desires or behaviors. It does not seem to fare much better than classical compatibilism.

Reasons-Responsive Compatibilism

Defenders of the reasons-responsive variant of compatibilism argue that humans are free when they act on the most compelling reasons for bringing about an action. However, the reasons-responsive variation does not seem

10. The most important work of Edwards in this regard is *Freedom of the Will* (1754). For a helpful exposition, see Wainwright, "Jonathan Edwards."
11. Cortez, *Theological Anthropology*, 106.

to hold up under serious scrutiny, one might argue, because one's action depends on the deliberation over what one will choose, which presupposes the indeterminacy in conscious experience. In this view, my volition is compelled to act on the decision that is the most rational. I act, then, not only when I have a reason to do so, but the reason actually contributes to the action of choosing one option over another. For example, if I am confronted with a college choice, I will choose the one that seems most rationally beneficial.

Critique of Compatibilism

Reflecting a host of literature on the subject, I will mention two of the objections to compatibilism in general that Marc Cortez advances. The first he calls the consequence argument: "1. No one has power over the facts of the past and the laws of nature. 2. The facts of the past and the laws of nature determine the facts of the future. 3. Therefore, no one has power over the facts of the future."[12] The second is called the ownership argument: Are my acts owned by me? Good question. There is a worry that on all variants of compatibilism, the acts that I do are not appropriately owned by me. Here is Cortez's summary of the argument: "1. A person acts freely only if she is the ultimate source of that action. 2. Determinism entails that no person is the ultimate source of her action. 3. Therefore, determinism entails that no person acts freely."[13]

There are other objections to compatibilism. One of the most important in a theological context comes from the problem of evil. On this sort of objection, God is the causal agent determining the specific or meticulous acts that constitute a whole state of affairs in one possible world (namely, this possible world in which you and I live). Not only is God aware of all the states of affairs, but also he causally brings them about. He may do so for arguably good reasons, but nonetheless *he* does so. However, other versions of compatibilism see Adam and Eve as libertarianly free prior to the primal sin (construed as a choice-based event or a source-based event) but compatibilistically free after the primal sin (i.e., post-fall), which might avoid the present objection. If we couple the objections above by affirming that human agents have no control over their future and that the future actions that human agents bring about are not properly owned by them, then we have compelling reasons to think that there is an agent bringing about these actions (although these actions are commonsensically attributed to me). If we include evil actions, then it seems to follow by necessity that God is the causal determiner of evil actions

12. Cortez, *Theological Anthropology*, 106.
13. Cortez, *Theological Anthropology*, 109.

as well. You and I are not causally in control of the actions that we bring about. If we take it as intuitive that I am responsible for any action I commit, it follows that I am also capable of not committing that action. Having looked at compatibilism and concerns that have been raised about it, let's move on to libertarianism.

Libertarianism

Several scriptural passages have been advanced that arguably favor a libertarian understanding of human action and freedom. Recall that on this view, humans are responsible because they are free to choose otherwise. There are different understandings of libertarianism, but this is what essentially makes it a position distinct from compatibilism. Once again, while the following passages have been propounded as support for libertarian conceptions of human agency, the scriptural data, on my view, are underdetermined, which requires that we consider the whole of Scripture and what it teaches about human freedom in light of the wider set of theological authorities (creeds and ecumenical statements, church divines, reason, and experience) in the task of systematically tying all the data together into a unified whole.

Several Old Testament passages, arguably, presuppose a libertarian conception of freedom wherein humans are conceived of not only as responsible but also as able to respond one of two ways.[14] The first passage of Scripture that is suggestive in the direction of libertarianism is Genesis 2:16–17: "And the LORD God commanded the man, saying, 'You may surely eat of every tree of the garden, but of the tree of the knowledge of good and evil you shall not eat, for in the day that you eat of it you shall surely die.'" In the creation story, Adam and Eve have the option to choose between good and evil. We know where the story turns from here, which sets the stage for God's redemption of humanity.

In a second passage from Genesis, when God speaks to Cain, he seems to suggest that there is an option for Cain: "The LORD said to Cain, 'Why are you angry, and why has your face fallen? If you do well, will you not be accepted? And if you do not do well, sin is crouching at the door. Its desire is contrary to you, but you must rule over it'" (Gen. 4:6–7). In the Mosaic covenant, Joshua intimates the same truth: "And if it is evil in your eyes to serve the LORD, choose this day whom you will serve, whether the gods your fathers served in the region beyond the River, or the gods of the Amorites in

14. I use the ESV translation in this section.

whose land you dwell. But as for me and my house, we will serve the LORD" (Josh. 24:15). This is consistent with the Mosaic theme of receiving blessing for obedience and curse for disobedience: "See, I am setting before you today a blessing and a curse: the blessing, if you obey the commandments of the LORD your God, which I command you today, and the curse, if you do not obey the commandments of the LORD your God, but turn aside from the way that I am commanding you today, to go after other gods that you have not known" (Deut. 11:26–28).

Furthermore, throughout the prophets, humans are called to serve God, which again presupposes, arguably, not only the responsibility to do so but also the ability to fulfill that responsibility. An example is Isaiah 55:6–7:

> Seek the LORD while he may be found;
>   call upon him while he is near;
> let the wicked forsake his way,
>   and the unrighteous man his thoughts;
> let him return to the LORD, that he may have compassion on him,
>   and to our God, for he will abundantly pardon.

A classic passage used in support of libertarianism is Ezekiel 18:30–32: "Therefore I will judge you, O house of Israel, everyone according to his ways, declares the Lord GOD. Repent and turn from all your transgressions, lest iniquity be your ruin. Cast away from you all the transgressions that you have committed, and make yourselves a new heart and a new spirit! Why will you die, O house of Israel? For I have no pleasure in the death of anyone, declares the Lord GOD; so turn, and live." The assumption is that God judges on the basis of one's actions, which some will argue depends on the ability to do otherwise. Even more, the passage presumes that after one has disobeyed, there is an opportunity to respond in repentance.

Several New Testament passages are theologically appropriated in the service of libertarianism. There is often a general call to all humanity to respond to God's gift of Christ in the new covenant. One famous example is Revelation 3:20, where Christ says, "Behold, I stand at the door and knock. If anyone hears my voice and opens the door, I will come in to him and eat with him, and he with me." Another famous New Testament passage that seems, or can be garnered in a theological reading, to support the notion that humans are libertarianly free is 1 Corinthians 10:13, where Paul explains, "No temptation has overtaken you that is not common to man. God is faithful, and he will not let you be tempted beyond your ability, but with the temptation he will also provide the way of escape, that you may be able to endure it."

Once again, theological interpretations of these passages in the libertarian direction have a long and sophisticated history. These are not determinative of what is *the* scriptural teaching on the topic of human freedom. As I have said, the Scriptures are underdetermined and require the information from other theological authorities taken up in a systematic presentation of the issues. How to explain these passages in a libertarian way is an open discussion. Let us consider some of the ways to interpret libertarian freedom.

Event-Causal Libertarianism

Compatibilist accounts of free action are typically event-causal views, invoking event-causal accounts of action. The simplest event-causal incompatibilist (i.e., philosophical libertarianism) theory takes the requirements of a good compatibilist account and adds that certain agent-involving events that cause the action must nondeterministically cause it. When these conditions are satisfied, it is held, in performing an action the agent exercises a certain variety of active control (which is said to consist in the action's being caused, in an appropriate way, by those agent-involving events), the action is performed for a reason, and there remains, until the agent acts, a chance of not performing that action. (It might be required that there remains, until the action is performed, a chance that the agent will perform a different action instead right then.) The action is thus said to be open to the agent to do otherwise, even given that (it is claimed) its being so open is incompatible with the truth of determinism.[15]

Event-causal libertarianism has some overlap with compatibilist views. The strengths of this variation of libertarianism in contrast to compatibilism are quite clear. On this view, the source and the control of actions are more closely linked with the agent, even if they are connected to previous events in the agent's history.

Agent-Causal Libertarianism

By contrast, it is the agent as a substantial self or I, not some state in the agent, that brings about a free act. By "substantial self" I mean a member of a natural kind, an essentially characterized particular that sustains absolute sameness through (accidental) change and that possesses a primitive unity of inseparable parts (parts that cannot exist and retain their identity when outside the wholes of which they are parts), properties, and capacities/powers at a time.[16] This strong view of substance is required for libertarian agency for at least three reasons:

15. Clarke and Capes, "Incompatibilist (Nondeterministic) Theories of Free Will."
16. Another term for an inseparable part is *mode*.

1. Libertarian agency is possible only if there is a distinction between the capacity to act or refrain from acting and the agent that possesses those capacities.

2. The type of unity present among the various capacities possessed by an agent is the type of unity (i.e., a diversity of capacities within an ontologically prior whole) that is entailed by the classical Aristotelian notion of substance.

3. Free acts take time and include sub-acts as parts, and an enduring agent is what gives unity to such acts by being the same self who is present at the beginning of the action as intentional agent, during the act as teleological guider of means to ends, and at the end as responsible actor.[17]

As noted, libertarianism has a long history of theological interpretation. Several passages have been used by theologians in support of a case for a libertarian view of agency. It is a commonsense view of agency and arguably supports responsibility. As with the exposition of compatibilism given above, the discussion here is not decisive. There is more work of a theological nature at the intersection of other disciplines (e.g., philosophy, cognitive science) to be done on personal agency. With that in mind, the notions of substance and personal identity are important to the free-will debate. Once again, there are some significant concerns with physicalism. To these we turn.

Freedom and the Problem for Physicalists[18]

Throughout the discussions I have frequently addressed the relevant underlying ontology of the human. In what follows I will offer some reasons for rejecting physicalism and reasons to endorse some version of immaterialism or substantial dualism, where freedom is predicable of persons as immaterial agents (i.e., minds or souls). Unpopular though it may be in the present climate, where physicalism seems to dominate in the philosophical and scientific literature, there are good reasons to reject physicalism. Saying this, I realize that there are sophisticated reasons for considering some version of monism or emergent materialism, and these are still live options for consideration.

17. Moreland, *The Recalcitrant* Imago Dei, 45–46.
18. A variety of resources touch on the link between free will and the mind-body relationship. For a sampling, see Swinburne, *Mind, Brain, and Free Will*; Swinburne, *Free Will and Modern Science*; Lowe, *Personal Agency*; Steward, *A Metaphysics for Freedom*; van Inwagen and Zimmerman, *Persons*; Gibb, Lowe, and Ingthorsson, *Mental Causation and Ontology*; Goetz, *Freedom, Teleology, and Evil*; Corcoran, *Rethinking Human Nature*; Madden, *Mind, Matter, and Nature*; Murphy and Brown, *Did My Neurons Make Me Do It?*

Assuming that consciousness is an emergent property/capacity from the natural physical world, physicalist agents do not bear top-down causation. All choices are causally brought about by their underlying physical properties. In the context of discussing John Searle's views of physicalism and libertarianism, J. P. Moreland offers a response that physicalism is incompatible with libertarianism.

> Searle's appeal to gaps at the neurobiological level that reflect gaps at the level of consciousness and which entail that the unfolding states of the brain are not sufficient for the next state does not work. . . . Without such gaps, the top-down causation is pre-empted. This is fundamentally due to the ontological dependency of emergent states/events on subvenient [i.e., base for which something stands] ones. The relation of ontological dependency is a transitive one just as is efficient causality. Now, if we grant the presence of the appropriate gaps at the brain level, this does not solve anything, for two reasons:
>
> 1 Given quantum theory, if we accordingly take causal laws to be probabilistic, each state of the brain still fixes the chance of the next state and this would not be the case if top-down causation occurs (in which case, the bottom effect would be guaranteed by the necessitating exercise of active power at the top). So there is a conflict with top-down causation and quantum gaps due to indeterminacy.
> 2 A conscious state qua event is (a) not a continuant, but rather, a fleeting event and (b) entirely caused by the subvenient event with the result that at the level of consciousness, we have a series of mere shadows as far as causality is concerned. Only a substantial continuant can solve the problem, but Searle eschews such if it is taken to be real.[19]

If we grant that physical agents lack libertarian free will, Moreland offers a persuasive argument for the necessity of the soul as a precondition for free will. He puts it this way:

1. If I am a physical object (e.g., a brain or a body), then I do not have free will.
2. But I do have free will.
3. Therefore, I am not a physical object.
4. I am either a physical object or a soul.
5. Therefore, I am a soul.[20]

19. Moreland, *The Recalcitrant* Imago Dei, 65.
20. Moreland, *The Soul*, 128.

In keeping with our commonsense view of the self, the commonsense view of freedom is libertarian freedom—likely agent-causal libertarianism or noncausal libertarianism. The arguments from personal identity come into play here when discussing free will because, as described above, the agent must have a unified consciousness in order to adjudicate between the options available. For the existence of free will depends on an agent that endures through time, has memories that are continuous and grounded in the enduring self, is metaphysically simple (i.e., a noncomplex entity), not constituted of separable parts, and has a consciousness about its own mental states.

Whether we affirm libertarianism or compatibilism, physicalism encounters some significant challenges for an explanation of freedom. Richard Swinburne explains,

> A mind-brain theory . . . would need to deal with things of very different kinds. Brain events differ from each other in the chemical elements involved in them (which in turn differ from each other in measurable ways) and in the velocity and direction of the transmission of measurable electric charge. But mental events do not have any of these properties. The propositional events (beliefs, desires, etc.) are what they are, and have the influence they do in virtue of their propositional content (and strength—to which I'll come shortly), often expressible in language but a language which . . . has a content and rules differing slightly for each person.[21]

Later he sums up his understanding by saying that defenders of mind-brain theories offer explanations of beliefs and desires in terms of brain events that occur prior to those mental events. The challenge for the materialist is that these mental events are not measurable in any statistical sense. Rather, the contents of mental events are distinguishable by subjects and their experiences of what it is like to have this or that thought or this or that experience.[22] This is important to note because while many compatibilists are also physicalists, this is not true of all compatibilists. In many cases the connection between physicalism and compatibilism (or even hard determinism) is a natural connection because actions are causally governed by general physical laws and causally determined by physical properties. However, once again, theists can affirm compatibilism for other theological reasons without affirming some variant of libertarianism. The governing laws or properties would be explicable in ways other than the physical subvenient base found in physicalist personal ontologies.

21. Swinburne, *Mind, Brain, and Free Will*, 189–90.
22. Swinburne, *Mind, Brain, and Free Will*, 189–90.

Before moving on to another theological topic, it is important that I take some of this data and bring it into a brief discussion with the systematic theological literature on the subject of human agency and freedom. While it is not clear that most theologians have moved on from substance dualism and immaterialism, some theologians have shifted away from substance dualism to some variant of monism or materialism.

Theological Construals of Freedom

Recent theological treatments of freedom have eschewed the philosophical discussion or, at a minimum, have suggested that it is a by-product of modernity. In other words, they have suggested that philosophy is an inappropriate way of approaching human freedom. As the notable systematician John Webster reflects on the philosophical discussions concerning freedom, he implies that these kinds of discussions are distinctly contingent in nature on modern philosophical practices: "Modern understandings and practices of freedom are a central feature in one of the most important shifts in Western culture which began before the Renaissance and Reformation in the rise of nominalist philosophy and which continues to shape our socio-economic and political order as well as our reflective images of ourselves."[23] Theologian Hans Schwarz reflects this perspective when he states,

> "Freedom" is a catchword of modernity, starting with the Declaration of Independence in North America, reverberating through the French Revolution in continental Europe, and surfacing again in the various theologies of liberation. Yet are humans actually free? We have already noticed that from a biological perspective humans are predisposed in many ways, their wings are clipped, and their strides are fettered. When we now look at that which humans often consider their inner sanctum, their brain and their psychic makeup, the answer is not very different. We are not actually beings who pursue our very own path. And if Frank Sinatra (1915–98), at the end of his life, sang, "I did it my way!" he was just telling half the truth. Only within certain limits can we really pursue our own way. This is of course most evident for those who suffer from bodily or psychic handicaps, and are severely challenged in pursuing their lives. Even those without such problems have difficulties pursuing their own path or even discerning what that path ought to be.[24]

There are two contexts in which theologians commonly discuss freedom: the first is that of sin and evil; the second is that of redemption. In the first,

23. Webster, *Confessing God*, 216.
24. Schwarz, *The Human Being*, 123.

there is a growing tendency to understand human freedom in the context of evil as a product of biological evolution. In other words, many theologians are working within a physicalist framework altogether.[25] Schwarz reflects this tendency when he discusses humans in the context of sin and evil. Upon an initial raising of the question, he summarizes his findings from the wider scientific community:

> Sigmund Freud resurrected this notion by juxtaposing *eros* and *thanatos* when he was confronted with the destructive human forces unleashed by World War I. Konrad Lorenz, too, emphasized that there is an aggressive drive in nature, perhaps reflecting Herbert Spencer's insistence on the survival of the fittest. In sociobiology that struggle for survival is seen on the level of genes where altruistic behavior is essentially egotistical, assuring the survival of one's own genetic material against foreign material. In neurobiology we detect the notion that violence results from neurobiological defects that are either inborn or acquired. But neurobiology, as we have seen, also shows that humans are not just biologically determined, but have a "faculty of deliberation." This human faculty of deliberation can be used in a destructive way. While on the one hand humanity had no chance of surviving unless individuals cooperated and helped one [another], as can be seen in the organization of the family, humans have at the same time become crueler than any other species when it comes to inflicting harm on, or even killing, its own kind.[26]

While it must be appreciated that Schwarz has brought the scientific data to the forefront of the theological discussions, these findings, which often find their way into contemporary theology, are part of a larger naturalistic and physicalist framework. However, as we have seen above, we have reasons to reject this framework in favor of a traditionalist view of humans that highlights an immaterial soul. To be fair, Schwarz assumes that the consensus from the scientific data is done in the context following creation and assuming the fall of humanity. He recognizes that the creational state of humans is

25. See Green, *Body, Soul, and Human Life*, 72–103. Green, too, discusses that nature of human freedom in the context of evil with the assumption of a physicalist (and pseudonaturalist, which presumes an ontology of causes and effects that are largely within the domain of the natural world, explained by natural causes, and occur in a regular lawful manner) personal ontology reflected in the sciences. See also the interesting discussion on human freedom by philosopher Nancey Murphy, *Bodies and Souls*, 71–109. I am not suggesting that Murphy discusses freedom in the same way as many contemporary theologians. She does not, because she desires to talk about human freedom in terms of human autonomy (see *Bodies and Souls*, 109). However, she reflects this assumption of physicalism and the preponderant direction or consensus coming from the biological community.

26. Schwarz, *The Human Being*, 156.

"consonant" with God's purposes for humanity before the fall.[27] While this is an interesting proposal, it is not clear where Schwarz stands on the actual nature of human freedom. As is common in much of contemporary theology, the metaphysical nature of human freedom is often left unaddressed or considered out of place in Christian theology. Schwarz may be assuming some variant of compatibilism, which could consistently make sense of his claims about humans in creation and humans in the fall. Alternatively, he may affirm a stronger version of determinism in both cases. A form of libertarianism, however, may prove challenging when reconciling it with all of his comments from the sciences (e.g., "determined"). While the biological data suggest that humans have evil dispositions—and this is not, strictly speaking, contrary to libertarian notions of free will—the claim that human actions are determined is inconsistent with libertarianism.[28]

In fact, most contemporary theologians consider freedom in the context of redemption, where humans are united to Christ. Often the assumption is that the philosophically nuanced discussions are unhelpful and miss the point of the scriptural determination of true freedom. John Webster describes human freedom in the context of God's action and, particularly, in the context of divine redemption. He states, "What of the freedom of the creature? For Christian theology, that question can only rightly be answered after the question of God's identity as the free creator, reconciler and perfecter has received an answer. To begin by determining the conditions of creaturely freedom in advance of an understanding of God, and then inquiring into the compatibility of human freedom with God's freedom, is simply to remain captive to the destructive convention of human freedom as self-government. A theology of evangelical freedom will work from an understanding of God's freedom toward and anthropology of freedom."[29] Pushing against what he understands as a modernist notion of human freedom, Webster is convinced that human freedom can be understood only in the context of divine action toward the human. Rather then seeing humans as substances with powers, he understands humans as communicative products of divine action in creation and redemption.[30]

In contrast to the Reformed evangelical tradition within which Webster is working, Ingolf U. Dalferth works out a similar understanding of human freedom in the Lutheran tradition. Consistent with some ways of working out a Neoplatonic understanding of humans as coming into being rather than

27. Schwarz, *The Human Being*, 158.
28. Schwarz, *The Human Being*, 156.
29. Webster, *Confessing God*, 223.
30. Webster, *Confessing God*, 217.

simply existing as static entities that can be counted, Dalferth advances an understanding of human freedom as situated in a broader causal and ontological context of redemption. Rather than highlight the actual substances with structural capacities that comprise the divine image (e.g., reason, free will), Dalferth begins in possibility. Humans are passive beings that receive life from the divine in their participation in him. Dalferth does not stray from what the consensus believes are the implications of biology and neuroscience, but he sees these as peripheral to the fundamental discussion of freedom. For him, human freedom is the reception of divine gifts to human life. He says, "To be free means that one does not have to want what one wishes for: one can want what one ought to. This capacity for freedom is the rock to be defended against every neuroscientific attempt at debasement."[31] Freedom, in other words, is a gift from God.

It seems to me that the lack of engagement among theologians with the philosophical literature on human agency and free will, which I have noted above, is a missed opportunity to clarify what is meant by personal agency.[32] As with other topics (e.g., human constitution), the philosophical literature provides the theologian with several resources worth taking into one's constructive theological work. Theologians, however, have raised some concerns with the philosophical conceptions of freedom. In order to facilitate this discussion, I will lay out four of these concerns briefly.

First, some will argue that the philosophical distinctions are modernist distinctions that are out of bounds in theological discourse. In some cases, this concern is one that distinguishes a premodern worldview from a modern worldview.

Second, and related, there is a common objection that the modern views of freedom miss the point of Scripture. More than that, the objection is that an articulation of freedom reflected in the analytic philosophical literature raises concerns that are foreign to the scriptural development of freedom. In theological articulations of biblical categories, the emphasis on freedom is one of joy or flourishing, according to which freedom is nearly synonymous with the blessing of a complete life. It is a life that is characterized by God's blessing to his chosen ones, which includes existence, relationship, land, and communion with God. Whatever the merits of this objection to common developments of freedom in philosophy, at best it is an objection that is misplaced.

31. Dalferth, *Creatures of Possibility*, 190.
32. We do find some discussions in the analytic theology literature. Thomas McCall is one example; see his *Analytic Christian Theology*.

Accordingly, it seems to me, it is a category mistake to apply this objection to discussions of free will from the philosophical literature. These are two distinct discussions on freedom, and they should be treated as such, yet they are not unrelated. One, the common philosophical discussion, concerns causation and/or control over one's actions. The other is a discussion about the end or purpose of humanity. While there is a connection between these discussions, they are not strictly identical discussions.

Third, and relevant to the modern concern above, some argue that the discussion of free will is beholden to substantial or structural conceptions of the *imago Dei*. This argument has been advanced in several forms by contemporary theologians.[33] Dalferth is objecting to the ever popular and traditionally common view of the *imago Dei* often called the structural view. Herein humans are image bearers of God, and as such they bear one common property or feature with the divine: rationality. Rationality, as defined by Dalferth, is a property that describes other capacities (e.g., free will and self-determination). The driving idea that Dalferth seems to be after, in addition to its incompatibility with recent scientific findings, is that rationality or free will is a property that is properly God's to own. It is not ours to own. To suggest otherwise would detract from the divine and elevate the creature to a state that is indistinguishable from the divine.

By way of response, it can be said that whatever the merits of the structural view of the image, to argue that humans are creatures that share in rationality or freedom does not seem to mitigate against God's being the ultimate owner of rationality and freedom. Assuming that humans were to instantiate rationality and free will in a way that is analogous to God's nature, this would not undermine or take away from God's being God and not creaturely. Nor would it elevate humans in such a way as to be indistinguishable from the divine. Humans remain creatures created by God. God is infinite in being, self-sufficient, immutable, and independent from all other beings. God needs no other being for his own existence. God is not dependent on other beings. The same is not true of humans. At best, Dalferth's objection or, more modestly, his worry concerning this traditional and popular conception of humans as creatures seems to overstate the implications of the status of creatures.

Fourth, with Dalferth, some also argue that the substantive view is a form of Western individualism. This sort of objection comes in many forms as well. Marc Cortez raises this common concern to the structural *imago Dei*,

---

33. Dalferth, *Creatures of Possibility*, 13. This has become almost normative in the scientific and scientifically influenced theological literature. However, there has been some recent pushback from philosophers of religion and theologians also trained in the sciences. For one example, see Visala, "Theological Anthropology."

which applies here to free will as a defining feature of the image. Cortez lays out the problem along the following lines: "Structural approaches can also be criticized for developing their perspective in highly individualistic terms. To the extent that the *imago* is understood as a capacity possessed and expressed by individual human persons (e.g., rationality), it fails to recognize that the emphasis in Genesis 1.26–28 is on humanity as a collective whole. Although we do not need to deny that the *imago* has application to particular individuals (Gen. 9.6; Jas 3.9), we should recognize the emphasis in the creation narratives is on humanity as a whole as that which images God."[34]

In particular, the capacity of free will could suggest this idea that individuals have the power within themselves to achieve their desired ends. This impulse crops up in discussions about our creational potential for fulfilling the creation mandate as well as discussions regarding justification and sanctification.[35] As with the response above to structural views, one need not affirm a structural view of the image, all the while respecting the unique capacities that we as humans exhibit. Even so, one might still want to affirm a variation of the structural view that highlights these unique capacities (e.g., consciousness and free will) as essential properties of human nature more generally—namely, construing human nature along abstractist lines.[36] By doing this, a structuralist can affirm both the holistic communal sense of the creation narrative's teaching on the image and the distinct properties of human nature. However, as promising as this line of thought is, it will need further elucidation in another context.

Theological Models of Divine and Human Agency

The broader context of theological discussions, which often see the modern Western discussions as out of bounds theologically, is concerned with how to theologically situate human freedom. Theological discussions are often consumed with the who of autonomy. Many theologians, at least those mentioned above, are concerned with giving God autonomy. Coupled with this, or

34. Cortez, *Theological Anthropology*, 20.
35. Tanner, *Christ the Key*. See specifically chaps. 2 and 3, where Tanner discusses the nature of grace in Protestant and Roman circles regarding justification and sanctification. She is particularly critical of individualist models, which highlight individual creaturely capacities that are pointers to grace in the new covenant and the supernatural. Tanner is particularly critical of the nature/grace divide that is so prominent in Roman Catholicism and to a lesser degree in Protestantism. For some modest pushback, see Farris, "A Substantive (Soul) Model."
36. In contrast with what the philosophical-theology literature calls a concretist approach to natures as grounded in concrete particulars that have powers.

ancillary to it, is the theologians' concern that by giving humans autonomy, we are in effect demoting God and elevating humans inappropriately.

The fear seems to be that if both God and humans are autonomous, then it follows that we have a competitive model of divine-human interaction. Such a model of the divine-human relation is called a heteronomous model. On this model, God's actions are in competition with human actions. In other words, if individual creatures are autonomous over their actions, then God is not in control over their actions. But this can't be! God is the Creator of the universe and is the owner of autonomy, hence the perceived theological problems with speaking of human autonomy. Such an understanding not only subtracts the power that is rightly owed to God, some have argued, but also inappropriately situates human nature and action.

In place of such a model, some have advanced a nonheteronomous model of the divine-human relation. On this model, otherwise called a noncompetitive model of divine-human interaction, divine action is ultimate and foundational in such a way as to make possible human action. So the idea is that somehow God's being and action appropriately situate human nature and action in their rightful order. Such a model allows God his rightful place in the created order, and humans are radically dependent on their Creator for everything.

The models regarding divine agency presented above emerge from a more basic discussion about how we should conceive of the divine being. Is the divine being a person? This and other questions are important not only to how we understand God but also to how we understand the human. On the one hand, if God is a transcendent agent, not a person in a commonsense way of understanding persons, then ascribing personality to God would fail to be a positive property of God. Rather, one would need to understand the ascription of personality as a characteristic extrinsic to God's actual nature (i.e., as a fiction or as an analogy for how God interacts with his creation). Understanding God's relationship to humans in this way has ramifications for how we understand human nature. On the other hand, if we take it that personality or personhood is a property positively ascribed to God, then we would describe God's attributes and actions in a way that is analogous (grounded in at least one univocal understanding of God and humans) to human agents. One of the ramifications of this understanding is that humans become analogues for understanding the divine nature. Is this a problem or an advantage?

Although I am open to a transcendent view of divine agency that allows for created freedom in its proper place, at present I am inclined to see divine action along the lines of theistic personalism, which retains an appropriate place for human freedom. On this construal, the discussions of divine freedom and human freedom are distinct and not muddled by a higher-order causation that is inaccessible to humans.[37]

Is Freedom a Pointer to the Divine?

Some theologians suggest that freedom, like other properties, or capacities, is a pointer to the divine. Not only is it a creaturely capacity, but also it is a transcendent capacity that points us to God, for God himself is a free being and provides the ground for our freedom. If we assume a personalist paradigm where God and humans fit the same paradigm, then we could understand this capacity as a common capacity of persons. Some have understood it as one of the person-constituting capacities or features that makes up the *imago Dei*. For example, Gerald Bray holds something like this view when he describes the image as a person-property—that is, the property distinct to individual persons that humans share with the divine being. Naturally, this human property is most clearly and fittingly exemplified in the person and work of Jesus Christ, but it is present from the very beginning in created human beings—later to be glorified.[38]

In keeping with the substantive or structural model of the image, J. P. Moreland has advanced a thoughtful reason for preferring the ontological understanding of the *imago Dei*. He says,

> As image-bearers, human beings have all those endowments necessary to represent and be representative of God, and to accomplish the tasks placed before them and exhibit the relationality into which they were meant to live, such as endowments of reason, self-determination, moral action, personality and relational formation. In this sense, the image of God is straightforwardly ontological. Even if we functionalize the image or treat it in largely relational terms, something that I am loath to do, it is still true that a thing's functional abilities or relational aptitudes are determined by its kindedness. Thus, even the functional, relational aspects of the image of God have ontological implications.[39]

Moreland is clear that both the functional approaches and the relational approaches to understanding the image specifically, and humans generally, are always undergirded and made sense of by the ontological. Humans that relate to God and other creatures may do so because of the kinds of beings they are

---

37. I realize that such a view is in tension with Reformed distinctives on God in the classical sense. I hold the position on this issue tentatively.
38. Bray, "God's Image in Man."
39. Moreland, *The Recalcitrant* Imago Dei, 4.

with the specific capacities they have. Humans that serve as God's covenantal representatives on the earth, according to Genesis 1:28, are capable of doing so because they have the powers that they have in virtue of the kinds of beings they are. Moreland makes this argument in the context of discussing human persons as products of natural physical mechanisms. He is convinced that these unique properties that constitute persons (e.g., consciousness, free will, moral conscience) are inexplicable in a naturalistic framework and require some theistic grounding.

Others take it that free will is the defining feature of human images. This is particularly common in Eastern patristic thought. Representing this common tendency, Kathryn Tanner defends and develops such a view when she describes humans as dynamic passive receptors who are also open and porous to the divine in contrast to what she would call the Augustinian view where humans are stative substances. She describes the Eastern position by claiming,

> The early Eastern church's stress on free will as the image—or often secondarily, rule in the sense of self-rule or self-oversight—could now be taken in a new light, not as the promotion of some vaunted power in a positive sense, an imitation of divine omnipotence, but as an interest in the unusual plasticity of human lives absent of any predetermined specification by nature. Free will becomes a sign of unusual variability. Powers of self-direction mean humans can rework what they are given by nature so as to imitate almost anything along the continuum of ontological ranks, from the bottom to the top.[40]

Tanner highlights the nature of human beings, again, not as static, isolated selves with intrinsic power but rather as open, dynamic selves ready to receive. From what? Well, that depends on the where from which the will receives. In this particular tradition, and consistent to some degree with Dalferth as described above, the human soul is a rather porous individual ready to receive. This is clearly in contrast to what some would call the Western or Augustinian view, as it is commonly construed. Rather than an emphasis on a strict soul-body dualism where the body is changeable and the soul is fixed, Tanner stresses the importance of the malleability of both soul and body. On her understanding, rather than the actualization of specific soulish properties, humans, as embodied souls, are being remade in Christ's body.[41] Instead of the definable cataphatic (i.e., positive) theology, where humans exhibit attributes and characteristics of God's actual nature, Tanner approaches the human from an apophatic (i.e., negative) theology, wherein humans image

40. Tanner, *Christ the Key*, 50.
41. Tanner, *Christ the Key*, 50.

God. Humans image God only by exhibiting mysterious characteristics that are received from God and point us back to God.[42] So our free will is not a positive property that accurately overlaps with God's freedom, for that is something beyond our grasp, but it is a freedom that points us to what we are not: the divine being. It is here that Tanner's anthropology is truly a christological anthropology because Christ is the archetype of which we are ectypes.[43] Christ shows for us what we are not as we become what we are not yet.[44]

In the end, theologians could reject a structural view of the image and Tanner's variation of the christological doctrine. Theologians might still wish to retain something distinct about free will as pointing to the divine. Distinguishing free will as the image is not necessary. Nonetheless, it is arguably a transcendent feature of human beings, like first-person consciousness and moral conscience. It is inexplicable in terms of a naturalistic physicalist framework and distinguishable from other created entities, as Moreland has carefully argued. It requires theistic grounding. Alternatively, theologians may prefer an apophatic approach to freedom, wherein freedom is not the defining feature, in some positive sense, of the *imago Dei*, but it does point us to that which we are not and that which we are becoming via Christ.

However one slices the anthropological cake, apophatically or cataphatically, it is clear that humans are unique and decisively different from other creatures. On both views, humans are unique eschatologically in terms of what they are not yet (at least those that are united to Christ). Yet humans might also exemplify cataphatic distinctions that set them apart from the rest of creation (despite what recent theological literature suggests [see Dalferth]). An even stronger claim, although not foreign to the tradition of theistic personalism, is that humans exemplify attributes that reflect God's nature protologically (i.e., at creation).

Conclusion

In this chapter I have explored the concept of freedom philosophically and theologically. I argued that a philosophical conception of freedom is important to the theological task because it shapes how one reads the relevant passages of Scripture and affects how the systematician organizes the data of human freedom. With this in mind, I have also shown that there are positive reasons

42. Tanner, *Christ the Key*, 51–52.
43. Tanner, *Christ the Key*, 58. See also the useful development of a christological doctrine of the image in Crisp, "A Christological Model of the *Imago Dei*."
44. Tanner, *Christ the Key*, 55–57.

to reject physicalist ontologies of the human person and to take up some variation of substantial dualism or immaterialism. Toward the end of the chapter, I interacted with the systematic theology literature on the topic and showed that a philosophical conception of freedom is not in tension with the theological data and that in fact theologians do not have good reasons to ignore the philosophical data; instead, how they conceive of the human presumes some philosophical stance on human freedom and responsibility.

5

Who Am I at Birth?

Original Sin and Creaturely Failure

Surely I was sinful at birth,
sinful from the time my mother conceived me.

Psalm 51:5

It is a corruption of the whole human nature—
an inherited depravity which even infects small infants
in their mother's womb,
and the root which produces in humanity
every sort of sin.

Belgic Confession, article 15

What is it that makes us tick as human beings? It seems that from the moment I can recall my conscious waking years of life, I was caught up in temptations to sin. My life is marked by tendencies and proclivities, some of which are probably commonplace with most people, but others of which some would find rather warped. Why is this? I am often perplexed at trying to answer that question. In fact, this tendency to sin in general is something universal to all human beings at some level and to varying degrees in varying ways. Many times I wrestle with myself in a manner that resonates with Paul in Romans 7:19: "For I do not do the good

I want to do, but the evil I do not want to do—this I keep on doing."[1] With the psalmist, I recognize the stain that is placed on my life, for I have been "sinful from the time my mother conceived me" (Ps. 51:5). It is certainly true to say that I have never experienced my creaturely nature more than in my own sinfulness, but this is the life of all human beings.

In chapter 2 I began the discussion of humanity's fundamental problem by considering an important anthropological doctrine: the historicity and theological meaning of Adam. Adam, as we saw, is important for one's doctrine of the anthropos because Adam serves as the covenantal head for all of humanity, according to the scriptural story line. Adam is, according to many Reformed theologians, our federal head (and, in some cases, our natural head), and for some non-Reformed theologians, he is merely our natural head. In that chapter we saw the various views on Adam and examined the importance of this doctrine for the primal sin (i.e., the first sin). This serves as the narrative starting point for understanding a doctrine of sin. Furthermore, we seem to have some metaphysical connection, or important theological connection, to Adam in our own story as the biological products of Adam's lineage.[2] But precisely what this means is unclear. I suggest one way forward by considering versions of Augustinian realism.

In the present chapter I focus on the doctrine of original sin. It seems like a natural place to begin because, no matter how one describes or defines sin, original sin is that condition, state, propensity, environment, or actual participation in which all humans exist. Whether one affirms that sin is an act, a disposition, a behavior, an intent, an existential angst, or something else, if we take both the scriptural narrative and the tradition seriously, it all begins with our connection to Adam and the original sin that follows from our relationship to Adam.

Where It All Begins

"She took of its fruit and ate, and she also gave some to her husband who was with her, and he ate" (Gen. 3:6 ESV). This is the first sin, what theologians

1. There are two common ways of interpreting this passage that I will not explore here. The first interpretation, and some argue the most natural, is that it is a reference to the Christian struggling to live according to the law but failing at times. The second interpretation says that this is Paul discussing his preconversion state to Christianity, where he is struggling with the law.

2. Earlier I discussed the term *human* in a variety of ways, and I was working with an understanding of *human* that represents all humans (in a biological sense) on the earth as connected in some way to Adam, the first human, who originates sin at the fall. There is a sense of *human* that excludes the genetic understanding and allows for the possibility of other biological humans (i.e., hominids) that would allow for our connection to Adam. See Swamidass, "Overlooked Science of Genealogical Ancestry."

call the primal sin. The most immediate result of Adam's partaking of the fruit that God has commanded him not to eat is that he faces mortality and will die. The author seems to be intentionally ambiguous, pointing to the detrimental effect following from the choice to violate God's command. The text also indicates that Adam is exiled from the garden of Eden, which may be indistinguishable from the death that follows from Adam's sin. Some immediate aspects of the text deserve spelling out. First, Adam and Eve, while experiencing life and blessing in a perfect sanctuary setting, are now exiled from that perfect setting to a place of death and curse. Second, the present state of Adam and Eve suggests that they are outside God's presence. Third, they are no longer partakers of the land, which brings life. Now, we know what follows in the story: all of humanity is affected by this event. Adam's one sin causes a ripple effect in the whole of humanity. I am reminded at this point of Garcin's question in Jean-Paul Sartre's *No Exit*: "And can one judge a life by a single action?"[3] Such a question most humans have no doubt raised with reference to their own lives and actions. Certainly, many Christians have raised this profound question concerning Adam's first sin and its devastating effects on humanity. How is this really possible? Now all of humanity is in this sad state of exile and death. Rather than blessing and life, humans experience death and curse. And all of this follows from Adam's first sin. The scriptural story seems to indicate in various places that certain sins do often characterize people for a long time. This is often the case in our own experiences. Certain kinds of sin characterize and attach a long-term stigma to our lives and in some cases are nearly permanent in this life. Some obvious cases come to mind. Those who are charged and found guilty for murder will inevitably have that on their record for the rest of their lives. The same is true for certain sexual offenses, which often come with a stain of shame. The stain of Adam's sin is something like this, according to the scriptural story.

We realize as much in the scriptural story in Genesis 6, where God makes a declaration about the state of all of humanity. "The LORD saw that the wickedness of man was great in the earth, and that every intention of the thoughts of his heart was only evil continually. And the LORD regretted that he had made man on the earth, and it grieved him to his heart. So the LORD said, 'I will blot out man whom I have created from the face of the land, man and animals and creeping things and birds of the heavens, for I am sorry that I have made them'" (Gen. 6:5–7 ESV). It is important to note that in the preceding verses the author establishes the connection between

3. Sartre, *No Exit*, 43.

humanity and Adam. If that were not clear enough, the author establishes several parallels between Adam's situation and that of humanity in general. God declares that the state of humanity is wicked and that each individual heart is wicked. We have already seen this pattern of wickedness in the life of Adam's progeny, and it does not end here. Consider, for example, the jealousy between brothers in the stories of Cain and Abel, Isaac and Ishmael, and Jacob and Esau, which turn into jealousy between nations. God says that he "will blot out man . . . from the face of the land," which is another way of saying that God brought about exile for humanity. All of humanity is in this state of exile and death.

At this point, it is important to note that there is a common discussion in theological anthropology about what it is that humanity loses at the fall. Do humans lose a relationship to divine presence, or do they experience some loss of structural capacities? As I have developed the conception of humans in keeping with Reformed catholicity, it is clear that both effects are present with humans post-fall. As stated above in Genesis 6, not only do humans lack access to God's presence in Eden, but also they experience noetic (i.e., intellectual) effects and volitional problems ("their foolish hearts were darkened" [Rom. 1:21 ESV]). And, once again, all of this is a result of Adam's primal sin.

The connection is clearly established in other passages of Scripture, both in the Old Testament and in the New Testament. We have considered one Old Testament passage already. In Romans 5:12 Paul states, "Sin came into the world through one man [*henos anthrōpou*], and death through sin, and so death spread to all men [*pantas anthrōpous*] because all sinned" (ESV). Paul's usage of the contrast of *henos* and *pantas* in 5:18 (and in 5:19 a direct parallel is made) reflects a deep patterned parallel between the particular Adam as the representative head and Christ as the particular head of people, and the logic of the concrete particular having some metaphysical relation to humanity depends on some causal originator in both cases (Adam for humanity, and Christ for humanity). Paul says that sin came into the world through one man to whom all humans are linked. Death comes through sin. However, this opens the door to different interpretations of how it is that we are related to Adam. The Scriptures do not offer a plain meaning on the precise metaphysics of our relationship to Adam. This is not to say that there is not a "biblical" meaning of that relationship that can be clearly inferred from all the biblical teachings once taken into account, but simply that there is not a proof text that clearly, obviously, and definitively states or explains the doctrine of our relationship to Adam.

The Post-fall State

What truths can we discern about the biblical teaching on the post-fall state of humans? First, some have referred to the scope of sin as "inherited sin," "birth sin," and "race sin."[4] What these terms, reflected in the theological literature, intend to convey is that all humans, universally, are under the domain and power of sin.[5] The Scriptures, as is recognized by the tradition and by most contemporary interpreters, reflect this teaching explicitly and clearly.

A second truth about post-fall humans that theologians generally agree on is that humans exist as morally vitiated beings. Their condition or state is morally problematized in some significant and substantial sense. And in this environment humans are inclined to sin and will, almost necessarily, sin actually. But why is this the case? This is a question that theologians have wrestled with for a long time. There is no easy explanation on offer, but several explanations are worthy of our consideration and reflection. Once we take into account that *all* human beings are morally vitiated and that this has some connection, biblically, to the sin of Adam (and Eve), then we are left in a place to try to make moral and metaphysical sense out of the biblical material. Thankfully, we are not left alone; we have several philosophers and theologians (e.g., Augustine, Aquinas, Calvin, Turretin, Edwards) throughout the history of catholic Christianity leading us and guiding us to a better understanding. On this theologically complicated issue, we stand on the shoulders of giants, once again, who give us nuanced ways of making sense both of sin and of how individual sin relates to the first (what theologians call the "primal") sin, original sin, and actual sin.

What, Then, Is Sin?[6]

Sin is not entirely easy to define. Several definitions are worth a mention in this context as we think more carefully about humanity in light of sin. A common view throughout church history is the privation view, which is often described as the lack of some quality or the malfunctioning of some capacity. I am reminded of the old children's song "There's a Hole in My Bucket."[7]

---

4. Parker, "Original Sin."

5. I certainly do not deny the claim that there are degrees of the severity of sin.

6. For a helpful chapter on the topic of corruption, see Hamilton, "On the Corruption of the Body." See also Helm, *John Calvin's Ideas*, 93–129.

7. See "There's a Hole in My Bucket," Wikipedia, https://en.wikipedia.org/wiki/There%27s_a_Hole_in_My_Bucket. Also consider Jer. 2:12–13 and its discussion of broken cisterns that can hold no water.

In the song, two persons talk about a hole in the bucket used for taking up water from a well. As they work through various ways to fill the hole, they finally realize that they have a fundamental problem: they lack the resources to fill the hole in the bucket. Our original condition is illustrated by the hole in my bucket. I have a fundamental problem, and I fail to see how I can fix it. The reality is that I lack the resources to fill this hole in my bucket. But not every privation is a sin (e.g., some people are born with birth defects). Some say that it is the will that is deprived, and others affirm that it is the intellect.

Other theologians defend the view that sin is a violation of law. On such a view, it is argued that Adam sinned against God by violating a basic command to not eat from the tree of the knowledge of good and evil. This view finds support in a broad reading of sin in Scripture, where Adam is a representative of humanity who exists in covenantal relationship with God. Within that covenantal relationship, Adam lives in an environment where specified conditions are to be met. This view is not necessarily in tension with the previous view. The former highlights the metaphysics of sin, and the latter highlights the covenantal and relational dimension of sin.

Yet another view, common to modern theology, is that sin is the violation of persons. Here sin is neither a violation of law nor an abstract privation; rather, it is the undermining of personal rights and the construction of societal structural harm rather than a classical conception of sin.[8]

Adam and Original Sin

The doctrine of original sin is a central plank of catholic Christianity, describing the morally vitiated estate of all human persons that derives from their relationship to the sin of the first human, first pair of humans, or first group of humans. Part of the question that is of particular interest in what follows is how the transmission of original sin occurs from one individual human—Adam and his primal sin—to each successive individual human. Historically, there are three ways to think about sin and Adam's relationship to his offspring. These three include Pelagianism, the Augustinian view, and the Eastern view. Within each of these there are more complicated ways of working out how it is that humans are related to Adam, how sin is transmitted

---

8. For a summary of various views, see Nelson, *Sin*, 18–35. For a history of the concept of sin, see Fredriksen, *Sin*. Modern developments have opened the door to a diversity of subjective accounts of sin along with modern and contemporary accounts that give credence to victimhood, structural hierarchy, power struggles, and suppression of particular social groups.

based on one's personal ontology, and how one construes the nature of guilt and corruption.

Pelagianism, named after the monk Pelagius, is a view of humanity and sin on one extreme end of the spectrum. In its pure form, Pelagianism is the view that humans have no connection to Adam except through imitation. Thus, humans are not connected to Adam as one metaphysical whole, nor are they biologically affected by Adam's actions. Instead, as free agents created in the image of God, all humans have the resources within themselves to accommodate for any deficiency. Humans have the power to satisfy God's righteous demands. However, such a view is clearly out of bounds given what we have found in Scripture.[9] Defenders of Pelagianism deny that sin is transmitted from Adam to his progeny.[10] By taking a closer look at Romans 5, we see that more than death follows from Adam's first sin. Paul claims in Romans 5:18 that we are condemned in or because of Adam. Paul also claims in Romans 5:19 that we are made transgressors because of Adam's transgression. Now, the debate is vibrant as to what this actually means, and there are several options worth considering, which we will explore below.

On the other end of the spectrum from Pelagianism is the Augustinian view, named after Augustine of Hippo, according to which we are actually guilty in Adam. We are guilty in Adam because we are literally parts of Adam, as an Adamic humanity. Rather than understanding humans as individuals, defenders of the Augustinian view understand individuals as parts of a larger collective whole. Adamic humanity is one substantial whole composed of a complexity of parts, which excludes a simple view of persons but allows for a union of individual persons to one substance. Thus, the actions of Adam are transmitted directly to the parts that constitute his substance. In this way, I am guilty with Adam as a part of Adam. In order to account for this exotic view, we would need to think about individuals, not according to common sense, where individuals are simple discrete entities that exist completely and wholly at the present moment, but as existing across time and composing one larger substance that spans the time of the

9. Harent, "Original Sin."

10. Pelagianism has very few defenders, at least explicit defenders, having been condemned by the Western church (Council of Ephesus; Council of Trent; Council of Orange; Council of Carthage) as well as the Reformed theological tradition (Second Helvetic Confession; Canons of Dort; Anglican Articles; Augsburg Confession; Gallican Confession; Belgic Confession). However, there are some explicit defenders, or sympathizers, and it is arguably the case that modern humans tend to exalt the ideas of Pelagius in contrast to Augustine. Following Walter Bauer's progressive teachings on Christian theology, Elaine Pagels was quite sympathetic in *Gnostic Gospels* and *Adam, Eve, and the Serpent*. For a recent and helpful overview, see Charlotte Allen, "Pelagius the Progressive."

universe. Such a view has been parsed in at least two ways. First, some in the Reformed tradition, following John Calvin, understand Adam to be the covenantal federal head for all of humanity, and we are found guilty because of Adam's federal representation of humanity. Jonathan Edwards has famously argued, quite passionately and persuasively, that the mere federal headship view entails a "legal fiction" and cannot be taken seriously, but, instead, Adam's federal headship is based on what is metaphysically real.[11] Second, as a way forward, others have suggested moving in a realist direction, which seems to be precisely what Augustine has in mind. On this realist understanding, we are literally guilty in Adam precisely because we are parts of Adam, where Adam is one metaphysical whole that has inherent individual persons as parts of himself. Consider the analogy of a tree and its branches. Adam is the tree and we are likened to the branches that are a part of the tree, but the parts are temporal. The present view draws a bit from the metaphysics of time and space to make sense of *how* it is that individual human beings can literally compose parts of Adam. Adam, on one view, is a space-time worm wherein all the slices of time compose one larger metaphysical whole across time. This is called the perdurantist view of persistence, which allows a complexity of space-time slices to compose a whole. There is another view that only sees the present as existing parts that are fissile and come to fuse and form persons across time. This is called the exdurantist or stage theory of time.[12] As Adam sins, so it follows that we sin in Adam. In other words, we are liable and guilty for Adam's first sin, so the first sin constitutes our original condition.

Another option is the Eastern patristic theory of original sin. It does not deny the doctrine of original sin, as we find with Pelagianism. Defenders of the Eastern patristic theory instead deny the transmission of original guilt. So, rather than a property of original guilt actually transferring from parents to their offspring, only original sin is transferred. Original sin, though, is construed in a weaker sense as a disposition or a stain or a general condition of which we are participants. But it never rises to the status of original guilt without our explicit and conscious free consent.

This raises the question of how it is that this first sin of Adam is actually transmitted from one generation to the next. Secondarily, how is it transmitted in light of our bodies and souls? Rather than offer up a direct answer to this question, I will lay out several models for how sin is transmitted

---

11. Crisp, *Jonathan Edwards and the Metaphysics of Sin*; Rea, "The Metaphysics of Original Sin."

12. Hawley, "Temporal Parts."

in the context of the soul's origin. I also will briefly touch on other issues germane to the discussion of what one means by the term *original sin*.[13] The purpose of this next section is to situate the reader in a variety of differing conceptualities in order to explore original sin more carefully in our contemporary context.[14]

Romans 5:12–21 on Adam and Original Sin

Therefore, just as sin came into the world through one man, and death through sin, and so death spread to all men because all sinned—for sin indeed was in the world before the law was given, but sin is not counted where there is no law. Yet death reigned from Adam to Moses, even over those whose sinning was not like the transgression of Adam, who was a type of the one who was to come.

But the free gift is not like the trespass. For if many died through one man's trespass, much more have the grace of God and the free gift by the grace of that one man Jesus Christ abounded for many. And the free gift is not like the result of that one man's sin. For the judgment following one trespass brought condemnation, but the free gift following many trespasses brought justification. For if, because of one man's trespass, death reigned through that one man, much more will those who receive the abundance of grace and the free gift of righteousness reign in life through the one man Jesus Christ.

Therefore, as one trespass led to condemnation for all men, so one act of righteousness leads to justification and life for all men. For as by the one man's disobedience the many were made sinners, so by the one man's obedience the many will be made righteous. Now the law came in to increase the trespass, but where sin increased, grace abounded all the more, so that, as sin reigned

---

13. For two classic discussions, see Taylor, *The Scripture-Doctrine of Original Sin*; J. Edwards, "The Great Christian Doctrine of Original Sin."

14. For two contemporary discussions on the compatibility of original sin with an original Adam (i.e., Adam-and-Eve pair), see Kemp, "Science, Theology, and Monogenesis." Kemp proposes that the biological species human could be distinct from the first human representatives in God's covenants. This or some variation could supply an explanation for why there seem to be humans, or hominids, prior to Adam and Eve. See also Rahner, *Hominisation*, 37–38; Rahner, "Theological Reflexions on Monogenism." In his writings, Rahner offers a coherent way to make sense of original sin in light of polygenesis (the view that humans were generated not from one original pair but from many) so that humans remain united as humans in a way that is consistent with Vatican II. Thus, monogenesis is not strictly required if it is understood as physical or biological descent. For help on some of the concerns with "original sin," see Copan, "Original Sin and Christian Philosophy." For a thorough and exceptional layout of the doctrine of sin in general and of original sin in particular, see McCall, *Against God and Nature*.

in death, grace also might reign through righteousness leading to eternal life through Jesus Christ our Lord. (Rom. 5:12–21 ESV)

The first question we must ask is, According to Paul, what do we know about Adam's relationship to original sin? Paul makes clear that death as condemnation is related to Adam and the fall precipitated by Adam's primal sin. Classically, this passage has been taken to yield a doctrine of the fall, a literal Adam, and the doctrine of original sin, which has some connection to condemnation for all human beings. Minimally, there are two lines of evidence that suggest that Adam was literally present at some point in history. First, the parallel between Adam and Christ is established by Paul as a causal connection between Adamic humanity and Christic humanity, even if the gift of Christ is greater than the condemnation from Adam. Second, there is a causal connection, which supports that Adam was the cause that originated the condemnation for all human beings, as stated in verse 12 ("sin came into the world through one man, and death through sin, and so death spread to all men because all sinned") and stated more explicitly in verse 18 ("one trespass led to condemnation").[15] The latitude of options for making sense of the causal connection between Adam's first sin and all of human condemnation is quite open to a variety of systematic options.

How Is Original Sin Transmitted?[16]

I take it as a natural intuition that humans bear a property of original sin that is passed down from one human to the next. The challenge becomes more complicated when one reflects on the nature of human constitution, as soul-body compounds. For if the property of sin originates in the soul given the nature of sin as beginning from personal agents (a common view within the Reformation), how is it transmitted? Is it transmitted from soul to body? How can this be if it is from each successive body that is generated that the property of sin is transmitted, soul to soul? Many such questions emerge from reflecting on the transmission problem as it is related to human constitution. Below I address these problems related to sin's transmission, and I offer some possible solutions by a careful consideration of various models of dualism and the origination of souls. Before we look at the various options in light of the soul's origin, I will systematically summarize at least some of the models of original sin.

15. Moo, *The Epistle to the Romans*, 334.
16. With significant modification and adaptation to the present volume, I draw from my previously published article on the subject. See Farris, "Originating Souls and Original Sin."

Models of Original Sin[17]

MODERNITY AND ORIGINAL SIN (EXISTENTIALISM)

Two guiding principles in the modern development of the doctrine of sin are important for us to note: biological evolution and the supplanting of traditional authority with Enlightenment rationality. These guiding principles gave rise to revisionist forms of reading the texts of Scripture. With the rise of historical-critical theory applied to the text of Scripture, several items impinge on the development of the doctrine of original sin. Motivated in part by a growing trend in science that questions the historicity of Adam and Eve, historical-critical theory raises several questions about the authenticity of the historicity of the Creation narrative. The literal Adam is replaced in favor of a mere narrative type. Sin is relegated to a status of existential importance, but it is not a matter of spiritual importance that is an inheritable trait beyond the mere fact that biological accidents occur in the genetics of *Homo sapiens*. And, with this, it was inevitable that the doctrines of Adam, the fall, heredity sin, and sin itself are reinterpreted as mere symbols, metaphors, and subjective existential realities, because the doctrine of sin requires a reinterpretation of traditional doctrine consistent with the findings of science.[18]

It is the assumption of the present work that science does not rule out the traditional doctrines of Adam, the fall, or a concept of sin that is hereditable. There are several options on offer that are consistent with the dogmatic deliverances of the Christian tradition, broadly, and the Reformed tradition, specifically, that are, arguably, consistent. To these we turn.

MERE CORRUPTION (NO GUILT)

It is common belief that the explicit account of guilt as somehow transmitted from Adam is not present prior to Augustine. Patristic Christianity, represented in Athanasius, presumes inheritable corruption but not explicitly a doctrine of original guilt. J. N. D. Kelly comments on Athanasius's view by saying that "sin has passed to all men." And Athanasius "never hints that we participate in Adam's actual guilt."[19] There is not a clear doctrine of original guilt during this period, which says that humans share in Adam's

---

17. For a more detailed and excellent exposition of many of the views, see McCall, *Against God and Nature*.

18. For a representative sampling, see Tennant, *The Origin and Propagation of Sin*, 4–5; Williams, *The Ideas of the Fall and of Original Sin*, 40–51. Some of the most important modern figures of this time include Tillich, Schleiermacher, and Macquarrie. The full flowering of modernity is seen in the philosophical anthropologies of Hegel and Heidegger.

19. Kelly, *Early Christian Doctrines*, 347.

condemnation—death, yes, but not guilt. This becomes the inheritance of the Eastern Orthodox tradition. Eastern theologian Timothy Ware supports this when he describes his own tradition by saying, "Humans (Orthodox usually teach) automatically inherit Adam's corruption and mortality, but not his guilt: they are only guilty in so far as by their own free choice they imitate Adam."[20] A mere corruption view is not solely in the provenance of the Eastern tradition. It is also commonly found in Arminianism, Wesleyanism, and much of contemporary theology.[21]

Beyond this, the Reformed theological tradition typically has endorsed a stronger view of original sin in the human narrative. Motivated by Augustine with his doctrine of original guilt, the tradition has maintained that humans are not merely corrupt via Adam nor do they experience mere solidarity with the actions of Adam, having a shared corruption.

Mere Federalism (Representationalism and Original Guilt)

Common to the Reformed theological tradition is a commitment to a theology of federalism. According to federalism, Adam is the head of the human race as the chosen figure to act as the legal representative for all of humanity through the creational covenant spelled out in Genesis 1–2. As our federal head, Adam's sin is not our sin, but his guilt is legally imputed to us in having been elected by God to act on our behalf. Reformed theologian Michael Horton supports this: "Adam's covenantal role entailed that he was the representative for his whole posterity. In fact, every person is judged guilty in Adam, and the effects of this curse extend even to the rest of creation (Ge 3:17–18; Ro 8:20)."[22] The challenges then are quite obvious. There is the fairness concern, first. It is hard to reconcile how it is fair that all humans could be held liable for the sin of one man. Second, there is the concern that humans did not have the choice to endorse Adam as their federal representative, as with so many leaders in our time (e.g., consider the elected dogcatcher for the city, a congressional representative, or a state senator). Third, the doctrine appears to be a legal fiction, and, at least, in some cases it is not possible to impute the sins of one individual to another individual (e.g., in the case of murder). For these and other reasons, the mere federal theological view of the human story seems insufficient, and, thankfully, many Reformed theologians

20. Ware, *The Orthodox Church*, 224.
21. For a representative sampling of Arminian theology, see Stanglin and McCall, *Jacob Arminius*, 149–50; Miley, *Systematic Theology*, 1:522. For a sampling of contemporary theology, see Swinburne, *Responsibility and Atonement*, esp. 73–147; Wyma, "Innocent Sinfulness, Guilty Sin."
22. Horton, *The Christian Faith*, 415.

do not develop a mere federal theological view but often buttress it with an Augustinian realist metaphysic or a participatory metaphysic that takes more seriously our connection to Adam in addition to a robust conception of heritable corruption.

REALISM AND GUILT

Following Augustine, Reformed theologians will develop a conception of our legal and covenantal relationship to Adam in a way that is metaphysically grounded in something actual or in some real relationship to Adam. Thereby, Adam's guilt is our guilt. There are two obvious ways to work this out: immediate guilt or mediate guilt. In *City of God*, Augustine describes the realism of Adam's sin:

> For we were all in that one man, since we all were that one man, who fell into sin. . . . For not yet was the particular form created and distributed to us, in which we as individuals were to live, but already the seminal nature was there from which we were to be propagated; and this being vitiated by sin, and bound by the chain of death, and justly condemned, man could not be born of man in any other state.[23] (13.14.2)

Augustine, then, initiates a tradition of the sin doctrine that illuminates humanity's profound connection to Adam that furnishes a coherent ground for making sense of original guilt. But that connection is open to further analysis.

Immediate Guilt (Augustine and Edwards). The first view is that of immediate guilt. Accordingly, the doctrine of original sin includes both Adam's corruption that is transmitted and his guilt being our guilt by virtue of our being literally parts of Adam that constitute one metaphysical whole for which Adam is the head. The clearest account of this doctrine is articulated in Jonathan Edwards, who affirms the reality that Adam is our federal head, but this legal relationship is rooted in a real relationship we have to Adam. Edwards bears this out in one famous passage:

> [Thus] both guilt, or exposedness to punishment, and also depravity of heart, came upon Adam's posterity just as they came upon him, as much as if he and they had all co-existed, like a tree with many branches. . . . I think this will naturally follow on the supposition of there being a *constituted oneness* or *identity* of Adam and his posterity in this affair.[24]

23. Augustine, *City of God*, 251.
24. J. Edwards, *Original Sin*, 220.

Notice that Edwards affirms that we are guilty in Adam, that we are condemned to be punished, and that we have a depraved heart in virtue of Adam's actions. Further, he uses a common organic example of a tree and its branches to make sense of our being constituted as one metaphysical whole, where the parts (i.e., the branches, all humans) are united to the whole (the tree) with Adam as the head. The obvious bite of such a view is that I am literally guilty for the sin of Adam.

Mediate Guilt (Anselm and Calvin). There is a second, more promising view that is able to take seriously federalism and realism without biting the bullet of saying that all humans are guilty for Adam's sin. On the mediate view, humans are guilty for their own sin, which is a consequence of Adam's sin and our inheriting either sinful dispositions or a corrupted nature. In other words, humans are guilty for their own sinful actions or, even better, their own sinful dispositions. Anselm states, "I do not think that the sin of Adam descends to infants so that they ought to punished for it, as if they had each personally acted as Adam did, although because of his sin it came about that none of them is born without sin, or the condemnation following it."[25] Calvin endorses a similar view when he describes our condemnation as our own consequentially from Adam. For Calvin, Adam's work of sin "produces" in us the "works of the flesh."[26]

There are other ways to work out a mediate view that take into account the fact that we are guilty in virtue of the nature we inherit. It is this nature that requires that justice be satisfied in some way, even if we will not be held accountable for someone else's sin. There is another view that is often not incorporated in the discussion of original sin but nonetheless finds a nice home in the mediate realist view.

Is Participatory Realism an Alternative?

Participatory realism, recall, is the view that humans partake of "Being" through participation in the immutable ideas that God communicates to his creatures. In other words, there are abstract objects that God brings about that act upon Adamic humanity.[27] And it is by negation, or by virtue of not

25. Anselm, "On the Virgin Conception and Original Sin," 378.
26. Calvin, *Institutes* 2.1.8. For a thoughtful treatment of Calvin's views of sin as it interfaces with personal ontology and faculty psychology, see Vorster, *The Brightest Mirror of God's Works*, 35–58. Calvin comes off rather strong when he discusses sin and the image bearer. He speaks so strongly in places that his words make one think that he views sin as eliminating the image in individual humans and humans collectively, but in his later writings he clarifies by saying that the image is retained in some small capacity and that glimmers of the image remain in corrupted humans. See Calvin, *Institutes* 2.1.16–2.2.25.
27. This is reminiscent of Plato's view of the relationship between concrete instantiated things and abstract objects. See Kraut, "Plato." Naturally, one can work out an understanding

partaking in that reality, that humans experience privation of nature—that is, a loss of their own nature. In a Reformed covenant context, humans participate in that reality through the covenantal obligations that God gives to the covenant members. Yet, when humans fail to do so, they experience a privation of their nature, and this is a lack of justice; that is, the consequence of Adam's sin is that humans are mediately guilty and justice must be satisfied.

Models, Original Sin, the Soul

In what follows, I am working with an understanding of anthropological models and models of the soul's origin for making sense of the transmission problem. For a layout of the views, see chapters 1–2 above. One of the big questions concerning the transmission of original sin is whether it is actual transmission, a resultant transmission, or merely an imputation.[28]

Minimally, the doctrine of original sin asserts that humanity shares some sort of solidarity or unity, and that all humans in relation to other humans bear corruption and will likely or necessarily eventually sin. Maximally, original sin means that all humans share not only in corruption but also in original guilt. The challenge here is to provide an account for the transference relation between Adam (as a metaphysical placeholder, not necessarily a historical Adam), through whom sin entered the world, so to speak, and other individualized souls, which come to bear original sin, and to do so in such a way that addresses the problem concerning the precise nature of the relation between body and soul, and how souls, bodies, or souls and bodies relate to Adam.[29] And while there are unique problems facing each view, I wish to examine two problems in particular: first, how human natures relate in terms of the propagation of souls from Adam's soul, and second, how the soul and body are united. Additionally, some of the views can only account for some variation of original sin in transmission. One view says that original sin is not so much transmitted as the environment itself is transmitted successively to humans. A second view says that original sin is construed as corruption—that

---

of abstract objects as an Augustinian who sees these objects as held eternally in the mind of God or as a Thomist wherein God creates these objects from eternity as immanent in the creation.

28. Moreland, *Consciousness and the Existence of God*, 29. For a helpful treatment of original sin, see Rea, "The Metaphysics of Original Sin."

29. Even though I assume that humans exist in some sort of solidarity with a literal Adam, theologians do not necessarily need to assume that Adam was a literal historical figure in order to make sense of the scriptural narrative or to make sense of human sin; he could be a literary figure for an actual historical first human. In other words, there are coherent ways to make sense of original sin and the transmission of original sin from an original population of people or from a couple prior to the historical referent in Genesis. It could be that original sin was transferred from an original human population (where Adam is a metaphysical placeholder).

is, human nature begins to malfunction. A third view, which we saw above, is a stronger form of original sin called "original guilt," whereby individual humans bear, in some sense, actual guilt and are held liable for the malfunction or sin of Adam, mediately or immediately. In what follows, I take each view of origins in turn and briefly discuss some of the options available for making sense of the transmission of sin. While each of the four views below can offer some explanation to the two problems noted above, emergent creationism provides what appears to be the most satisfactory account of the doctrine of the transmission of original sin.

Traditional Traducianism

Defenders of traducianism traditionally have charged the creationist with an inability to respond to the problem of divinely created souls that bear the property of original sin. Traducianism, recall, is the view that souls are generated successively (i.e., diachronically, not synchronically), and this generation establishes a fine-grained relationship between souls. The strength of traducianism is that it provides the theologian with an account of the transmission relation. Unlike creationism, traducianism has resources, its defenders argue, for a clear and definite answer that averts charging God with the responsibility of creating the soul sinful and averts the notion that the originally created soul is arbitrarily made sinful, followed by each successive soul after Adam. The traducianist proposes that the human soul bears the property of original sin without invoking God as the direct cause of and explanation for sin. Most often traducianists affirm one of two different kinds of souls in their rejection of the soul's simplicity, something commonly attributed to creationists. Metaphysical simplicity is the view whereby souls are noncomposed, noncomplex, and not reducible to a complex of parts.[30] Traducianists affirm either that the soul is *fissile* or *parturient* (for this discussion, see chapter 2), both of which, I suggest, are liabilities to the traducianist.

Now, despite these dissenting comments, the virtue of traducianism is that it provides a solution that coherently allows for the generation of sinful souls and Augustinian realism. Augustinian realism is the notion that all souls exist in one metaphysical substance: the Adamic soul. On this view, a natural and generative mechanism unites all individualized souls to the originally created Adamic soul. The Adamic soul bears a generative relation to all other

---

30. There are, in fact, at least two different ways of construing simplicity. First, the weaker view is that souls are simple in the sense that they have inseparable parts (mind, will, etc.), and the whole is indivisible. Second, the stronger view is that souls are literally metaphysically simple and have no parts, except the one mental or soulish part.

human souls. In this way, it is justifiable to predicate original sin (or guilt, as it is sometimes argued) to individualized souls in virtue of their relationship to the Adamic whole, of which they are parts.[31]

Some have raised a problem for the traducianist view concerning human nature and the view's solution to the doctrine of original sin. The problem for traducianism is not in offering an explanation for transmission but rather in preserving the *natural* experience we have of soul and body in relation. Prima facie, the problem for the traducianist is being able to affirm a sufficiently dualistic view of human persons without slipping into what one might construe as nonreductive physicalism or a version of property dualism, which says that there is only one substance—a physical or material substance (a property bearer)—with higher-order properties of mind (some of which are simply properties of a material thing and others of which are novel emergent properties of the same substance).[32]

While Augustine saw this tendency in traducianism, it remains to be seen whether this is a knockdown objection against traducianism. Certainly, it prompts defenders of traducianism with a difficulty requisite of further clarification. What may perhaps be a bigger problem for the traducianist, or some versions of it, is the mysterious nature of how the soul generates another soul and yet remains metaphysically distinct from physicality and physically generating mechanisms. Souls and immaterial entities do not seem to have physical parts, but the language of the traducianist is likened to a physical mechanism giving off parts (alternatively, fissile souls) and fusing with new parts, but this is a concern worth taking up in another context.

In light of the traducian option and the challenges raised to creationism, let us now consider traditional variations of creationism.

Traditional Creationism (Simple Creationism)

Traditional creationism, or simple creationism, is distinct from traducianism. Simple creationism says that God creates souls directly and immediately and that he provides the metaphysical grounding for the relationship between the body and the soul. This view is unique in that it satisfies the creationist intuition that souls are distinct from bodies, resulting in the soul having a sufficiently distinct essence from physicality. Added to that, the difficulty on a simple creationist view for conceiving the unity and interaction of the soul and the corresponding physical part is greater than on other accounts. The soul, on

31. See Burnell, *The Augustinian Person*, 35. For more on William G. T. Shedd's discussion of sin's transmission, see Crisp, *An American Augustinian*, chap. 1.
32. Burnell discusses this problem in *The Augustinian Person*, 36.

this view, is unique in that its nature is distinct from the brain. Consequently, the virtue of this view seems to entail a vice concerning the soul's relationship to original sin, which is the problem of the soul's relationship to the brain/ body, the problem in accounting for evolution, and the empirical problems. Given this, the defender of simple creationism has no obvious or intuitively available solution to the problem concerning original sin and transmission. However, creationists seem to have a problem offering a sufficiently robust relation for the soul and brain/body. It is not enough to simply assert the intimately integrated unity of brain/body and soul. It requires a robust relation that unites the two as one, which is naturally explained in terms of origins. The problem for the traditional creationist is not only that God would seem to create souls corrupt but also that souls would not seem to bear a sufficient relation to Adam to account for the transference of corruption or sin.[33]

The defender of pure substance dualism with creationism would need to affirm that sin, rather than being a positive property that is transferred, is a derivative property from the body. In this way, the view could make some sense of original corruption, yet not of original sin where actual sin is transmitted. Even if the proponent of simple creationism defends the view on this basis, simple creationism with pure substance dualism can only affirm original corruption in the sense of a soul inhabiting a body and living in the environment of sin.[34] The reason for this should be quite clear. On simple creationism with pure substance dualism, the person is essentially and strictly a soul, not a soul plus a body. Therefore, the person is not literally a bearer of original sin but lives and functions in the environment of sin because the body is the bearer of corruption.[35] The defender of simple creationism may have another way out of this problem by affirming a variation of compound substance dualism if in fact compound variations are compatible with simple creationism.

Now, the proponent of simple creationism with compound substance dualism may have the resources to rebut the objection by affirming that the soul-part inherits original sin in virtue of the body-part as a derivative property. On this view, the human person is a compound of both body and soul (i.e., construed

33. For a development of the challenge with creationism, see Crisp, *An American Augustinian*, 17.

34. The defender of traditional creationism might opt for a stronger view of original sin by arguing that souls bear this property derivatively such that souls are originally corrupt and bear injustice of a previous sin but do not bear original guilt. The only way one could affirm original guilt is mediately by way of ratification of Adam's sin (e.g., in Arminianism).

35. I do not believe that the body can be the literal bearer of sin and guilt, but it can be corrupted. I say this because the locus of sin is predicable on personal identity and a moral agent. Thus, if persons are strictly identified with souls or are essentially souls, then souls are the locus of sin (if *a* and *b*, then *c*; *a*, therefore *c*).

along the lines of property-nature emergence). If the human person is a compound of body and soul, then one might think that God creates the soul-part and attaches it to a body-part. The body completes the human person and is literally a part of an individualized human nature. If this is true, then the soul can be the bearer of original sin in light of embodiment, but this would require one to construe original sin more loosely as original corruption, not original guilt. In this case, the soul would be a divine creation that is logically, though not temporally, prior to embodiment, according to which the human person in virtue of the body inherits original sin. Additionally, this provides us with a stronger view of original sin than the person's situational grounding in the environment of sin. It actually provides the ground for saying that the person, minimally, has sinful dispositions via the body. It is stronger than the previous view, which is likened to a saint stumbling into an environment of debauchery. On this story, the saint is in the corrupted environment, but this does not entail that the saint himself or herself is in fact corrupt. For this reason, the overall difficulty for simple creationism seems fairly significant.

It is difficult to see how the defender of simple creationism can affirm a natural relationship between the body and the soul that would allow for the person as a soul-substance to inherit original sin via the body or in a way that is connected all the way back to Adam. The advantage of the simple creationist view, in which the soul and the body have sufficiently distinct natures such that the two do not overlap or mix, also carries with it a problem. On such a view, it appears that divine arbitration brings about the soul-body relationship; hence it appears that the transmission of original sin would make God culpable for these sins. Or, on one view, if all humans are liable for their individual sins without any relation to Adam, then it may amount to Pelagianism. There are ways around Pelagianism for the creationist. Certainly one could affirm the idea that Adam's dispositions are somehow passed down from generation to generation or that there is a common curse on the environment for which we are all inheritors. Finally, one could construe the transmission of original sin in a covenantal context where Adam is the federal representative for all of humanity, yet without the existence of any metaphysically real connection between Adam and his progeny. The next two views do not encounter the problem facing simple creationism because of the strong notion of emergence and, by extension, an emergent relation between body and soul and human nature more generally.

EMERGENT SUBSTANCE DUALISM WITH MATERIAL ORIGINS

Emergent dualism, as it is normally construed, takes it that minds, or souls, emerge from a suitably complex neural and biological structure. Elsewhere,

I have called this ESDMO ("emergent substance dualism with materialistic origins"). This view says that human persons are souls with a body, and those souls emerge from suitably complex neural structures, as soul or mind is dependent on the brain and the central nervous system. While ESDMO in conjunction with the doctrine of original sin remains undeveloped, it can be spelled out in a similar manner as the traducianist view of the soul's origin, in that it posits that a human soul is generated from a body or alongside a body that is metaphysically related to other human organisms. The difference here is the specific generative relation. On ESDMO, the physical/neural part generates the soul at a level of suitable complexity in contrast to souls generating other souls directly. On this anthropology, God creates the physical matter with the appropriate mechanisms for conscious individuation. Thus, an individual human person (Adam) appeared for the first time, and the fall occurred shortly thereafter, which brought about a chain reaction whereby all souls proceeding from the first soul (and the primal sin) were successively generated from the first soul, or the first pair. Accordingly, each individual soul inherits original sin and bears a metaphysical relationship to every other human soul. In this way, one can avoid the problem of a divinely created corrupt soul and provide a metaphysical explanation for original sin.

That said, it is doubtful that souls can exist in a "realist" way in which souls exist as one whole, possibly providing an explanation for original guilt. Rather, ESDMO posits a relation between soul and body such that souls are related to other souls mediated by their material parts. At most, then, it seems that the defender of ESDMO could naturally affirm original corruption and corrupt dispositions of the soul (i.e., the dispositions of the soul or the faculties are effects of corruption that could be directly generated from previous bodies biologically, and given the close relation between the soul and the body, one could see how the dispositions and functioning of the body would affect the soul).

Now, while ESDMO may have the resources to provide an accounting for the transmission of original corruption, there is an apparent problem with this view. ESDMO posits a variation of origins that is out of sync with traditional discussions on the soul's origins. According to the tradition, it seems that God creates, at minimum, one soul that has the capability to generate additional souls. However, on ESDMO, where souls are generated in and through biological evolution, it appears that God does not directly create any souls, nor do souls generate other souls (e.g., as in traducianism), which, minimally, seems in tension with the traditional views on soul origination. The defender of ESDMO may be able to affirm an orthodox view of original sin, but can do so only in a weak sense. What is more, ESDMO does not affirm a traditionally recognized view of the soul's origin. And this leads us to the final option for our problem relating to the transmission of original sin.

EMERGENT CREATIONISM

According to emergent creationism, God creates the human soul directly (i.e., the sufficiency condition for the soul), yet the soul's coming into existence is mediated in some sense because souls, while substantial, exist in a larger dynamic and functional framework of inputs and outputs (i.e., the necessary condition). In this sense, emergent creationism is distinct from simple creationism. On emergent creationism, the soul has a natural connection to the body in terms of the soul's coming into existence with the body and its mediation via a properly functioning body.[36] The body may mediate the soul in terms of existence or may mediate the soul's functioning, but on this view, the soul does not come into existence isolated from its so-called physical part. The two are, in one sense, designed for each other and function as an integrally related dynamic compound.

According to one variant of emergent creationism, God creates all souls directly as one divine creation, but these souls come into existence at discrete times as effects of one divine cause, and souls can bear a uniting relationship as one concrete whole, which emerges as discrete individualized effects. The soul, then, bears an important relation or property that unites it to all humanity in virtue of the emergent relationship that exists between souls, bodies, and their progenitors. This view has the immediate benefits found in simple creationism without the problems, in that the soul is directly created and sufficiently distinct from the body yet has a unity relation with the concrete physical part—minimally, in terms of property-nature emergence. Following from this, the emergent soul has the unity and uniqueness of simple creationism, arguably, in terms of the soul's metaphysical simplicity or indivisibility. Furthermore, this does not require the defender of emergent creationism to affirm either a fissile or parturient soul, as with traducianism, because of the emergent relation that holds between the physical and immaterial particulars. Additionally, emergent creationism bears the benefit of ESDMO, wherein souls have a naturally intuitive relationship to bodies, but it averts the "gappy" problem found in ESDMO, wherein souls have no direct relationship to one another because the existence of souls is produced by the body/neural structure. For this reason, the soul's relationship to the body concerning origins allows the proponent to confidently affirm that there is a natural relationship

36. Souls come to exist with the physical part and have first-order properties actualized in terms of the body.

between the soul and the body, such that the body really is a part of human nature, albeit contingently—something that proponents of simple creationism struggle to defend. On simple creationism, it is difficult to ascertain what it is that ties *this* soul to *this* body, but on emergent creationism, there is a natural explanation or story that suggests that *this* soul is tied to *this* body via divine design as well as an explanation for the manner in which the soul bears an essentially originative relation to the particular body. One additional benefit for emergent creationism seems to follow.

On emergent creationism, one has the resources to tell a story about the transmission of sin from one soul to the next on the basis of a unity relation with other souls via generation through or with biological means. It appears that emergent creationism provides a mechanism for allowing individualized souls to bear a property that unites them to Adam's soul on the basis of the connection between bodies construed as parts of one holistic compound of body and soul. As stated above, the soul and the body bear a functional relationship such that the two function naturally together as an integrated whole. In this way, the property of original sin passed on is passed not solely biologically or spiritually but to a compound that is teleologically and functionally one unit. For this reason, one can affirm a natural transfer relation between souls that are united to Adam and his initial act of sin (the primal sin). Additionally, we might say that God creates all the souls at once, related to one metaphysical whole, and that they come into existence at discrete phases of time, but this would require additional metaphysical work to construe the nature of concrete wholes and individual instantiations of the parts in relation to time. This begins to approach Augustinian realism, but in affirming Augustinian realism, of an immediate sort (in which case it wouldn't be "transmission" technically but simply instantiated in the self-same substance), the defender must affirm a stronger union than humans sharing a common nature, even a common nature that is instantiated by individual natures via some sort of generative succession, where souls come into existence with or on the basis of the material aggregate (i.e., the body) in time. Instead, the defender could affirm that all humans compose a concrete or, we might say, a moral whole, but this could be worked out as an immediate or mediate version of realism.[37] This would allow for a kind of individualism, wherein

---

37. Crisp, in *An American Augustinian*, suggests something like this for creationist souls toward the end of chap. 1, but he offers no detailed story or even initial lines for consideration. What I have done here is situate this view with the other views on offer, and I have suggested initial lines as to how one could tell a story that is creationist but has some of the benefits of traducianism because of the souls' unique kind of generative relation, yet it is unlike ESDMO's delayed emergence view of the soul.

the individual bears teleological relations to the collective whole. Potentially, then, one could conceive of a story wherein God holds each individual sufficiently responsible for original sin or a more modified story concerning corruption (similar to ESDMO) to individual human souls on the basis of this metaphysical story.[38]

What I have briefly shown here concerning emergent creationism is one way in which it provides resources for a satisfying account of the transmission of original sin from soul to soul via the connection each has to the other as an effect of one divine cause in creation. Yet the individual appropriations of sin or corruption are derived in terms of the unity relation that each soul shares in its generative relationship (unlike both ESDMO and traditional traducianism). Even if one were to shy away from telling a story that included Augustinian realism, where each individualized soul was a part of one larger concrete whole, a story could be told that allowed for the direct transmission of original sin (construed in terms of corruption) because of the intimate relationship of souls to bodies and of souls to other souls connected through one long biological chain. This is unlike simple creationism, in which souls have no obvious relationship to the body or the generation of the body successively linked together. Additionally, it is distinct from ESDMO in that it more naturally coheres with the traditional inclination toward creationist souls and has the resources to ground the transmission of original sin.

In the end, it seems that all four views have at least some resources to provide a metaphysical explanation for the transmission of original sin, but the explanation may only account for a weaker notion of original sin (e.g., an originally corrupt environment or original corruption). Additionally, each view of origins carries certain liabilities. I suggested that this is especially true of the first three options. I also suggested that emergent creationism might provide the theologian with a more satisfying solution based on the *naturalness* criterion, but this would depend on a variety of other doctrinal and theological commitments—such as one's commitment to the soul's simplicity or the strength of original sin. On emergent creationism, one has the resources to account for an immediate realist view (depending on how one construes the relationship an individual soul has to the whole; recall the analogy of a tree, a mediate realist view, and/or a participatory realist model where the soul participates via Adam's sin of failing to meet the covenantal demands established by God). My aim has been to motivate additional theological and

---

38. It is debatable whether this would allow for a full-blown doctrine of original guilt where souls instantiate original guilt in relation to Adam. This is an interesting question deserving more reflection. See Crisp, "Original Sin and Atonement."

philosophical reflection on the soul's origin in relation to the transmission problem concerning original sin, where the discussion seems to be minimal in both the philosophical literature and the theological literature.

What, Then, Is Original Sin?

There is not a widely agreed upon definition of original sin spelled out in a creed, nor do the scriptural passages yield an obvious view of what is meant by original sin, yet there are parameters within Scripture and within the wider tradition's development of the doctrine that allow us to construct some descriptive statements about the doctrine that are consistent with the wider Christian tradition, of which the Reformed tradition gives us additional parameters. In order to arrive at an orthodox doctrine of original sin, we often need an explicit scriptural statement or a creed. If we do not have those, then we must seek to organize the doctrine in relation to other orthodox doctrines guided by authoritative theologians within one's own tradition. The Council of Trent offers some information about the doctrine of original sin with its assumption that sin is transferred from Adam, at the fall event (i.e., the primal sin), to the rest of the human race. For theological authorities, Irenaeus's *Against Heresies*, battling the gnostic tendencies influencing the doctrine of original sin, is one of the most important; but Augustine's *On Original Sin* is possibly the most important document in the history of the church's understanding of original sin. As with many doctrines within Christianity, and more specifically catholic Reformed Christianity, one needs to press further by developing a coherent systematic account that takes into consideration several theological sources of knowledge by pressing into the metaphysical explanations of doctrines. This is by no means an easy task. In order to do this successfully, one must take all the relevant biblical data into account along with the broader dogmatic claims of the church catholic. Beyond this, if there is not a creedal or confessional statement that speaks with clarity on the particulars of the doctrine, one ought to take into account the moods and tendencies and leanings of the wider confession of the church catholic when guided by the theological authorities of the Reformed tradition. Even more, one must consider the doctrine as it is informed by the experiential data regulated by reason. Then, hopefully, we can come to a better understanding of the doctrine in question.

What seems clear from Scripture and the voice of the church catholic is that humans bear original sin. What this means, however, depends on a wide set of debated issues and on what particular subtradition one inhabits, along with various interlocking assumptions made from other theological sources of knowledge. By delineating some of the variants and models, we have several to choose from and reflect on in our theological constructions concerning the human. We have seen that such a doctrine impinges on our origin story and our condition. However, as insightfully pointed out by David Parker, while important, apart from the stronger versions of original sin (e.g., original guilt), the doctrine does not exclude or undermine personal responsibility or the need to discuss depravity and personal or actual sin.[39] In the end, sin dirties the image of God in humans, but it does not eliminate it, if we affirm that the image is a structure or a substance. Sin blurs the eyes from seeing God and God's hand in the world, and it is this problem that we find satisfied in the union of God and humans—that is, in Christ.

39. Parker, "Original Sin."

6

Who Am I in Christ?

Humans, Descended and Ascended

The Son is the image of the invisible God, the firstborn over all creation.

Colossians 1:15

He is given to us for our salvation, and "is made unto us wisdom, and righteousness, and sanctification, and redemption": so that if we refuse him, we renounce the mercy of the Father, in which alone we can find a refuge.

The French Confession of Faith (1559)

One of the fundamental questions of theological anthropology is where to begin. It's been said before that "Christology is anthropology," but it is not clear what the statement means.[1] There are several ways to interpret this statement. A more specific question will help us make sense of the statement: Do we begin with Adam or Christ?[2] Theological anthropology is the study of humanity, all would say, but the more profound question is this: Who is it that accurately defines humanity? In one important sense, all Christians would say that Christ is the proper starting point for our

1. Peoples, "The Mortal God."
2. In his Barthian-influenced way, Jason Maston gives one answer to this question. See Maston, "Christ or Adam."

anthropology. But why should this be the case? Christ is the one who reveals humanity's purpose. Humanity's purpose is union with the divine, and it is in Christ that humans see perfect union of God and human. As a survey of this exciting, growing field, I will lay out some of the broad issues involved in the subject and how it helps us conceive of humans. Particularly, I will look at Christ's person and Christ's work, two traditional dogmatic categories. Both give us some important insight into the doctrine of humanity.

My hopes for this chapter are unlikely to satisfy those who wish to see developed what I will later call the more robust versions of christological anthropology, but here I will lay the groundwork for further constructive work that takes its starting points from a robust christological anthropology. What I intend to do here is to move beyond making modest claims about humanity concerning the image of God and ethics—topics common to theological anthropology discussions—by considering anthropology in light of the christological data. I am dubious about constructing a totalizing or comprehensive vision of humanity from Christology, as seen in the more robust accounts. I take it that we have a legitimate starting point for anthropology in the creational narrative as well as in first-person philosophy and natural law. As a result, I am reticent to start with Christology and work all the way down to the level of anthropology.

What I offer here is more modest than the robust accounts but more ambitious than developing a theology of the human from ethics or the image of God. I wish to answer three questions in our study of the human via Christ: What am I? Who am I? Who are we as the church? As I have been answering these questions throughout the present book, how one understands christological anthropology will yield an answer to the questions of what I am, who I am, and why I exist. On some christological anthropologies, I am what I am in relation to Christ, which means that I am substantially human only as I am united to Christ, and without that union my substantial existence is only partial. On all christological anthropologies, true humanity (minimally, in an epistemic sense) is revealed in Christ, hence answering the who question. Finally, Christology indicates an answer to the why question of anthropology, as we will see toward the middle and end of this chapter. What is at stake in articulating an orthodox account of Christ's divinity and humanity is an account of both God and humanity. Failing to articulate our Christology entails that we have also failed to articulate the means and purpose of humanity. Given that there is perfect unity between God and humans in Christ, the doctrine of "union" is central to an orthodox anthropology. By working through the scriptural, conciliar, and philosophical issues, I will lay out a variety of christological views within the boundaries of orthodox Christology and discuss the failings of those views that catholic Christianity has deemed heterodox and heretical.

Christological Anthropology Defined

Redeemed humans are expressed most truly in the person and work of Jesus Christ. What it means to be truly or fully human is explained in Jesus Christ. In other words, by looking at Christ, we may see the human as God ideally intended. This is often called the study of christological anthropology, because the study of anthropology is properly understood in light of one's Christology. There are several ways one might understand the discipline of christological anthropology.

Minimally, christological anthropology is a study of the human through the study of Christ. Apart from sympathetic Pelagians (who hold the view that humans are free, unhindered by sin, and unaffected by Adamic sin), nearly all Christian theologians work with some minimalist christological anthropology. We know this because Jesus Christ is the divine-human who lived a perfect human life. He brought divinity to humankind and humanity to divinity. I refer to sympathetic Pelagians because they do not see Christ actually doing anything to humanity apart from providing a moral example. However, even Pelagians have some minimalist christological anthropology in that Christ is a primary moral example, or *the* moral example, for humanity.

A stronger variant of christological anthropology contains the idea that Christ is fundamental to one's anthropological understanding. In other words, our anthropology is metaphysically tied in some substantial sense to our Christology, or Christ provides the fundamental epistemic lens by which to understand much of anything about human nature. However, this stronger notion is still a topic of great interest in the contemporary theological anthropology literature. This is certainly where the more robust versions of christological anthropology are interestingly different from the more minimalist versions. Many practitioners of christological anthropology are committed to more robust versions, claiming that Christology justifies or warrants some fundamental ideas about humanity.

One of the more recent and important theologians to develop christological anthropology in the contemporary literature is Marc Cortez. Cortez has recently published two works specifically fleshing out what he means by the method.[3] Drawing to some degree on David Kelsey, he offers a working

---

3. See Cortez, *Embodied Souls, Ensouled Bodies*. See also his more recent work, *Christological Anthropology in Historical Perspective*.

description: "In its most basic form, the fundamental intuition of a christological anthropology is that beliefs about the human person (anthropology) must be warranted in some way by beliefs about Jesus (christological)."[4] He proceeds to marshal the help of theologian Ian McFarland, saying, "Ian McFarland expresses this fundamental intuition well when he argues that if Jesus is 'the criterion' for Christian talk about what it means to be human, no argument about humanity 'can be theologically binding unless it has a clear christological warrant.'"[5]

Cortez builds on the description above by providing two conditions for what he calls an "initial definition" or a minimal definition: "A *minimally* christological anthropology is one in which (1) Christology warrants important claims about what it means to be human and (2) the scope of those claims goes beyond issues like the image of God and ethics."[6] With this stipulation, Cortez takes it that there are two conditions, not simply the first, which is what started the discussion. Christ must warrant important claims, and the scope must be broad enough to include a wide net of anthropological issues. However, it is not clear that this is an improvement on his working definition with the first condition. Why is it that one must move beyond the image of God and ethics? Cortez describes the role that Christology has and does play in theological understandings of the image and ethics. He notes that this has occurred in theological literature for some time.[7] He also notes several important and recent theological anthropologies that have some christocentric focus to their systematic work, but only insofar as the christological data seems to inform the Christian worldview.[8] The idea may be that focusing on the *imago Dei* and ethics is insufficient. To push back just a bit, it seems that any theological claim that is not made on a creational basis alone or from the framework of natural law or some other framework, but rather is a sui generis (i.e., novel) claim about the anthropos via Christ, would seem to yield a stronger variation of christological anthropology, but I think what Cortez has in mind is something a bit stronger, even comprehensive. Cortez has a wider vision as to how Christ is central not only to a Christian worldview but also to a vision of humanity. In this way, merely making claims about humans as image bearers or arriving at ethical claims is insufficient for a christological anthropology, comprehensively construed. Cortez, then,

4. Cortez, *Christological Anthropology*, 20. See also Kelsey, *Eccentric Existence*, 9.
5. Cortez, *Christological Anthropology*, 20–21. See I. McFarland, *Difference and Identity*, 115.
6. Cortez, *Christological Anthropology*, 22.
7. Cortez, *Christological Anthropology*, 21.
8. See Sherlock, *The Doctrine of Humanity*; Schwarz, *The Human Being*; Jewett, *Who We Are*.

representing several theologians, has a more totalizing and comprehensive vision in view for humanity.

The discussion here will proceed as follows. First, after some contextual remarks, I discuss how to make sense of Christ's human nature. This is important as a way to *confirm* our anthropological theories of constitution (i.e., what we are made of). If our theories of constitution lack the resources to account for our Christology or have some significant challenges, then we should consider rethinking our anthropologies in light of our Christologies. Furthermore, this is the starting point for many more robust christological anthropologies, as I have defined them above, and is important for further reflection on the project. Second, I will discuss the work of Christ. This is often called the work of atonement or justification. What is it that Christ does on the cross? Noting the importance of atonement studies is not my primary intention. My primary intention is to say something about the anthropological question from our atonement study. Third, I will make some final comments by drawing from two representatives on the nature of hearing and seeing via Christ.

Scripture and Christ's Nature

The significance of the incarnation for humans is great. The uniting of two distinct natures was an act of cosmic proportion. The incarnation brought two competing worlds together. Not only did it allow for the two worlds to enter into a peaceful interaction by carving out a new humanity from dead humanity, but also it brought God's presence to humanity in the most intimate way. The picture of the divine assumption of human nature is a picture grafted into the minds of Old Testament believers, in which the divine would take up a dwelling place in the ark of the covenant and the temple. God was uniquely present insofar as his glory was stationed in these locations in a way distinct from the glory that God had shown in other places (e.g., victory in battle or the Holy Spirit's presence on Old Testament leaders).

The scriptural data linking the divine and human natures is quite strong. In the context of a new cosmic shift from the old order, John describes the act of incarnation by first pointing to the Word (what we later realize is identical to Jesus Christ [John 1:14]), who was God (John 1:1). This Word, the Second Person of the Trinity, spoke into the darkness of a fallen world, a world that was deaf and blind to the things of God. The Word invaded our world so as to make a new world. He did so, initially, by becoming one of us both in nature and by taking on all general characteristics of humanity, except for sin. As we find in John 1:14, "The Word became flesh and dwelt among us, and we have seen his glory, glory as of the only Son from the Father, full of grace and truth" (ESV). In keeping with the glory theme of the Old Testament, the glory of God the Father has shifted from the location of the temple in the land to a person who has assumed flesh (i.e., human nature). The parallel is overwhelming and strikes one as, potentially, in the human author's understanding, but even if it was not, it is there in seed form ready for development within the tradition (even if the author was unaware of later doctrinal implications and developments).

Several passages support the union of divine and human natures in the person of Jesus Christ. Hebrews 1:3 provides one important example: "He is the radiance of the glory of God and the exact imprint of his nature, and he upholds the universe by the word of his power. After making purification for sins, he sat down at the right hand of the Majesty on high" (ESV). The church has come to understand and appropriate this passage as signifying that Christ owns the glory of God, that Christ is God (i.e., the exact imprint of his nature), and that he has the power ascribed only to God.

The Church on Christ's Human Nature

We do acknowledge a distinction between Christ's divinity and his humanity so as not to fall into the problem of ancient Greek gods, who were mixed beings of the divine and the human. The flowering doctrine of the incarnation is expressed in the church's confession at the Council of Chalcedon. Herein Christ is a divine person who has assumed a human nature without confusing the two natures. In so doing, Christ reveals God to humans and communicates something new about humanity. Chalcedon is recognizably the most important statement on the person and nature of Jesus Christ. Representing the systematic teaching of the Scriptures, the catholic (i.e., Nicene) tradition confesses this statement with assurance that it is accurate in all its details regarding Christ's divine and human natures in relation. For our purposes here, we will take this as a launching point for discussing Christ's human nature so as to gain some insight into our own nature.

> Following, then, the holy fathers, we unite in teaching all men to confess the one and only Son, our Lord Jesus Christ. This selfsame one is perfect both in deity and also in human-ness; this selfsame one is also actually God and actually man, with a rational soul [i.e., human soul] and a body. He is of the same reality as God as far as his deity is concerned and of the same reality as we ourselves as far as his human-ness is concerned; thus like us in all respects, sin

only excepted. Before time began he was begotten of the Father, in respect of his deity, and now in these "last days," for us and on behalf of our salvation, this selfsame one was born of Mary the virgin, who is God-bearer in respect of his human-ness.

(We also teach) that we apprehend this one and only Christ—Son, Lord, only-begotten—in two natures; (and we do this) without confusing the two natures, without transmuting one nature into the other, without dividing them into two separate categories, without contrasting them according to area or function. The distinctiveness of each nature is not nullified by the union. Instead, the "properties" of each nature are conserved and both natures concur in one "person" and in one *hypostasis* [reality]. They are not divided or cut into two *prosōpa* [persons], but are together the one and only and only-begotten Logos [Word] of God, the Lord Jesus Christ. Thus have the prophets of old testified; thus the Lord Jesus Christ himself taught us; thus the Symbol of Fathers [the Nicene Creed] has handed down to us.[9]

As a part of the dogmatic teaching of the church catholic, Christ is the divine-human, but first he is a divine person who assumes a human nature—thus truly human and divine. On this ground, the framers of Chalcedon confess that Christ reveals God's nature to humans, and Christ reveals humanity as God intended. The articulation of orthodox Christology here, which is within the Nicene tradition, is important for at least two reasons. First, it concerns our salvation. According to the Nicene Creed, Christ came "for us and on behalf of our salvation." Second, it concerns revelation. Christ is the Word (referring to John 1:1), who perfectly articulates the nature of the divine and human. He is the Word that God intends for humanity. These twin concerns of salvation and revelation conjoin when we understand that a part of salvation is our hearing God's word and our seeing and knowing God's nature in the divine-human. A common patristic principle reflecting Chalcedon claims that what Christ does not assume, he does not save. According to St. Gregory of Nazianzus, "For that which He has not assumed He has not healed; but that which is united to His Godhead is also saved."[10] Thus, it is important that Christ be God because that is the goal of humanity, and it takes divinity to save humanity. It is also important that Christ be human so that he can save humanity.

In its christological definition, Chalcedon seeks to avoid multiple heresies. First, Chalcedon states, consistent with the Nicene Creed, that Christ

9. Leith, *Creeds of the Churches*, 35–36 (brackets in the original have been changed to parentheses; my additions are enclosed in brackets); for a useful description and analysis, see 34–35.

10. See Gregory of Nazianzus, "To Cledonius the Priest Against Apollinarius," New Advent, http://www.newadvent.org/fathers/3103a.htm.

is consubstantial (i.e., of the same nature) with the Father. In other words, the person of Jesus Christ—the Logos, the Second Person of the Trinity—is of the same nature as the Father. The statement in John 10:29–30, arguably, confirms this: "My Father, who has given them to me, is greater than all; no one can snatch them out of my Father's hand. I and the Father are one." Christ is, then, first divine in nature, and by uniting to human nature, he reveals something about our destination.

Christ does not just have a nature similar to that of God the Father; rather, he bears all the essential properties of God the Father in the Old Testament. *Arianism* is the view that Christ is not fully or optimally God but is a lesser being than God. Some variants of Arianism state that Christ is not God at all but instead is a unique human being with special capacities.[11] The importance of his being fully God concerns the nature of salvation and who it is that he is bringing to humankind. If he is not fully God, then God is not fully and intimately present with humanity in the way understood by the fathers of catholic/Nicene Christianity or Scripture's teaching that "God is with us."

Next, Chalcedon affirms that Christ is composed of two distinct natures without "confusion." *Eutychianism*, otherwise called *monophysitism*, is a view that affirms that Christ is a *mix* of two distinct natures, not that a union occurs that respects both natures. I like to call this "the blender view."[12] When you put the various ingredients such as milk, carrots, and wheat germ in a blender and mix them, you have a new, mashed-up creation, otherwise known as a tertium quid. In the same way, with Christ, on the blender view, we have a sprinkling of the divine and a sprinkling of humanity, which makes a distinct third kind of nature, a nature that is composed of elements of both humanity and divinity. However, on Eutychianism, the divine nature was sustained, and humanity was relegated to being less important. Contra Eutychianism, and according to orthodoxy, Christ is a divine person who remains with a divine nature and assumes a full and complete human nature without the confusion of the two.

Chalcedon also states that Christ has two *natures*, one divine and one human. There are not two *persons*, which is the heresy called *Nestorianism*.[13] It is important that the union of the two natures are conjoined in a way that humanity can be united to the nature of God, for this is the goal of humanity,

11. For a helpful survey, see Barry, "Arianism."

12. See J. Chapman, "Eutychianism."

13. Some have argued that if a particular anthropology does not allow for the Second Person of the Trinity to assume a human being without the emergence of a distinct person, then we have a christological reason to reject that anthropology. For example, Jonathan Chan argues precisely this against Cartesianism in "A Cartesian Approach to the Incarnation."

and it is actualized in the church's union with Christ. Establishing these two natures allows for a sufficient union but maintains the distinctions between the two natures by not merging them (where this is the case with other ancient portraits of deification).

Last, Chalcedonians confess that Christ is both fully divine and fully human. He is not somehow divine and partially human, but rather he has a complete human nature. To suggest that Christ is partially human would be to fall into the trap of *Apollinarianism*. On Apollinarianism, the Logos already had a mind, so all he needed to assume was a body. In keeping with a natural interpretation of John 1:14 according to Apollinarianism, the Logos only assumes the body of human nature; however, as we find in other parts of Scripture reflected in Chalcedon, Christ bears a complete human nature. If Apollinarianism is true, then it seems to follow that Christ saves only a part of humanity: the bodily part of humanity.[14]

Two schools of thought, namely, Alexandrian and Antiochene, take different perspectives on the emphases of the union and the difference between the human and divine natures of Christ. These schools of thought, prior to their logical extremes, are arguably within orthodox Chalcedonian boundaries but impinge on how we understand humanity as united to the divine or differentiated from the divine. It is by means of the union that we have the divinity dwelling with humanity.

How do we begin to make sense of the union of the two natures? This is an important topic because if we lack a satisfying model to explain the union, then the model could yield an inadequate anthropology.

Let me say a bit more about what seems to be the general consensus in catholic or Nicene Christianity. There is a tendency to affirm dyothelite ("two wills") Christology—for example, in the Sixth Ecumenical Council of the Church in Constantinople (680–81)—as reflected in Luke 22:42 ("not my will, but yours be done").[15] Even if one does not accept the authority of this council, the majority of the Reformed tradition has affirmed that Christ had two actual and distinct wills, one divine and one human. This, then, excludes two-part Christologies of a divine soul ensouling a human body, but this also depends on a more complicated issue about how we construe Christ's human nature—more on that in a moment.

There is another question about the use of the Chalcedonian statement (along with other creedal and dogmatic statements) relevant to human nature.

14. See Gregory of Nazianzus, "To Cledonius the Priest Against Apollinarius"; "Against Apollinarius; The Second Letter to Cledonius," New Advent, http://www.newadvent.org/fathers/3103a.htm.
15. For a helpful treatment, see Stamps, "Atonement in Gethsemane."

As the framers use the language of "rational soul," referring to a rational nature, their background assumption seems to be a hylomorphic (construed as monism or dualism, but it is arguable that this excludes contemporary versions of materialism, as I have discussed previously in chapter 1) anthropology. Some might argue that catholic theologians ought to assume the same anthropology assumed in the minds of the framers, but this seems too strong. Insisting that we must hold the background assumptions of the framers concerning conciliar dogma seems to hold too high a standard for orthodoxy.

Beyond serving as a normative standard for what it means to be God and human, Christ does more. Christ prescribes for us how humans ought to live before God. Christ peels back the veil to expose God's nature to us. In this act by Christ, God becomes intimately present to us in a way that is unique to the human story.

Our Creaturely and Divine Nature (Personhood)

Most theologians today would agree that humans are not, strictly speaking, divine in nature. To use a tautology (i.e., repeating the same concept or idea), humans are human in nature. While some theologians throughout history may see our immaterial natures as having a divine element or spark (e.g., Plato), Christian theologians, especially in the Reformed tradition, highlight the strong distinction between our natures as creatures and the divine nature of the Creator. I have suggested throughout this book that our immaterial nature has some important overlap with the divine nature. Or, more modestly, human nature transcends normal creaturely functioning in the earth and points us to the divine as the direct causal explanation for creaturely existence.

While this transcendent part of our created nature may point to its compatibility with the Logos's assumption of a human nature, it is debatable that our human nature necessitates or implies such a radical event as the incarnation. What we have in the incarnation is quite radical. It is a sui generis property or relation, by which I mean to convey its novelty in the created realm. There is no other event or act that is metaphysically like it. It is new in the history of God's providential care of his creation.

The incarnation of the Logos is an event that changed history. It changed humanity as well. Humanity entered a new arena. This was a radical change in the human narrative. The idea of God becoming human is something of a heresy in some Greek philosophical perspectives, but in Christianity the incarnation is the central defining moment of God's initial redemption of his creation.

Christological anthropology offers us an important insight into an overarching vision of humanity. Given the novelty of this divine act in which the Father sends the Son and the Spirit concretizes the divine and human natures to one divine person (i.e., the Logos, the Second Person of the Trinity), something radically changes in the human realm. I suggest that something metaphysically and epistemologically changes in humanity. Metaphysically, Christ carves out a new humanity. He does not do this in the sense that a distinct human race is literally created, but, on the assumption that there is an Adamic humanity, there is now a new humanity—what I will call "Christic humanity." Christ carves out a new humanity in the sense of carving out a new order of humanity (i.e., a new path, a cosmic shift, a new moral order, as the writer of John is so careful to expound). In addition, Christ supplies new information about humanity that is otherwise inaccessible, hence an epistemological change in human knowing.

I will argue below that no anthropology should contradict claims germane to Christ's human nature. More than that, any additional claims beyond a created or natural understanding of humanity must be made in virtue of understanding Christ. Christ is the link between God and humans in a robust sense. Christ metaphysically unites humans to the divine without merging the natures. Christ also adds an epistemic link for humans to the divine. In an important sense, Christ transforms our knowledge of the divine. As human creatures with frailties and epistemic weaknesses even apart from sin, we, in ourselves, are incapable of seeing God's nature and of responding to God's call. But in Christ, the divine-human with flesh, we see God. As I have previously defined this notion of seeing, or vision, as a capacity of the soul, it is only through Christ that we come to see God in a redeemed way. I have likened the experience of seeing God to those ectypal (i.e., copies or representations of the archetype, Christ, in God's redemptive economy) moments when we have a fresh and overwhelming sense of divine majesty in our lives, when our cognitive faculties are awakened and we see the world with clarity. In a similar fashion, the metaphor of hearing is unlocked in Christ's speech to us.

The issue of the philosophical ontology (i.e., the structure of being) of Christ's human and divine natures bears on the anthropocentric question insofar as what it is that is united to the divine nature through Christ must be made sense of in light of the ontologies of essence. There are two ways to make sense of Christ's human and divine natures: abstractist and concretist.[16] Alvin Plantinga gives a helpful description of the terms:

16. The literature on this subject is growing, and the finer distinctions are complicated. See Loke, "On the Coherence of the Incarnation"; for a response, see Arcadi, "Kryptic or Cryptic?";

In this context, the terms "nature" and "human nature" get used in two analogically related but very different senses: in the first sense, the term "human nature" denotes a *property* (or, if you like, group of properties): the property P which is such that necessarily, every human being has P, and necessarily, whatever has P is a human being. In the second sense the term "human nature" denotes a *concrete human being* rather than a property. In this second sense, the thing denoted by "human nature" and that gets assumed is a human being, a concrete object, not an abstract object like a property. I'll therefore call the first view the "abstract nature" view, and the second the "concrete nature" view. Aquinas apparently endorses the concrete nature view; Augustine appears to accept the abstract nature view, although he also sometimes speaks as if it is the concrete view he holds. John Calvin follows Augustine in being a little ambiguous here, usually suggesting the abstract view, but sometimes falling (or ascending, depending on your preferences here) into the concrete view.[17]

Notice the distinction made between a property view and a concrete particular view. In other words, does a set of properties entail a kind-membership relation ("kind" referring to a common nature of a thing in question) or does the kind-membership of a thing entail that it has certain properties and powers? Let us see if we can parse these distinctions out more carefully.

As the name suggests, abstractist views of natures begin with abstract properties. In this way, natures are properties or a specified set of properties. Birds are described by the natures they possess in virtue of the properties they instantiate. Fish are described by the natures they possess, as well, in virtue of the properties they instantiate—fish have gills. Dogs, apes, and humans are the same in that they, too, are described by the properties they have as part of their common natures. They all bear different natures, and natures are construed in terms of properties or a set of properties. For example, a bird's nature is not in virtue of the concrete particular body it has but rather in terms of the kind-nature it participates in, which is characterized, in part, by flying.

Concretist nature views are different. Concretism says that we are or have our natures in virtue of the particulars that compose the thing in question. Birds are the kinds of things that have wings. Humans are composed of body and soul and are bipedal, versus apes that (usually) walk on all fours. Also noteworthy is that the concrete particular is what endows the individual with particular powers and liabilities. For example, birds are endowed with wings that endow those birds with the power to fly (most birds, anyway, as some

for a response to the response, see Loke, "On the Divine Preconscious Model of the Incarnation." See also Plantinga, "On Heresy, Mind, and Truth," 183–84; Crisp, *Divinity and Humanity*, 41; Hill, introduction to *Metaphysics of the Incarnation*, 11; Morris, *The Logic of God Incarnate*.
    17. Plantinga, "On Heresy, Mind, and Truth," 184.

have wings but are flightless). They also have liabilities in that their frames and bones are lightweight and birds are generally limited in their ability to walk on the ground. Humans, on the other hand, are composed of body and soul, and the soul endows the individual human with powers of imagination, rationality, moral awareness, and volitional capacity for free choice.

This question, too, impinges on Christology in particular. The ontology of Christ's natures, divine and human, is the ground for human union with the divine or participation in the divine attributes given to us through Christ. How we understand the relationship between the two-natured Christ will have an impact on the coherence of anthropology and carries with it implications for that anthropology. In the case of Chalcedonian and Nicene Christology, I am taking it for granted that Christ is a divine person with a divine nature that he shares with the other two persons of the Trinity. In this way, it cannot be that Christ's divine nature is merely a set of properties that Christ shares with the other two persons of the Trinity; rather, it is a concrete particular—deity—that he shares with the other two persons of the Trinity. According to Chalcedon, Christ is, properly speaking, a divine person, with a corresponding divine nature, which undergirds and assumes a human nature. The question of relevance here is how we construe the human nature of Christ. Is the human nature of Christ construed according to abstractism or concretism?

On abstractism, Christ is human not in virtue of assuming two concrete particulars but rather by assuming the properties necessary and sufficient to being human. A variety of options are available for construing an abstractist view of Christ's human nature. Thomas Morris offers a famous abstractist option where he describes Christ's human nature as a set of essential properties that entail his membership into a kind—human. On Morris's view, the divine person Logos, Second Person of the Trinity, assumes a conscious perspective or power that is distinct from the higher-order divine consciousness had by the Christ's divine nature. Morris makes helpful distinctions between Christ being merely human and fully human, which is at pains to show, on his view, that Christ is fully human because he meets all the necessary and sufficient conditions via the properties he has in the incarnation. Morris states,

> In the case of God Incarnate we must recognize something like two distinct minds or systems of mentality. There is first what we can call the eternal mind of God the Son, with its distinctively divine consciousness . . . encompassing the full scope of omniscience, empowered by the resources of omnipotence, and present in power and knowledge throughout the entirety of the creation. And, in addition to this divine mind, there is a distinctly earthly mind with

its consciousness that came into existence and developed with the conception, human birth and growth of Christ's earthly form of existence.[18]

Morris takes it that his view not only is coherent but also satisfies the New Testament data. Christ exhibits properties of an unlimited consciousness, via his divine nature, and a limited conscious perspective, via his human nature. And each of these properties is predicable of the respective natures in question.

Richard Swinburne offers what is a distinctive abstractist view of Christ's human nature. Although similar to Morris's view, Swinburne is quite clear that the Logos, Second Person of the Trinity, does not assume an additional created mind but rather assumes a power that is limited in nature. On Swinburne's account, in order for Christ to be essentially human, he must assume a body for which his human consciousness operates. He advances a "divided mind" view that allows Christ to hold within his personhood two ranges of consciousness, one human and one divine.[19] The benefits of Swinburne's view is that it avoids Nestorianism (i.e., the view that Christ's two natures entails two persons), but it appears to be a version of Apollinarianism (i.e., the view that Christ is a divine person with a human body).

Both views are distinct from a concretist view in that a set of properties entails a kind-membership relation rather than a concrete particular endowing one with a set of powers and properties. One might argue that an abstractist view presupposes concrete particulars that endow one with powers. This is one advantage of the concretist view. There is another potential benefit. As stated above, the natural reading of Chalcedon is that the Logos assumes two concrete particulars—a body and a rational soul—in order to avoid the heresies listed earlier and to uphold a coherent rendering of the biblical material on the fact that Christ instantiates what appears on the surface to be incompatible properties.

The question for the concretist is whether Christ has one or two parts. Materialists argue that Christ has one part: a body or brain that gives rise to higher-order neural properties of consciousness.[20] The Logos, then, needs only to assume one part to become human—not just any old body but rather a body that carries higher-order properties of consciousness. Assuming that this is within the parameters of Nicene and Chalcedon, one would need to construe a "rational soul" as a set of properties tied to a brain. And this would avoid Apollinarianism in virtue of the fact that the properties would serve to satisfy the role for "rational soul." So, on this view, we have a two-part

18. Morris, *The Logic of God Incarnate*, 169.
19. Swinburne, *The Christian God*, 61–66, 196.
20. See Crisp, *God Incarnate*, 137–55. Peoples, "The Mortal God."

Christology. The obvious challenge for a two-part materialist Christology comes from the doctrine of Christ's persistence upon somatic death. Upon Christ's human body dying, Christ would cease to be human. The concern that he persists raises significant worries about his representational work on behalf of humans during the intermediate state of disembodied existence. Without a human body, on a materialist account, there is no part that would sufficiently make Christ a human. Nonetheless, it is this crucial step in the redemptive process that is sustained on a dualist account of human nature.

On a dualist concretist account of Christ's human nature, we have a three-part Christology. Three-part Christologies naturally account for a reading of Chalcedon's statement about the Logos assuming a "rational soul" and a body. But there is a challenge for some dualist accounts that is not a challenge for abstractists or for materialist concretist accounts. That challenge is for dualist accounts that take it that the individual human just is identical to his or her soul or that the core of the individual human is the soul—that is, broadly Cartesian accounts of human nature. The challenge for this account is that minds or souls just are persons, generally speaking. Two solutions are available.

The first solution is that Christ's human nature is impersonal in itself and depends on the divine particular mind of Christ. Arbitrarily, God simply stops the process of a Cartesian soul from becoming a *personal human*, and Christ's divine personhood personalizes the human mind. The view amounts to an exception in the human realm. Only one human mind fails to be a personal human mind.[21]

The second solution is Cartesian abstractism. Rather than the Logos assuming a particular mind, he assumes a body, and the relation between the divine mind and the human gives rise to a human nature that is sufficiently and essentially human. What makes Christ fully human is that he has all the properties sufficient for being a member of the human kind.[22]

I have canvassed a representative sampling of some of the important christological views of human nature by considering them in light of one's ontology of materialism or dualism in relation to concretism and abstractism. The complex combination of these views impinges upon anthropology. Developing a coherent account of Christology, particularly the human nature in relation to the divine nature, is necessary if we are to make sense of humanity both as a coherent account of human nature and as one that sustains the union between the two natures. Without an appropriate Christology, we cannot make sense of how it is that humans are humans and how it is that humans are united

21. Crisp adopts this view in *Divinity and Humanity*, 68, 94.
22. Chan, "A Cartesian Approach to the Incarnation."

to God. The discussion of abstractism and concretism concerning Christ's human nature coupled with Christ's redemptive work also has implications for the anthropocentric concerns of redemption.

Christological Anthropology (Work)

Central to the Christian story of redemption is not only the incarnate life of Christ but also his death and resurrection. For it is the incarnation and Christ's death that represent for us Christ's descent, and our descent, so that, in the beatific vision and resurrection, we might with Christ ascend to God as our rightly intended destiny. Christ's work of death and resurrection is important to our understanding of God. God is just and requires justice in his moral order (e.g., Lev. 11:44–45; Deut. 6:25; Matt. 5:43–44, 48; John 3:19; 1 Pet. 1:15–16). God is also loving, and he chose to send his Son in the form of a creature to die for other creatures so as to save them from the effects of sin (e.g., John 1:10–14; 3:16; Rom. 3:25; 5:1; 8). Christ's work of death and resurrection is significant to how we understand the human story. What does the atonement teach us about humans?[23]

What I am interested in is the anthropocentric issues in the context of christological work. We can learn several things about the anthropos via a better understanding of Christ's work. For example, Christ points us forward in understanding the nature of both human death and human resurrection. In this context, I will explore the nature of Christ's death as it impinges on the anthropocentric question. Generally speaking, the atonement is held up by a covenantal structure in both the Old Testament and the New Testament. As we have seen previously, the creational covenant contains within it the basic structure for succeeding covenants (e.g., Abrahamic, Mosaic, Davidic, and the new covenant). This is also true of the atonement insofar as it works within the basic structures of the previous covenants, wherein Christ consummates the new covenant, bringing about new life and blessing to that life (paralleling the creational covenant).

Given the covenantal nature of the atonement, it is important to note the covenantal nature of human identity (broadly construed in terms of narrative identity). Several implications follow from the heart of the atonement's covenantal structure. First, humanity is construed both communally and individually.[24] Any theory of the atonement must have the resources to adequately

---

23. An interesting attempt at this is Woznicki, "Atonement and Anthropology."

24. See Boersma, *Violence, Hospitality, and the Cross*, 166–67. See also Wright, *Jesus and the Victory of God*, 561.

capture this notion of the atonement and uphold this understanding of humanity.

Second, human beings are beings of justice.[25] The atonement reveals such a truth about humans in multiple ways. As a reflection of God's nature, the atonement reflects God's heart for justice in governing the human world. And humans are designed to satisfy and uphold God's law as dignified beings (see Gen. 9:6). The nature of this justice flows right out of a covenantal structure. The maintenance of the covenantal structure via the law is important for the sustaining of humanity. The nature of this justice is retributive in that punishment often follows the violation of covenantal demands. It is restorative in that God acts to bring to life what was lost through lawful violation. It is rectoral in that God is conceived of throughout the Old Testament as the King of a nation who has entered into covenantal relationship. God is the Creator and King of his universe, and he is the one who governs it through law. We humans are designed to live and breathe in the context of covenant with the King. This results in the shape of human purpose.

Third, then, humans are purposeful beings who are called to honor God in his provenance. Some would thus argue that what is fundamental in human sin is not merely the violation of covenantal demands but the violation of the king. By not giving God what we rightfully owe to him, we have violated the covenant. It is important to note that social justice, too, is a concern of God's covenantal structure, as forcefully presented by Old Testament prophets. While social justice is not the central or fundamental concern of the divine-human covenant, it is nonetheless important to it.

Fourth, a more obvious, yet not unimportant, feature of human identity is that humans are relational beings.[26] Humans are intended for relationship. As reflected in the creational covenant, humans are designed for horizontal relationship with other humans and the rest of creation, as well as vertical relationship with God himself. This relational feature is a necessary condition of covenant. When we violate God's covenantal demands, we breach a relational connection once established between God and humans.

Each one of these four features is important to the theories of the atonement. How each of these features is understood will depend on how the systematician works out the logical and metaphysical connections between them in a theory of atonement. No doubt each atonement theory will, to some degree, bear out

25. See Vidu, *Atonement, Law, and Justice.*

26. For a useful collection of essays that highlight the relational nature of human identity, see Schwöbel and Gunton, *Persons, Divine and Human.* Nearly every chapter in the collection highlights and expounds on this understanding of humans as relational beings. Many of the authors see a relational ontology as fundamental to substantial ontology for theological anthropology.

these features (or it should), and each theory has an emphasis that has something to contribute to our understanding of humanity. But this is not an endorsement of an atonement theory that does everything (e.g., the eclectic or kaleidoscopic view), nor will I offer an endorsement to any single theory of atonement.

Christ and Human Death

Here we will answer the big question, What happens in death?

On a moral theory of atonement, the central motivation is, arguably, love. Christ, motivated by love, provides for us a moral example of what it means to follow God. This theory exalts one primary attribute: God's goodness. The aim or object of atonement is the motivation of human-to-human interaction and human-to-divine interaction that subverts and transforms the meaning of death.

On sympathy theories of the atonement (i.e., *Christus dolor*), the central motivation is divine sympathizing with humans. The death of Christ, then, reveals or illuminates something about the practice and function of what it means to be human. Fundamental to our coming to know God is the practice of suffering and sympathizing with other humans in their suffering. As God through Christ identified with us, we are to identify with others.[27]

Anselmian satisfaction is another prominent theory of atonement that distinguishes itself from the previous atonement theories in that it focuses on some fundamental lawful relationship between God and humans. On Anselm's understanding, the central motivation for the Logos's becoming human is the love that the Son has for his Father's honor, primarily, and, secondarily, the love God has for covenantal relationship with humans. God's aim is to satisfy the fundamental objective of the covenant and its laws. Christ's death, then, is the culmination of his life that is given up to God in service. The purpose of the laws is not so much retributive as rectoral—that is, the restoration of God's honor in the moral universe.[28] On this view, humans have a primary purpose of honoring God in the moral universe, of which God is the governor.

Prominent to some degree in the Reformed tradition, one atonement theory that has gained more acclaim is the penal substitution theory. On such a theory, Christ dies to pay the debt of punishment that we owe to God for our sins. Depending on various constructions, the central motivation for the atonement

---

27. For a recent development of this theory, see Mouw and Sweeney, *The Suffering and Victorious Christ*.

28. For a development of a Reformed version of Anselmian atonement, see Farris and Hamilton, "The Logic of Reparative Substitution"; "Reparative Substitution and the 'Efficacy Objection.'"

is either divine wrath (i.e., the satisfaction of divine anger toward sin) or divine justice (i.e., the satisfaction of God's moral law meted out through the penalty of death).

These and other questions about Christ's work reveal something of what it means to be human. Humans exist in a narrative where God redeems humanity through the God-man. What it is that Christ does for humanity reveals human nature and its functioning in relation to God. The atonement discussion, then, raises several questions about how humans ought to live and how to understand human death. It also points us to something greater and higher: what happens upon death. Christ gives some insight into what it is that ideally happens to humans after death.

How it is that humans are united to Christ, historically, comes about for many theologians by way of the beatific vision of God. And, in some Reformed articulations, it is not merely that we are united by way of seeing God in Christ, but we are united by way of seeing God in Christ manifest in the flesh.

Christ's Ascension (Human Ascension)

Christ first reveals humanity in his descension to live among us as the incarnate divine-human who dies on our behalf. Christ reveals human purpose in the ascension. Christ's ascension after death and resurrection further buttresses the victory over death in the resurrection and Christ's achievement in taking us to be with the Father in heaven. Christ's ascension is our ascension. In the beginning of the book of Acts, Christ is not conquered by death but ascends to life in heaven, and this signifies the purpose for his church.

> So when they had come together, they asked him, "Lord, will you at this time restore the kingdom to Israel?" He said to them, "It is not for you to know times or seasons that the Father has fixed by his own authority. But you will receive power when the Holy Spirit has come upon you, and you will be my witnesses in Jerusalem and in all Judea and Samaria, and to the end of the earth." And when he had said these things, as they were looking on, he was lifted up, and a cloud took him out of their sight. And while they were gazing into heaven as he went, behold, two men stood by them in white robes, and said, "Men of Galilee, why do you stand looking into heaven? This Jesus, who was taken up from you into heaven, will come in the same way as you saw him go into heaven." (Acts 1:6–11 ESV)

The significance of the ascension to understanding a doctrine of humanity relates to understanding human purpose, as the redemptive story in Scripture bears out. As promised, the Holy Spirit will come with power and authority upon Christ's ascent, which we see following this portion of Acts. Christ's act of ascent is not only significant as another fact in the story. Nor is it simply that Christ must eventually go back to be with the Father as planned. The significance is not only the glory he brings to the Father in his work but also the anthropocentric implications of his human nature transcending in power, authority, and status as Christ moves into the presence of God. At this point in the narrative, the disciples have heard the Word of God and they understand. They have also seen the divine in the flesh of human nature. Both hearing and vision are present because he spoke to them and they responded as witnesses and because they saw him ascend in glory.

The ascension impinges on several doctrines relevant to an anthropocentric focus. Calvin discusses what is, arguably, deification in the context of sacramental discussions: "In sum, God comes down to us so that then we might go up to him. That is why the sacraments are compared to the steps of a ladder."[29] Calvin raises a christological distinction from the medieval emphases. He argues that the medieval doctrine of ascent and descent seems to invert the process, highlighting not God's coming to us but our going to him. Julie Canlis helpfully comments on Calvin's understanding, "If human life has been brought 'up' into God without change or confusion and our 'partaking' of his very humanity is raising us up into God's triune koinonia, then we see just how essential the Eucharist is as a confirmation of Calvin's doctrine of participation."[30] Christ's ascension is our ascension into the triune life of God, where we participate in the divine life through the resurrected and ascended one.

Canlis accurately points out that in Calvin's view, humans ascend in their union to Christ. This union occurs in the covenantal (even sacramental) context of the redemptive story in the New Testament. Through the means of grace, after baptism—the initiation into the new-covenant church—humans participate in God's giving of redemptive gifts (and sanctifying gifts) in Christ by the power of the Holy Spirit. The sacraments (the Lord's Supper), and prayer, reaffirm our union with Christ and are instrumental in our participation in the life God gives to us—his life through grace.[31]

Michael Horton has made much of this distinction of ascent and descent. On his view, representing what he takes to be the view of Calvin, Bavinck, and of the Reformation in general, we do not so much ascend as disembodied

---

29. Calvin, "Lessons from the Death of Uzzah," 234.
30. Canlis, *Calvin's Ladder*, 160.
31. Canlis, *Calvin's Ladder*, 164.

souls in a purely Platonic sense, but we are passive receptors of trinitarian action. Bavinck, working within the Reformed theological tradition, shares an overlapping traditional space with Calvin and reflects the themes listed earlier found in Calvin. Summarizing what he has argued, in one article, for Calvin's view, Horton says, "Over against the Neoplatonism that has frequently infected theology, writes Bavinck, 'in Reformation theology' the antithesis to grace is not nature but sin. Grace is not simply 'an aid to humans in their pursuit of deification'; it is 'the beginning, the middle, and the end of the entire work of salvation: it is totally devoid of human merit.' Like creation and redemption, so also sanctification is a work of God. It is of him and through him, and therefore also leads to him."[32] It is arguable that Horton overstates the difference between Calvin, as well as the Reformed tradition, and the medieval tradition. While it is important to highlight the trinitarian nature and foundation of human participation in God for deification, it is not the case that humans are inactive in the process, according to much of the Reformed tradition—as we will see below in the discussion of Owen and Edwards on the beatific vision. Furthermore, with the medieval tradition, it is important to emphasize a theology of glory, where souls participate in God's glory.[33]

Christ as Abstract Humanity or Concrete Humanity

An important ground for making sense of Christ's death, resurrection, and ascension is the ontology of Christ's human nature. Drawing from the abstractist and concretist discussion given above, I will parse out some of the options for how we are to think about anthropology in light of human union to God. How we make sense of Christ's human nature furnishes a ground for how it is that the benefits of Christ's death, resurrection, and ascension are imparted to *redeemed* humans. Undoubtedly, Christ's relationship to humans, especially redeemed humans, amounts to more than a mere representationalism or federalism. Christ does more than simply represent redeemed humanity as God's chosen one who acts on humanity's behalf, or part of humanity's

32. Horton, "Atonement and Ascension," 249.
33. See Farris and Brandt, "Ensouling the Beatific Vision." Herein we show that Reformed theologians have a tendency to highlight the immaterial and intellectual aspects of anthropology and the beatific vision. While many Reformed theologians had a place for the trinitarian action of resurrecting Christ, this does not somehow do away with the immaterial nature of God or of humans in the act of vision or becoming like God. How both of these work together is unclear. What is clear is that Christ is the means by which to unite the twin impulses as reflected in some Reformed theologians. It is important to note this because the Reformed tendency is often taken as starkly in contrast to Neoplatonism (and the whole package that comes with it) and medieval Christianity, but things are a bit more nuanced in the Reformed tradition.

behalf. There are two ways to make sense of Christ's covenantal work that grounds the benefits of his representational work and extends those benefits to redeemed humans by way of union.

On one account, Christ assumes humanity, or an elected part of humanity, as a concrete entity. Individual human beings are concrete parts that compose a larger concrete whole. Assuming humans persist as four-dimensional space-time objects, Christ assumes the four-dimensional object that composes what I have earlier called Christic humanity. As parts of his concrete nature, Christ becomes human by assuming the four-dimensional object. The legal union on this account is insufficient to account for the nature of the union between Christ and redeemed humanity, but, instead, redeemed humanity becomes part of Christ's compound substance. The nature of union is an actual union and is a way of working out Augustinian realism. However, there is an alternative way to construe the union between God and humans that is not uncommon in the history of Christian thought, but it assumes an abstractist understanding of Christ's human nature in relation to individual human beings.[34]

On the second account of union, the Logos assumes an abstract property: humanity. He is a human in virtue of his membership into a kind-nature. As a human, Christ's humanity is given to humanity, or one part of humanity, for which this select group is able to participate in the life had by the divine-human being. As found in the discussion on original sin, where humans participate in Adam's sin in some way, humans participate in the reality of the heavenly forms that are given to us by God. In this case, rather than participating in the privation of Adam's sinful humanity, redeemed humanity participates in the reality of Christ's humanity, which shares in the divine nature of Christ. Again on this account, similar to Plato's account of universals, properties have causal efficacy in the world, so what Christ does as the archetype of humanity causally effects individually redeemed humanity.

The Beatific Vision

"Jesus said to him, 'Have I been with you so long, and you still do not know me, Philip? Whoever has seen me has seen the Father. How can you say, "Show us the Father"?'" (John 14:9 ESV).

There is a tendency to think that the medieval tradition has sole rights to the beatific vision and that the Reformed tradition has largely left the doctrine

---

34. Crisp, "Original Sin and Atonement."

behind.[35] This is just not true. In fact, vision is present throughout the Reformed tradition when Reformers describe this transcendent knowledge of God and union with God in Christ. Unlike Thomas Aquinas, according to a common reading of him, many of the Reformers who explicitly developed the doctrine did so in a christological way. In contrast to what is a common understanding of Aquinas, and medieval theologians, that the disembodied self has a static vision of God himself, without explicit development of a vision of the Trinity, the Reformed theological developments emphasize a dynamic vision of the incarnate and resurrected Christ made physically manifest. And this vision culminates in our physical resurrection. That said, several Reformers worked from a basic understanding of Aquinas yet built on him and moved in a christological and trinitarian direction.

Thomas Aquinas is typically understood to describe the beatific vision as a stative power of the soul after sloughing of the body of flesh during the intermediate state of soulish existence. In this state, saints will see God through the eyes of the soul. They will behold the glory of God. Aquinas describes this as an intellectual and immaterial exercise. Following Aquinas, one notable Reformed theologian, Francis Turretin, understands the vision as a seeing and knowing of God's highest goodness in and through love that leads to joy. For him, this process begins in the intellect and then moves to the will.

The christological nature of the vision is certainly true of John Owen. He bears this out: "The beholding of the glory of Christ is one of the greatest privileges and advancements that believers are capable of in this world, or that which is to come."[36] Note that, for Owen, it is Christ that is central to the beatific vision. Christ is that which we behold in the vision. Also, most important, it is God who is made manifest in Christ. "The enjoyment of God by sight is commonly called the beatifical vision; and it is the sole fountain of all the actings of our souls in the state of blessedness. . . . Howbeit, this we know, that God in his immense essence is invisible unto our corporeal eyes, and will be so to eternity; as also incomprehensible unto our minds. For nothing can perfectly comprehend that which is infinite, but what is itself infinite. Wherefore the blessed and blessing sight which we shall have of God will be always 'in the face of Jesus Christ.'"[37] Owen gives unique attention to the resurrected Christ as the means by which we experience the beatific vision. For Owen, it is not a human achievement of beholding the face of God;

35. We have seen this sentiment to some degree already. See also Bauckham, "The Vision of God," 711.
36. Owen, *Works*, 1:287.
37. Owen, *Works*, 1:292–93.

rather, it is brought by the Son of God, who reveals the Father to us. It is in the humanity of Christ that we see and behold God in Christ.

Again, Christ is central to the vision. By seeing Christ, we see God, and for Owen, this is the source for the believing saints to act in redeemed ways or, as Owen puts it, in "blessedness." What is invisible is now available in Christ. Divine blessing is seen "always" in the face of Jesus Christ. Owen declares that the gospel is most fully revealed in the face of Christ. Part and parcel of this gospel, for Owen, is the seeing of the Father in the person and work of Jesus Christ.[38] While the vision is christological, the vision is intellectual and immaterial.[39]

Suzanne McDonald summarizes Owen's understanding. She states that it is one of beholding Christ. For Owen, the vision is composed of content directly from Christ, specifically the content of the mysterious union. And this union is made manifest to us in the work of Christ.[40]

Kyle Strobel, in a helpful expository paper, develops Jonathan Edwards's Reformed doctrine of the beatific vision. In it, he summarizes Owen's understanding as it impinges on the anthropocentric question.

> By focusing his doctrine of the beatific vision on Christ, Owen connects the vision in glory with the vision had through faith. Faith perfected, as it were, is sight. This necessitates anthropological perfection—the addition of new *faculties* of sight—as well as the immediacy only available in glory. Furthermore, heaven is, in a sense, tethered to what has already been revealed on earth: "No man ought to look for anything in heaven," Owen evinces, "but what one way or other he hath some experience of in this life." Owen's account is grounded in Christ's eternal mediation and the faculties available to truly *see* Christ in his divinity (and not only see him as the disciples did).[41]

Edwards improves on Owen by highlighting the christological nature of the vision while developing its trinitarian nature. Edwards does not depart from an understanding of God as immaterial or humans as immaterial, hence prioritizing the immaterial and intellectual nature of the vision (with Aquinas and Turretin), yet he also says that the vision will occur by seeing God in the flesh of Christ. Here Edwards touches on several anthropocentric themes.

First, the nature of the vision will be complete according to human kind. Edwards says, "The soul has in itself those powers, whereby 'tis sufficiently

38. Owen, *Works*, 1:378.
39. Owen, *Works*, 1:379.
40. McDonald, "Beholding the Glory," 149.
41. Strobel, "Jonathan Edwards' Reformed Doctrine," 174.

capable of apprehending spiritual objects, without looking through the window of the outward senses. The soul is capable of seeing God more immediately and more certainly, and more fully and gloriously, than the eye of the body is."[42] Reflected here and elsewhere, Edwards highlights the capacities of the soul as sufficient for seeing God, far more than the capacities of the physical eyes. It is immediate in the way that the physical eyes see the sun. In other words, this novel kind of knowledge is not something that is known from nature alone in creation, nor is it arrived at by way of inference, but rather it is known immediately in experience. When humans see God, they do so in a way that is definitive, decisive, and full. By complete and full, Edwards seems to indicate something about the nature of humanity, but he is not suggesting that humanity can see in the same way that an individualized infinite nature can see.

Second, the nature of the vision reveals the motivation of humans and their purpose: love and glory. Edwards states that, upon the vision, humans will have an experience of God's love toward them, which is directed toward God's glory. He expresses this in the following: "This very manifestation that God will make of himself that will cause the beatifical vision will be an act of love in God. It will be from the exceeding love of God to them that he will give them this vision which will add an immense sweetness to it. . . . They shall see that he is their Father and that they are his children. . . . Therefore they shall see God as their own God, when they behold this transcendent glory."[43] This act of God's love causes the vision to occur for the Christian (i.e., the saint, the elect). The flowering of God's covenantal love toward his image bearers is fully experienced in the vision of God. Herein God's children experience God's glory, which for Edwards means that they experience joy and happiness—in accord with their natures.[44] Yet this experience of love, while brought about in a covenant with humans, is the ushering of the human into the love shared by the trinitarian persons. Edwards makes note of this when he describes the Father as the cause, Christ as the means, and the Holy Spirit as the actualization. Edwards says, "By the Holy Ghost a spiritual sight of God is given in this world, so 'tis the same Holy Spirit by which a beatifical vision is given of God in heaven."[45]

More could be said about the christological nature of the beatific vision, but my purpose here was to touch on Christology as it impinges on the

42. J. Edwards, *Works of Jonathan Edwards*, vol. 50, "373. *Rom. 2:10.*" Thanks to Kyle Strobel for pointing out this sermon. Quotations from it here follow the transcriptions of the sermon in Strobel, "Jonathan Edwards' Reformed Doctrine," which he edited for readability.

43. J. Edwards, *Works of Jonathan Edwards*, vol. 50, "373. *Rom. 2:10.*"

44. See J. Edwards, *Works of Jonathan Edwards*, vol. 17, "The Pure in Heart Blessed."

45. J. Edwards, *Works of Jonathan Edwards*, vol. 50, "373. *Rom. 2:10.*"

anthropological. Interestingly, when following Reformed theologians such as Owen and Edwards, we have examples of how the christological affects the anthropological questions. Humans, as covenantal relational beings, are motivated by God's love toward God's glory, according to Edwards. Humans, as primarily immaterial beings, experience God with the eyes of the soul, yet they see the immaterial God in the flesh of Christ. And this vision is an experience of God's transcendent glory, symbolized and typified by God's glory in the temple of the Old Testament, all the while surpassing it. The glory that we experience is full, satisfying, and complete—according to human nature and its limitations.

7

Who Are We in Culture?

Creaturely and Divine in Work, Race, and Disability

*After this I looked, and there before me was a great multitude that no
one could count, from every nation, tribe, people and language, standing
before the throne and before the Lamb.*

Revelation 7:9

One aspect of the "Who am I?" question is the relationship that individual humans have to culture.[1] To this point, I have touched on
the topic of culture to some degree already in the introduction and
the chapter on personal identity when discussing narrative identity. Culture
is both constructed by earlier generations of people and sustaining of later
generations. Culture is important to who we become as a people, as a society,
and as communities. Culture is a product of society and communities, which
includes ideas, actions, customs, and artifacts as the carriers of meaning for
the purpose of sustaining society.

Several important questions impinge on the nature of culture in relation
to Christianity and who we are as human beings. For example, is Christianity in conflict with culture? Should Christianity transform culture? Is
there a paradoxical relationship between Christianity and culture? Should the
church act in a subservient way to culture? These are complicated questions.

1. One of the more constructive contributions in recent years is Tanner, *Theories of Culture.*

While I give some answer to them indirectly, I will not address them directly. Instead, I will address three other topics relevant to culture that have become important in contemporary theological anthropology. First, I will offer some broad theological characteristics of vocation and work. Second, I will lay out various theories on race. Third, I will lay out two models for thinking about disability.

Before pressing on, we should note some broad principles with which to think about Christian culture. Divine revelation, as it is received by the church catholic, gives us several ideals for thinking about culture. First, a Christian culture is characterized by a singular kingdom under the order and authority of Christ on the throne. As we look at the Old Testament, one thing is clear: God intended to be the King of the earth. When we come to the New Testament, we find that God is ruling as King in the church. Second, and following from a monarchy, the final kingdom will be one nation composed of a plurality of previous nations, ethnicities, and cultures. Third, Christian culture is distinctly covenantal. This is the case in that humans relate to one another and to God through covenants, which include pacts, rules, promises, blessings for obedience, and curses for disobedience. Fourth, Christian culture is ordered. God has created the world with order, as we find in the creation story and as the psalmist proclaims: "He set the earth on its foundations" (Ps. 104:5). Fifth, it follows that Christian culture is lawful in that a society is governed and ordered by God's law. Sixth, Christian culture is peaceful. These six principles inform our understanding of work, race, and disability.

Work/Vocation

Work is basic to everyday life, and it, too, is spiritual. Vocation is similar to work, but it is more intimate as it is integrated with our contingent identities. Often when people are identified, they are identified by what they give of themselves to projects that influence society in some way. It is important, as these topics are given greater exposure, that some theological reflections on work and vocation are offered. Our work as human beings is creational and covenantal, theistic, trinitarian, and pneumatological. We will explore each of these in turn.

Creational and Covenantal

Each individual has value and meaning in the creational context, where God has created all human beings as his image bearers. The creational and covenantal context manifests and presupposes that all humans are valuable and dignified (see, e.g., Gen. 9:6). The literature on the image of God and ethics has securely established this precedent, and it has become normative in evangelical literature that humans are dignified agents responsible for their own actions.

It is also true that we are communal agents designed for covenantal community, as exemplified in Genesis 1:26–28, with its emphasis not on one human agent but on humanity as a whole. Additional evidence in the same passage for the covenantal, communal nature of the *imago Dei* is expressed in the fact that we are created to represent the community of heaven ("Let us make mankind in our image"). Buttressed by later revelation, in Genesis 5, where humans are described as part of a royal lineage, human beings are covenantal images that share in this broader royal community that is transmitted from generation to generation through the covenants. We need one another to fulfill the creation mandate because, among other reasons, individuals are unable to procreate alone. And from this one relationship between a man and a woman, other relationships ensue (e.g., father-mother, parent-child, wider family, community, society, nation).[2]

These covenantal relationships establish a pattern for life, a life cycle. From the most basic community of husband and wife with God, to children, to a larger family, and finally to a community, these relational structures are fundamental to our humanity. We exist as created covenantal beings, we give birth to new life (that God has blessed, consistent with Gen. 1), we create community, and we die. These patterns characterize basic creaturely existence on earth.

That is not the end of the human story. We were created for something more, but that "something" is only signaled in the Old Testament story. As God the Father "breathes" life into human bodies (Gen. 2:7), that same "breath" that makes humans whole living beings is designed to return to the Father who gave it (Eccles. 12:7). No doubt the Old Testament pattern of human community beginning with creation and procreation and leading to death (at least somatic death) is firmly entrenched in the Hebrew mind. A view that takes into account a larger story of the afterlife and communion with a trinitarian God who exists in heaven becomes plain only when we come to the New Testament and the early church. In the new-covenant community we find continuity with the old-covenant community, specifically the creational covenant. Human dignity, value, responsibility, life, blessing, and the cycle of

2. For a resource developing the relationship of body to personhood and a foundation for a theology of community, see John Paul II, *Man and Woman He Created Them*. In this work, John Paul II develops a philosophy of personalism that is deeply embodied.

life are not somehow undermined and expelled in the new covenant, but rather they are expanded and clarified, even transfigured. Human life is expanded and clarified by the redemptive community.

Our vocation is specifically located in a covenantal context of caring for the world and producing a royal dynasty, and it is carried out in community.[3] In this way, it is both bodily and soulish.[4]

Theistic

Our vocation, our work, and our culture are characterized by monotheism. Consistent with our confession of Deuteronomy 6:4 ("the LORD our God, the LORD is one"), all of life is unified by the one true God who enters into covenantal relationship with his creatures. Thus, our vocation and work are characterized by monarchy, but not just any monarchy; rather, the monarchy is a singular kingdom under the authority of Christ on the throne that is characterized by perfect order, love, and joy under the authority of God the Son as King. God functions as the King of the universe, and we exist as servants in his kingdom.

Trinitarian

In classical Reformed theology, as well as in Lutheran theology, there is a tendency to talk about our vocation and work in the context of the creation and in the context of the natural kingdom. Often "work" is described not as an end itself but as an instrumental means to some other end. And this natural work contrasts our work in the context of redemption, explicitly, or in the new-covenant kingdom.[5] While not inconsistent, these two ways of approaching vocation provide contexts for exploring the topics involved. More recently, there have been attempts to address work/vocation in the redemptive context in which we find ourselves. More to the point, our work/vocation is described in a trinitarian and pneumatological context. How is it that the Trinity and the Spirit shape and form our work now, and how does this relate to that which is to come: the new heavens and new earth? These broad questions frame the present discussion, and how one answers these questions will impinge on the anthropocentric questions—that is, who we are in relation to one another and why we exist.

3. For a helpful collection that helps motivate many of the discussions surrounding vocation and work, see Loftin and Dimsdale, *Work*.
4. For a chapter that explores the bodily and soulish dimensions of work, see Richards, "Be Fruitful and Multiply."
5. See Cosden, *A Theology of Work*; Cosden, *The Heavenly Good of Earthly Work*.

Theologian Miroslav Volf gives us some footing for thinking about work in the context of the new creation brought about by God the Father, Son, and Holy Spirit: "When the ascended Christ gave the Spirit," the Spirit was released into the world. "The Spirit of the new creation cannot be tied to the 'inner man.' Because the whole creation is the Spirit's sphere of operation, the Spirit is not only the Spirit of religious experience but also the Spirit of worldly engagement. For this reason it is not at all strange to connect the Spirit of God with mundane work."[6] With Volf's emphasis on the new kingdom found in redemption, it is the Spirit that infuses all aspects of life, including one's work. What is unique about Volf's theology of work is that he situates that which was once thought of as situated primarily in the natural or creational kingdom in the redemptive kingdom with the infusion of life by the Spirit.

In the Christian life, another kingdom is added as an outgrowth within the natural kingdom. You might think of this kingdom like a flower that begins to grow in the fertile ground of an old tree bed. There is nothing particularly wrong with the tree bed (even if the tree that was once there in full force is now dead and most of the wood is now rotten), but there is something new that grows in the same bed that carried an old, now dying, tree.[7] The new emergent product is a beautiful, sweet-smelling flower. The kingdom of God is something like this flower, emerging within the natural kingdom that throughout human history has moved in multiple directions, in many cases bad directions. The flower emerges within a dead old tree. For the purposes of this discussion, I do not wish to delve deeply into the "two kingdoms, one kingdom" discussions concerning the Christian life and politics. However, I do want to recognize that in some minimalist sense, there are two kingdoms. To the extent that they overlap, there may be some sense in which Christians could argue for one kingdom that emerges within an older kingdom by showing the natural relationship between the two and the superiority of the latter.

For a potentially better analogy for the new-covenant kingdom (i.e., the kingdom of God), let us consider the natural kingdom as transformed by the kingdom of God. Consider the use of a tree spade, where the spade digs down deep into the roots of a tree and uproots it from its context by winnowing away the bad

6. Volf, *Work in the Spirit*, 104.
7. This will depend on several important biblical-theological commitments. For one commitment, it depends on how much continuity is seen between the Old Testament and the New Testament and how the covenants of each are related. Are the covenants, as I have assumed, building on the previous covenants progressively and thereby reaffirming the previous covenants and the good of each covenant yet improving upon them, or are the covenants that follow largely disparate, which subvert or replace the older covenants?

soil. Then the tree is transferred to a bed of new fertile soil. The tree is analogous to the human transferred from one kingdom to another kingdom (Col. 1:13).

Whether you endorse a one-kingdom or a two-kingdoms theology, one thing is for sure. The Christian is looking at present toward the kingdom of God and its full manifesting power. The Christian is not satisfied with the natural kingdom, or the kingdom of humans, but instead looks forward to the presence of the Father, Son, and Holy Spirit.

In our desire for God's presence, the redemptive community is marked by the conjoining of heaven and earth in the incarnation. No doubt the death and resurrection of Christ are central and defining events in the Christian life, but the picture of redemption's effects is seen in the Logos's union with human nature. It is here that humans take on a new life sent forth by the Father and imparted by the Holy Spirit. As the Nicene Creed reflects, it is the Father's sending of the Son and the life-giving power of the Spirit that make the human alive to the things of heaven. In the redeemed community (i.e., the church) we experience not merely a reconciliation and restoration of the old fallen life but, more importantly, a transformation by virtue of the union of the human to the divine. We now experience and are affected by the trinitarian God, who makes himself known centrally in the person and work of Christ.

Christians cannot live the life intended on their own. What is clear from the new covenant is that our capacity, our identity, and our purpose are wrapped up in the new community. The new community provides for us the necessary causal conditions that shape our heavenly identity, grant us access to the throne of God, and give us the purpose of engaging with the divine Trinity in a personal encounter.

The new community is characterized by three unique practices: baptism, the Lord's Supper, and the ministry of the word (through preaching and teaching). All three activities reflect the union of the two-natured Christ. Baptism signals and seals death to the old life and resurrected new life in the Spirit (Rom. 6:4). In the Lord's Supper we experience a new meal, continuous in many ways with the meals we eat on a daily basis, in which we partake in a new life. The ministry of the word is a proclamation of the realities of heavenly life that we have now and a pointing to the realities of our presence with the Father, Son, and Holy Spirit in the future. And all of this furnishes fertile soil, not merely for the end of which our work anticipates, but for a renewal of our work in the present age.

Pneumatological

Taking a trinitarian theology further, we give attention to the Holy Spirit's role in our work. Miroslav Volf helps us begin to understand the nature of the Holy Spirit's function in our work. Volf describes different models and shows the benefits of the interaction model of charism and calling, which brings together creation and redemption for the purposes of understanding our vocations. In this context, he advances a model for thinking about the relationship between the creational (particularly the capacities at creation) and redemptive aspects of work, when he says that, according to the interactional model,

> a person who is shaped by her genetic heritage and social interaction faces the challenge of a new situation as she lives in the presence of God and learns to respond to it in a new way. This is what it means to acquire a new spiritual gift. No substance or quality has been added to her, but a more or less permanent skill has been learned. We can determine the relationship between calling and charisma in the following way: the general calling to enter the kingdom of God and to live in accordance with this kingdom that comes to a person through the preaching of the gospel becomes for the believer a call to bear the fruit of the Spirit, which should characterize all Christians, and, as they are placed in various situations, the calling to live in accordance with the kingdom branches out in the multiple gifts of the Spirit to each individual.[8]

There is something about the nature of our vocation that is transformed by the Holy Spirit's impartation of the divine life. Theologian T. F. Torrance has discussed this subject in the context of vocation and anthropology. It is worth our time to survey some of his thoughts.

Torrance has rightly pointed out that humans are social/relational beings. As such, in both creation and redemption, humans depend on other humans to fulfill their purpose and calling. Relations become causally necessary for human beings to actualize the potential that they have and to function in the manner in which God has called them to function. While it may be difficult to see and understand human transformation in particular social contexts, the social contexts are necessary for human transformation. This in no way undermines the need for created capacities as part and parcel of the redemptive transformation, because these are functionally necessary for the change to occur. Relations necessarily require relata (i.e., that which stands under relations and upholds them—namely, particular concrete things) and do not exist apart from relata. In other words, we need substance. Excising substance is destructive to the whole project of Christian theology because it undermines the explanation for the relational structures present in Christian thought. Christian theology presupposes substantial ontology.

8. Volf, "Work as Cooperation with God," 100–101.

What does the Spirit do to transform our work? Myk Habets and Peter McGhee offer some explanation: "The work of Christ and the Spirit does not override humanity but recreates, reaffirms, and enables one to stand before God as his beloved child. Accordingly, in accepting the truth of Jesus Christ, we become more human not less; our lives, and therefore our labour, take on new meaning and importance as we participate in God's divine love and plan for creation. Here we might say we require not only a theology of work but a theology of workers."[9] In other words, there is a harmony between creation and redemption in our work, as rooted in the creation, which is not replaced or overridden by God's work in the kingdom of the new covenant. Instead, our work, in its multiple expressions, is reaffirmed and energized by the work of the Holy Spirit.

Humans can work in several diverse contexts in order to fulfill their calling. It does not require one particular context neatly fitted for each individual, as Volf has insightfully pointed out.[10] No doubt there are tensions in what theologians have called "external vocations" and "internal vocations." Let me offer some analytic clarification on these terms. "External vocation" refers to our jobs that we publicly devote our time to in order to earn a living. "Internal vocation" is a term for the set of religious values, or ultimate philosophical ideals, that we hold to be true and reflective of our purpose. When the two callings are in deep tension, it could lead to a kind of schizophrenia or the elevation of work over religion.[11] When work consumes one's thoughts, motivations, time, and energy, work inevitably becomes religion.

We are "priests of creation" and "mediators of order," according to Habets and McGhee.[12] Scott Harrower describes our creational and redemptional role in similar terms: "vice-regents."[13] One of our purposes as stewards of the earth is to represent God to creation. In part, this means directing humans and the rest of creation to their goal by way of upholding their value. Again, a theology of work finds its blueprint in the creation narrative of Genesis, which is not overtaken by the work of the new covenant but, instead, is reaffirmed; Christians are energized by the Holy Spirit to perform with excellence, and there may be a sense in which our work in this life is given a purpose that finds expression only in the next life.

Romanian Orthodox theologian Dumitru Staniloae describes our work, or workers in relation to God's work. He prefers to describe men and women

9. Habets and McGhee, "TGIF!," 35.
10. Volf, *Work in the Spirit*.
11. Jensen, *Responsive Labor*.
12. Habets and McGhee, "TGIF!," 34.
13. Harrower, "Christian Vocation," 225.

as creation's "master" (Greek, *archōn*), its created "cocreator," "coworker," or "continuator." Staniloae considers the world as God's gift to humanity in order that humanity may gift it back to God. In this way, argues Staniloae, the sacrifice offered to God by men and women is a Eucharist, making every person a priest of God for the world. The language of Eucharist reminds us of priestly duty, specifically the priestly duty of humanity to represent the world to God. Such is a vision for a rightly ordered concept of work; it is priestly labor, freely offered to God.[14] In the hands of Torrance, the concept of the priest of creation captures what he means by the image of God being a calling. As creation's priest, humans exist to "assist the creation as a whole to realize and evidence its rational order and beauty and thus to express God."[15] Torrance is clear that our work as divine representatives, priests, and cocreators is to help lead others in their work and in our own work to see its rational order as it is connected to God's creation.

Unfortunately, our vocation is often met with boredom or with the desire to satiate some idolatry—wealth or power. We often find ourselves unmotivated to work. We lack the energy to put in the best work we can. That said, when we understand and experience the vocation-transforming work of the Spirit, we have a new vitality for work. Volf states that a person, through his or her work,

> can destroy either human or natural life and hence contradict the reality of the new creation, which preserves the old creation in transfigured form. The circumstance that the gifts and energies that the Spirit gives can be used against the will of the Spirit results from the Spirit's condescension in history: by giving life to the creation, the Spirit imparts to the creation the power for independence from the Spirit's prompting. Because the Spirit creates human beings as free agents, work in the power of the Spirit can be done not only in accordance with but also in contradiction to the will of the Spirit; it can be performed not only in cooperation with the Holy Spirit who transforms the creation in anticipation of the glorious new creation, but also in collaboration with that Unholy Spirit who strives to ravage it.[16]

In a real sense, we are the stewards that bring the rest of creation to God by bringing rational order to the creation. As rational creatures with a first-person perspective, we have the capacity and the charge (from God) to order the world appropriately as we represent divinity to creation and we represent

14. Staniloae, *The Experience of God*, vol. 2.
15. Torrance, *The Christian Doctrine of God*, 213.
16. Volf, *Work in the Spirit*, 122.

creatures to God. We do so through our physical labor and through casting a vision for the rest of creation.[17]

Again, there is not a division between our created purpose and our redeemed purpose. The redemption enlivens and sheds light on creation. While distinct, there is a deep harmony between creation and redemption. This is true of our jobs on earth and our religious commitments. The two, when ordered correctly, for the most part work harmoniously.

As beings uniquely created in the image of God, humanity occupies an exclusive place on the boundary between the natural and the supernatural. As priests of creation, humanity has the function and privilege to assist the creation to realize and evidence its rational order and beauty and thus to express God's beauty and being back to God.[18]

It is possible to take an anthropocentric view, a solely pneumatological view, or a trinitarian view on individual giftedness. The anthropocentric view is that taken by Gordon T. Smith, who argues that people have a birth vocation that is inherent to them particularly. Smith argues that people have a lifelong vocation that does not change. A practical outworking of this is his view that vocation probably cannot be truly discerned until a person is in his or her mid-thirties. Fred Sanders's theology as a whole is a helpful corrective to the anthropocentric view. He writes, "A Christian, especially . . . is somebody who is already immersed in the reality of the Trinity, long before beginning to reflect on the idea of the Trinity."[19] Thus, Sanders lays the basis for a corrective to the anthropocentric view for two reasons. First, Christians do not live in a reality that can be a priori considered apart from God's particular gifts. Second, each Christian vocation must be addressed in light of God's desires for the church and the world.[20]

For the Reformers, grace and the divine gift of life and blessing in the new covenant are the means by which humans flourish in culture and in their vocations. Because we are dependent beings, we need one another. Relatedly, the diversity of ethnicities sheds light on how we are to understand the creational intentions for humanity. This also includes those who are disabled. While

17. See Habets, *Theosis*. Habets links the notion of work and theosis (45). It is often the case that theological developments of work and vocation lack a robust ontological system and a value system. Andrew J. Spencer points this out in "The Inherent Value of Work." He helpfully describes the distinction between intrinsic and inherent value as applied to the discussion on vocation, following C. S. Lewis. Dorothy Sayers, in *The Mind of the Maker*, 21–31, certainly has something to say with respect to the value system undergirding our work when she describes the value of the product. For one recent article, see W. Harrison, "Loving the Creation."

18. Habets and McGhee, "TGIF!," 39.

19. Sanders, *The Deep Things of God*, 26.

20. Harrower, "Christian Vocation," 8. See also Sanders, *The Deep Things of God*, 171.

people who are disabled are not able to actualize their full bodily potential as human beings, at least not in this life, they serve to show us, in a deep way, our need for one another. People with disabilities also show us that life is a gift from God, which excludes pride and boasting. When we understand our culture and our vocations in this gift-giving context, we are most free.[21]

It is important to note that human work in this life is not the final end or purpose of humanity. Given the time we spend at work and in our vocations, work is important to our purpose. It is not insignificant. While some have chosen to discuss vocation in the context of human destiny, I have chosen to discuss it in its creational and redemptive contexts because both provide information on the nature of our vocation and contribute to human destiny.[22] One of the themes, especially in our modern contexts, concerning the value of work (and the workers) is diversity, which leads to another important aspect of a theology of culture: diversity of peoples in terms of ethnicity and race.

Race

We have already noted that humans are created in the image of God. What this means, in part, is that humans are dignified (see Gen. 1:26–28; 9:6). We have also shown that humans are intended to develop as human beings in light of Christ; that is, christological formation is in order (see Rom. 8:29; 1 Cor. 15:49; 2 Cor. 3:18; Col. 3:10). These aspects of human identity and purpose serve as the foundation for thinking about groups of humans, including different races.

Most scholars concur that race is a modern phenomenon. The discussion emerges in the context of growing biological discussions on the origins of people groups (e.g., monogenesis [of the same source or biological origin] and polygenesis [of different sources and biological origins]) along with the philosophical attention given to common characteristics, dispositions, and values ascribed to broad ethnic groupings based on the tone or color of skin and rooted in heredity. It is commonly argued that the older view of race is one of naturalistic bent, where humans are grouped according to a biologically essential category. These categories of people share similar attributes and characteristics that are perceived to have given rise to particular distinctions, which in the modern period led, in some cases, to racism (i.e., the

21. For a treatment of how freedom and vocation are related, see O'Callaghan, "Luther and 'Sola Gratia.'"
22. See Schwarz, *The Human Being*, 344–54.

undervaluing and mistreatment of particular broad groups of people, which was often triggered by the tone or color of their skin).[23]

In the Reformed heritage, especially in Europe and the US, there is a long and complicated history concerning race, racism, and slavery. While slavery was and has been a near universal feature of societies throughout history, it is arguable that slavery in the West took on a particularly racial character and impacted the anthropological discussions in profound ways. Historically, and the Reformed heritage is not unique in this way, people groups, nations, and ethnic boundaries have been the starting points for evaluating individuals in terms of values, ideals, and dispositions. At times, the Reformed heritage has been marked with a particular kind of injustice toward certain people groups. Unfortunately, theological justification for race-based slavery has, arguably, been a common value from Reformed theologians. Reformed theologian Charles Hodge has been highlighted as particularly noteworthy in this respect, given his justification for slavery as an institution of the natural order; he argued for the gradual freedom of slaves (which is an improvement on some who argued for no emancipation of slaves whatsoever), rather than an immediate freeing of all slaves, for the sake of society's structure and for the sake of the stability of churches.[24] But, in order to get a handle on the practical and theological implications for anthropology, one needs to clarify the notion of race and racism, which is not a simple task given the state of the literature.

Race is related to our bodily life, as I intimate below, because it is a social concept that has some relationship to biology and culture. Race reflects ethnicity, culture, and customs that are deeply cherished. Furthermore, a conception of race has implications for nation building and politics. In what follows, I will merely sketch some of the theories regarding race.

Race has become an important concept in theological discourse as well as our everyday discourse. One of the questions deserving our attention is this: To what extent should "race" function in theological discourse? There are three broad answers to this question. First, some are eliminativists in that they endorse the idea that race should be discarded as a concept in discourse. Some eliminativists opt for color-blindness because it averts any of the discriminatory results of identifying different groups of humans.[25] Second, some are conservationists, arguing that we should retain concepts about racial distinctions. For one reason or another, the notion of race is important to

23. For a helpful summary, see James, "Race."
24. For a helpful article, see Wallace, "The Defense of the Forgotten Center."
25. For one challenge to this view, see Alexander, *The New Jim Crow*.

upholding the dignity of all human beings in their diversity. Third, some opt for revisionism, which is the view that we should think about race as a social concept rather than a biological concept.[26]

Other questions that will affect how we answer the question above are these: Is "race" a real feature of human beings? If it is a real feature or property of human beings, then how do we account for it as such? There are several answers to these questions that require some analytic clarity, which will help theologians think more carefully about how it is that race functions in our understanding of humanity.

The broad categories for thinking about race are realism and antirealism. Realism is the view that race has some ontological status in that it exists independently from our thinking about it and our subjective proclivities. Antirealism states that race is not real or that it is an illusion.

One realist approach maintains that race is a biological reality. According to this view, there are several different ways of understanding race as a biological reality. One is that humans are distinctly classified merely in virtue of their skin color—a rather shallow understanding. Another is the genetic approach, which defenders argue relies on the fact that races are not only biologically rooted but each race, and all the various dispositions, is rooted in some traceable gene(s). Another view is that race is a category for genetic distinctions within humankind. Finally, another theory is that there are genealogical populations that might account for similarities within clusters of breeding groups and distinctions with other genealogical pools.[27]

Another question within the realist discussion has to do with essentialism. Are individual humans essentially one particular race? Am I essentially white or black, or are these properties of race predicated contingently? There have been numerous challenges to a biological or naturalist essentialism as a ground for race, but there remains some arguable yet loose connection to particular ethnic groups and shared similarities across genealogical populations.[28]

A second realist approach sees race as a construction. It is a social construction of human making. This does not eliminate race or make it an illusion but instead requires the fact that the notion of race represents a thick cluster of relevant cultural resemblances that are grounded in societies. It might be oversimplified to describe race as cultures because that would tie together

26. Glasgow, *A Theory of Race*, 1–3.
27. For a discussion of these positions along with some of the variations of the genealogical view, see Mallon, "Passing, Traveling and Reality"; Mallon, "'Race': Normative, Not Metaphysical or Semantic"; Mallon, "A Field Guide to Social Construction."
28. See Zack, *Race and Mixed Race*. Also see Zack, *Philosophy of Science and Race*; Zack, *The Ethics and Mores of Race*; Zack, *White Privilege and Black Rights*.

culture, subculture, ethnicity, and some feature of human groups that encompass more than cultural distinctions.[29]

Several implications follow from how we understand race. I will mention only a few in this context. First, if race is primarily a biological reality and, further, that biological reality is an essential property of specific groups of humans, then it would seem to follow that some specific groups bear essential marks that are consistent with biological and genetic realities, which has been a sore subject of discussion as it concerns the putative biological advantages or disadvantages of various races. This is accommodated if we take it that humans are essentially souls that have contingent relations to their biology, and the value or dignity due to specific groups is not dependent on a sliding-scale property reflected by intellectual, physical, and volitional capacities. By moving race to a contingent property, we are not setting it aside as somehow unimportant.[30] Second, if we are eliminativists with respect to race, then we take it that race language should not be incorporated into our discourse. This has one obvious downside: it tends to downplay the value that various ethnicities and races bring to the table of human flourishing—that is, the significance in the diversity of humanity. This certainly leads to some sort of conservationism of race language in our theological discourse, because we desire to give some sort of accounting of difference as it helps us see God's intentions for humanity at creation and in redemption.

The fact is that God created a rich diversity of people who share, universally and generally, in humanity. Furthermore, this diversity has some role to play in God's redemptive plan for the church, where various expressions of worship, languages, customs, and rituals will contribute to the lively interaction of humans in the new kingdom. Some element of revisionism is necessary if we take it that throughout most parts of the world in history the value and honor of specific people groups have been denigrated or violated. If this is a tendency throughout most of the world (e.g., in most of the world, enslavement of people groups has been commonplace), then there are, arguably, long-standing and ingrained habits and dispositions in human history toward racism (i.e., the intellectual and affective disposition to view and treat some ethnicities or groups of people as essentially inferior in their value or dignity).

29. For some theological implications, see Jennings, *The Christian Imagination*; Carter, *Race*; Sowell, *Black Rednecks and White Liberals*.

30. I can conceive of my having been born in a different ethnicity or race, which would yield the fact that race is contingent and not essential to who I am as an individual human being. I can conceive of a possible world where I was Middle Eastern, but I have a harder time conceiving of my being female. The latter may be harder not because it is essential, though, but because it is a more deeply ingrained feature or property that stamps itself on the structure of my soul.

A mixture of views seems to be the best way to think about race: bringing together aspects of race as a biological reality that is tied to a social-constructive reality. While I am not convinced that race is purely a social-constructive reality, I do think that how we commonly think of particular ethnicities (e.g., Africans, Asians) is shaped and formed by social customs both inside one's particular ethnic context and from an external vantage point looking into an ethnic context. Instead, these social realities do seem to be tied loosely to biological, genetic, and environmental conditions, and so excising the biological component altogether is unrealistic.

Beyond defining the notion of race, and by extension racism, there are a set of important anthropological questions that deserve the attention of philosophical and systematic theologians. Moving forward in our contemporary context, it is important that theologians treat the subject of race and ethnicity not only from a philosophical perspective but also from a theology of creation and redemption. How should we conceive of different races in the creational order, and how does this relate to the redemptive order? As a matter of justice or injustice, what ought to be done ethically to justly treat other races and ethnicities fairly? Does the justice issue require reparations for past sins, and on what basis? Further, in an ecclesial context, does the church have a responsibility to engage in social and political justice? Is social and political justice an extension of the church's, or an individual church's, responsibility? Rather, is it an extension of the gospel mission for churches? In the redemptive order, it is arguable that in a local context, the sins of one's particular culture and history should find some redemptive measures in the context of the church, but the depth and extent is a matter of more specific attention. Finally, should churches seek to become racially diverse communities based on the eschatological reality that the new heaven and new earth will be diverse (e.g., Rev. 7:9)?

Disability

Another topic relevant to culture and work is disability. Often descriptions of people with disabilities in Scripture are implicitly unfavorable toward the state of being disabled. In one case in the Gospels, Christ heals a blind man so that he can see once again (Mark 8:22–25). In another case, a man is unable to walk, and Christ heals the man so that he can walk (John 5:1–9). In both of these cases, the state of completion or wholeness is presupposed as desirable or, at least, preferable to the state of being disabled. And part of Christ's kingdom work is redeeming what is lost. Arguably, this is one sign of what it will be like in heaven.

In our contemporary culture, it is not clear that there is a higher ratio of people with disabilities compared to the past, but disability has become a feature that impresses itself on our consciousness more clearly. In part, this is because we now discern a greater number of distinct kinds of disabilities. And discussions about the nature of people with disabilities emerge in the context of social policy, politics, work environment, and everyday common courtesy. But two theological topics come to the fore in the discussion concerning those who are disabled. First, what is the role of people with disabilities in the kingdom of God now and in the future? Second, what will it be like in heaven for those who have disabilities? I will briefly sketch two answers to the second question because how we answer the second question will give us some insight into the first question.

There are, broadly speaking, two models for thinking about disabled people in heaven. The first one might be called the Aristotelian model, and the second one I will call the alternative model. On the first model, it is assumed that all or nearly all disabilities are by their nature undesirable states and are not preferable to the state of being capable to perform a task that otherwise the individual cannot. This is so because, on an Aristotelian model, parts function in light of the whole substance. Parts have a certain telos, and when they achieve that telos, they are said to perform the function for which they are designed. To lack the ability to perform tasks otherwise teleologically intrinsic to the part in question is tantamount to a malfunctioning part, in which the person cannot achieve the part's purpose. Presumably, as in the biblical cases above, it would be better, in principle, to obtain those abilities (seeing and walking) if the option were available. Furthermore, it seems that, all things considered, one's life would be more fulfilling if one were to have the power to utilize the respective part to achieve its function.

On the alternative model, one might conceive of things in a different way. Some have claimed that on the one hand there is a sense in which they would like to have their disability disappear, but on the other hand they cannot imagine life without their disability. In other words, their disability has become so normal to their way of life that to live otherwise would be unthinkable. It has, one might say, become a part of their narrative identity. Another claim is that some disabilities do not detract from happiness and that in fact the happiness of the people who are disabled is on par with those who, perceivably, lack a disability.

To answer the questions earlier, we do have reason to think that humans with disabilities are part and parcel of the redemptive order. Given the fact that Christ redeems those in need and those who are incapable of accessing God's redemptive blessing apart from God's grace in Christ, we have a paradigm for thinking about specific instances of humans with disabilities in the kingdom. And we have concrete cases where Christ heals those with what would be considered disabilities—the lame, the mute, and the deaf—and this is characteristic of Christ's kingdom (e.g., Matt. 9:27–33; 12:22; 21:14; Mark 7:31–37; Luke 7:21–22; 14:13–14; cf. Isa. 42:16; Gen. 25:21; Exod. 23:25–26; Mic. 4:6–7).

A great deal more discussion is necessary to flesh out each model. For now, I set this out so that readers might find some traction in the present anthropological discussions that are brewing in the literature.

Culture, work, race, and disability tell us much about our narrative identities. They represent our life as bodily and soulish, and in many ways they give us insight into an understanding of who we are in relation to one another. They reveal something about our purpose in life, and they may unveil something about the nature of what is to come.

The differences of work, race, and disability in a variety of cultures serve two clear theological purposes. From the perspective of "hearing" God, different cultures, arguably, grant us epistemic access to the diversity within God's creative and redemptive purposes, but also the creational diversity of humans reveals something about the goodness of God that is otherwise hidden or disguised in one's own culture. From the perspective of "seeing" God, since God reveals himself through his image bearers, each individual person and, to varying degrees, each individual culture points in some way to who God is and to God's polyphonic plan for the redeemed world.

8

Who Are We as Male and Female?

Humans as Gendered and Sexual

He created them male and female and blessed them. And he named them
"Mankind" when they were created.

Genesis 5:2

Marriage is to be between one man and one woman: neither is it lawful
for any man to have more than one wife, nor for any woman to have
more than one husband, at the same time.

The Westminster Confession of Faith, "On Marriage and Divorce"

The Genderbread Person is an educational tool that gives us a picture
of the complicated issues involved in parsing out sexuality.[1] The
picture represents different items that intersect on the questions of
sex and gender. According to the picture, there is a distinction between sex
(associated with the anatomical parts of our biology), gender (associated
with our brain), expression (associated with the whole body), and attraction or sexual orientation (associated with the heart). To this point, I take

1. "The Genderbread Person," https://www.genderbread.org.

it that "expression" and "attraction" are both dispositions that are tied to something: a substance with a common nature. In other words, I have to this point assumed that there is something of what it means to be human. And I have argued that humans are soul-body compounds. With that said, I will limit myself to giving some description to sexuality and gender. In what follows, I argue that gender is unavoidably tied to biological sex, and while biological sex is fairly stable, gender is either an essential property of the soul that is discernable only via biological sex or gender is an essential property of the body (and human nature) that is a common, albeit an important, property of the soul.

Taking my cues from a theological description of sexual orientation and gender, I begin, as I did with all the topics previously, with the various theological authorities (Scripture as the norming norm, tradition, reason, and experience). Where to begin is difficult, but begin we must. The challenge is that there is no creedal statement that clearly adjudicates for us a metaphysic or theology of sex and gender. In part, this has to do with the fact that until recent history, the tie between gender and sexuality was fairly well connected as a fixed and permanent feature of the human race.

Let me offer some workable descriptions of the terms. While there is no agreed upon definition of the term *gender*, the term *sex* is a descriptive term of biology.[2] The term *gender* is often loosely used in reference of human identity to perceptions of masculinity and femininity that are based, at least in part, on social constructions.[3] Gender is also, in part, based on sexual identity, and for two reasons. First, social constructions, while contingent, give us no reason to designate any sufficient specific content to gender without some other criterion. Second, *gender*, if it is a term for social behavior, is rooted in biological reality. If gender is a purely social construction, then it is unclear why we should assign any fixedness to a person's being either male or female. However, if gender is partly rooted in and explained by biological sex as a manifestation of it, then we have grounds to designate a soul as either male or female. But, if one prefers to use the term *sexual identity* rather than *gender identity*, then in what follows one may feel free to read gender as meaning sexual identity—so long as sexual identity is not taken in a strictly biological reductive sense. I use the terms *gender* and

2. To get a sense of some of the complexity in contemporary Christian theology that is fairly uninformative but offers some insight into the overlapping issues and questions relevant to gender identity, sexual identity, and sexuality, see Toth, "Gender." For a complex set of essays on a variety of subjects concerning sex and sanctification, see Walls, Neill, and Baggett, *Venus and Virtue*.
3. For a masterful historical treatment, see vol. 2 of P. Allen, *The Concept of Woman*.

sexual identity somewhat interchangeably, and I think that there is good reason for doing so. Sexual identity has implications for certain kinds of behaviors and ways of our relating to one another that are essential to what it means to be human. And, when we consider the traditional data along with the scriptural data, we see a close tie between gender and sexual identity. To avoid being charged with anachronism, let me simply state that the term *sexual identity* does all or most of the work we need for thinking about these social realities.

Here is the basic structure of the chapter. I will show: (1) gender (as social expression or behavior) is not reducible to either a social construction or a preference but rather is dependent on biological sex; (2) the "one-flesh" union of the complementary sexes is a necessary condition for God's giving of life and blessing that life through the covenants; (3) one necessary condition is the assumed productive function of the complementary sexes, hence "kinship" is insufficient as a condition; (4) this kind of union yields a permanent, holistic, and comprehensive union; (5) biblical law, reflecting natural law, puts parameters on the expression of sex in a way that guards the "one-flesh" union from violation. By surveying some of the traditional and scriptural data, I will be giving some description of gender and sexuality, which I see as mutually informing. That said, I offer two models of gender (i.e., sexual identity). With my use of substance dualism ontology, I will lay out a Thomistic model and a Nyssa model in the later part of the chapter in the section titled "Two Models of Sex and Gender." From here, I will spell out several implications and raise additional questions that I am unable to address due to space constraints.

Unsettling Contemporary Assumptions about Gender and Sexuality

Invoking scientific authority is often tantamount to playing a trump card. When it happens, you can hear the pin drop in the room. Regardless of whether the arguments are sound and worthwhile, if the argument resonates as true in present company, then it follows that it must be true, or at least that is the perception. Something like this is the case with popular assumptions about the nature of gender and sexuality. There is a growing sense that a set of interrelated assumptions actually undermine the traditional consensus about gender and sexuality. But is this the case? Have traditional views been unsettled by scientific consensus on gender and sexuality? In short, my answer is no to the assumption that the scientific consensus, if there is one, has undermined traditional understandings of gender and sex. For the sake of space, we will consider one popular assumption that, if true, has the potential to undermine the essentiality of gender binary in human nature and expand gender options as well as provide a foundation for reconceiving sexuality.

One common assumption is that biology is, strictly speaking, nondeterminative of who we are by nature because biology is insufficient to ground gender or biology complicates the gender binary. Biologically, various conditions make one either male or female, or so it is assumed traditionally. First, there is "chromosomal sex," which is the notion that one's genetics, one's chromosomes, determine sex. Second, there is "gonadal sex," which is the notion that one's chromosomes, at the most fundamental biological level, determine the development of testes (sexual organs determinative of being male) and ovaries (sexual organs often associated with being female) and that it is these structures that determine sex. Third, there is "fetal hormonal sex." This refers to the dominant hormone, either estrogen (for female) or testosterone (for male), that is developed in the womb. These factors are crucial to later stages of development of the organs in the fetus and later on during the development of hormones in puberty. By using "determinative," I am not intending to convey that all future outcomes, choices, or possibilities are determined but rather that these are determinative conditions that give some description of human nature and, in this case, human gender. In fact, there are several studies that show a strong link between our biological sex and our gender behavior.[4] Based on the biological conditions listed here (chro-

---

4. Udry, "Biological Limits of Gender Construction." Though complex and nondeterminative for social behaviors, the biological data show a strong link between biology and gender behaviors. Furthermore, much of the data can be favorably accounted for from a traditionalist binary view of gender. See Geffen, "The Genetics of Sex Differences." There certainly is a popular assumption that gender (as a sociocultural construct) has no connection to biological identity and that gender is completely malleable, but this is not supported by science, nor is there any good philosophical or theological reason for accepting the claim. It may be true that our sexual desires are malleable to some extent, but this is distinct from gender behavior. See Cohen-Bendahan, van de Beek, and Berenbaum, "Prenatal Sex Hormone Effects." Marc Cortez states, "Drawing on biology, psychology, and theology, essentialists present a convincing case that sexuality is fundamental to human nature and identity and is not simply some 'extra' factor added onto a more fundamental human nature. Essentialism also points us toward the many ways in which sexuality is grounded in the biological givens of life. Despite our Enlightenment emphasis on the self-created and autonomous individual, who can become anything he or she wants? Essentialism forces us to realize that much of who we are results from the bodies with which we are born" (Cortez, *Theological Anthropology*, 55). Note also this observation made by Lawrence Mayer and Paul McHugh: "In summary, the studies presented above show inconclusive evidence and mixed findings regarding the brains of transgender adults. Brain activation patterns in these studies do not offer sufficient evidence for drawing sound conclusions about possible associations between brain activation and sexual identity or arousal. The results are conflicting and confusing. Since the data by Ku and colleagues

mosomal sex, gonadal sex, fetal hormonal sex), in most cases there will be a fact of the matter to an individual's sexual identity. With some exceptions of exceptional ambiguity, constructing a new gender category against traditional consensus seems to apply the logic of inverting the rule for the exception.[5] To make determinative conclusions about the nature of gender and sex, we need to bring God's perspective on the subject.[6] We do that through a consultation of Scripture via the confessing church and with rigorous philosophical tools of clarification.

Traditional Material

There is no dogmatic creedal statement on the nature of sexuality and sexual behavior. However, there are several catholic and Reformed symbols that establish the priority, normativity, and essentiality of the male and female sexual identities as conditions for sexual activity within marriage, which excludes revisionist accounts of gender and sexuality.

---

on brain-activation patterns are not universally associated with a particular sex, it remains unclear whether and to what extent neurobiological findings say anything meaningful about gender identity. It is important to note that regardless of their findings, studies of this kind cannot support any conclusion that individuals come to identify as a gender that does not correspond to their biological sex because of an innate, biological condition of the brain" (Mayer and McHugh, "Part 3: Gender Identity," 102). There is an assumption that the brain and the true self are somehow connected, which is a safe assumption even according to most versions of substantial dualism where the soul or mind is somehow functionally dependent on or, at a minimum, significantly influenced by the brain (and vice versa). Saying this, I realize that on Cartesian dualism, there is a metaphysical possibility that the soul, if souls are gendered, could have inhabited an incompatible body; for example, a woman could be in a male body. However, it's not clear that Cartesian dualism necessitates this state of affairs. In raising this scenario, one must make some substantive assumptions about the fixity of gender and the supposed connection between it and the sexual body. Otherwise, what is the point in claiming that the soul is in the wrong body? For a nontechnical article on the subject, see O'Neil, "What Does the Bible Say?"

5. Mayer and McHugh, "Part 3: Gender Identity," 91, 96–97. While there may be empirical ambiguity, it does not undermine a fact of the matter about sexual identity. However, one could argue that sexual identity should be sharply distinguished from gender identity, such that there is a fact of the matter regarding sexual identity (apparent by the scientific evidence), but this should not be confused with gender identity. Some will treat gender identity like a wax nose that can be manipulated and is wholly a social construction, but as Mayer and McHugh make clear, our sexual identity yields some context about specified traits that are common to being male or female (Mayer and McHugh, "Part 3: Gender Identity," 105). For a thoughtful response to the transgender movement written for a broader audience, see Anderson, *When Harry Became Sally*. In other words, the empirical data for a new category of sex or gender are inconclusive.

6. See Kevin Vanhoozer's reflections on the topic in "A Drama-of-Redemption Model," 191–97.

The *Catechism of the Catholic Church* states,

"The intimate community of life and love which constitutes the married state has been established by the Creator and endowed by him with its own proper laws. . . . God himself is the author of marriage." The vocation to marriage is written in the very nature of man and woman as they came from the hand of the Creator. Marriage is not a purely human institution despite the many variations it may have undergone through the centuries in different cultures, social structures, and spiritual attitudes. These differences should not cause us to forget its common and permanent characteristics. Although the dignity of this institution is not transparent everywhere with the same clarity, some sense of the greatness of the matrimonial union exists in all cultures. "The well-being of the individual person and of both human and Christian society is closely bound up with the healthy state of conjugal and family life."[7]

While the Catholic catechism is not an ecumenical statement for all Christians, it does represent definitive or normative teaching among Christians.[8] In it, there is an understanding of gender and sexuality as tied to marriage. As found in the catechism, marriage depends on the complementarity of the sexes—male and female. This institution is established by God and is not contingent on a human perspective of it but rather undergirds culture, society, and spiritual practices. Central or essential to the description of marriage is the notion of "conjugal" (i.e., think of the *conjoining* of two differing but complementing substances) union of the complementary sexes of male and female. Complementarity of similarity and difference is essential to the core of gender and sexual ethics codified in catholic Christianity and represented in several Reformed symbols.[9]

7. *Catechism of the Catholic Church* 1603, http://www.vatican.va/archive/ccc_css/archive /catechism/p2s2c3a7.htm. The *Catechism* also states, "Homosexuality refers to relations between men or between women who experience an exclusive or predominant sexual attraction toward persons of the same sex. It has taken a great variety of forms through the centuries and in different cultures. Its psychological genesis remains largely unexplained. Basing itself on Sacred Scripture, which presents homosexual acts as acts of grave depravity, tradition has always declared that 'homosexual acts are intrinsically disordered'" (*Catechism of the Catholic Church* 2357, http://www.vatican.va/archive/ENG0015/__P85.HTM).

8. "[Homosexual relations] are contrary to the natural law. They close the sexual act to the gift of life. They do not proceed from a genuine affective and sexual complementarity. Under no circumstances can they be approved" (*Catechism of the Catholic Church* 2357, http://www .vatican.va/archive/ENG0015/__P85.HTM). See Protestant philosopher J. Daryl Charles, *Retrieving the Natural Law*, 109, 194. Instead, as pointed out in my introductory chapter above, the Reformed catholic or catholic Reformed tradition parted with Roman teaching concerning its ecclesiological and soteriological dogmas (e.g., papal teachings and Marian dogmas), not with respect to its broader teachings on ethics.

9. Unfortunately, Eastern Orthodoxy has not developed a definitive theological understanding or a dogmatic statement on sex and gender as we find in catholicism, in the West,

There are two Reformed symbols that I will mention as a sampling of the confessions that support the essentiality and normativity of gender and sexual complementarity. First, the Westminster Confession of Faith states, "Marriage is to be between one man and one woman: neither is it lawful for any man to have more than one wife, nor for any woman to have more than one husband, at the same time."[10] The framers of the Westminster Confession attend to the fact that marriage, as a divinely designed covenantal institution, is between the complementarity of the sexes—male and female. And, as we will see below, this emerges from a theological reading of various key texts of Scripture that hold gender, sexuality, and marriage in a close relationship but also exclude the possibility of an expansive notion of sexuality that is not mutually informed by the binary of male and female within marriage.

In the Second Helvetic Confession, chapter 7, we find the same core teaching: "Moreover, God gave him a wife and blessed them." The confession highlights the "difference" between husband and wife. It also states, in the context of the "image" of God, that God blessed them—both male and female. Echoing the biblical language of Genesis 2:20b–24, it states that God gave a wife to the man, and they were to become one flesh.

In several mainline denominations, revisionism of traditional teaching on gender and sexuality is predicated on the belief that the Scriptures are unclear, or underdetermined, and that the tradition is offering a descriptive rather than prescriptive account.[11] Consider a recent revision of the complementarity of the sexes in the liturgy of marriage.

---

and Roman Catholicism (a forthcoming work by David Bradshaw is titled "Sexual Difference and the Difference It Makes: The Greek Fathers and Their Sources"). There was, however, commonly assumed consensus that essential to humanity is the gender binary of male and female. In several cases, it appears that the Greek fathers saw gender/sex as not an essential property of the soul, but the soul is gendered in virtue of its relation to a sex/gendered body. Souls, then, have a structure to them via the body.

10. The Westminster Confession of Faith, chap. 24. James S. Spiegel has recently discussed what he calls "moral heresy" (i.e., false teaching), conveying the notion that one who affirms, propositionally, some moral action or behavior that falls outside orthodox boundaries is then committed to a heresy. Following Eleonore Stump's definition of heresy simpliciter, Spiegel lays out his definition of moral heresy. He gives the following as a way to assess beliefs of moral behavior that is unacceptable: (1) X constitutes a central claim in W. (2) S claims to embrace W, but rejects X. (3) There is a long-established consensus affirming X by experts in the W tradition. Moral heresy refers to "doxastic error on eternally pivotal (that is, salvation- or damnation-determining) moral matters." Those who claim to be Christians and identify with a Christian view of humanity who go on to deny or reject a clear Christian moral teaching, thereby affirming the opposite, commit moral heresy. Homosexuality makes the list. See Spiegel, "Moral Heresy," 405, 410; drawn from Stump, "Orthodoxy and Heresy," 158. Spiegel lists homosexuality as an act or behavior (i.e., public tacit acceptance, implicit or explicit).

11. For one important instance of this, see Rogers, *Jesus, the Bible, and Homosexuality*.

The United Church of Christ 2012 revision makes allowances for same-sex marriages as acceptable, yet its liturgy retains the language of the marriage as a pointer to (i.e., at a minimum, a pedagogy to) Christ and his bride.[12] The challenge here is that the richness of the complementarity of the sexes is lost as a parallel or type for Christ and his bride, a theme eagerly picked up in Scripture and in the wider tradition. In the Episcopal Church, the 2015 addition to the Book of Common Prayer revises the language by replacing male-female complementarity with gender-neutral language, thereby losing the Christ-bride parallel.[13] In addition to the parallel between Christ/bride and husband/wife faltering, the scriptural data signifies the sexual identity of male and female as essential to the human story, which is predicated on biological difference as well as similarity for the "productive" function of bringing about a "dynasty" through the covenants, and the "one-flesh" union is guarded by the lawful commands not to partake of sexual relations outside of this union. Hence, the gender and sexual identity of male-female as expressed in sexual activity in the context of marriage preserves the traditional teaching as both descriptive and prescriptive.

Scriptural Material

Genesis 1:26–28 states,

> Then God said, "Let us make mankind in our image, in our likeness, so that they may rule over the fish in the sea and the birds in the sky, over the livestock and all the wild animals, and over all the creatures that move along the ground."
>
> So God created mankind in his own image,
>   in the image of God he created them;
>   male and female he created them.

12. United Church of Christ, *Book of Worship*, 323–46. It is important to look at the revised version of 2012. On page 327, the language of Christ and his bride is used and Ephesians 5 is one of the suggested readings.

13. Episcopal Church, *The Book of Common Prayer*, "The Witnessing and Blessing of a Marriage," and "The Celebration and Blessing of a Marriage 2." The former can be used with any gender couple and the latter uses gender-neutral language, but, unfortunately for marriage revisionists, the parallel of Christ and his bride with a homosexual couple falters. For an explanation of these, see "Church Publishing Inc Has Released the New Marriage Rites for the Episcopal Church's Trial Use," Episcopal Café, December 5, 2015, https://www.episcopalcafe.com/church-publishing-inc-has-released-the-new-marriage-rites-for-the-episcopal-churchs-trial-use; "Liturgical Resources 1: I Will Bless You and You Will Be a Blessing," Church Publishing, accessed September 3, 2019, https://www.churchpublishing.org/products/liturgicalresources1. The revised version actually excised Genesis 2 with its "A man shall cleave to his wife and they shall become one flesh."

God blessed them and said to them, "Be fruitful and increase in number; fill the earth and subdue it. Rule over the fish in the sea and the birds in the sky and over every living creature that moves on the ground."

Genesis 1:26–28 gives us an initial blueprint for thinking about the human story and, more specifically, the biblical take on gender, sexual identity, and sexuality. As we have noted previously, humans are created in the image of God, signifying their unique place in the created order. This unique place is not subverted in the new covenant but instead is reaffirmed in a variety of texts and elevated in relation to Christ. The meaning of the image is nearly synonymous with a particular species, and not just any old species but the human species, which is composed of soul-body beings. Image indicates a covenantal representation meaning, although, as I argued earlier, it is not limited to that but instead has some ontological foundations.

Two tasks are given to God's covenantal representatives. The first we find in Genesis 1:26, where God commands humanity, specifically Adam in this context, to take "dominion" (ESV) over the earth. Dominion over the earth entails that humans are to care for it, tend it, cultivate it, cause it to grow, and serve it in a way that brings about its flourishing. The second task is that of procreation. Procreation is given to us as part of the creation mandate in Genesis 1:28. Procreation is the act of bringing about children through sexual activity. Notice that in Genesis 1:27 the author gives one of the conditions for making sense of sexual activity: "male and female." The picture that is already beginning to form in the human story is that "male and female" is an essential feature of the image of God. For God created them in his image—male and female. Sexual activity itself presupposes the image-bearing reality of humanity as male and female.

It is not a coincidence that the author places procreation and dominion together. Instead, these are integrally related to the human story and central to God's covenantal blessing of life to the world. For it is by dominion through the means of procreation that God gives life and blesses the life of his creation. The male-female formula of procreation is positively fitting for how God chooses to bless his creation.

Genesis 5 reflects this covenantal formula. In Genesis 5 we find the same blueprint of God's design for fulfilling the creation mandate laid out in the creational covenant of Genesis 1:26–28 to all of humanity. Genesis 5:1–3 states,

This is the written account of Adam's family line.

When God created mankind, he made them in the likeness of God. He created them male and female and blessed them. And he named them "Mankind" when they were created.

When Adam had lived 130 years, he had a son in his own likeness, in his own image; and he named him Seth.

Notice that the use of "image" and "likeness" are reintroduced, thus pointing us back to Genesis 1:26–28. It is through the "family" predicated on the "He created them male and female" that God's purposes are carried out through the family line. In other words, what we have here is a dynasty, a royal family, the line for which God carries out his plan to give life and bless his creation. Dominion is satisfied through the dynasty that God creates and "blessed." The image described in the early chapters of Genesis is transmitted through the dynasty that God will later expand to the rest of the earth. But it is here in this formula of male-and-female complementarity that God reveals to us the interrelated nature of sexual identity, sexual activity, and the creation of culture.

It is through God's covenantal blueprint that he gives life to the world and blesses that life, as confirmed in Genesis 1:28: "God blessed them." Genesis 2:24 picks up on this blessing of procreation. Marriage is instituted in Genesis 2 as the covenantal context for sexual activity and procreation. But we notice something else in Genesis 2:24 that is relevant for a biblical understanding of sexual activity and sexual identity: "That is why a man leaves his father and mother and is united to his wife, and they become one flesh." Again, note the binary of male and female as that which complements the other in the covenantal story. It is they, in the context of the marriage covenant, who are joined. Male and female become one flesh.

This "one-flesh" union needs to be highlighted because it, too, provides the blueprint for our understanding of sexual identity and gender identity. The "one-flesh" union is not characterized by kinship alone, as some would have us believe, but rather it depends on the procreative complementarity of the sexes to fulfill God's covenantal design for the world. That said, let us consider, however briefly, one recent and popular revisionist of Genesis 2:24, which, if correct, creates some conceptual space for a more elastic and expanded notion of sexual activity and gender.

James Brownson has recently argued in favor of a revisionist understanding of "one flesh." He summarizes his position contra the traditional position of complementarity discerned through biology, which has in mind specifically Genesis 2:24 (and, for that matter, Gen. 1:26–28):

> By contrast, I have argued that the language of "one flesh" refers not to complementarity but to kinship. The relationship of kinship is not based on complementarity, but on similarity and mutual obligation. Kin are those who have

something essential in common with each other, and who accept the obligation to help and support each other in distinctive ways. Moreover, nowhere in Scripture is the notion of anatomical or biological complementarity of male and female explicitly portrayed or discussed. The absence of confirming texts calls into question whether this vision of gender complementarity truly underlies the antipathy Scripture shows toward the same-sex erotic relationship it addresses.[14]

Brownson pivots to his positive exposition of "one flesh" by undermining the assumption for male-female complementarity. He states that this complementarity is not explicitly mentioned in the text, but this is an argument from silence. More importantly, it is an argument from silence that purports to open up space for other sexual relationships. But the reason the text does not mention alternative sexualities is precisely that they are taboo and abominations according to the Old Testament law.[15] However, Genesis 2:23 indicates complementarity when the husband describes his wife as both similar to and different from himself. She is similar in that he states, "This is now bone of my bones"; she is different in that "she shall be called 'woman,' for she was taken out of the man." The contrast is found in the "woman" juxtaposed with "man." The two are helpfully different. That said, while verse 24, according to Brownson, does not state explicitly what is excluded in the meaning of the "one-flesh" union, it is made sense of in light of its surrounding context in the creation mandate to create a dynasty through procreation.

Brownson argues that his reading of "one flesh" as meaning "kin" is at the core of what is going on in the scriptural narrative and that biology is not necessarily a determinative feature for the nature of the "one-flesh" union. While related Scripture passages often refer to male and female, this actually is incidental to what is conveyed. Furthermore, although the biblical authors may have commonly had in mind the notion of males and females, this does not yield the idea that this is all that is conceived or acceptable in God's mind. This opens the door, then, to the acceptability and viability of same-sex relationships, assuming that marriage in a legal sense is a reality.

This argument fails to take into account all that we find in Genesis 1–2. The complementarity of male and female is central to the vision that God has of his human creatures. This is clear in the fact that the "one-flesh" union is a reference to the blessing of procreation found in Genesis 1:28. God gives life and blessing in creation, and the manner in which he gives life to the rest of

14. Brownson, *Bible, Gender, Sexuality*, 260.
15. I thank Old Testament scholar James K. Hoffmeier for reminding me of this truth and bringing out this powerful point, which is made sense of in context and is further buttressed by the Old Testament law.

humanity is through male and female union. God blesses that union by giving humans the ability to procreate. The sexual difference between male and female is integral to the blessing that God gives to his humans. The ability to fulfill the covenantal blessings that God intends occurs only in the covenantal context of relationships between male and female. Sexual difference, then, is biological difference. This is not to say that sexual difference is reducible or fully capturable in biology, but it is not less than biological difference.

Christopher Roberts forcefully argues for the importance of interpreting "one-flesh" union as including sexual and biological difference. He summarizes his position when he says,

> We will not know what it means until we allow God to tell us what it means. The tradition has claimed that we do not know who we are and what it means to find ourselves differentiated as men and women until we allow the premises and practices of revelation to unfold. In the tradition, stretching from Augustine to John Paul II, sexual difference is not mute, inert, nonexistent, or indifferent. In this tradition, God brings man to woman and tells the two sexes something they would not otherwise know: that their creation is good, that their creation as two sexes is for the sake of enabling a church and a covenant, and that, despite their fallenness, their twoness can in itself become a witness to reconciliation and redemption through marriage. Marriage gives this aspect of our creation the power to testify, and the nonmarried offer supporting testimony through their chastity, which creates the social ecology supporting marriage.[16]

Grasping the meaning and significance of the "one-flesh" union as predicated on the productive power in the union of the binary and complementary sexes (which are, at a minimum, biological in nature) points us to a social ecology and the flourishing of the covenantal reality for which God has designed human beings. As Roberts pointedly notes, the tradition has not been unclear on the necessity of sexual difference as significant and publicly attested to. Genesis 2:24 bears this out in the immediate context as well as in reading it in light of other relevant passages already mentioned.

Most importantly, the sexual activity described in Genesis 2:24 is set in a particular covenantal context that depends on one condition being met:

16. Roberts, *Creation and Covenant*, 247. For a classical natural-law account that helpfully grounds and offers additional support to the biblical data, see Feser, *Neo-scholastic Essays*, 378–415. See also a video where Feser develops the argument: "Edward Feser: Natural Law & Sexual Ethics," YouTube video (1:49:30), published by TheAnscombeSociety, April 13, 2015, https://youtu.be/rynlfggqAcU. Feser buttresses the scriptural portrait of sexual deviations by advancing an argument from the perversion of faculties. If our bodily parts have a telos, then it does seem to follow, in some way, that one can misuse those parts in ways that are unhealthy or fail to achieve the purpose of the substance.

the collective capacity of "procreation" or the "productive" capacity that depends on the male-female complementarity of the sexes.[17] Without this complementarity, the blessing is simply not present.

Another feature is relevant to our contemporary discussions. The creational passages give us insight into the "normativity" of the sexes and by extension the gender complementarity of male and female. As stated earlier, I take it that *sexual identity* and *gender identity* are overlapping and interrelated terms, and the scriptural story of humans embodies this same assumption. Gender, having to do with the social dimensions or behaviors of humanity, is rooted in a biological reality. In other words, the biological complementarity of male and female sexuality is tied to and implicates social reality. Lest we think that this is a matter found only in the creational story, let's consult other key representative texts that share the central vision of sexual identity therein.

Song of Songs, representative of the Wisdom literature, continues with the assumption of the gender complementarity of male and female both as normative for sexual activity, confined to marriage, and as embodying a normative social reality dependent on biological sex. Song of Songs is a celebration of the romantic and sexual love between a husband and a wife.

17. The present reading is quite compatible with natural-law theory, which argues that there are natural realities that are teleological in nature. On these accounts, the "one-flesh" union is nearly synonymous with a "conjugal union" understanding of marriage, which presumes the sexual complementarity of male and female as having productive teleological capacities. The following gives a representative set of the "new" natural-law literature. See Finnis, *Natural Law and Natural Rights*, 95. Finnis is drawing from Nozick, *Anarchy, State, and Utopia*, 42–45. This also reflects Aristotle's ethics of the good. Within this natural-law framework, all decisions or determinations are carried out by considering the basic goods of life, knowledge, play, aesthetic experience, friendship, practical reasonableness, and religion. For similar arguments, from a modified traditional natural-law perspective, see Budziszewski, *What We Can't Not Know*, esp. 86–87, 100, 190, 205, 208–9, 214–15. Budziszewski argues that homosexual acts cannot obtain certain basic goods. Minimally, then, these provide evidence that the acts are not good and represent reasons for thinking that we are outside our covenantal boundaries in relationship to God, or so one could argue. Budziszewski gives a clear understanding of the good as "natural" in *The Line through the Heart*, 70, 175. He distinguishes acts that are unnatural in a trivial and nonnormative sense from acts that are unnatural in a nontrivial and normative sense. Coffee drinking would describe the former, and homosexual acts the latter. See also Girgis, Anderson, and George, *What Is Marriage?*, 23. In a more technical academic treatment, Patrick Lee and Robert P. George defend what amounts to the same view of marriage. See Lee and George, *Conjugal Union*, esp. chap. 3. In connection to their own preferred anthropology, Lee and George develop their view of sexuality and marriage in light of their concept of body-self dualism, which is really just a version of Thomist dualism—not quite substantial dualism. See Lee and George, *Body-Self Dualism*, esp. chap. 6. They are quite critical of substantial dualism; however, a substantial dualism that maintains the distinct substances with powers/capacities that are either enhanced or actualized when the two parts are joined could fit with this view of sexuality and marriage.

The prophetic literature of the Old Testament bears witness to the necessity of the "one-flesh" union of the complementary, and distinct, sexes as the means by which God has designed humanity to experience blessing and life through the covenants. And, as we have seen, this reality is not reducible to a biological one alone; it has implications for social reality that impinges on gender complementarity. One of the most significant prophetic passages that buttresses the same continuous meaning of sexual identity and the parameters for sexual activity, but also gives us additional insight into that union, is Malachi 2:13–16.[18] The prophet states,

> Another thing you do: You flood the LORD's altar with tears. You weep and wail because he no longer looks with favor on your offerings or accepts them with pleasure from your hands. You ask, "Why?" It is because the LORD is the witness between you and the wife of your youth. You have been unfaithful to her, though she is your partner, the wife of your marriage covenant.
>
> Has not the one God made you? You belong to him in body and spirit. And what does the one God seek? Godly offspring. So be on your guard, and do not be unfaithful to the wife of your youth.
>
> "The man who hates and divorces his wife," says the LORD, the God of Israel, "does violence to the one he should protect," says the LORD Almighty. So be on your guard, and do not be unfaithful.

As noted, the passage presumes the complementary, and distinct, sexes of male and female as necessary conditions for marriage and sexual intimacy— "the man who hates and divorces his wife." Other notes on the passage are sufficient for establishing the fact that the "biological" condition for "productivity" in procreation is nonreductionistic in the covenantal relation, but in fact it extends to social realities between the male and female. Both male and female are joined in such a way that the relationship is permanent and not intended to be broken. The relationship extends to the whole of the persons—"You belong to him in body and spirit." This points in the direction of a "comprehensive" relationship that is conditioned by biological complementarity.

Old Testament law maintains this covenantal story as central to sexual behavior, not only in its prescriptions but also in its commands. Leviticus 18:22 precludes other kinds of sexual unions being acceptable in practice: "Do not have sexual relations with a man as one does with a woman; that is detestable." And the command to not have sexual relations is reiterated in

---

18. James K. Hoffmeier has stated that this may be the lens by which both Christ and Paul are working when they comment on marriage and sexuality.

the New Testament, carrying along the same vision of sexuality.[19] In Romans 1:26–27 Paul likens the violation of sexual complementarity to idolatry, which is condemned: "Because of this, God gave them over to shameful lusts. Even their women exchanged natural sexual relations for unnatural ones. In the same way the men also abandoned natural relations with women and were inflamed with lust for one another. Men committed shameful acts with other men, and received in themselves the due penalty for their error."

Christ reaffirms the created order of sexual identity and, by extension, sexual behavior. In fact, he explicitly quotes the creation story in the context of his discussions on the unnaturalness of divorce: "But at the beginning of creation God 'made them male and female.' 'For this reason a man will leave his father and mother and be united to his wife, and the two will become one flesh.' So they are no longer two, but one flesh" (Mark 10:6–8).

Paul carries along this vision of human sexuality when he describes the relationship of Christ to his bride using the creation story of male and female in marriage: "In the same way husbands should love their wives as their own bodies. He who loves his wife loves himself. For no one ever hated his own flesh, but nourishes and cherishes it, just as Christ does the church, because we are members of his body. 'Therefore a man shall leave his father and mother and hold fast to his wife, and the two shall become one flesh.' This mystery is profound, and I am saying that it refers to Christ and the church" (Eph. 5:28–32 ESV). Paul carefully uses the marital relationship as the type for understanding the "mystery"—Christ and his bride.[20] And it is important to note that Paul

19. Other passages directly bear on this subject that put guards to preserve the "one-flesh" union and that yield a prescriptive, not simply normal pattern, for sexual behavior. Christian philosopher Richard Swinburne supports this, helpfully, when he states, "Various biblical texts forbid performing homosexual acts; Romans 1:24–27 does so very clearly, and so fairly clearly does 1 Corinthians 6:9–10. These take up Old Testament prohibitions—Leviticus 18:22 and Deuteronomy 23:17–18. Nineteen centuries of unanimous church tradition supports this prohibition, and denying it would surely have been deemed heretical. So again I suggest that it must count as a central Christian doctrine" (Swinburne, *Revelation*, 303). See also his larger argument (303–5). See also Gagnon, *The Bible and Homosexual Practice*. Gagnon offers the authoritative biblical treatment on the subject. For a discussion on some of these topics, see Sprinkle, *Homosexuality, the Bible, and the Church*. For a popular treatment that offers a revisionist perspective, see Vines, *God and the Gay Christian*. See also Song, *Covenant and Calling*, 81. Song's work applies in this context as well. Song argues for the tentative possibility that there is another category for sexual activity that is allowable in Scripture. But this conceptual possibility is ruled out when we understand the meaning of "one-flesh" union and the lawful commands that serve to preserve it.

20. Ephesians 5 gives us some textual indication of the sacramental nature of marriage because the typology is, arguably, used by Paul as a means not merely to illustrate Christ and his bride but to point to, press into, and participate in the mystery via marriage in the new covenant. There is a sacramental tapestry that is inclusive of marriage.

does not subvert the creational reality of male-female complementarity of the sexes in marriage as the condition for the productive flourishing of humans.[21] Paul reaffirms the reality of the creation, and he uses it as a positive foil for which to unpack the reality of Christ and his bride, the church.[22]

Theological claims begin with an authority structure. And this is true when attending to gender and sexuality. Guided by traditional teaching, I maintain that Scripture affirms the five claims that I made earlier. Gender, as a social expression of sexual identity, is nonreducible to biology, as gender is informed by and central to the covenantal structure of the Old Testament means by which God gives life and blesses that life. It is even arguable that gender is essential to the human story and essential to what it means to be human. Gender identity is also made sense of in light of the "one-flesh" union, which is a kind of union that is more than "kinship" and is dependent on the sexual complementarity of the two biological sexes and their dynamic power of "productivity" (see especially Gen. 2:13–14). The complementary dynamic of the sexes is a necessary condition to the union described, as it is the means

21. An important passage for reflecting on this question in the new covenant is 1 Cor. 7. There, some might take it that Paul suggests that marriage is merely a means to fighting sexual temptation, which seems out of sync with an Old Testament understanding of the reason for marriage. However, in Eph. 5 Paul offers a much more explicitly positive view of marriage in the new covenant that is continuous with the Old Testament, not by subverting or eliminating it but by reaffirming and elevating it to a status that leads us to understand the "mystery" of Christ, even transfiguring it. How one interprets these passages will depend, in some measure, on what role the interpreter gives to the wider "catholic" tradition's reception of it, one's own particular subtradition, and the amount of continuity or discontinuity found between the old covenant(s) and the new covenant. For an exploration of some of these issues, see Schwarz, *The Human Being*, 290–317. Schwarz talks about the openness to interpreting the marriage relationship seen in Eph. 5 as sacramental (even a "lesser" sacrament—subordinate to baptism and the Lord's Supper) and participatory in a supernatural reality (317). An understanding of marriage as a lesser sacrament is consistent with Anglican catholicity and with some ways of working out Reformed theology. Schwarz discusses some of the distinctions between theological developments in the Reformed tradition in contrast to ancient Christianity along with Roman Catholicism (esp. 317–39).

22. One of the important questions that this raises concerns identity—not personal identity but narrative identity. For example, should a person who experiences same-sex attraction but is committed to singleness identify as being gay or having gay inclinations? This and related questions have encouraged a body of literature offering different responses. Some have said that there is too much at stake and that we should not be defined by our sexuality, because we are so much more. Others take it that identifying with our inclinations is important for being honest about who we are as we await redemption. There are more fundamental questions that bear on these issues. For example: What kind of description can we give to sexuality and marriage? For one answer, see N. Collins, *All but Invisible*. One answer is to suggest that there is too much at stake in identifying with same sex-attraction and that there is far more to our identity as Christians than our sexual attraction, exemplified precisely in our constitution as embodied souls with a higher purpose.

for producing a dynasty. The nature of the union is not merely biological, and Malachi 2:13–16 crystalizes our understanding of the union as a developed Old Testament concept as permanent, holistic, and comprehensive. The lawful commands buttress the centrality of these concepts as an interrelated cluster of gender, sex, sexuality, and marriage. The intent of these laws is to preserve the "one-flesh" union of male and female and to exclude other kinds of sexual union in the preservation of God's people, which, once again, is not intended merely as a biological preservation but also as a covenantal preservation of families, societies, and nations.[23] Gender is essential in some way to the human story, but there are two ways to account for gender.

Two Models of Sex and Gender

I have established that sex and gender, where gender is tied in some determinate way to one's sexed body, are not just significant to the human story but even essential to that story. In the way that sexual complementarity of male and female is necessary for marriage and God's ongoing giving of life and blessing that life, the binary of male and female is an integral part of the story about marriage and sexuality. The question of interest here does not have to do with the essentiality of male and female to God's intentions about the human story but rather with how it is that one metaphysically accounts

23. This does raise a series of questions for those who are same-sex attracted, and Scripture does have another category, but it is not another category that allows for alternative sexual activity outside of a complementary male-female union in the context of marriage. See Shaw, *Same-Sex Attraction*. Shaw lays out a case in favor of the celibate life, which applies to those who have sexual inclinations that are out of step with Christian teaching. Celibacy is also relevant for those who have no desire for the opposite sex whatsoever and desire the single life. Shaw shows that our identity is not wrapped up in our sexuality alone but that we have an identity in our relationship to Jesus Christ. He also shows what it looks like to live a celibate life devoted to the mission of the gospel. It is possible to live this life and to do so in a meaningful and satisfyingly fruitful way. Roman Catholic Eve Tushnet complements many of the ideas found in Shaw's work. However, Tushnet represents a slightly nuanced position of identifying as gay while identifying and living a devoted life under the authority of the church's teaching. Tushnet identifies as gay or lesbian and sometimes as same-sex attracted. She also identifies as a Roman Catholic. She is aware of the tension and reveals it in her autobiographical experience of struggling with her desires while seeking to submit to the authority of the church. Upon offering her own journey, Tushnet advances several helpful ways that one can live a celibate life. Rather than highlight the negative of lacking the freedom to participate in this wonderful gift of sex, she highlights the single person's identity with God and in community. Life as a single person is possible if it is lived out in a loving community where the virtue of friendship can be developed. Friendship, she argues, is a virtue that has been lost in the church, but it is one that finds rich traction in church history and deserves to be revived. See Tushnet, *Gay and Catholic*, esp. 88–119.

for being male or female. Here we are interested in the particularity question often confronting modern reflections: Am *I* male or am *I* female?

Gender and sexuality raise a complex of issues for all anthropologies, but they raise some unique issues on the view that humans are composed of both body and soul. Presumably, if I am essentially my soul, then it is conceivable that I could ensoul a different body. One can see where this might lead. On substance dualism, it is natural to have some body-swapping intuitions. Consider the movie *Being John Malkovich*. In the film there is a secret portal that mysteriously leads to the inhabiting of John Malkovich's mind and to experiencing what he experiences as if in his body, and, in some cases, the characters are able to manipulate his body through some sort of mental trying and intending. While an "actual" body swap may not occur here, there is something relevant to body swapping in this movie.[24] Granted the individuals inhabiting Malkovich's mind and experiences are not, arguably, taking ownership of his body, but it is not entirely clear what a body swap would be beyond that of experiencing one's place through the body of another. Now, on this scenario, not only can one person inhabit the mind and experience the body of John Malkovich and experience the world from his place in it, but also multiple individuals can experience being embodied by John Malkovich's body at the same time and experience the world from his place in it. What is also interesting in the movie is that different genders could mentally occupy the bodily place of John Malkovich, including what it might *feel* like to experience a masculine body. The movie illustrates the body-swapping intuitions had on a view where humans are souls with bodies. That being said, it is important to clarify two items. First, the illustration most apparently serves to aid our ability to think about the possibility that we could conceive of swapping bodies, even bodies of the opposite gender. Second, it raises the question about the possibility of swapping out different genders.

On the first item, we must distinguish the aspects of our conscious experience about body swapping. I could conceive of my swapping my body out for another body, and this is not altogether exotic if we consider the fact that, according to science, I exist through the changes of my present body. As my body changes, and on the assumption that it changes entirely after a seven-year period, I am still the thing occupying the differing changes of the body in and through time. If I am swapping out bodies, as it were, then it appears that I could occupy a different body. Drawing on Alvin Plantinga's

---

24. Other movies that might help shore up our intuitions about body swapping include *Big*, *Avatar*, and *Freaky Friday*. In *Big*, a child inhabits the body of an adult. In *Avatar*, individuals are able to inhabit the bodies of avatars through a computer simulation. Whether these are real bodies depends on the natures of bodies. In *Freaky Friday*, a child and a parent swap bodies.

replacement argument developed in chapter 1, we see that slowing down the process or accelerating the pace significantly would not undermine the modal intuition that I could, and do in fact, swap one body for another or replace one for another. I grant that the continuity of one body for another body, from the perspective of biology, has a different set of interesting questions, but the simple point of body swapping on this understanding of persons as souls remains. If a soul could swap one body for another body, then there is reason to think that one could swap one gender instantiated in one body for a different gender instantiated in a different body. Hence, person X could occupy body *a* that happens to be anatomically male at time *t* (say, 1990), and person X could come to occupy body *b* that happens to be anatomically female at time *u* (say, 1991).

This raises another question—the second item. It could follow that one person's metaphysical assumption of a distinct gendered body means either that *that* person's gender changes or simply that person experiences a mismatch with his or her body. How one accounts for these contingencies depends on the underlying ontology of gender, and gender in relation to sex. Certainly, if we take some version of physicalism as our starting point, then it follows that when the sex of my physical part (i.e., the body) changes anatomically (along with the right sort of hormone supplements), then I am the sex/gender that is instantiated in my physical part because I am either my physical part (with higher-order neural properties) or I am constituted by my physical part in a way that my physical part determines my sexed nature. But, if I am my soul or a person who has a soul—a belief that I, along with much of the Christian tradition, take as true—then the ontological facts of gender and sex are more complicated. I might have difficulty imagining that I could become the opposite gender, but the conceivability or possibility of gender transformation depends on our ontology of gender.[25] There are two models of the ontology of gender in the history

25. The present set of issues impinges on a rather important topic in the contemporary and academic cultures on transgenderism (i.e., those who have a gender identity or gender expression that differs from what they have been assigned). This is also related to transsexualism for those who seek to transition from one biological sex to another biological sex. There are several common assumptions in these discussions that are mutually inconsistent because they depend on the conception of gender binary, but they also claim that the binary is undermined by science or their first-person experiences of their gender and/or sexual identity. See Arbour and Gilhooly, "Transgenderism." The models listed here also have different answers to the worry about those who are intersex—that is, anatomically ambiguous. In *Sex Difference in Christian Theology*, Megan K. DeFranza offers some data that serve to problematize the gender binary position. While it is impossible to deal with all the complicated empirical data, there are a couple of responses that do not undermine or cause a collapse to the binary view at work in the tradition. First, one can argue, with the Roman Catholic Church, that all

of the church that will give different accounts, which have different theological implications.

The Thomistic Model: Gender Is an Essential Property of the Soul

On the Thomistic model, I am essentially my soul that informs some matter. Arguably, my soul is essentially gendered as male or female.[26] The descriptive content of what makes one male or female is a natural property essentially instantiated by each individual.[27] As such, each individual is either male or female necessarily and essentially. The bodily sex type is a manifestation of a deeper fact about the person: he is a *he* and she is a *she*, and the two cannot be confused. On this model, then, one could conceive of a possible world where one could assume a body that is anatomically distinct from the soul's gender, but one could not conceive of being a different gender. In other words, if one were a male, then one could not conceive of being female in a different world. One could, however, conceive of being mismatched with a different body that is anatomically female. The deeper question about the naturalness or unnaturalness of that mismatch depends, in part, on the ontology of the relationship between souls and bodies.

The Nyssa Model: Gender Is an Essential Property of the Earthly Body and a Common Property of the Soul[28]

The Nyssa model is different. On the Nyssa model, gender is not an essential property of the soul but rather is a common property of the soul and, if in fact a body has essential properties, then an essential property of the body. Nyssa states in the context of his discussion of the *imago Dei*

---

individual humans are intrinsically either male or female, even if anatomically there are some ambiguities. And, in many cases, there is a fact of the matter that is differentiated by way of genetic information. Second—and this is a more modest response—in extreme cases there is no clear empirically verifiable fact of the matter, and for such individuals there is in Scripture a nonsexual and nonmarriage category.

26. Pruss, *One Body*.

27. This does raise the question as to what descriptive content is applied to the distinct genders. There is, on some traditional ways of construing gender, an essentialist hierarchical distinction between male and female. This opens up to contemporary discussions about egalitarianism and complementarianism. See Pierce and Groothuis, *Discovering Biblical Equality*; Piper and Grudem, *Recovering Biblical Manhood and Womanhood*.

28. For an exploration of Gregory of Nyssa, see Boersma, "Putting On Clothes." See also N. Harrison, "Male and Female in Cappadocian Theology." For a useful introductory and constructive exploration of the Cappadocians, see N. Harrison, *God's Many-Splendored Image*, 107–23; Cortez, *Resourcing Theological Anthropology*, 198–202; Cortez, *Christological Anthropology in Historical Perspective*, 31–55.

as participating in the divine, "I presume that every one knows that this is a departure from the Prototype: for 'in Christ Jesus,' as the apostle says, 'there is neither male nor female.'"[29] Gregory's Platonic influence colors how he perceives the soul in relation to gender. Gender and sex are necessary in this life, as we saw earlier in the scriptural story line, but ontologically they are so because sexes are "divided according to distinction."[30] For the sake of the argument here, I will avoid a discussion about the specifics of Gregory's Platonism concerning the division of the sexes only to be united in the afterlife. On this account, one could conceive not only of swapping a male body, for example, out for a female body but also of the soul transitioning, as it were, from a male body to a female body. In order to do this, one would need to tell a story about the "narrative" identity of the soul but not the strict identity of the person. On a narrative identity of the soul, one could make sense of the fact that souls are gendered as derivative properties. For example, as a soul, I bear the derivative properties of my body, such as height, hair color, skin color, and weight. These derivative properties are, to varying degrees, important to my narrative identity and shape my self-concept.

Theological Implications of the Two Models

Each model has several theological implications that impinge on how we think about practical daily living and the afterlife. Let's consider each model as it is guided by what I have set out above in both the wider "catholic" tradition and the basic covenantal structure in Scripture. Arriving at a theologically developed version of gender and sex necessitates that we work within the parameters given above. To depart from the tradition, and the common confession of the church that humanity is primarily male and female and that the binary of male and female is central to the story line of Scripture, would situate our speculations about gender in a different ordering of theological authorities, possibly with scientific deliverances or the deliverances that follow from our traditionless reason, but it is not clear why starting here would lead us any closer to the truth about gender. If we were to speculate about each of the models quite apart from both Scripture as the norming norm and tradition as the normative parameters for scriptural interpretation, then it is possible that we could construct some quite radical conclusions about gender.

29. Gregory of Nyssa, "On the Making of Man," 16.7.
30. Gregory of Nyssa, "On the Making of Man," 16.7.

Epistemology of Gender and Sexuality

In one way or another, the epistemology of gender depends on our knowledge of biological sex. The scriptural link of covenantal blessing confined to marriage depends for its fulfillment on biological complementarity in the "productive" role, but this "productive" role is precisely what is missing in other understandings of sexual behavior.

The question is about the possibility that one's particular instantiated gender could be otherwise. This is certainly a worry. The concern with this worry is an epistemic one. How would we know that I am a gender other than my biological sex? How could I or we make determinate that a soul is mismatched with its body? Is there some feature or property that one could point to in order to make determinate one gender that is distinct from biological sex? It is not entirely clear what epistemic resources one could point to in order to determine a fact of the matter about one's gender that is not consistent with one's biological sex.

Gender and Sexuality

Gender and sexuality are related, if, in fact, sexuality is a manifestation of gender identity. This may sound circular at first, until we realize that gender is not reducible to a physical reality, but the physical reality is the obvious epistemic evidence for gender and is lawfully connected to it. In this way, biological sex places limitations on gender, and biological sex yields specified social realities. And sexuality is tied to both biological sex and gender.

There is an initial worry on a strict substance dualism account of human nature. If gender is a property of the soul and the soul is actually independent from the biological reality of sex, then it follows that there is a possibility that one person could be mismatched with the wrong biological sex (hence, what is oft called gender dysphoria). And, as we have seen above, intuitions of body swapping do seem initially conceivable, but its conceivability is also dependent on both the models listed above (e.g., Thomas Aquinas and Gregory of Nyssa) as well as one's personal ontology.

If we assume that the Nyssa model is true and that souls do not instantiate one gender essentially but only derivatively as a common property, then there is one advantage here. The advantage is that our souls could not be somehow mismatched with the wrong body because gender or sexual identity is determined by one's biological reality not by the possibility of some invisible reality. In other words, the body that I inhabit is, literally, the gender that I inherit when I am born. The possibility that I could be otherwise is already determined by the biological structure given to me. This is not the same on the Thomistic model.

On the Thomistic model, it is initially possible that I could be mismatched with a sexual identity that is not compatible with the gender instantiated by my soul. In other words, I could come to assume a body that, properly speaking, is a functional mismatch for my soul. However, this becomes less likely depending on the personal ontology that one is working. Consider two personal ontologies where it would be unlikely, even impossible. If we assume hylomorphism, where all matter, actually, is informed by a form (i.e., a soul of a particular kind), then the possibility for a functional mismatch does not seem possible. Persons are matter-form composites, and persons are not, properly speaking, identical to their souls alone apart from the matter the soul informs.[31] The body is the matter that a soul informs. Some would call the soul the "configured configurer."[32] On such an account, it is not clear that a soul could be mismatched with the opposing gendered body. Instead, the soul and the matter would simply be two constituents that constitute the person, and the gender is made manifest in the body.

The mismatching problem would also falter on an emergentist account of the soul—that is, person. Emergent substance dualism is the view, recall, that the soul comes about from a suitably complex neural structure and, at a minimum, functionally depends on that neural part that serves as the soul's proximate cause. The biological development of sexuality, then, would consist of the ground for gender as its causal contributor. It is not clear what other cause would contribute to the emergence of a mismatching soul with body.[33]

But let us take the most obvious case where mismatching at the origination of the soul is a conceivable possibility. If we take a strict substance dualism, without the emergentist mechanism at play, then the possibility for such a mismatch seems possible. In this case, the soul originates in one of two ways, traducianism or creationism. On the creationist account, God creates the soul directly and immediately and attaches it to a body.[34] God would then be directly responsible for placing a male soul in a female body or a female soul in a male body. Traducianism seems like a more likely possibility. Traducianism takes it that, on most accounts, God creates the first Adamic-soul or the first

31. For an excellent defense of Aristotelian ontology that undergirds at least some interpretations of Thomas Aquinas that challenge some of the contemporary scientific conclusions that would unsettle the intimate connection between gender and sexuality, see Feser, *Aristotle's Revenge*.

32. Stump, *Aquinas*, 200.

33. A strange proposal could be advanced that God somehow intervenes or occasions that this soul would be mismatched with this body.

34. Earlier, in chapter 2, I proposed a hybrid of emergentism and creationism, where the soul is created directly by God as the occasion for the emerging soul.

pair, Adam and Eve, with a mechanism for splitting off potential souls at the moment of conception. The contributing cause outside of biological development would come from the parents who contribute what, on one account, is called soul-stuff. Let's assume for the moment that this is a possibility. There are several complicated questions that remain unanswered.

Even if we assumed that a mismatch between soul and body is a possibility, we could tell some story that the cause for mismatch would be due to the problem of original sin somehow messing about with the biological process.[35] What sort of origination story is needed to explain this possibility? In order to tell this story, one needs a plausible account of the origination process that separates the splitting off of future souls in that it is unaffected by the biological origins of the body. Presumably, one could take up one of the origination stories given above with a more robust story concerning the problem of evil as a way forward, but these, at first sight, are exotic. There are other questions that complicate this possibility.

The present scenario of gender dysphoria depends on a private solipsist account of gender. While there are some truths about persons that are directly accessible only from one's own private access, it is not clear that this is the case with gender. As we consider the scriptural and traditional data, we see that both are predicated on a public account that is biologically determinate and not solely privately accessible by one's own internal states. In these unique cases, why should one privilege the first-person account of a mismatch? This amounts to a unique problem of evil within divine providence that raises all sorts of epistemic implications that are not easily resolvable. By what means with a sufficient criterion could one discern his or her gender? What appears unlikely, if it were true, would raise the further question of what could be done in this case. For the reasons listed here, the *improbabilities* of an actual mismatch should still any violence done to a body.

Gender and the Afterlife

Matthew 22:30 raises a set of questions about gender, sexual identity, and sexual behavior in heaven: "At the resurrection people will neither marry nor be given in marriage; they will be like the angels in heaven." Several questions have been and continue to be part of the discussion surrounding gender in a theological anthropology. Does it follow that there is no sexual activity in

---

35. Ironically, traducianism is often posited as a way to avoid charging God as the active agent who transfers original sin from the parents to the child as with creationism, but in this unique situation, traducianism faces a different kind of problem of evil.

heaven? The text neither states this nor precludes the possibility. Does it follow that gender distinctions will no longer exist? If so, then the Nyssa model makes sense of this fact. Our account of Christ complicates these questions, however.

Christological Gender and the Problem of Particularity

What about Christ? I take it that Christ, in his humanity, exemplifies what humans will be. Christ persists as a male in his resurrected state, so it follows that we will remain as gendered in the afterlife. Can both the Thomistic model and the Nyssa model supply an ontological explanation for the fact that Christ appears male? It seems they can. On the Thomistic model, where creational realities are not subverted or replaced by another reality, Christ just is male. On a Nyssa model, the story is not as simple.

Nyssa's model can still account for our gendered natures if we take it that bodies instantiate a sexual identity in heaven. Souls have a structure that develops through interaction with biology, relationships, and environment, and through one's own memories and character development. In other words, the choices that souls make, in fact, contribute to the structure that a soul will come to have. In the same way that we can, arguably, say that souls assume derivative properties from their bodies, we can say that souls assume a sexual identity that is grounded in the body. Souls are not strictly colored, long, and wide. Souls are derivatively colored, long, and wide. It is not untrue to say that Michael Jordan is six feet six inches tall, because he is so in virtue of the body he is attached to. In a similar way, souls carry with them a structure that bears properties via the hunk of matter. And some of these properties have a deeper impression on the soul than others. For example, you might have a scar on your forehead that is marked by an event where you tripped over your own feet, or you might have a scar on your forehead from an incident that leaves not only a physical scar but also a deep emotional scar, such as from being personally attacked. Similarly, you might think that hair color is rather unimportant to one's internal structure, but this is not always the case. You might have striking red hair that has stayed with you your whole life, and over time it becomes a mark of pride that shapes how you think about yourself and how others think of you. In a more profound way, the sexual identity that the soul carries with it from the body that it originated in and lived in would carry a deep mark on the structure of the soul. This will likely stay with us in the afterlife, and if we have resurrected bodies that are continuous with our earthly bodies, then one's sexual identity will continue to shape one's self-concept.

Conclusion

The biblical and traditional material gives us a picture of human identity that is essentially gendered. And the biblical and traditional material establishes categories for the normativity of sexual identity in relation to gender identity. In what preceded, I argued that the essentiality of gender to the human story and the normativity of sexual identity and gender identity are rooted in a biological understanding of the complementarity of the sexes that is biologically nonreductive and has implications for social practice. The Old Testament law as communicated in Scripture intends to preserve the "one-flesh" nature of sexual complementarity in marriage by excluding alternative sexual practices. Finally, I addressed the challenge of body swapping and, by implication, the nonessentiality of gender to individual humans, intuitions for ontologies that take it that persons are souls that are modally and actually distinct from their bodies. Within this discussion, I suggested that gender and sexuality are pointers to the purpose of human nature, and they give us a glimpse into the mystery that Christ preserves for the saints.

9

Why Am I Here?

Creaturely Living, Dying, and the In-Between

I remain confident of this:
I will see the goodness of the LORD
in the land of the living.

Psalm 27:13

I eagerly expect and hope that I will in no way be ashamed, but will
have sufficient courage so that now as always Christ will be exalted in
my body, whether by life or by death. For to me, to live is Christ and
to die is gain.

Philippians 1:20–21

As all Christians believe in the resurrection of the body and future judg-
ment, they all believe in an intermediate state. It is not, therefore, as to
the fact of an intermediate state, but as to its nature that diversity of
opinion exists among Christians.

Charles Hodge, Systematic Theology

The portion of the present chapter on the intermediate state is a modified and updated version
of my article "Christianity" in *The Palgrave Handbook of the Afterlife*, ed. Yujin Nagasawa
and Benjamin Matheson (London: Palgrave, 2017). For another volume that is more specific in
focus yet touches on similar topics, see Cushing, *Heaven and Philosophy*.

Lisa is a middle-aged woman who has worked all of her life as a server in a café. On one rainy and cold day, as she drives to work, she has a bad car accident with an eighteen-wheeler. The truck slams into the side of her car, pressing her against the side rails. She loses a lot of blood and is rushed to the hospital. Her husband meets her there. Realizing that it is too late and that death is near, he comforts her with these words: "Your pain will be gone soon." June is ninety years old. One day her daughter, Becky, comes to see her. June conveys to Becky that she will be leaving soon. Becky, in an attempt to comfort her, says, "You will have a new body one day, and I can't wait to see you again." Frank is forty-five years old and has lung cancer. While he is on his deathbed, his son Joel meets with him and says, "Dad, you will be with God in heaven soon, and I look forward to the day that I can see you again." All three stories represent a different view of the afterlife. My objective is to explore the variety of Christian views on the afterlife.

The Christian view of the afterlife includes two states: the interim state and the everlasting state. The former is, at present, underexplored in the literature, so my goal is to explore some of the options situated in its wider eschatological context, advance one underappreciated view in the literature, and discuss its ontological implications concerning the everlasting state. I recommend a view that I call "disembodied hope with resurrection hope," in which immortality and hope are achieved, in one sense, during the disembodied interim state and the process is completed in the physical resurrection. I suggest that this view is in keeping with the Protestant Reformation concerning the afterlife, yet it is also commonly held in medieval scholasticism and is represented in Roman Christianity.

In the present chapter, I will answer two questions concerning anthropocentric afterlife, one primary and the other secondary. First and primary, I give an answer to the question on the nature of Christian hope and immortality (from a Reformed perspective). Second, I answer a question that is ancillary to the first question and a corollary to it: What does it mean to be a human? The second will shed light on the first and offer an accounting of the first. To the first, the debate surrounds the question of whether Christian hope/immortality is concerned with immortality of the soul or the resurrection of the body, which correlates with the question of whether humans are souls, bodies, or souls and bodies. By specifically addressing the intermediate state, I argue, instead, that we have both dogmatic and philosophical reasons that recommend both the doctrine of the immortality of the soul and the physical resurrection of the body. The consensus of Reformed Christianity favors the intermediate state and the immediate presence of God after somatic death with its ancillary doctrine of the soul.

I begin by situating the discussion of the afterlife in Christian theology. Next, I address what seem to be unacceptable views of the Christian afterlife. Finally, I advance an underappreciated model of the intermediate state in light of its alternatives and suggest which corresponding ontologies provide a satisfactory accounting.

Eschatology and the Afterlife

In what follows, I take it that all of Christian thought presumes theological realism with respect to the afterlife. By this I mean that when I make a statement that persons exist in some state beyond the present earthly state, I am making a statement that is actual and obtains as a state of affairs regardless of whether other human minds believe it to be the case.[1] Where x is a term for something, there is a y that x exists in, within, or in a larger framework. As Michael Rea articulates it, "Where 'T' refers to the linguistic expression of some claim, theory, or doctrine, to *interpret or treat T realistically* is (a) to interpret T as having an objective truth value (and so to interpret it as something other than a mere evocative metaphor or expression of tastes, attitudes, or values); and (b) to interpret T in such a way that it *has realist truth-conditions*—in other words, it is true only if realism about the xs [which refers to propositions] and Fs [which refers to facts] putatively referred to in the theory is true." When a particular claim, say in theology, is true or real is when it obtains in the world.[2] For example, where x (representing the claim that persons will die somatically yet live on in a different state) is related to y (where y is reality) as obtaining in y, so x is interpreted within a larger framework and is not constrained by a particular discipline; it is not humanly mind-dependent nor is it an illusion.[3]

With that in mind, the afterlife is situated in a larger framework called "eschatology." Eschatology is the study of last things or the summing up

1. The reader may ask, "What about divine idealism?" In this case, it is true to say that all things are ideas in the mind of God (as in Berkeley or Edwardsian idealism), but we ought to make a distinction between ideas that God has of actual things that exist and ideas of fiction and ideas that God publishes and ideas that he does not, to use a bit of language from Berkeley.

2. See Rea, "Realism in Theology and Metaphysics," 323–24.

3. I realize that by making this claim up front, I am necessarily ruling out Friedrich Schleiermacher, an important figure in the Protestant Reformation tradition who affirmed an antireal view of the afterlife. I suggest that there is reason to affirm a realist view of the afterlife. First, it seems rather natural and intuitive to read divine revelation (as codified in the Christian Scriptures) as speaking of a real afterlife. Second, there is no reason to think that prior to modernity (Schleiermacher is the father of modern theological liberalism) theologians would have spoken of the afterlife in antirealist terms.

of all of God's actions. More specifically, eschatology is the study of God's redemptive actions. The Apostles' and Nicene Creeds teach us that the center of all God's action concerning his creation is redemption in Christ, which culminates in God's consummative act of bringing his church to glory. As the Nicene Creed states, "For us and for our salvation he came down from heaven." In other words, given that God's actions are centrally located in Christ (i.e., the Christ event), and Christ came to save us, humans, the story of eschatology is about the summing up of redemption. As the Nicene Creed states toward the end, "We look for the resurrection of the dead, and the life of the age [or world] to come," and the Apostles' Creed refers to the final state as "life everlasting." This is the purpose or expectation of our redemption. The afterlife, then, is related to God's consummative action of redemption as it pertains to the state of humans in the afterlife.

There are two ways to look at eschatology: spatially and temporally.[4] Spatially, we are considering God's actions, from his vantage point, as he invades the life of humans in the Christ event and brings to conclusion the end and purpose for which he created humanity. Temporally, we can consider eschatology in a manner consistent with linear or historical progression toward the end of the world, the present world. In this way, humans are concerned not only with God's eschatological actions that affect the present but also with his actions that affect the future of the human race and the rest of God's creation. We are asking here: What is going to happen eschatologically in the future? Part of the answer is given in the creed, as stated above: we are looking forward to the resurrection of the dead and the life of the world or age to come. God's spatial activity is centered on Christ as redeemer consummated in Christ's resurrection, which has effects in the afterlife of humans (i.e., temporal eschatology). More specifically, I am concerned with what is called "personal eschatology" (i.e., the state of humans in the afterlife).[5] Where do humans go when they die? What is the hope of where we are going when we die? Such questions, while related to the creation story, are not merely a

---

4. See Tanner, *Jesus, Humanity and the Trinity*, chap. 4, esp. p. 99.

5. The literature on this subject is growing. The following is a representative sampling. See entries on survival and the nature of the afterlife in Walls, *The Oxford Handbook of Eschatology*, particularly chaps. 5, 13, 21, 22, 23, 24, 27, 31, 36. Walls is one of the foremost defenders of the "traditional" Christian view of the afterlife; see Walls, *Hell*; Walls, *Heaven*; Walls, "A Philosophical Critique of Talbott's Universalism"; Walls, "A Hell of a Choice"; Walls, "A Hell of a Dilemma." See also Murray, *Reason for the Hope Within*; Hick, *Death and Eternal Life*; Küng, *Eternal Life?*; Swinburne, "A Theodicy of Heaven and Hell"; Talbott, "The Doctrine of Everlasting Punishment."

repetition of what we find in creation but are greater.[6] Before addressing the main concern of the chapter via the intermediate state, I address a series of afterlife views that are inconsistent with the Christian afterlife.

Christian Afterlife: What It Is Not

Stephen T. Davis suggests—rightly, in my opinion—that there are four broad ways to carve up the concept of afterlife: (1) death ends all, (2) reincarnation, (3) immortality, and (4) resurrection.[7] The death-ends-all theory might be associated with what is often referred to as a naturalistic theory of death and the afterlife (well, not really an afterlife at all).[8] Naturalism is the view that the world is a closed physical system, and all physical/biological things exist in a causal nexus of physical causes and effects closed off from the outside. Such a view is necessarily excluded from the Christian vantage point; if we are to assume the creation narrative and the church's reception of it, then there is a Being that transcends the natural causal framework as the ground for it (as an atemporal being). Furthermore, that Being (which we call God) is the agent that gives life and blesses that life in creation and throughout all of redemption. Characteristic of God's actions are the giving of life and blessing to his creatures in the eschaton (i.e., the age to come), so the death-ends-all theory sits outside the boundaries of Christian afterlife.

Other theories affirm naturalism but see death not as the complete end of all but rather as the extension of some kind of life force (e.g., Buddhism).[9] Generally speaking, the continuation of a life force is antithetical to what the Christian Scriptures and the broader teaching within church history have

---

6. The story of creation itself implies that the image has purpose and destiny, but the specifics are left for later parts of revelation to unfold. See Cortez, *Theological Anthropology*, chap. 1. Cortez shows that the concept of covenantal representation is central to the meaning of "image" and that this has a function throughout Scripture because God is using his image bearers in the context of covenant to bring about his final plan. See also Kilner, *Dignity and Destiny*, esp. the latter part of chap. 3 and chap. 6. Kilner convincingly makes the case that the image concept is fulfilled in the age to come, where the incarnate one enters the human world—where Christ becomes the perfect representative to carry out God's plan and, in a sense, restates the intentions of creation.

7. See Davis, "Eschatology and Resurrection," 386.

8. For a unique naturalist view of the afterlife, see Steinhart, "Digital Afterlives." He affirms that we can affirm the possibility of a personal life after death by adopting not scientific materialism but digitalism. Digitalism is the view that rejects substance metaphysics and affirms that information and computation are fundamental to substance, matter, and energy. Thinking about bodies and persons as composed of "bits" allows for the possibility of some kind of survival so long as the necessary and sufficient "bits" are gathered together.

9. See Johnston, *Surviving Death*.

affirmed. Instead, they affirm that there is a real afterlife in which persons persist either in a loving community that is able to experience the goodness of the triune God everlastingly or in a state of punishment.

Similar to the life-force-continuation view is the notion of reincarnation. Raynor Johnson offers a description of reincarnation: "(By the term 'soul' we mean that individualized aspect of the Self, including buddhi—the Intuitive self—and Higher Mind, all of which are regarded as immortal.) We should of course bear in mind that what is meant by the phrase 'have lived before' is not that the physical form Raynor Johnson has lived on earth previously, but rather that Raynor Johnson is only a particular and temporary expression of an underlying immortal soul which has adopted previous and quite possibly different appearances."[10] Such a view has been subjected to numerous philosophical objections, from the simplicity of the soul as substantial self to the unlikelihood of actual persistence from this life to the next. More important for our purposes, while reincarnation has a few adherents within Christianity, it is generally treated as antithetical to Christian theology because the church's reception of the creation narrative has tended toward the view that human life was created with the creation of the world, and persons will persist as numerically identical objects.

What, then, is the hope of the Christian?

"Life Everlasting"

The Apostles' Creed describes the afterlife as "the resurrection of the body: and the life everlasting." Similarly, the Nicene Creed speaks of "the resurrection of the dead, and the life of the age [or world] to come." Recall that the divine action in redemption occurs through the Christ event, whereby God brings about life and blessing for his chosen people consummately. But what does it mean to experience life everlasting? Some understand it to mean immortality of the soul, and others understand it to mean explicitly immortality through the resurrection of the body.

Oscar Cullmann, reflecting on a long-standing question in Christian thought, raises this famous question: "Immortality of the soul or resurrection of the body?" He argues that the Christian view is tied to the resurrection of the body as the hope of humanity. He says,

10. Johnson, "Preexistence, Reincarnation and Karma," 192–93. See also Hick, *Death and Eternal Life.*

> There is a radical difference between the Christian expectation of the resurrection of the dead and the Greek belief in the immortality of the soul. . . . Although Christianity later established a link between these two beliefs, and today the average Christian confuses them completely, I see no reason to hide what I and the majority of scholars consider to be the truth. . . . The life and thought of the New Testament are entirely dominated by faith in the resurrection. . . . The whole man, who is really dead, is brought back to life by a new creative act of God.[11]

As Cullmann sees things, the immortality of the soul is a product of Greek thought and not a product of Christian thought as it is depicted in the New Testament.[12] Often the notions of immortality of the soul and the resurrection of the body are pitted against each other. These divisions commonly emerge between philosophers (reflecting more on the philosophical coherence of survival and persistence) and theologians (reflecting on the quality of the life eternal), or so it has been suggested where contemporary religious philosophers are interested in the immortality of the soul for making sense of mere persistence beyond the grave and theologians take up greater interest in the physical resurrection as central to Christian theology of the afterlife, but the two are not mutually exclusive.[13]

The question of immortality and resurrection is at the heart of God's intentions for humanity. But what do these mean within the Christian story? Immortality minimally means "endless survival," as Peter Geach articulates.[14] Given, however, the fact that human persons seem to die physically, one must first ask the question as to whether it is sensible for persons, or some part of persons, to survive physical death (i.e., where the physical organism ceases all functionality).[15] What does it mean, then, to live forever according to Christianity? I take it that this claim includes both the immortality of the soul and the physical resurrection of the body, as I will argue in a moment. Yet what

11. Cullmann, *Immortality of the Soul*, 6.

12. The charge of unnecessary or unhealthy Greek influence on Christian theology is a common one that is still at work today. First, it is unwarranted because Christian theology as communicated in the Old and New Testaments is, generally, unsystematic and requires systematization. The Bible itself does not articulate metaphysical issues but instead yields certain metaphysical views or requires a metaphysical grounding. Second, given Second Temple literature, it is nearly impossible to separate Greek philosophical categories from Jewish tradition, which is part of the background behind the New Testament. See Levering, *Jesus and the Demise of Death*, chap. 1, esp. p. 9; see also Daley, *The Hope of the Early Church*.

13. See Harris, "Resurrection and Immortality," 51.

14. Such a question is taken up in the classic and useful treatment given by Geach, "Immortality," 225.

15. Geach, "Immortality," 225.

one means by immortality will vary depending on how one construes the interim state in relation to the everlasting state.

What most Christians mean by immortality is, arguably, distinct in some important respects from the ideas of the most influential Greek defender of immortality, Plato. Plato held to a strong substantial dualism, where the person is the soul that happens to exist in a body, which is a variation of what I have called "pure substance dualism." Pure substance dualism is the view that persons are essentially souls that happen to interact with bodies, contingently, and there is no obvious or intuitive relationship uniting the two substances together.[16] Yet Plato makes an additional claim in the *Phaedo*, as in other places, that the soul is made of the same stuff as what composes heavenly beings like God and is a part of the heavenly universal realm. Thus, Plato moves beyond what some might construe as natural immortality to a kind of necessary and essential immortality, such that souls have existed prior to embodiment and will, by necessity, continue existing unhindered after the body dies (hence, arguably, violating the Creator-creature distinction in the creation narrative). Instead, some Christians have held that persons as soul substances will naturally exist forever, assuming that the divine being does not act in such a way as to snuff the soul out of existence (i.e., natural immortality). Alternatively, some might construe the existence of the soul as contingent on an additional divine act in which God extends life to the soul as a gift; otherwise the soul would simply cease to exist at biological death or at some time after biological death—say, in hell (i.e., annihilationism).[17] While Christians often disagree with Plato, I suggest that the immortality of the soul and the resurrection are not incompatible Christian concepts, but the contemporary inclination is to exclude the soul and its immortality altogether.

Mere Resurrection Afterlife

Characterizing the contemporary Christian ethos, there has been an overwhelming emphasis on the body and the physical world as the primary emphasis of the afterlife (and its correlating creational emphasis). A contemporary tendency is to see humans as solely material creations of God and the nature of hope as material resurrection. There are other potential reasons for such an emphasis on the body and the physical world, but for our purposes here I will set aside this question in favor of the task at hand: the traditional

16. See Farris, "Pure or Compound Dualism?"; Farris, "Considering Souls."
17. For a recent collection, see Date, Stump, and Anderson, *Rethinking Hell*. For the classic treatment, see Fudge, *The Fire That Consumes*.

balancing of both soul and body.[18] The interim and everlasting states have corresponding relations to or correlate to various human personal ontologies as their ground. Both states are situated in this age and the consummation of the final age, that which is to come. The intermediate state or stage is that stage that occurs in between the present life, which ends at somatic death, and the next life—the everlasting state.

Several views are on offer that I categorize under a "mere resurrection" model of the afterlife, including soul sleep, temporary nonexistence or extinction and re-creation, and immediate resurrection.

First, "soul sleep" is the view that persons in the afterlife exist in the mind of God or something similar. Some materialists refer to their view of the interim period as "soul sleep." This seems mistaken, however. As Davis has pointed out, "The term is misleading because (1) the soul does not actually sleep during the interim period; it simply does not exist; and (2) sleeping is essentially a bodily activity, and during the interim period the body is incapable of any activity (except perhaps rotting away, if that is an activity)."[19] In other words, the materialist variation of soul sleep really is not the view that the soul or person is actually existing anywhere in some real sense.[20] A mind-body dualist might refer to soul sleep in which the soul exists in some attenuated sense as a nonfunctioning entity.[21] That said, the materialist is simply affirming that the soul/person ceases to exist, which leads more accurately to the next view.

Second, the "extinction and re-creation" (or "temporary nonexistence") view holds that humans, as material creations, die (i.e., cease to exist) at somatic death and must be re-created by God at the resurrection. The view espoused above by Oscar Cullmann is one example of this understanding. John Hick advocates a view called the "re-creation view." He argues that humans are psychosomatic wholes and persist only as whole beings,[22] such

18. For interesting proposals on this topic, see Bynum, "Why All the Fuss about the Body?"; Eagleton, *The Illusions of Postmodernism*, chap. 4, esp. pp. 75–79; Coakley, "The Eschatological Body."

19. Davis, "Redemption," 299. For example, Oscar Cullmann has affirmed "soul sleep" as the teaching of the New Testament; see Cullmann, *Immortality of the Soul*, 57. John Cooper has helpfully pointed out in the context of discussions of 1 Thess. 4:13–18 that the reference to sleep is simply a metaphor for death. See Cooper, *Body, Soul, and Life Everlasting*, 137.

20. See Davis, *Risen Indeed*.

21. This is a rather strange view.

22. Calling humans "psychosomatic wholes" is rather fuzzy, although not uncommon in the theological literature. When philosophers or theologians use this term, they are referring to the integrity of both the mind and the body in operation. While this term is often used to distance human nature as ontologically holistic or monistic from substantial dualistic conceptions of human nature, it is not entirely clear to many substance dualists that it does create the kind of distance suggested. However, substantial dualism can, arguably, account for a psychosomatic

that when the body dies, the soul seems to die as well; thus if we are to uphold traditional Christian belief in the afterlife, we must affirm some kind of re-creation. But the position encounters significant challenges, which Hick recognizes. Drawing from Derek Parfit in *Reasons and Persons*, he lays out the problem in part:

> Suppose, for example, that the cells of my brain are surgically replaced one by one, under local anesthetic, with physically identical cells. My consciousness and other characteristics continue essentially unchanged throughout the operation. When only 1% of the cells have been replaced we shall probably all agree that I am the same person. But what do we say when 50% have been replaced? And when 99% have been replaced? And what when they have all been replaced? Is this still me, or do I no longer exist, and this is now a replica of me? Or again, consider the teletransporter (somewhat as in *Star Trek*) which scans my body, including the brain, records its state in complete detail, and then destroys it, the next moment forming an exact replica on Mars. The Mars replica's consciousness is continuous with that of the earthly me; but nevertheless, is it me on Mars? Have I been teletransported, or has someone different been created in place of me? This is a question for decision. My contention is that the best decision, the one that best satisfies our intuitions and that gives rise to the fewest practical problems, is that the replica on Mars *is* me; and also, that the John Smith "replica" in the resurrection world is John Smith.[23]

Hick argues that a decision must be made to determine that the resurrected person is the same person or a different person, but a move of this sort reveals what is lacking in materialism. There is no fact of the matter concerning the persistence of material objects across long periods of time.

This view has come under attack in the recent literature, and rightly so, for it amounts to a "closest continuer" theory of personal persistence. The person just is not the same person, even if the physical parts have been gathered up and the person looks the same. The defender may respond and claim that the closest continuer is all we need to make sense of persistence.[24] Additionally, one might attempt to account for some loose continuity between the presomatic death person and the postresurrection person by suggesting that some of the bits of matter hold continuously between the states, but I hardly think that

---

whole if in fact the mind and body are treated as functionally integrated, although not ontologically identical.

23. Hick, "The Recreation of the Psycho-physical Person," 241.
24. See Olson, "Immanent Causation and Life after Death."

this is what we are after.[25] No, instead, our *desire*, and the presupposition of Scripture, is that we would exist as the same individuals here and in the life to come. So we will consider other options.

Third, the theory called "immediate resurrection" is the view that humans, upon somatic death, are resurrected. The defender of immediate resurrection could tell a story wherein God resurrects the corpse that previously composed the person and makes it alive once again (similar to the creational description in Gen. 2:7). The advantage attending the immediate resurrection of bodies/persons is that it can account for passages of Scripture that seemingly yield an interim period of personal existence between somatic death and somatic resurrection by either collapsing the intermediate state into resurrection or by advancing a distinct kind of resurrection from the final resurrection, thus coherently making sense of material intermediate state existence.[26]

What most of these "mere resurrection" views have in common is that they yield, or are made sense of by or are motivated by, materialist views of human nature. That said, there is a challenge for these views. If Eric Olson is right that what dies is, strictly speaking, not able to be created again, then the materialist lacks the resources to sustain personal persistence in the afterlife. There is not much *hope* here without some sort of immortality. In fact, some sort of ground that persists between somatic death and somatic resurrection is required to account for numerical identity before somatic death and after resurrection.[27] What is required, arguably, is a soul to account for the continuity between the two stages. In fact, most divines in Christian tradition assume something other than nonexistence of the soul or soul sleep; most affirm a literal persistence of persons or souls.[28] While these views listed here are commonly cited as ways of making sense of the afterlife for the materialist, it is

---

25. This is something like a Stoic view of humans, which, while not wholly materialist in the modern sense, has some similarities to materialism, but the material world exists eternally. This is different, however, from the view that persons exist forever, as is what we are after in Christian afterlife.

26. Kevin Corcoran advances an "intermediate bodily state" view in *Rethinking Human Nature*, 130–34.

27. See Olson, "Immanent Causation and Life after Death."

28. In fact, the belief in the afterlife as two stages, where the first is an interim state of disembodied existence, while not held to creedal standards as an essential Christian truth, is held to the standard of dogma in both Roman Catholicism and Eastern Orthodoxy. Furthermore, it is the common view within Protestantism. See Nichols, *Death and Afterlife*, chap. 3. He shows that it is the common view throughout church history. Mathew Levering has shown that this is a dogmatic truth in Rome and in the East. See Levering, *Jesus and the Demise of Death*, chap. 1, esp. pp. 20–25. Levering argues that, taking Christology as the starting point, Rome dogmatically affirms that Christ descended to preach to those in hell. With that, the views of hell, heaven, and even purgatory are dogmas.

important to note that there are dualist defenders of these sorts of views that are, arguably, motivated by other concerns. Before turning to a case for an interim state of disembodied soul persistence, let me mention one important dualist version of immediate resurrection.

J. T. Turner is one notable defender of the "immediate resurrection" view. He argues that a view of the afterlife as developed in the creational purpose for humanity will yield a distinct portrait from what is often construed as the traditional view, which includes the disembodied interim state of human existence. Rather, the creational purpose, according to several biblical scholars discussed early on (e.g., N. T. Wright, G. K. Beale, J. Richard Middleton, John D. Levenson, Benjamin L. Gladd, John H. Walton, and Anthony Hoekema to some degree), in contrast to what he sees as a large consensus among philosophers and theologians, yields a holistic, embodied, this-worldly approach rather than a dualistic, other-worldly understanding of humans. In this context, Turner is quite convinced that the scriptural story motivates a portrait of humans and their purpose as one of creational holism that yields an eschatological holism; this holistic view precludes a strict decoupling of the soul from the body but rather upholds a picture of humans as eschatologically visible creatures of the divine—as it is impressed on us protologically. He states this in the following way:

> Moreover, against the backdrop of the Ancient Near East, and its popular theology within which the cult image "is a precisely localized, visible, corporeal representation of the divine," we have good reason to think that the Genesis creation story presents *humankind* as the *embodied* and *visible* expression of Yahweh's rule, in contradistinction to the various wooden, stone, and what have you, cult images of competing Ancient Near Eastern deities. Yahweh's image is crafted by Yahweh Himself, rather than by human hands. If one supposes that the property "being a localized, visible, and corporeal representation of Yahweh" is an essential property of human beings, then a human cannot—so long as she exists—fail to be localized, visible, and corporeal. If that's right, humankind lacks the ability to exist in a disembodied state.[29]

29. Turner, "The Intermediate State, 273." Turner is drawing from a set of biblical-theological literature that has tended to highlight a this-worldly, earthly, or horizontal understanding of eschatology rather than as I have intimated through *An Introduction to Theological Anthropology* for a robust grounding of a this-worldly eschatology in an other-worldly, heavenly, and vertical reality that is, arguably, theocentric rather than anthropocentric. See Middleton, *The Liberating Image*, 25; see also Green, "Eschatology and the Nature of Humans," 48–49; Middleton, *The Liberating Image*, 121–30; Beale, *The Temple and the Church's Mission*, 152.

Once again, Turner represents a common and growing trend in contemporary Old Testament studies (it is widely disseminated in biblical studies more generally) to see humans as whole embodied beings, visible and functioning as one unit, which would seem to exclude a disembodied state of creaturely existence. Saying this, I think that it is important to note that variations of substance dualism that allow for soulish persistence from bodily demise do not entail the denial of holistic creatures (with souls and bodies), but rather most contemporary substance dualists would affirm the functional integrity of the human as a soul-body unit. Such a claim is not an ad hoc response to those pushing against substantial dualisms but instead points to the reality that the soul is limited and diminished in its powers and functioning during the disembodied interim state. This would mean that, on these versions of substance dualism, humans are normally and naturally embodied and physically visible, because there is something about the nature of the soul that depends on or requires a body for its complete and full functioning.[30] I would also point out that such a view lacks the characteristic makeup of humans as centrally immaterial beings at their core in a way that enables such creatures to interact with God in unique ways. The scriptural creation story highlights not merely this physically visible representation of human beings but also the importance of knowing, hearing, and seeing God (who is immaterial in nature). If the later narrative is correct by accurately representing the scriptural story line on humans, then we have some reason to consider a wider or broader understanding of the creaturely story that allows for a telos that is inclusive of both soulish realities and bodily realities. Via this route through creaturely afterlife, we can indirectly come at a picture of humans. Keeping with a traditioned understanding of humans as soulish beings that persist in an intermediate state between somatic death and somatic resurrection, let us consider this alternative picture.

The Intermediate State

The intermediate state often described by the church is normally understood to convey not nonexistence but soulish or personal existence. The support for

30. J. T. Turner advances an account of a Thomist model that provides some rationale for understanding the human as dying somatically; that is, the human goes out of existence, yet the human being is resurrected immediately as an embodied being. Without looking at his model in detail, it would seem that such a view still requires some kind of persistence (namely, a soul as form), even if it is not a temporal kind of existence.

such a view is found in several passages of Scripture commonly garnered as support for the intermediate state of disembodied existence.[31]

With Davis, I affirm the immortality of the soul as a metaphysical precondition for affirming the intermediate state of disembodied existence. In disagreement with Cullmann, Davis summarizes Cullmann's rejection of the soul's immortality: "He radically separated the two theories and argued that only resurrection is a genuinely Christian notion. Immortality of the soul, he claimed, is an alien concept. It was imported from Greek philosophy by certain church fathers, played no role in biblical or primitive Christian conceptions of the afterlife, and ought not to be part of Christian thinking about the afterlife today."[32] If in fact the Christian view includes an intermediate state of personal or soulish existence between somatic death and somatic resurrection, then it follows that some variant of the doctrine of the immortality of the soul follows.[33] To go back to Geach's insight, if the body dies, then the natural question is whether the person or some part of the person persists; if so, then immortality of the soul follows because the body dies. If the theologian wishes to distinguish this kind of immortality from the one described in the scriptural story line, then he or she could affirm a weaker-immortality thesis (i.e., disembodied souls, where souls persist without their bodies) and a robust-immortality thesis (i.e., where souls exist in union with God, experiencing all the blessings God intends for his image bearers) to account for the distinctions.

In keeping with these immortality distinctions, Joseph Ratzinger has summarized quite well the church's position that unites the assumptions of philosophers with those of theologians. He says, "Clearly, then, what the Church had to maintain was, on the one hand, the central certainty of a life with Christ that not even death can destroy, and, on the other hand, the incompleteness of that life in the time before the definitive 'resurrection of the flesh.'"[34] In other words, some *thing* must account for the persistence of persons as the ground for resurrection hope, where humans experience all the blessings that God intends.

31. For a defense from the biblical material, see Cooper, *Body, Soul, and Life Everlasting*. See also Cooper, "Biblical Anthropology," 227–28. For a contrary opinion on the biblical data, see Green, *Body, Soul, and Human Life*. Green delivers a strong case in favor of the biblical data yielding not dualism but monism, but dualists do not find his case finally persuasive. It is important to note that Green's interpretation of the biblical data is revisionist in nature from the common traditional interpretations of Scripture.

32. Davis, "Eschatology and Resurrection," 389.

33. Davis, "Eschatology and Resurrection," 389.

34. Ratzinger, *Eschatology*, 147.

One important symbol of the Protestant tradition representing a common conviction in church history is the Westminster Confession of Faith, which supports the immortality of the soul as the ground for intermediate disembodied existence. It states,

> The bodies of men, after death, return to dust, and see corruption: but their souls, which neither die nor sleep, having an immortal subsistence, immediately return to God who gave them: the souls of the righteous, being then made perfect of holiness, are received into the highest heavens, where they behold the face of God, in light and glory, waiting for the full redemption of their bodies. And the souls of the wicked are cast into hell, where they remain in torments and utter darkness, reserved to the judgment of the great day. Beside these two places, for souls separated from their bodies, the Scripture acknowledges none.[35]

John Calvin supports the belief in the immortality of the soul as a central tenet of the Christian faith. He says the following:

> Furthermore, that man consists of a soul and a body ought to be beyond controversy. Now I understand by the term "soul" an immortal yet created essence, which is his nobler part. Sometimes it is called "spirit." For even when these terms are joined together, they differ from one another in meaning; yet when the word "spirit" is used by itself, it means the same thing as soul; as when Solomon, speaking of death, says that then "the spirit returns to God who gave it" [Eccl. 12:7]. And when Christ commended his spirit to the Father [Luke 23:46] and Stephen his to Christ [Acts 7:59] they meant only that when the soul is freed from the prison house of the body, God is its perpetual guardian.[36]

Several scriptural passages, arguably, support the doctrine of a disembodied interim state.[37] Knowing that bodies die excludes the possibility of persons as bodily substances persisting, but why think that persons as souls might persist?[38]

35. Westminster Confession of Faith, chap. 32, art. 1. This statement excludes purgatory, but my intent is not to exclude purgatory, necessarily, from the interim state but rather to highlight the emphasis on the immortality of the soul.

36. Calvin, *Institutes* 1.15.2.

37. Passages traditionally appropriated as signaling the intermediate state include the following: Gen. 3:19; Eccl. 12:7; Luke 16:23–24; 23:43; Acts 13:36; 2 Cor. 5:1, 6, 8; Phil. 1:23 with Acts 3:21; Eph. 4:10; Heb. 12:23; 1 Pet. 3:19; Jude 6–7.

38. For a general appraisal of substance dualism, there are five recent collections, three of which are more negative critiques of materialism and two of which are a positive defense of substance dualism: Koons and Bealer, *The Waning of Materialism*; Göcke, *After Physicalism*;

The great nineteenth-century Reformation theologian Charles Hodge, dealing with many of the scientific concerns confronting us today, albeit in seed form, affirms the doctrine of the intermediate state and its ancillary doctrine of the soul as that affirmed by all Christians. He says, "As all Christians believe in the resurrection of the body and future judgment, they all believe in an intermediate state."[39]

Why Think That Souls Would Survive the Death of Bodies?

I have to this point, to some extent, taken it for granted that if materialism encounters overwhelming problems concerning the nature of survival in the afterlife, then one ought to affirm the doctrine of the soul (i.e., the immortality of the soul) to account for the transition from somatic death to somatic resurrection. I have done so because the doctrine of the soul is often described as a commonsense view that seems naturally compatible with survival in the afterlife.[40] To motivate this conception of the afterlife, I will briefly look at analytic philosophy of mind, which comes into play when we consider the subject of survival and the afterlife. Both issues emerge in the context of discussing either disembodied existence or bodily resurrection.

Charles Taliaferro offers an argument in favor of dualism (i.e., substance dualism). He says, "1. If I am the very same thing as my body, then whatever is true of me, is true of my body. 2. But my body may survive without me (it may, for example, become a corpse), and I may survive without my body (I might have a new body or exist in a disembodied state). 3. Therefore, I am not the very same thing as my body."[41] If this is true, then there is no problem in suggesting that persons survive in the afterlife. The crucial premise is premise 2, which can be buttressed by the experiences that one has of self in contrast to body. Upon reflection, I intuitively believe that I am not, strictly speaking, my body but rather could be separable from my body. One can motivate this intuition by considering the various objects of the body in

Loftin and Farris, *Christian Physicalism?*; Lavazza and Robinson, *Contemporary Dualism*; Loose, Menuge, and Moreland, *The Blackwell Companion to Substance Dualism*.

39. Hodge, *Systematic Theology*, 3:724. Another important modern Reformed theologian is Karl Barth, but his view of the afterlife is less than clear.

40. For a defense of substance dualism for the conceivability of the afterlife, see Hasker and Taliaferro, "Afterlife." Hasker and Taliaferro are not exclusively concerned with a Christian view of afterlife, but they are concerned with afterlife teaching more broadly concerning the possibility of survival. The authors suggest that dualism is the commonsense view often naturally assumed as an accounting for the afterlife; see esp. section 2, "The Possibility of Survival—Dualism."

41. Taliaferro, "Human Nature," 539.

relation to who I am as a soul. I instinctively believe when I look at my feet, I am distinct from my feet, and, in fact, I could lose my feet and still be me. If this is true, then dualism (construed as the soul having a distinct kind of substantial existence) can conceivably account for the doctrine of an interim state. Added to this, if the soul is distinct from the body as a metaphysically simple thing and does not divide like material entities, then the ontology of souls allows for the possibility and conceivability of persistence.

Taliaferro's argument is helpful in that it motivates the coherence of dualism and the intermediate state. But what about the distinction between a soul that is severely diminished while disembodied and a soul that is able to flourish, in some sense, while disembodied? Two distinct models seem to emerge. Davis, in a recent article, agrees that there is an intermediate state of disembodied existence, thus requiring the soul and its immortality, but he proceeds to articulate what I call a "mere resurrection hope" view of the afterlife.

Mere Resurrection Hope

Stephen Davis has defended the immortality of the soul as an accounting for the interim state in addition to the physical resurrection doctrine, but, for Davis, the nature of Christian hope is the physical resurrection of the body alone.[42] Toward the end of his recent article on the afterlife, Davis summarizes his position as follows: "Once again, resurrection points the way for us. If you believe both in a general resurrection that is essentially bodily and in the continuing incarnation of the second person of the Trinity, you will have no trouble accepting the idea that the blessed, in the eschaton, can literally see God. But will the blessed also see the Father and the Holy Spirit? Here Christian theology comes to the end of its tether. The only answer we can give is perhaps."[43] Davis describes the hope of humanity as physical resurrection, not the heavenly state of disembodied existence. While he recognizes an interim state, he does not say much about it but views the state as a highly deficient kind of human existence.[44] In another place he favorably cites Aquinas on

42. Wright has a similar perspective. See Wright, *Surprised by Hope*.
43. Davis, "Eschatology and Resurrection," 396.
44. Assuming that we do much of anything, it is not clear what we do. On this view, the interim state is treated as a kind of holdover until we get to the good stuff: physical resurrection of the body. As noted earlier, the tendency to highlight the physical world and the body is common today, which is reflected in this view. Davis, however, is only one representative contemporary example affirming this "mere resurrection hope" view. See also Wright, *Surprised by Hope*. See also the interpretation of 2 Cor. 5 in Witherington, *Conflict and Community in Corinth*, 391. Witherington recognizes that 2 Cor. 5 yields an intermediate-state interpretation, hence

the need for the soul's resurrection body: "Man cannot achieve his ultimate happiness unless the soul be once again united to the body."[45] Davis understands Aquinas to affirm that the hope of the Christian is the beatific vision, which occurs in the resurrection state. However, the key word for Aquinas is "ultimate." Aquinas does, in fact, hold a kind of hope for the Christian that one can experience during the intermediate state, which has an intimate relationship to the everlasting state. To this we turn.

Disembodied Hope with Resurrection Hope

Jason Hentschel readvances one respectable traditional theological reading of 2 Corinthians 5:1–10 by retrieving it from Thomas Aquinas's works.[46] Contrary to the contemporary sentiment that the interim state is bleak, dark, and nonfunctional, he suggests that one way to read 2 Corinthians 5 is to understand that Paul is laying out a hopeful intermediate state. For Paul, on such a reading, the hope of the believer is to experience union with God as the initial beatific vision. I suggest that we have here a model of the afterlife distinct from Davis's model. Instead, on this model, humans can truly function and even experience union with God during the disembodied state. Thus, on one's deathbed one can rest in the hope of *immediate union* with God.

Aquinas is not the only one who views the interim disembodied state as desirable. Terence Nichols has convincingly shown that disembodied hope is a common traditional view and is reflected in the martyr's hopeful expectation to be drawn up immediately to heaven upon death.[47] This model is the common Protestant view. The Westminster Shorter Catechism says, "The souls of believers are, at their *death*, made perfect in holiness, and do immediately pass into glory [the Larger Catechism (86) and Confession (1) say "into the highest heavens"]; and their bodies, being still united to Christ, do rest in their graves till the resurrection. At the *resurrection*, believers, being raised up in glory, shall be openly acknowledged and acquitted in the day of judgment, and made perfectly blessed in full enjoying of God to all eternity."[48] Theological eccentric William Shedd summarizes and codifies the

---

substance dualism, but does not view the state positively. Thomas Aquinas, too, recognizes a view of this sort in the famous commentary called the *Gloss* in his *Summa Theologiae* III.59.5.

45. See Davis, "Redemption," 299. He is referring to Aquinas, *Summa Contra Gentiles* IV.79. However, this needs to be balanced with Thomas's claim that at least some humans experience the beatific vision during the disembodied heavenly state.

46. Hentschel, "Thomas Aquinas," esp. 73–77.

47. Nichols, *Death and Afterlife*, 57.

48. Westminster Shorter Catechism, answers to questions 37, 38 (emphasis mine).

Reformation view: "The substance of the Reformed view, then, is, that the intermediate state for the saved is Heaven without the body, and the final state for the saved is Heaven with the body; that the intermediate state for the lost is Hell without the body, and the final state for the lost is Hell with the body. In the Reformed, or Calvinistic eschatology, there is no intermediate Hades between Heaven and Hell, which the good and evil inhabit in common. When this earthly existence [is] ended, the only specific places and states are Heaven and Hell."[49] Charles Hodge, in agreement with the Reformed tradition, states, "The common Protestant doctrine on this subject is that 'the souls of believers are at their death, made perfect in holiness and do immediately pass into glory; and their bodies, being still united to Christ, do rest in their graves till the resurrection.' According to this view the intermediate state, so far as believers are concerned, is one of perfect freedom from sin and suffering, and of great exaltation and blessedness."[50]

In other words, the common Reformed view of hope is heaven, which begins upon death and finds completion in the resurrection. Naturally, this raises the question as to the nature of Christian souls that are not prepared for heaven. Some have argued that the Reformation view, which I will call the "immediate glorification upon death" view, is incomplete, possibly incoherent, requiring a doctrine of purgatory.[51] My contention is not to rule out either purgatory or immediate glorification upon death but rather to consider these as variants of the model advanced. My only point is that the nature of Christian hope is not mere resurrection hope but is disembodied interim hope, which has fallen into disrepute in the contemporary discussion.

The model that I propose not only carves out a place for the immortality of the soul as disembodied interim existence but also construes the interim state as the initial hope of the Christian. This leads to the final question worth considering.

Anthropological Models and Disembodied Existence

Thus far, I have shown that immortality of the soul grounds the interim state in relation to the resurrection state, making materialism an unlikely option for Christian afterlife. Furthermore, I advanced a "disembodied hope" view

49. Shedd, *Dogmatic Theology*, 831–63.
50. Hodge, *Systematic Theology*, 3:724.
51. Purgatory is commonplace for Roman Catholicism. For a definitive Protestant treatment, see Walls, *Purgatory*. Walls presents a persuasive case for the doctrine of purgatory that, he argues, is consistent with Protestant doctrine.

of the afterlife. In light of this there are several anthropological models worth considering, all of which have an immaterial essential core and could broadly be construed as variations of mind-body dualism.[52]

The first is substance dualism. Substance dualism is the view that humans are composed of two substances (i.e., property bearers) that are separable. There are variations of substance dualism. I mentioned two in chapter 1. One is what one might call "pure substance dualism," because it maintains the strict integrity of the substantial soul from the bodily substance. While not off the table for consideration, the view has difficulty accounting for a unity of body and soul, which the intermediate state only exacerbates. Another view is what I call "compound substance dualism."[53] I suggest that the two substances are distinct and separable, as with pure varieties, but that one can tell a story that maintains a more natural and intuitive relationship between soul and body. One could construe souls as bearing a kind-nature related to bodies. By way of contrast, a relational soul is a soul that has no kind-nature but can adapt to a variety of differing biological organisms. Kind souls, then, naturally exist in a larger dynamic structure inclusive of the body. One would have a distinct option from pure or relational varieties of substance dualism. While the body is, technically speaking, contingent, it is necessary for a complete human nature.

Alternatively, one could affirm some variant of Thomism.[54] Thomism, similar to compound substance dualism, holds a stronger unity of body and soul.[55] That unity is one where the soul exists as an organizing principle for the matter it inheres. On this view, souls can persist between somatic death and somatic resurrection. The challenge for the view is its ability to make sense of personal persistence, because both soul and body are required for a human being to exist.

Finally, a view that is almost completely excluded from discussion is idealism. By "idealism," I am referring to an Edwardsian or Berkeleyan variant of idealism, which says that only minds and their ideas exist. Both Edwards

52. I am less inclined to describe idealism as mind-body dualism because there is nothing substantial about bodies on this view, but some would categorize it in this way. I prefer to describe idealism as a variation of monism that has the benefits of substance dualism because of the person's immaterial nature.

53. See Swinburne, *Mind, Brain, and Free Will*. See also Taliaferro, *Consciousness and the Mind of God*. Taliaferro refers to his position as "integrative dualism" to maintain the functional integrity of soul and body. His view, as I construe it, is a variation of compound dualism.

54. I use the term *Thomism* to avoid confusing the view with substance dualism. Although there is some debate about whether Thomas Aquinas was a materialist or dualist, I take it that materialism is an odd coupling with Thomism because of his clear assumption that humans are composed of an immaterial part that can exist separable from the body.

55. See Stump, *Aquinas*; Leftow, "Souls Dipped in Dust."

and Berkeley affirm that God exists along with other created minds, and the only thing that is substantial is the mind, which is an immaterial substance.[56]

One immediate objection or worry comes to the fore. How do we make sense of the bodily resurrection if disembodied souls experience Christian hope without the body? It is a fair concern, and for the sake of space I will very briefly offer a response.

The first way to respond is to suggest that the soul's powers are weakened or diminished during the intermediate state, yet the soul's state of being objectively in union with God is not. So the resurrected body would complete the nature of the human person and enhance the subject's experience of its own state before God.[57]

Second, one could respond similarly by arguing that disembodied souls exist in a perfect state of existence in union with God but not in terms of the finite good attained via the kind-nature respective of the soul. In commenting on Thomas Aquinas's view of disembodied hope, Christopher Brown offers an interesting response to the worry of an insignificant body: "The takeaway from this text for our purposes is clear: St. Thomas teaches here that the separated soul's desire for the glory of the body *is not a desire for the essential reward*, since the desire for embodiment has a created good for its object and the object of the desire for the essential reward is the uncreated good, i.e., God. The separated soul's desire for embodiment is therefore a desire for a part of the accidental reward and so embodiment is a part of the accidental reward and not the essential reward."[58]

Added to this, it is fitting that God would supply the body to the soul at resurrection in order to complete the human. In the end, for Aquinas, the body is a finite, created, and accidental good, and so it follows that in the afterlife it is a finite, created, and accidental reward.

Conclusion

I began the chapter with a variety of stories that shape one's expectation of the afterlife. Recognizing its relevance to our creaturely condition as one that leads to death but doesn't end there, I proceeded to explore the relationship between the intermediate state and the final state within Christian thought. I argued that a Reformed view of the afterlife, dogmatically understood,

---

56. Things are slowly changing. See Farris and Hamilton, *Idealism and Christian Theology*.
57. Marc Cortez advances something like this solution in the context of defending Jonathan Edwards's idealist conception of the afterlife. See Cortez, "Idealism and the Resurrection."
58. Brown, "St. Thomas," 23.

affirms the immortality of the soul and the physical resurrection of the body. Furthermore, I surveyed a variety of models or views on offer concerning Christian afterlife. While not definitively excluding Christian materialism as an option, I did suggest that it encounters significant biblical and philosophical challenges and is in tension with what we find in the broad consensus of traditional Christianity. In this way, the immortality of the soul seems to be a necessary precondition for the resurrection of the body. Finally, I advanced one underappreciated model of the afterlife and its ancillary ontologies. The view or model that I recommend maintains not only that disembodied immortality of the soul is assumed in a doctrine of the afterlife but also that the initial hope of the afterlife occurs during the interim state of personal existence. Much more could be said about the assumed ontologies and their relationship to both the interim state and the everlasting state, but additional reflection on the implications of personal ontology and the afterlife remains a topic for another day.

Before we proceed to the next chapter, it is important to note that the present chapter has raised some questions about our final state. While we have explored our creaturely existence as weak, frail, and finite, we have also explored our divine existence as immaterial beings that are like God. In the context of this chapter, we have explored the meaning of our death, yet we have also explored the divine side of our existence as creatures that actually persist from one state (before somatic death) to another state (after somatic resurrection). A few questions are deserving of our attention as we seek to give some answer to the question, Why do I exist? These include the following: What is the beatific vision, and is it still relevant? When does the beatific vision occur—in the disembodied state or the resurrected state? What is the nature of human union with the divine (traditionally called "deification" or "theosis")? These, along with the contemporarily relevant question regarding transhumanism, will occupy us in the next chapter.

10

Why Do I Exist?

Creaturely Process and Divine Destiny

Through these he has given us his very great and precious promises, so that through them you may participate in the divine nature.

2 *Peter 1:4*

By a true and a real union, (but which is only passive on their part,) they are united to Christ when his Spirit first takes possession of them, and infuses into them a principle of new life: the beginning of which life can be from nothing else but from union with the Spirit of Christ; who is to the soul, but in a far more excellent manner, in respect of spiritual life, what the soul is to the body in respect of animal and human life.

Herman Witsius, Conciliatory or Irenical Animadversions
on the Controversies Agitated in Britain

How one understands the creation narrative affects how one understands the new-creation narrative. There is a growing set of literature, some of which I have referenced, that understands the new creation as one that is physical, holistic, and earthy. In fact, the notion of heaven is characterized as this-worldly rather than other-worldly. This contemporary impulse certainly has some value. However, there is another impulse present in the broader catholic Christian and Reformed traditions, which has always highlighted the other-worldly nature of heaven. Yet those who motivated this particular emphasis did not intend to devalue the this-worldly character of creation and new creation. Rather, their focus was the other-worldly character of heaven, where God resides, which is understood to be the life-infusing and suffusing power of this world.

We could think of an illustration to help distinguish a this-worldly model of eschatology from an other-worldly model of eschatology. Consider a waterfall that you may have experienced in your past or one that you have seen in pictures. You may have even visited this waterfall more than once in your life. As with the most beautiful waterfalls, this one is refreshing, beautiful, and energizing. When you see it, you want to dive into the water below and swim around in it. You may recall several fond memories you have had in relation to this waterfall with your friends and family, and the waterfall reminds you of the relationships you have had in the past. The waterfall helps illustrate two distinct pictures of our heavenly existence. On a this-worldly understanding of heaven, we will experience this waterfall again or one that is similar, just more magnificent. The waterfall will be pure, the most satisfying blue color, and clear. On an other-worldly understanding of heaven, the waterfall points us to another reality that finds its fullest expression and reality in God and his attributes. On the first picture, there is a tendency to elevate the physical and sensual reality of this earthly life (albeit with the clear intention of conveying the superiority of the next life) and to downplay, even miss, the reality that all these earthly things point us to God and his perfections. On the other picture, which highlights the other-worldly heavenly reality of God and his perfections, there may be a pristine waterfall, but even it fails to capture what it points to. On a heavenly model of the afterlife with its other-worldly emphasis, it is important to point out that this world was never intended to function alone or independent from the other world, but, instead, this world is made complete sense of by the other-world and points to the other-world. At times the difference between these two perspectives/models or ways of reading Scripture is not so much a difference in kind as a difference in emphasis. In the present chapter, I will lay out and describe what are often considered other-worldly aspects of human eschatology.

Human Purpose as an Experience of God

It is common in contemporary eschatological literature to place important emphasis on the physically embodied experience of God's intention for the newly created state, especially with its emphasis on the final state of humanity as physically resurrected. And it is this state that is contrasted with the beatific vision as articulated in much of the Christian tradition. The physical resurrection is, unfortunately, that which dominates much of the personal eschatological literature without a robust rootedness in the doctrine of the beatific vision. For example, the physical resurrection is often construed as the outcome or consequence of the beatific vision of God in Christ in the final state, which becomes the causal condition that brings about union with God and the elevation of our natures in the resurrection.[1] However, there is something important that could become suppressed or muffled in the present discussion but is necessary to the theological traditions mentioned above. That is that we as humans are designed to experience the living trinitarian God of Scripture who acts in creation and redemption. In his acts, God brings about new life and blessing to human beings. In some sense, this emphasis is fundamental in Scripture for understanding how we are transformed from our previous states as fallen humans to redeemed humans.

The vision in which we experience God in Christ is not a perception obtained by use of the eyes. The vision is traditionally understood to be a vision of the immaterial God by way of the intellectual eyes of the soul. The vision described and developed in the Christian tradition is, it seems, a metaphor for a set of interrelated capacities. It signifies the capacity to be fully human in that humans have acquired the completion of their divinely intended goals. It is a capacity for affectively experiencing God. It is a capacity for understanding and knowing God. It is a capacity for willfully being disposed toward God. It seems right to characterize the vision as a spiritual perception as well as a capacity.

Another metaphor that is commonly used in reference to the vision is theosis or deification. Humans are, arguably, designed for the end of becoming like God. Metaphorically, humans are designed to become God or gods. Theosis, or deification, means just that we will be like God through an elevation of our natures in union with God in Christ. Through the process of redemption,

---

1. As I have already mentioned, the most influential treatments on personal eschatology reflect this shift away from any notion of the human soul, beatific vision, and the related notion that we partake in the divine nature. For a small sampling of influential works, see Middleton, *A New Heaven and a New Earth*; Wright, *Surprised by Hope*; Turner, "Temple Theology, Holistic Eschatology, and the Imago Dei." This is also characteristic of Dutch Calvinism, which has influenced contemporary evangelical theology and continues to do so. The challenges to these contemporary trends from a more "theocentric" focus on God's attributes and our participation in them in contrast to a more anthropocentric and earth-centered focus are seen in the likes of Levering, *Jesus and the Demise of Death;* Boersma, *Heavenly Participation*; Boersma, *Seeing God*; Allen, *Grounded in Heaven*; Canlis, *Calvin's Ladder*; Billings, *Calvin, Participation, and the Gift*; Strobel, "Jonathan Edwards and the Polemics of *Theosis*."

saints become like God in that they exhibit attributes and characteristics that resemble their redeemer.[2] In some sense, the final end/completion of redemption is theosis. The larger systematic question is whether vision and theosis are, strictly speaking, synonymous or related in some important way. Some might take it that the vision is an aspect of this broader process of becoming like God; others might take it that the vision is the causal mechanism that brings about theosis. However one parses out the relationship, the two are closely related.

Scriptural Warrant for Beatific Vision and Human Souls[3]

In the First Letter to the Corinthians, Paul gives us perhaps the fullest description of the vision in Scripture. Paul's letter offers a warranted starting point for a theology of the beatific vision that is intellectual in nature yet guided by love. Paul writes, "For now we see in a mirror, dimly, but then we will see face to face. Now I only know in part; then I will know fully, even as I have been fully known" (1 Cor. 13:12 NRSV).

Anthony Thiselton confirms this theological reading of 1 Corinthians 13:12 as an indication of the beatific vision. He describes the metaphor used here as one that is common to the Platonic tradition, thus highlighting human immateriality and its corresponding relationship to the vision of an immaterial God.[4] Seeing God, in 1 Corinthians 13:12, is not only the end for which we see God in the eschaton but also the event that sums up the whole hope of the Christian and makes sense of the whole process leading to it. This is exemplified in 1 John 3:2: "When Christ appears, we shall be like him." And in John 14:9 Jesus says, "Anyone who has seen me has seen the Father." These passages point to the beatific vision and the connection with our union with God.

In the context of redemption and covenants, there are several types that point to the final vision, where we will be united to God by seeing God. One of the early types is found in Moses's statement to God, "Show me your glory, I pray" (Exod. 33:18 NRSV). God responds by claiming, "No one shall see me and live" (33:20). Then, after the glory of the Lord passed by while Moses was in the cleft of a rock (33:22), the Lord allowed him to gaze at

---

2. See Blackwell, *Christosis*.

3. For a fuller treatment of this subject from which I draw in this section, see Farris and Brandt, "A Theology of Seeing."

4. See Thiselton, *First Epistle to the Corinthians*. Thiselton offers a helpful exposition of the issues that are consonant with a beatific vision understanding of eschatology.

his back, though his face went unseen (33:23). At this point in redemptive history, Moses and humans in general are unable to see God, but our ability to see God will come about progressively as God reveals himself, which will ultimately climax eschatologically.

Later revelation gives us one example of the eschatological vision. Second Corinthians 5:6–7 says, "Even though we know that while we are at home in the body we are away from the Lord—for we walk by faith, not by sight" (NRSV). A traditional, albeit Thomist-inspired, reading of the passage takes it that this is a description not of the physical resurrection (1 Cor. 15) but of the disembodied intermediate state wherein the saints will see God upon somatic death. Paul shows that in this state the saints, rather than living by faith, will see God—not of faith but of sight.

Another passage, which progressively unveils the final state of humans (at least those tied to Christ in the new covenant), is 2 Peter 1:3–4, which unites beatific vision with deification. Peter says, "His divine power has given us everything we need for a godly life through our knowledge of him who called us by his own glory and goodness. Through these he has given us his very great and precious promises, so that through them you may participate in the divine nature, having escaped the corruption in the world caused by evil desires." The notion of sight, which traditionally corresponds to knowledge, is connected with union or participation in God through Christ.

The Medieval Tradition[5]

Briefly, the present section shows that there was an emphasis on both the immaterial and material aspects of the afterlife in the medieval period of Christian history. It is debatable whether the medieval tradition emphasized the immaterial to such an extent that it devalued the material aspects. Because the Reformers were working within the context of the medieval construction, it is helpful to note the propensity toward the immaterial and intellectual elements in both Peter Lombard and Thomas Aquinas. First, Peter Lombard prioritizes the immaterial over the material in his discussion of the beatific vision. While Lombard places his discussion of the beatific vision after the resurrection and judgment, it is not entirely clear in what state he imagines the vision taking place. However, the distinctions that he examines and the way in which he examines them show that he conceives of the vision primarily in immaterial terms, especially through the assumption that the vision is

5. Much of the following has been modified and synthesized from a previous publication. See Farris and Brandt, "Ensouling the Beatific Vision."

chiefly intellectual.[6] He begins by addressing the mansions in heaven and hell, respectively, concluding that "to have life is to see life, that is, to know God face to face."[7] The nature of the beatific state is one primarily of soulish, or intellectual, qualities. Indeed, to "have life is to know [God]."[8] The standing assumption that the vision is immaterial and intellectual is confirmed as he continues to consider the state of blessedness, which he defines in terms of willing and knowing the good—again, both soulish qualities.[9] He goes on to discuss the different degrees of knowledge and joy in the beatific state.[10] Interestingly, a discussion of the body's place in the vision is lacking, except for a reference from Augustine.[11] Lombard prioritizes the immaterial and intellectual in the beatific vision.

Thomas Aquinas also prioritizes the immaterial and intellectual. Like his predecessor Lombard, Aquinas focuses on the vision in terms of the intellect.[12] While he discusses the glorified body's role in the vision,[13] he does not grant the body particular weight in the discussion: "The intellect can perceive spiritual things, whereas the eyes of the body cannot: wherefore the intellect will be able to know the divine essence united to it, but the eyes of the body will not."[14] The bodily senses are thus limited in capacity compared to the immaterial intellect in the vision. Aquinas also suggests that we actually gaze at God in his essence: "God will be seen in His essence by the saints in heaven."[15] Aquinas prioritizes the immaterial in the beatific vision, but this does not end with him; instead, it is taken up in a large part among Reformed theologians.

The Reformation Tendency

Following Peter and Aquinas, many Reformed theologians have prioritized the immaterial and intellectual aspects of the beatific vision. Arguably, this is relatively straightforward in the tradition. No doubt, there were other aspects within the tradition worth exploring on the afterlife, and I do not intend to convey that the Reformed tradition was by any means monolithic. By considering some of the most significant Reformed theological authorities (John

6. See Rosemann, *Peter Lombard*, 118–44.
7. Lombard, *Sentences*, Book 1, 266.
8. Lombard, *Sentences*, Book 1, 266.
9. Lombard, *Sentences*, Book 1, 267–68.
10. Lombard, *Sentences*, Book 1, 269–70.
11. Lombard, *Sentences*, Book 1, 270.
12. Aquinas, *Summa Theologiae*, Suppl.93.1–3.
13. Aquinas, *Summa Theologiae*, Suppl.93.2.
14. Aquinas, *Summa Theologiae*, Suppl.93.2.7.
15. Aquinas, *Summa Theologiae*, Suppl.93.1, s. c.; cf. Suppl.93.1–3.

Calvin, Francis Turretin, Charles Hodge, Jonathan Edwards), I show some of the priorities highlighted throughout the tradition.

First, while John Calvin does not address the beatific vision systematically, the idea appears occasionally throughout his *Institutes*.[16] Calvin's emphasis on the immaterial is most clearly visible when he discusses human anthropology as an image of the divine. Calvin is committed to Plato's understanding of the human constitution, including the supposition that the soul or the mind is more fundamental than the body. He says, "Now I understand by the term 'soul' an immortal yet created essence, which is his nobler part."[17] For Calvin, it is the soul or the mind (henceforth "soul") and its powers that provide the appropriate connectedness to God in Christ, for the soul has primacy with respect to the *image*.[18] Based on the link between creation and redemption in Calvin on the "image," it is the soul as "image" that is the primary referent that participates in God's attributes for the *visio Dei* as he understands it in 2 Corinthians 3:18. The role of the body is, no doubt, important to Calvin's understanding of personal eschatology and Christology, but to what extent is open for additional exploration. Turretin especially reflects this closely.

Following the articulation of Thomas Aquinas, Francis Turretin offers the Reformed theologian a more explicit and developed treatment of the beatific vision than we find in Calvin. He places his discussion of the vision in the context of eternal life. The primary elements of eternal life, he avers, are sight, love, and joy: sight "contemplates God" and "perfects the intellect," love moves toward (and ultimately unites with) God and perfects love, and joy enjoys God and perfects the conscience.[19] In the context of these three, he describes the vision: the vision "implies the most perfect and clear knowledge of God and of divine things, such as can belong to the finite creature."[20] He contrasts this clear and distinct knowledge with the specular and enigmatical knowledge in the present state. On account of God's incorporeal nature, Turretin continues, he "accordingly cannot fall under a sense of the body because power is not carried beyond its own object."[21] In other words, Turretin explains that God cannot be seen by bodily eyes. Indeed, while the resurrection eyes will "become spiritual as to qualities, they will not be changed into spirits, but remain corporeal."[22] Thus, even after the resurrection, the bodily

16. Calvin, *Institutes* 2.14.3, 3.2.24.
17. Calvin, *Institutes* 1.15.2.
18. See Helm, *Calvin at the Centre*, 40–64; Helm, *John Calvin's Ideas*, 129–57.
19. Turretin, *Institutes of Elenctic Theology*, 3:609.
20. Turretin, *Institutes of Elenctic Theology*, 3:610.
21. Turretin, *Institutes of Elenctic Theology*, 3:610.
22. Turretin, *Institutes of Elenctic Theology*, 3:611.

eyes cannot see God's essence. Once again this is because, for the Reformers, God is immaterial in nature, and thus we are—at least at our core—immaterial in nature. In continuity with Calvin, Turretin understands the human constitution to be fundamentally immaterial.[23] The climax of our redemption, while inclusive in some sense of resurrection for Turretin, is the spiritual and thus immaterial vision of God: "God can be seen of man by a spiritual and internal vision alone."[24]

Thus far, there is an open question as to the state in which the vision occurs in Turretin. Is it the disembodied interim state or the final glorified state, which includes the physically resurrected body? While Turretin has not clarified the state in which the vision will take place, he has implicitly shown that the immaterial takes primacy in creation and redemption; thus, there is a seeming tension between the disembodied interim state and the physically resurrected state. A case might even be made that Turretin inconsistently moves from considering a disembodied soulish state to an embodied glorified state.[25] His inconsistency is evident in that after he discusses the vision in the context of soulish qualities (primarily if not exclusively), he concludes his discussion of the vision by saying, "Now from this communion with God will arise that wonderful glory with which the saints will be endowed both as to the soul and as to the body. And as to the former, indeed by perfect knowledge and holiness; and as to the latter, by a removal of all misery, pollution and weakness of every kind, arising not only from sin, but also from the condition of animal life which had obtained communication into a state of innocence and incorruption and spirituality."[26]

While Turretin clearly prioritizes the immaterial over the material, one wonders how he connects the beatific vision with the final bodily resurrected state. There is an interesting tension here. However, Turretin more likely than not places the discussion of the vision in the context of the disembodied state because of his close alignment with Aquinas. He clarifies this position by suggesting, as cited before, "God can be seen of man by a spiritual and internal vision alone." We can gaze at this now in the "specular knowledge of faith," but we will gaze at it later by an "intuitive and far more perfect beatific vision." In particular, Turretin clarifies, it is the soul itself that is gazing at God in this beatific state: "But whether the

23. For clear evidence along these lines, see Turretin, *Institutes of Elenctic Theology*, 1:482–88. Turretin clearly articulates the soul's priority over the body so that when the body dies, the soul continues to operate, subsist, and act independently of the body (see esp. 485–86).

24. Turretin, *Institutes of Elenctic Theology*, 1:485–86.

25. Turretin, *Institutes of Elenctic Theology*, 3:609–11.

26. Turretin, *Institutes of Elenctic Theology*, 3:612.

soul will immediately see the very essence of God or only some reflection of it (*apaugasma*), rather the brightness and glory suitable to the other life, because the Scripture does not disclose it to us, so neither should we rashly define anything concerning it."[27] He thus seems to be placing the beatific vision in the context of the disembodied state, which is to say not that the soul will cease in the vision once becoming reembodied but that it will be the soul alone that sees God. He also uses several adjectives to explain the nature of the vision that prioritize the immaterial qualities: mental, intellectual, internal, supernatural, intuitive, beatific, adequate, and comprehensive.[28] Afterward he moves to consider the transformation of the human soul in consequence to the vision.[29] His clear emphasis is on the immaterial and intellectual elements.

The famous nineteenth-century Reformed theologian Charles Hodge continues the tradition regarding the vision, also showing an impulse toward the immaterial. While he places the discussion after the final bodily resurrection, it lends clear priority to the soul in the vision. He begins by noting that the beatific vision is inconceivable, but then he states eight elements that we can know about the vision. In particular he notes, "This vision is beatific. It beatifies. It transforms the soul into the divine image; transfusing into it the divine life, so that it is filled with the fullness of God." It is telling that he directs the beatific elements toward the soul, not the body. Perhaps he is envisioning the beatific vision in the context of the disembodied state, or, more likely, he suggests that the vision, while taking place in the resurrected bodily state, primarily affects the soul. Either way, the lack of reference to the body is significant. Hodge also suggests that the vision consists of "the indefinite enlargement of all [the saints'] faculties" and the "constant increase in knowledge and in the useful exercise of all their powers." He does not clarify whether this involves bodily or soulish functions, though his use of "all" might suggest both if bodies have or are powers. Hodge then notes other aspects of the vision in terms of perfected love, happiness, holiness, fellowship, goodness, and blessedness.[30] While the tendency toward the soul might be less noticeable than in, say, Turretin, Hodge continues the same trajectory as before by prioritizing the soul over the body in his discussion of the vision.

Jonathan Edwards, likewise following catholic and Reformed tradition, also places the emphasis and centrality on the immaterial in his understanding

27. Turretin, *Institutes of Elenctic Theology*, 3:612.
28. Turretin, *Institutes of Elenctic Theology*, 3:612.
29. Turretin, *Institutes of Elenctic Theology*, 3:611–13.
30. Hodge, *Systematic Theology*, 3:860–61.

of the beatific vision.[31] Edwards is explicit that it is a sight not of the eyes but of the soul and the intellect. This is unsurprising in Edwards given the fact that he upholds that God and humans are essentially immaterial in nature, even if humans are normally embodied. For Edwards, the beatific vision is that which makes humans ultimately happy, which is primarily an immaterial state of being.[32] For example, in one place Edwards highlights the act of seeing God for who he is—without mention of Christ or the body—by isolating the soul as the object of transformation.[33] In another place he associates the vision closely with contemplation—hence an intellectual, emotive, and appetitive activity.[34] In several places in the *Ethical Writings*, Edwards seems to follow Aquinas in his understanding of the vision in the context of the disembodied state—hence an immaterial state.[35]

Edwards describes the general nature of the beatific vision as "immaterial" and "intellectual" precisely because the highest part of the human is such; furthermore, God is immaterial in nature and must be encountered not with bodily eyes but with the soul.[36] In other words, Edwards suggests that the vision is intellectual, a seeing with the eyes of the soul. This must be so, for God is spirit and cannot be gazed upon by physical eyes. While saying this, I do not want to leave the reader with the impression that these selections are all that Edwards mentions about the beatific vision. In fact, I believe that Edwards has much to say that deserves additional constructive attention in the literature. I will briefly explore these constructive elements at the end of this chapter.

In summary, the Reformed tradition prioritizes the immaterial and intellectual elements of the vision more than the material and bodily elements. This is not to say that the material elements were ignored; rather, it is only to say they were not explicitly and fully articulated in the context of the discussions of the beatific vision.

The Immaterial and Reformation Theology

With the Reformed tradition's inclination toward the immaterial with respect to the beatific vision (seen most clearly in Turretin) as the end or purpose of humanity, it is curious that the contemporary literature leans in the alternative

31. J. Edwards, *Works of Jonathan Edwards*, 8:723–24.
32. J. Edwards, *Works of Jonathan Edwards*, 13:490.
33. J. Edwards, *Works of Jonathan Edwards*, 10:324.
34. J. Edwards, *Works of Jonathan Edwards*, 8:94; cf. 8:534.
35. J. Edwards, *Works of Jonathan Edwards*, 8:720–25.
36. J. Edwards, *Works of Jonathan Edwards*, 8:720–25.

direction—that is, toward the material, the bodily (at times to the exclusion of the immaterial), and the final state of afterlife (i.e., the physical resurrection of the body). Arguably, both impulses resonate with the scriptural portrayal of humanity's end. Both impulses are present to some degree and deserve a place at the anthropological table. How one parses out the relationship of each and the degree to which both are present in personal eschatology are topics for further discussion.

The immaterial nature of humans and God seems right to highlight not only in the Reformed tradition but also from the experience that humans have of themselves. Intuitively, we have paradigm examples of material things, as mechanistic and spatially extended, that are paradigmatically different from persons as immaterial things. In most of the Christian tradition, God is seen as personal and immaterial. The Western and Augustinian tradition bears this assumption about God: God is a consciously thinking being with freedom, in the minimalist sense, such that the presuppositions that God is immaterial and personal are foundational to all theological reflections about God.[37] Such a claim is supported by the testimony of Nicene Christianity, in which God is described as the Creator of the world, the "Maker of heaven and Earth."[38] As practitioners of perfect-being theology, Reformed theologians understood God to have various characteristics that are not characteristics of material objects. The Athanasian Creed bears this out as well when it describes God as being uncreated, immeasurable, and eternal, which theologians often take to mean that God is a pure immaterial being. On this ground, it would seem to yield the notion that, in order for us to experience God, some interface with him would require immateriality.

The more challenging claim confronting Reformed theology is that human beings are essentially immaterial—that is, that they are immaterial at their core. The claim is especially challenging because, while most Christians today regard God as purely immaterial, that is not how they regard humans. Some describe humans as a mixture of the immaterial with the material, if not wholly material in nature. In fact, recently there has been a flurry of Christian defenses of the claim that humans are wholly material in nature.[39] However, I argue below that humans are not wholly material but rather are essentially immaterial; I do so by suggesting that when we experience the world as an object around us, we do so primarily as immaterial beings. The Reformed understanding of the vision as primarily immaterial, then, seems justified for

37. Farris, "Discovering God and Soul"; Lund, *Making Sense of It All*, 93; Swinburne, *The Christian God*, 126–27.

38. Wilhelm, "The Nicene Creed."

39. Corcoran, *Rethinking Human Nature*; Murphy, *Bodies and Souls*.

two reasons: (1) our experiences require an immaterial substance, and (2) our experiences are primarily mental.

The first reason that justifies the Reformed impulse is based on the fact that our experiences presuppose the first-person perspective, which requires an immaterial substance. I take it that vision is a kind of experience. Drawing from holistic empiricism or phenomenal conservatism, which claim that our first-person experiences give us some indication or grasp on reality, I argue for the Reformed claim that we are immaterial essentially and that this comes up as a primary feature in our experiences. Phenomenal conservatism is the view that we have knowledge of something based on what seems or appears to be the case in our experiences; thus, how it appears to be for a person carries with it some level of justification. When our faculties are functioning properly, our seemings are justified and reliably give us knowledge. Holistic empiricism, similar to phenomenal conservatism, is the view that we ought to take all our experiences as trustworthy until proven otherwise, so it encompasses more than the narrow empiricism often associated with the modern empiricist tradition (e.g., Francis Bacon, David Hume). Holistic empiricism rests on the assumption of a holistic anthropology, yet our experiences point us to the fact that we are primarily and essentially immaterial.[40]

This means that humans, while coming into existence with a body, are at their core immaterial beings, otherwise called "minds" or "souls." While it is true to say that the body is causally necessary in some sense for the soul's functioning, this would not entail the essentiality and constant requirement that the soul function as embodied. Take the following argument to ground the reality that we, humans, are essentially immaterial.

Consider the act of painting a picture of Jesus. Although a contemporary painter has never seen Jesus directly, she has some idea of what Jesus might look like through traditional data. With this background, she begins the imaginative process of conjuring up an image of Jesus. This process of imagination is not the same as a causal registering of Jesus via the eyes, but it is a mental process cognized. The painter has the ability to reflect more deeply and critically on the image in her mind. As she enters the process of painting, she experiences an interactive process between the mind's picture and what she sees painted on the canvas. Now, one can comfortably argue that the imaginative process itself is a process that is not ontologically dependent on material processes in the brain or in the central nervous system; rather, it is a process brought into being by the mind itself—requiring first-person consciousness.

40. Kwan, *The Rainbow of Experiences*.

For the painter to continue in the process of painting, two fundamental activities must occur. First, the painter must have a first-person consciousness ability. She must be able to imagine, yet in the process of imagining she is holding an idea in her mind. In fact, she is having a thought about the image of Jesus. What is important to note is that it is the person herself holding the thought in her mind. No one else owns the thought or has access to the mental picture of Jesus that the painter has. Contrary to the immaterial, the physical is potentially discoverable by agents. The idea the agent-painter holds in her mind is accessible directly and immediately only by the agent herself. Second, the painter must have the ability to endure through time. In order to causally bring the painting into being from an original mental image, the painter must be in the process of thinking, reflecting, and discriminating about the paint on the canvas. These are occurrent activities of the mind presupposed in the act of reflection on the painting. Other occurrent activities are present when the painter is moving her limb in the process of putting paint to canvas.

In contrast to what we believe to be a material object, the agent-painter exists in and through time as the selfsame individual with the capability of self-reflexively thinking and imagining a new reality. Whether it is the case that any material object can exist for very long through time, it is fairly clear that we have no positive reason to think that the material object knows that it exists or continues to know that it exists. In fact, it is not clear at all what material object is identical to the agent. Intuitively, we understand that the agent and the material object that she happens to be attached to, or interact with, are distinct.

This idea leads to the second reason: our experiences are essentially and primarily mental (i.e., immaterial) in nature. It is conceivable that I am a material object, and supposing I were, it is not clear what material object I would be identical to. It would not be the parts of the body. Conceivably, as I argued earlier, my body parts can be replaced. Further, I argued that I do exist in and through time as the same persistent individual and that there is some fact of the matter to who I am or a fact that makes me *me*, but what that is is not accounted for on a physicalist accounting of persons. I am not strictly identical to my body, for I am the kind of thing that endures through time as the same individual, but this is not the case for the body. In fact, it seems inconceivable that we would find a material object to adequately satisfy what it means to be me—the thinking and experiencing thing that I am. Yet the human agent is capable of such a capacity, natively, and can move through time with ease. While there is not a material object or part that can conceivably make sense of the human agents' conscious mental states, it becomes more significant to recognize that human beings gain and lose parts through the process of time while remaining the selfsame persons without those physical objects. This supposition finds support in a premise of faith. As articulated above, Christians traditionally are committed to the doctrine of an intermediate disembodied state in which humans experience reality. In this way, human beings are essentially immaterial substances that bear, at least, one essential immaterial or mental property: the property that I am a conscious, experiencing self.

As a consciously thinking and experiencing self that exists among other consciously thinking selves, I believe that we have a paradigm case for thinking about agents in general, including God, as I suggested above. God himself, so the tradition holds, is an immaterial being and not a material being.[41] The foundation for our "seeing," "experiencing," or "knowing" God, then, seems naturally to correspond to our immaterial natures as souls in relation to God, who himself is an immaterial being. God neither has nor needs a body. He is without material, which makes sense of the traditional belief that he is immutable (without change).[42]

However, it is true that in our present and normal experience of God, we are embodied beings. Our embodiment is important in two ways. First, arguably, it is necessary to the normal process of sense perception. During most of our lives as humans, we live as embodied beings, and we gain access to the physical world in and through the use of our bodies. Bodies provide for humans' additional powers that contribute to our knowledge of the world. Second, our embodiment is necessary to the full functioning or ordering of human nature. When some part of our body is malfunctioning, we seem to experience a malfunction in our whole being. When I experience a blow to the head, my states of awareness are dramatically affected.[43] If this is the case, then it follows that the body provides some sort of operational power that not only positively affects the soul of the human being but also situates that soul in a context where it can function properly.

The philosophical data above give us some reason to think that the traditional impulse is correct with respect to the priority given to the immaterial in the beatific vision. This is in part because of who God is and the fact that we will exist and experience disembodied states—pointing to the essentiality of the immateriality of our nature. Furthermore, even in our embodied experiences there is a logical and, seemingly, metaphysical priority given to the immaterial, given the data from our having the causal power to sustain

---

41. Aquinas, *Summa Theologiae*, I.1.2–13; Augustine, *On the Holy Trinity*, 65.
42. Augustine, *On the Holy Trinity*, 88; Lombard, *The Sentences, Book 1*, 46.
43. Swinburne, *The Christian God*, 154; Swinburne, *The Evolution of the Soul*, 10, 104.

a thought from one moment to the next and our ability to endure through time. The first-person perspective, which is distinct from the material realm, is what makes our encounter of the world unified and sustains our reflection across time.[44] My point is merely that the traditional impulse is correct, aside from any difficulties that might arise regarding the body.

In light of the descriptions of Reformed theology and the philosophical arguments above, the impulse toward the immaterial and intellectual in the beatific vision is well founded and helpful. Given the priority of the immaterial in both God and humans, it makes sense that the vision is also primarily immaterial in nature. The difficulty in the Reformed literature and the contemporary literature is that of striking a balance on these features of human beings in such a way as neither to devalue the body nor to neglect the immaterial and intellectual aspects of humans in the afterlife. As seen in the discussion of Christology in chapter 6, some Reformed theologians are able to balance both in their developments of anthropology through the lens of Christology.

Christology as Anthropology

Earlier I discussed the development within theological anthropology as christological anthropology. While I was dubious about its success as a totalizing systematic way to approach the anthropos, I do see the benefits of our reflections on the anthropos being guided by Christology. My bias, which is borne out in Scripture, has been to see the creation narrative as having some integrity as a starting point for thinking about humans as creaturely and divine and as embodied souls. As image bearers, humans have some natural/creational properties that set them apart as divinely dignified and destined beings. Such a design prompts them for something greater, all the while upholding the integrity and significance of their created natures.

The story starts in creation, but it ends in redemption. It is in redemption that we encounter a transition in the narrative of Scripture. The created nature finds its full expression in the New Testament story of redemption. Life is not merely a salvation from death; it is a new life. That new life is a life of union with the trinitarian God. And it is in the person of Jesus Christ that God is most intimate with humans. It is in the incarnation of the Logos (i.e., the Second Person of the Trinity) that humanity becomes divine. So rather than start with Christology from the beginning, an approach that seems to be fraught with some initial problems, we engage with Christology in two

44. Taliaferro, "The Soul of the Matter."

distinct ways. First, Christology retroactively shows us what it means to be fully human. Second, Christology shows us, in the context of redemption, what it means to be God. Rather than christological anthropology, we have a Christology as anthropology.

Eschatologically, the fulfillment of human nature is inaugurated by Christology. While I have touched on christological considerations earlier in this chapter, Christology is crucial to understanding the final state of human beings.

First, it is in our Christology that humans have a vision of God. In John's Gospel, Jesus bears this out when he says, "Now this is eternal life: that they know you, the only true God, and Jesus Christ, whom you have sent" (John 17:3). Jesus also says, "Have I been with you so long, and you still do not know me, Philip? Whoever has seen me has seen the Father. How can you say, 'Show us the Father'?" (John 14:9 ESV). These statements reveal several truths. We know from the context that Christ takes the Father to be identical to the God of the Old Testament. In fact, he sees no discontinuity between the God of the Old Testament and the God of the New Testament.

Second, Christ is the uniting of creatures and the divine. Taking these two passages together, we see the ultimate resolution of history reconciled in God's act of his Son. And his Son is identical to God. This decisive act in redemptive history uniquely brings together the divinity, so often conceived as distant, with humanity. Where the horizontal and vertical of Scripture come together in the person of Jesus Christ, we find the ultimate destiny and finality of humanity. Humans are intended for union with God.

One worry is raised against theosis and beatific vision. The worry concerns embodiment. We can offer an initial response to this problem motivated by what I have argued or expounded on throughout this book. Certainly, we have reason for thinking that embodiment is significant to human life because we are originally created as embodied souls (barring the assumption of Origenism in which souls originate in a preembodied state only to become embodied after sin). The significance of human embodiment is reflected in our generative relationships. The incarnation and resurrection, prima facie (i.e., on the surface), also point to the significance of embodiment to human life. But these theological reflections are insufficient for making a case for the meaningfulness and significance of human embodiment, and they require a more thoughtful constructive integration of the body in our doctrine of deification and the beatific vision. Previous reflections add a deeper perplexity to this. If in fact the disembodied human can experience and have a vision of God, then this seems to raise some questions about the significance of the body to the final state of human existence.

Again, finding this balance in the Reformed tradition in the ongoing attempt to construct our theologies of human beings is a difficult task. There are at least two challenges in the Reformed account, challenges that will need further parsing and nuance. First, Reformed theologians (excluding Calvin, Owen, and Edwards) have little to say about the role of Christ, specifically, and the role of the Trinity, more generally, in the beatific vision. Of course, they certainly were christocentric (especially in their soteriologies), but their accounts of the beatific vision minimize and even ignore at times the place of Christ in the vision. Their accounts tend toward an understanding of the anthropological nature of the vision alone. When they do mention God, they give credence to the oneness of God—and not his triunity. One might even say that Turretin's discussion, to mention one example, is devoid of the Trinity and the christological aspects altogether.

Second, and more central, while Reformed theologians correctly note that the vision lends a priority to the immaterial, many, arguably, improperly neglect or minimize the glorified resurrected state and its role in and relation to the vision. As noted, they have little to say about the body's role in the vision, and when they do speak about the body, it is unclear how the body and soul jointly cooperate in the vision itself. As shown above, some of them had a clear place for the vision in the disembodied intermediate state (e.g., Turretin following Aquinas). Others spoke somewhat confusingly about the vision as both disembodied and occurring in the physically resurrected state.

While Calvin brings some clarity to the discussion where other Reformed theologians are unclear, he is less than clear on the nature of the immaterial in relation to the material and its implications for the vision. I am not sure whether he, as well as the later tradition, knows how to coherently tie together the immaterial vision with the resurrected state. I am not even sure that they are aware of the tension between the two. For the Reformed tradition, the body, unfortunately, becomes deeply perplexing. What I have shown is that this impulse in the Reformed tradition is theologically and philosophically motivated, but it runs into a problem of what to do with the body. Fortunately, John Owen and Jonathan Edwards provide us with some constructive potential for thinking about the vision in relation to the final resurrected state.

Owen has some significant similarities to the Reformed theologians listed earlier, but he also significantly departs from those who are Thomistically motivated (e.g., Turretin). Interestingly, in keeping with his tradition, Owen highlights that the vision is primarily immaterial, but the way he does so is strikingly different. He does not describe the vision in the context of the disembodied intermediate state. Instead, he situates the vision in the resurrected state, which is the first unique contribution. Second, he moves in the material direction when he describes the vision as a vision of the fleshly humanity of Christ.[45] He took Jesus's words as programmatic for the vision: "Whoever has seen me has seen the Father" (John 14:9 ESV). Thus, he suggests that the vision entails a direct, physical sight of the glorified Jesus while we are in our glorified bodily state: "There will be use herein of our bodily eyes. . . . That corporeal sense shall not be restored unto us, and that glorified above what we can conceive but for this great use of the eternal beholding of Christ and his glory."[46] This is no generic gaze; it is a gaze directed at the person of Christ as fully God and fully human. Indeed, the vision involves "a continual contemplation of the glory of Christ."[47] Since "the glory of Christ is the glory of the person of Christ," Owen suggests that this vision is of the hypostatically united Jesus Christ as fully God and human.[48] In this sense, the gaze is both intellectual and physical (i.e., bodily sight). This is a rather unique departure from the Reformed tradition before Owen. Suzanne McDonald argues that the intellectual has priority here,[49] but Owen does not fall under the same criticisms of the other Reformed theologians mentioned here for two reasons: he has some role for the body in the vision, and the immaterial/intellectual vision coincides with the first-person experience of the physically embodied Christ. Yet it seems that for Owen, the only way that the glorified human person can apprehend the divinity of Christ (through a physical gaze of the human person) is through a redeemed and perfected intellect; so even Owen prioritizes the immaterial and does so in the embodied context. However, he does not offer a sufficient accounting or story for the link between the experience of the vision and the bodily glorified state.

Jonathan Edwards, arguably, has even more to say about the christological nature of the vision, all the while neither excising the immaterial nature of humanity nor devaluing the intellectual vision. In his extraordinary sermon on Romans 2:10, Edwards is clear that (1) Christ is central and mediates the vision of the Father (and the Trinity), and (2) the physical body has a significant role to play in the vision.

Edwards is thoroughly christological in his development of the vision. He begins by expounding on the nature of humans as encountering God through a kind of intellectual or spiritual (i.e., immaterial) seeing via Christ. Christ, from beginning to end for Edwards, is central to the soteriological means or

45. Edwards makes this move as well. J. Edwards, *Works of Jonathan Edwards*, 8:720.
46. Owen, "Meditations and Discourses on the Glory of Christ in His Person, Office, and Grace," in Owen, *Works*, 1:379.
47. Owen, *Works*, 1:277.
48. Owen, *Works*, 2:393; McDonald, "Beholding the Glory," 146–47.
49. McDonald, "Beholding the Glory," 156–57.

mechanism by which humans come to see and apprehend the Father. Indeed, it is in the context of our union to Christ that we have union with God, become children of God, are justified before God, and receive all the divine qualities in Christ. In other words, it is in virtue of our union with Christ that we are able to "apprehend" the nature of God. Christ, the divine-human, is the root by which we as soul images are grafted and bear fruit, and this is primarily an act where Christ is "instamped" on the soul of humans. Edwards is clear that such a state is immaterial: "Though it [the indwelling of the Spirit] be but small, yet it is powerful; it has influence over the heart to govern it, and brings forth holy fruits in the life, and will not cease to prevail till it has consumed all the corruption that is left in the heart, and till it has turned the whole soul into a pure, holy, and heavenly flame, till the soul of man becomes like the angels, a flame of fire, and shines as the brightness of the firmament."[50] The priority of the soul here is apparent. Yet it is the *embodied* Christ who mediates to human souls this new perception of God, for Edwards describes Christ—and not simply the Logos—in the present "earthly" and embodied state of humans. Saying this, Edwards elsewhere makes explicit that the embodied Christ is the medium by which the saints come to have an intellectual vision of God.[51]

While the immaterial/intellectual is the primary ontological component in the vision, Edwards assigns a role not only to the body but also specifically to the newly bodily resurrected Christ. In his usual fashion, Edwards uses several images signifying that we are seeing God via the embodied Christ during the disembodied state of the saints. Indeed, in one place Edwards is relatively explicit that it is the resurrected Christ who mediates such a vision; namely, in the context of talking about human souls ascending to heaven and obtaining a vision of God, Edwards states this clearly:

> There are some who say that there is no such place as heaven; but this is evidently a mistake, for the heaven into which the man Christ Jesus entered with his glorified body, is certainly some place. It is absurd to suppose that the heaven where the body of Christ is, is not a place. To say that the body of Christ is in no place, is the same thing as to say he has no body. The heaven where Christ is, is a place; for he was seen ascending, and will be seen descending again; and the heaven where the departed souls of the saints are, is the same heaven where Christ has ascended. And therefore Stephen, when he was departing this life, saw heaven opened, and the Son of man standing on the right hand of God. And he prayed to that same Jesus whom he saw, that he would receive his

50. J. Edwards, *Sermons*, 889–90.
51. J. Edwards, *Sermons*, 892.

spirit; i.e. that he would receive it to him, where he saw him, at the right hand of God. . . . Therefore, there is some place, where God gloriously manifests himself, and where Christ is, and where saints and angels dwell, and whither the angels carry the souls of the saints when they depart from their bodies; and this place is called Paradise, and the third heaven. 2 Cor. xii. 2, 4.[52]

Edwards makes it clear not only that God is immaterial and the vision is intellectual but also that heaven is a place. For in the fact that Christ, in his embodiment, takes us to God, it is precisely the humanity of Christ in his newly resurrected state that effectuates the disembodied vision for the saints. There is a tendency today to think of the disembodied intermediate state as a diminished state of existence,[53] but this is clearly not the case for Edwards. His understanding is that disembodied souls encounter the embodied Christ. He describes this state as "a state of exceeding glory and blessedness." Edwards seems to take up the anthropological realities of the vision through the lens of Christology with greater precision and depth than Owen.

Edwards also has some constructive comments on the disembodied vision in relation to the reembodied vision. He makes what seems to amount to two claims regarding the relationship between the two states. First, he claims that humans are normally and naturally embodied. In other words, human beings, while fundamentally or essentially soul beings, function as integrally whole beings when embodied. To give just one example, he points us to the embodied Christ, as we will see below. Second, Edwards claims that there is a higher or more intense state that we as humans enter into when we envision God as newly embodied beings. He describes this state as a more complete and blessed state. In fact, he uses the words "exceeding joy." Christ remains the medium by which saints experience the trinitarian God. It is with Christ, in his human form, that we ascend, but it is also with Christ that we descend back to the earth as resurrected saints.[54]

Toward the end of the sermon, Edwards advances some beautifully complex and somewhat perplexing statements about the interaction between bodily seeing and intellectual seeing. He describes the final state as one of seeing God in Christ, as in the disembodied state, yet with "exceeding strength"

52. J. Edwards, *Sermons*, 893.

53. Witherington, *Conflict and Community in Corinth*, 391; Wright, *The Resurrection of the Son of God*, 216, 312–74.

54. J. Edwards, *Sermons*, 894–95. It is important to point out that while Edwards gives a powerful place to embodiment, he does not understand the body to be a material substance but rather a set of phenomenological qualities that God uses to communicate glory to humans.

and "wonderful beauty."[55] Edwards offers links between the physical and the immaterial when he brings the embodied Christ into the discussion.

In this way, John Owen and Jonathan Edwards offer hope for a way forward. They provide some resources for making sense of the beatific vision in the context of the relationship between the intellectual and the physical. These resources need to be taken in constructive theological directions as theologians continue to reflect on the nature of human beings in the ongoing process of communicating the gospel as it concerns humans.

Defining Deification

Related to the beatific vision (where the vision is the cause for becoming united to God), the doctrine of deification has become of interest in Reformed and contemporary theology. What it means is a bit more challenging in our contemporary context and can be conflated with another important contemporary topic: transhumanism. In short, I am taking deification to be synonymous with "apotheosis" (i.e., "making divine") and glorification—the final outcome of the process of sanctification. Deification is the doctrine that we are united to Christ and, specifically, to God in Christ. Once we are united to Christ, we will be like him. But what this means deserves some clarification. A common confusion is that deification is conflated with another contemporary concept that is gaining traction in Christian thought and outside of it called posthumanism or transhumanism. But, to be clear, these are not synonymous terms.

Deification and Transhumanism[56]

A question often arises regarding deification and the transhumanism (i.e., human advancement through technology) movement that has peppered many of the discussions concerning the nature of humans. Transhumanism often overlaps with the study of artificial intelligence and the study of futurism (humanism about the future with the use of technology).[57] And, to some extent, we are experiencing transhumanism already when we think about all the technological aids that enhance our abilities (e.g., prosthetic legs, electrical artificial arms, the use of synthetic blood, and implants that enhance neural functioning). We are also getting an imaginative foretaste of what may come in

55. J. Edwards, *Sermons*, 894–95.
56. For a useful collection that touches on these themes in the "science and religion" literature, see Murphy and Knight, *Human Identity*.
57. For a useful collection on AI from a materialist frame, see Brockman, *Possible Minds*.

the future (e.g., Robocop, Iron Man). All of these advancements, and more to come, raise several questions about the human story. For our purposes, raising one question in order to illuminate the discussion on deification will aid the reader so that she might consider other contemporary issues in light of it.

As both are considered paradigms of human purpose, the similarity between transhumanism and deification deserves our reflection. Is transhumanism synonymous with deification? Or, asked another way, are the essential features and objectives of deification synonymous with transhumanism? These and other related questions will concern us here as we attempt to drill into the why of human nature and God's purposes for human beings. It is important to note that my most immediate question is not, Is transhumanism morally or ideologically consistent with deification or a Christian understanding of human purpose? Rather, it is a question as to the essential core of each and whether their objectives overlap significantly. It may be that the objectives of transhumanism, or some modified version of it, are consistent with the objectives found within Christian theology. It may be that there is not anything, strictly speaking, out of sync with divine goals concerning humans. We can answer that question only after more clearly describing each.

One working definition or description of transhumanism comes from Julian Savulescu and Nick Bostrom: "Transhumanism is a loosely defined movement that has developed gradually over the past two decades and can be viewed as an outgrowth of secular humanism and the Enlightenment. It holds that current human nature is improvable through the use of applied science and other rational methods, which may make it possible to increase human health span, extend our intellectual and physical capacities, and give us increased control over our own mental states and moods."[58] In other words, transhumanism is a movement that places some emphasis on the use of science and technology as a means of improving (qualitatively speaking, yet not in terms of essential properties) our physical and cognitive abilities. It is doubtful that the technology is directly contacting the soul, but via the body the soul's abilities are improved. Another definition comes from Sky Marsen: "Transhumanism is a set of dynamic and diverse approaches to the relationship between technology, self, and society. Since transhumanism is not a crystallized and static doctrine, my use of the term requires definition. The working definition that informs the subsequent discussion is this: transhumanism is a general term designating a set of approaches that hold an optimistic view of technology as having the potential to assist humans in building more equitable and

58. Savulescu and Bostrom, *Human Enhancement*, 55.

happier societies mainly by modifying individual physical characteristics."[59] As the reader can see, there is an overlap of meaning in these descriptions. Both Marsen and Savulescu and Bostrom highlight the importance of using science and technology (including medicine) to enhance and improve the physical attributes of human beings.

These modest descriptions are quite minimalist. In one sense, they are consistent with a broad form of humanism that highlights the acceptability of using medicine to help individuals improve their physical lives. On the surface, nothing is new here. However, there may be a difference if technology is used in such a way as to bring about a new species. Apart from this questionable and debatable move, transhumanism seems fairly tame. Engaging with the above definitions, Benedikt Paul Göcke argues in the affirmative that so long as it does not yield the creation of a new species, what he calls "radical transhumanism," but rather yields the improvement of external (i.e., bodily) abilities, or what he calls "quantitative enhancements," through scientific and technological means, transhumanism is morally acceptable (even encouraged) and consistent with a basic set of Christian ideas.[60]

It is clear that the descriptions above have little overlap with an understanding of deification. Deification is the ultimate purpose of human beings, where humans experience union with God as the gift of life and blessing. *Deification is another word for "immortality,"* construed in a Christian context.[61] As I suggested earlier, a minimalist understanding of immortality is a persistence of individual existence. This, I have also suggested, is a normal property of humans given by God, but it is insufficient to capture the whole meaning as we find it represented in Scripture and received by catholic Christianity. I will leave the question somewhat open here as to how often or to what extent we should allow technology to enhance human abilities. As with the use of medicine, there are surely times in which Christian wisdom steps in and prevents Christians from the unguarded and intemperate use of technology. With that said, I would like to state clearly that the descriptions given above are not the same as deification or the Christian understanding of human purpose.

59. Marsen, "Playing by the Rules—or Not?," 86.
60. See Göcke, "Christian Cyborgs," 9. Göcke is convinced that a "moderate transhumanism" is fully consistent with his minimalist understanding of Christianity. As he understands it, this form of transhumanism does nothing to undermine or contradict a unified Christian narrative in which God exists, Christ's death and resurrection has saving significance, humans will be judged on the basis of the moral value of their lives, and there are objective moral values.
61. Ziegler, *Eternal God, Eternal Life*. In this collection of essays, the authors describe immortality as basically synonymous with receiving the life of the Trinity or becoming united to the Trinity. This is not an uncommon understanding of Christian immortality in the theological literature.

While I find Göcke's analysis interesting and helpful, this is not the only way that transhumanism has been defined. Some have understood transhumanism (otherwise called "posthumanism") differently. English scholar Peter Mahon understands posthumanism as a kind of project that places the benefits of technology at the center of human advancement. Embedded in this understanding of humans is an understanding of humans as physical beings alone. In fact, Mahon says that one necessary condition of posthumanism, as he defines it, is functionalism. Functionalism says that physical organisms are essentially what they do. Drawing from David McFarland, Mahon says that this is a "key underlying concept." "Functionalism is the view that certain entities, including some mental ones, are best described in terms of the functional role that they play within a system. Thus, a word processor is a device that processes words. Physically, word processors have changed greatly over recent decades, but they remain best described in terms of their function, not in material terms."[62]

As functional beings, we are not wholly reducible to our material parts. However, material parts do function together in a holistic fashion as a part of a whole system. Through technological engineering we can bring about the advancement of human well-being and prolong the existence of human life. Functionalism is a form of physicalism. As I have argued throughout the book, a physicalist understanding of human persons is largely out of place within a Christian frame of reference. While I have left the door open to the acceptability of nonreductive physicalism (à la Nancey Murphy), I have significant doubt about its natural fittingness with Christian theology. That said, it is important to note that Murphy is not a global physicalist, and thus her view of human purpose might extend beyond the physical processes and functions of creaturely life. Physicalism, along the lines of functionalism, misses some important information about the human: the essential properties composing human nature and the immaterial properties composing the human telos.

What if we described transhumanism in a different way? What if we described it according to a common set of values, motivations, or purposes? Much of the transhumanist literature suggests that transhumanism is a movement to achieve immortality or extend the mere existence of humans through scientific and technological manipulation. Several Christian authors have argued that this is an unacceptable motive and uncharacteristic of mature Christian thinking.[63] As I have shown earlier, human life has a characteristic

---

62. Mahon, *Posthumanism*, 5. Drawing from D. McFarland, *Guilty Robots, Happy Dogs*, chap. 7, "The Material Mind."
63. See Mitchell, Orr, and Salladay, *Aging*; Meilaender, *Should We Live Forever?*

frame and shape to it. While there may be a desire for immortality among humans, that described by the Christian story is not a desire for mere unending existence at any cost. Rather, the Christian story describes humans as coming into existence via some biological generation, living a life to old age, and dying somatically. Something of life, as designed by God, is short-circuited when humans seek to continue existing for its own sake. The Christian story includes a real death that allows for physical resurrection and union with God. Within this context, transhumanism, described as a desire for unending existence, is unwise because it steals the shape and form of life that God intends for his creatures. We come into existence through a physically embodied generation, and we cease to exist embodied. Painful though it is, there is a reason and design to it that gives meaning to life now.[64]

Deification in Christian Tradition

Deification, the notion that we become united to God, has taken on a wider meaning and significance for the human telos. Thus, its meaning cannot be discerned from creation alone, although it may be hinted at in the creation story. Nor can it be discerned by the ontological constitution of the human, but, again, the ontological constitution of the human might point in this direction somehow. Neither can science find the meaning of deification through a dissection of human parts, hence ruling out reductive forms of humanity (along with other forms like behaviorism, or functionalism, that describe humans as either beings that are basically cogs in wheels that respond to stimuli or are defined by what they do).

While the Reformed and evangelical traditions are often characterized as understanding deification or theosis solely in terms of moral transformation, the Reformed tradition throughout history has had a more robust place for deification as holistic and describing human purpose eschatologically. And, in fact, the Scriptures as a whole, read theologically, point in this more robust direction. The most famously cited passage in support of deification is 2 Peter 1:4, where it says that we, the saints, "become partakers of the divine nature" (ESV). In other words, humans who are redeemed, or who are in the process of redemption, are partaking in, sharing in, or participating in the divine nature. This is not mere moral transformation but rather a holistic transformation reflecting the holism in the creation story culminated in the resurrection story. Other scriptural metaphors and passages situate our understanding of theosis and paint a more well-rounded picture of what actually happens to humans.

64. See Mitchell, Orr, and Salladay, *Aging*; Meilaender, *Should We Live Forever?*

Psalm 82:6–7 actually begins the discussion of thinking about humans as theotic when it refers to humans as "gods." Nicene Christianity has theologically appropriated the passage in such a way as to raise the question regarding redeemed humans. Rightly so, the whole discussion is already situated in a clear distinction between God the Creator and his creatures. There is never a sense in which humans become God literally or possess the attributes that essentially constitute God's nature. Several New Testament concepts build on this idea that our purpose is union with God, including adoption in Romans 8, Christ as the image of God in 2 Corinthians 3–4, immortality in 2 Timothy 1:10 and 2 Corinthians 5:1–5, and glory in Romans 2:7. These concepts are understood in the larger redemptive context, wherein God through the power of the resurrected Jesus brings about life and blessing to human creatures.

Christ, as the resurrected divine-human, gives us the perfect image of a deified human given that he himself in his resurrected state is a perfected human who is most intimately united to God. In Hebrews 1:3, Christ is described in this way: "The Son is the radiance of God's glory and the exact representation of his being." In Colossians 1:15, he is said to be "the image of the invisible God." As exemplified in the Scriptures and commonly interpreted by the church, it is the divine-human who joins redeemed humanity to God, and it is the resurrected Christ who takes humanity back to God in the ascension.

But how does this actually work with two conflicting natures? And can we say any more about the human? Space limitations in mind, I think there are figures in the history of Nicene Christianity who help point us forward when thinking about the deified human via Christology. Maximus the Confessor offers us one way to do that. As a Nicene theologian working within Chalcedonian boundaries, Maximus affirms the union of the divine and the human in the single person of Christ, similar in ways to Cyril of Alexandria. He also affirms not monothelitism but dyothelitism, where Christ has two distinct wills corresponding to two distinct soul-parts (i.e., the divine soul as person and the human soul). In this context, Maximus understands human deification. Redeemed humans are united to God without confusion of the natures. However, redeemed humans assume characteristics that reflect the divine nature.

Commenting on Maximus's understanding of deification, Ben Blackwell and Kris Miller provide some help:

> Christ's humanity takes on divine characteristics, and the divine nature assumes human characteristics in the incarnation. In other words, the communication of properties from this intimate union results in the deification of Christ's humanity. Maximus employs the illustration in *Opuscula* 16 of the sword and

fire to explain the nature of this hypostatic transformation. The iron sword placed in the fire does not cease to be iron, but it takes on the properties of fire as it emits light and heat. In the same way Christ's humanity remains human, but it also takes on the properties of divinity, such as incorruption, through an unconfused union. This transformation of Christ's own humanity is paradigmatic for the believers who follow him.[65]

It is helpful to see how Blackwell and Miller highlight both the mystical and the incarnational elements of Maximus's understanding of deification, which remains robustly Chalcedonian. Talk of properties may be less than fully accurate. It might be better to stick with the use of characteristics so as not to confuse the natures. At a minimum, Blackwell and Miller are using properties analogously between God and human. They conclude their description of Maximus on deification in the following: "Maximus understands deification as the fulfillment of God's creational intent expressed in the language of the 'image and likeness of God.' Like many that precede him, Maximus sees image and likeness as distinct. The image of God relates to 'being and eternal being' and refers to the *logos* of humanity at creation. Likeness regards 'well being' and entails sharing divine attributes through the *tropos*. The eschatological culmination of salvation is 'eternal well being' where believers participate in God's incorruption noetically and somatically, reintegrating image and likeness."[66] Helpfully, Maximus gives us a model for thinking about deification of the human that is consistent with Chalcedonian Christology. His view is also holistic in nature in that it highlights the nature of redemption of the whole person and not simply the human intellect or the human body.

The Reformed tradition resembles some of the aspects found in Maximus. True to its Christology, Reformed theologians have typically interpreted and appropriated Chalcedonian Christology in a distinctive way. Reformed theologians tend to highlight the distinction between the divine and human natures of Christ, and this affects how Reformed theology describes the culmination of deification (i.e., redemption). Reformed theology tends to highlight our union with the humanity of Christ through his body, rather than a union with his soul or a merging of the natures. These debates about Christology, sanctification, and how they impinge on the culmination of redemption become rather complicated and would take us too far afield from the task at hand.[67]

65. Blackwell and Miller, "Theosis and Theological Anthropology," 306. For other versions of deification, see Cortez, Farris, and Hamilton, *Being Saved*, esp. chaps. 6, 8, 9, 17.

66. Blackwell and Miller, "Theosis and Theological Anthropology," 307.

67. For a helpful study on distinctions in the Reformed and Lutheran debates on Christology and the Lord's Supper, see McGinnis, *The Son of God beyond the Flesh*.

Deification, in general, is distinct from what often characterizes trans-humanism. Deification, unlike transhumanism, highlights the fact that redemption is a process that begins in divine action, primarily in the Christ event of the Logos becoming one of us in the incarnation. Furthermore, the process of redemption that culminates in deification has been providentially ordered by God for our good. Short-circuiting the process through a mere extension of that life fails to appreciate the process of human origination, physical suffering, physical death, the disembodied intermediate state, and the physical resurrection of the body. These are all part and parcel of what it means to be creaturely. In contrast to the Maximus model, let us consider some alternative models.

One model states that humans become absorbed into the divine. You might think of a common analogy where a droplet of water is absorbed into a large body of water, never to be found again. Alternatively, one might think about how the branch is absorbed in a fire. The branch does not remain a branch but is transformed into something else and ultimately eliminated by it. But this model fails in at least two ways. First, it fails to maintain the all-important Reformed distinctive of the distinction between Creator and creature. Second, and logically entailed by the first, the creature fails to be a creature in the afterlife but, instead, becomes what it is not. With that, let us consider an alternative.

Another model would highlight the human nature of Christ as that which is "deified." You might think of this model as the Hercules model. Consider that Hercules is, in many cases, an ideal human being with powers that succeed other normal human beings. These powers were achieved with the help of the immortal gods. On this model, it is Christ's human nature that expresses fully what it means to be human.[68] In virtue of Christ's human nature being personalized by the divine, the human nature actualizes all the capacities relevant to its nature. Christ expresses a human life fully alive, and this is one way of thinking about deification. On this model, deification is the human nature fully and completely expressed in the state of glorification and physical resurrection, but the human nature does not take on any properties properly attributed to the divine, nor does the human nature participate in the divine essence.

A better way to think about deification is to think about God as somehow enlivening human nature. Jonathan Edwards, in the *End of Creation*, describes a similar view: "God, in glorifying the saints in heaven with eternal

---

68. Carl Mosser develops a similar view in "The Metaphysics of Union with God," 4 (unpublished paper, cited with permission).

felicity, aims to satisfy his infinite grace or benevolence, by the bestowment of a good infinitely valuable, because eternal: and yet there never will come the moment, when it can be said, that now this infinitely valuable good has been actually bestowed."[69] Again, we can look to Christ as the exemplar. Christ was deified not only in his resurrected state but also prior to it (e.g., the transfiguration). Accordingly, Christ is deified because the life of God is full in him and protrudes his human nature. Drawing on an analogy that I developed elsewhere for one model of the "image of God," I like to think of deification along the lines of a light bulb.[70] Consider that a light bulb has the outer casing, receptor, and the filament wire through which the power to express light is sent. The filament wire, like that of the human nature, isn't somehow changed, at least not essentially, by the light flowing through it, but it can express the light to varying degrees and in varying intensities depending on the source of power to which the light bulb is attached. In a similar way, Christ's human nature expresses the light and life of God through his human nature. But, properly speaking, Christ's human nature or his properties are not somehow absorbed into the divine, nor is the human nature simply a fully functioning actualized human nature.

In keeping with the substantive human nature model of the image of God developed earlier, there is a question about what happens to human nature on this later model of deification. One might be inclined to think that God simply shines through the human nature of Christ and, by extension, the human natures of the redeemed. While this is true, it is only partly true. It seems to me that the substantive human nature model of the image combines the last two models by claiming that the human nature is actualized in its full capacity as a fully flourishing and functioning human, yet this is done primarily by the action of God shining through the souls of humans, as with the filament wire of the light bulb. However, it would follow that something would happen to the structure or capacities of the human soul. The capacities of the soul would be elevated in a fashion that the light and life of God were expressed in creaturely form. Here we are guided by a key verse that combines the doctrine of beatific vision and deification: "We know that when Christ appears, we shall be like him, for we shall see him as he is" (1 John 3:2). It is in seeing Christ that we are united to him and we become like him.

Deification, once again, is the final culmination of redemption, whereby humans are united to God in Christ. In this way, redeemed humans are raised above their created natures and partake of attributes that are not,

69. J. Edwards, *Works of Jonathan Edwards*, 8:527.
70. Farris, "A Substantive (Soul) Model," 171–78.

by created nature, theirs. Properly speaking, there remains a distinction between Creator and creature, and the attributes that humans partake of are properly God's attributes. In the truest theological sense, this is where humans partake of immortality: the life that God has by nature and the life that we have by grace.

Conclusion

Where Do We Go from Here?

*Be diligent in these matters; give yourself wholly to them, so that everyone
may see your progress.*

1 Timothy 4:15

We have come a long way. Our present journey must end, but that does not mean that the larger journey must end. I began with discussing humans as both creaturely and divine. By creaturely, I conveyed that humans are earthly in the sense that they are embodied, and they exist dependent on other humans in patterns of birth, life, and death. By divine, I intended to convey that humans are more than mere dust, more than their bodies, and they have a destiny that moves beyond the earth into heaven. Heaven is not merely a place; it is God's residence. We have worked through the prolegomena and methodological issues concerning theological anthropology, where I offered a way forward in approaching a massive set of data. Addressing the topics of theological anthropology requires information from several different sources. I have sought to give the reader a heavy dose of traditional theological anthropology and a heavy dose of the literature in philosophical anthropology that overlaps with those traditional categories in theology. I have also, where it was relevant, drawn from the scientific and social-scientific data on humans.

Beyond methodological and prolegomena topics, I have touched on all the topoi traditionally found in theological anthropology. I have surveyed some of the important Reformed and evangelical literature on the subject, offered

283

some of the biblical data, and then moved on to more specific philosophical and theological topics—some traditional and some contemporary in nature. The traditional topics include human constitution, human origins, original sin, corruption, Christology, salvation, free will and personal agency, Adam, sexual identity, traditional sexual ethics, the intermediate state, beatific vision, and deification.

We have also explored new areas of interest to contemporary philosophers and theologians. Some of these issues intersect with traditional topics, but these traditional topics have been complicated by recent findings in biology and other contemporary discussions (e.g., the social sciences and cognitive science). For instance, recent theological discussions on human origins and Adam have been complicated by biology and paleoanthropology. These disciplines not only suggest that humans are older than many throughout history might have assumed, but also show, some will argue, that there are other humans or hominids that are nongenetically connected to humans today. This means that not all hominids are connected to Adam genetically. I argued, briefly, that we should not sharply separate, even if these *conceptual* distinctions are helpful for discussion, the theological human spoken of in the creation narrative from the biological or genetic humans as they are tied to the original person, pair, or set of original humans. In fact, there are several metaphysically complicated ways to harmonize the data from Scripture with the biological data from science, to which I gave the reader some exposure.

Another development within traditional theological anthropology is the discussion concerning gender and sexuality. Popular opinion has it that gender and sexuality can be decoupled one from the other, leaving open the possibility that one's gender identity may have nothing to do with sexual identity, which is otherwise biologically stable. Other more recent questions relevant to our sexual identity have been raised as viable revisions of traditional views. For instance, is homosexuality permissible as a lifestyle for the Christian? And what is the nature of marriage? Is it merely a binding contract recognized by one's country? Or is there something divinely ordained about marriage? Are there other vocations relevant to our sexual identity beyond that of marriage between man and woman? What about the nature of singleness? To all of these questions I gave some answer, but further discussion beyond what I have briefly developed here is necessary.

Some traditional positions have been helped by recent developments in other academic disciplines. For example, the plausibility of personal persistence beyond the grave has been aided as a viable and warranted belief by developments within the philosophy of mind. No doubt, developments in the brain sciences seem to suggest a tight and intimate dependence between the soul and the body; something that was not immediately clear throughout all of church history is now apparent to scientists and philosophers reflecting more deeply on the deliverances of the sciences. These and other related topics at the intersection of science, philosophy, and theology have been given some exposure in the present introduction.

The discussion must not and cannot end here. My hope is that readers will take up these topics with greater appreciation and facility and reflect on what it means to be human. For philosophical and theological reflection on anthropology is part and parcel of the ongoing task of the theologian to communicate Christian truth afresh to the needs of the contemporary church and to address the concerns in our world.

Appendix

Philosophy and Theology in Anthropology

A Review of Recent Literature

As the present study is marked specifically by the relationship between philosophy and theology concerning human constitution, recent noteworthy works on theological anthropology deserve pointing out. In the philosophical literature, several works specifically in the philosophy of religion have relevance to the study of theological anthropology. Kevin Corcoran advances a revisionist interpretation of Christian anthropology, what some call "Christian materialism," in *Rethinking Human Nature: A Christian Materialist Alternative to the Soul*.[1] Here he addresses several relevant topics, such as the soul, materialism, ethics, life after death, and other biblical considerations. A traditional interpretation of Christian anthropology is advanced by J. P. Moreland; in two recent publications, *The Soul: How We Know It's Real and Why It Matters* and *The Recalcitrant* Imago Dei: *Human Persons and the Failure of Naturalism*, he defends what Christians

---

1. It is important to note that most Christian materialists are materialists with respect to local objects but not with respect to their global ontology. So they can understand angels and God to exist as immaterial beings but can also affirm that humans are material. Some Christian materialists take it that the whole of reality is fundamentally material; for one example, see Webb, *Jesus Christ, Eternal God*.

have defended for most of church history: some variant of dualism, where humans are compounds of both soul and body. In *The Soul*, Moreland advances a defense of substance dualism. This book is similar to Corcoran's work in that Moreland addresses the soul in the Bible, philosophical evidence for the soul, ethics, and the afterlife. In *The Recalcitrant Imago Dei*, Moreland defends the substantial soul as the essential part of humans by arguing abductively from various properties and faculties (e.g., reason, consciousness, freedom of the will, morality).

In addition to Corcoran's defense of Christian materialism, two other defenses of Christian materialism deserve mention. Joel B. Green, in *Body, Soul, and Human Life: The Nature of Humanity in the Bible*, defends Christian materialism as the most natural interpretation of a theological anthropology based on his integration of the neuroscientific data and the biblical data. Both sets of the data naturally highlight humans as embodied physical beings. In a similar vein from the vantage point of thinking about humans in a communal context, Warren S. Brown and Brad D. Strawn, in *The Physical Nature of Christian Life: Neuroscience, Psychology, and the Church*, defend Christian materialism as the best explanation for the life of individuals in the practice of the church. They contend that the soul is not necessary and that the embodied life of the human being is central. The soul is not unorthodox, they contend, but neither is it needed to work out Christian doctrine and practice.

John Cooper's work is the most thorough biblical defense of dualism (e.g., substance dualism, Thomist dualism) in the literature to date. Cooper's famous work moves through the biblical material and finally concludes in favor of substance dualism. The linchpin of his argument depends on the biblical teaching of the disembodied intermediate state. He reasons that if the Bible clearly teaches a disembodied intermediate state, then a version of dualism is entailed by the biblical material. By carefully working through Old Testament, intertestamental, New Testament, and ancient writings, Cooper shows quite plainly that the metaphysical implication of the biblical data is dualism, not monism.

Few works have defended the soul in a holistic theological framework, but two come to mind. Matthew Levering defends substance dualism (or some position near it) in a recent work, *Jesus and the Demise of Death: Resurrection, Afterlife, and the Fate of the Christian*. Here, Levering gives a defense of the immaterial nature of human beings as that which the scriptural narrative yields concerning humans. However, Levering's focus is not so much anthropology as the afterlife. I have recently defended one version of substance dualism (in *The Soul of Theological Anthropology: A Cartesian Exploration*) in an explicitly theological context where I advance several arguments for the soul. In this way, I build on the successes of Cooper's famous work with closer attention given to philosophical specificity and systematic scope.

Several authors move beyond the question, What am I? to, Who am I? and put forward more comprehensive treatments of theological anthropology. John F. Kilner, for example, has recently defended, in *Dignity and Destiny: Humanity in the Image of God*, two big ideas from the biblical story line concerning the *imago Dei*. He contends that the *imago Dei* is a covenantal term referring to humans generally and universally. As a covenantal term, the *imago Dei* signifies the whole of the human as the covenantal bearer of God's interactions with the rest of the world. For Kilner, humans as images are dignified because of their covenantal role in the world and find their destiny in Christ.

In one recent introductory theological anthropology, *Theological Anthropology: A Guide for the Perplexed*, Marc Cortez surveys some of the big issues. He concerns his investigation with methodology, *imago Dei*, mind and body, free will, and reflections for this burgeoning field. He is less concerned with offering a distinctively evangelical slant on the subject, and his investigation is limited to these topics.

There has been a resurgence of interest in theological anthropology from a christological vantage point. Kathryn Tanner advances a theological vision of humanity in *Christ the Key*. Tanner considers the human through the lens of patristic Christology as a way to salvage humanity from modernity's fragmented picture of the divine and human. She develops a vision of humanity via Christology. This theological mode of reasoning is not uncommon in the literature. Marc Cortez, too, capitalizes on some of the recent developments in christological anthropology in his *Christological Anthropology in Historical Perspective: Ancient and Contemporary Approaches to Theological Anthropology*. Cortez explicitly develops a christological method motivated by his inclinations toward Karl Barth. He defines this method by arguing that it is Christ who concretely warrants specific claims about the human in ways that go beyond a generic understanding of the *imago Dei* and ethics. The remainder of the book gives expression to this method by showing how it is that theologians have practiced christological anthropology in history.

The why of humanity—that is, the reason for human existence—has received more attention than other topics in theological anthropology and is connected to the afterlife (Where will I go when I die? What will happen to the redeemed and the nonredeemed when they die?). In Christian dogmatics, the theological topic in focus is often called "personal eschatology." Jerry L. Walls offers up a persuasive and insightful vision of human persons in the afterlife in his book *Heaven, Hell, and Purgatory: Rethinking Things That*

Matter Most. Walls generates a vision of humanity's purpose in light of the divine drama of redemption in the afterlife, which includes three possible locations or events for humans (heaven, hell, and purgatory). A theme in some theological works on personal eschatology that is receiving additional attention in the literature is deification.[2] Herein the idea is that the final end of humans is not simply a creaturely embodied life on the new earth but a partaking of the divine life in heaven.

Normally, anthropology logically follows the doctrine of God and the doctrine of creation. Theological anthropology is often construed as a subset of the doctrine of creation in the broader Christian vision of reality. However, it seems to me, especially in light of the modern emphasis on the subject, that theological anthropology deserves its own substantive place in systematic theology. Anthropology not only is informed by almost every theological locus but also has some role to play in our understanding of nearly every doctrine, including the doctrine of God.[3]

2. See one example in Blackwell, *Christosis.* Blackwell shows us the relationship between Paul and his patristic interpreters. Blackwell is loosely working within a Reformed theological tradition, but his interlocutors are primarily patristic sources and New Testament reception.

3. For a useful introduction to modern systematic theology, see Kapic and McCormack, *Mapping Modern Theology.*

Bibliography

Alexander, Michelle. *The New Jim Crow: Mass Incarceration in an Age of Color-blindness*. New York: New Press, 2012.

Allen, Charlotte. "Pelagius the Progressive." *First Things*, April 2019.

Allen, Michael. *Grounded in Heaven: Recentering Christian Hope and Life in God*. Grand Rapids: Eerdmans, 2018.

———. "The Visibility of the Invisible God." *Journal of Reformed Theology* 9, no. 3 (2015): 249–69.

Allen, Michael, and Scott R. Swain. *Reformed Catholicity: The Promise of Retrieval for Theology and Biblical Interpretation*. Grand Rapids: Baker Academic, 2015.

Allen, Sister Prudence. *The Concept of Woman*. 3 vols. Grand Rapids: Eerdmans, 1997–2016.

Anderson, Ryan T. *When Harry Became Sally: Responding to the Transgender Movement*. New York: Encounter Books, 2018.

Anselm. "On the Virgin Conception and Original Sin." In *Anselm of Canterbury: The Major Works*, edited by Brian Davies and G. R. Evans, 357–89. Oxford World's Classics. Oxford: Oxford University Press, 1998.

Aquinas, Thomas. *Summa Contra Gentiles*. Translated by Charles J. O'Neill. Notre Dame, IN: Notre Dame University Press, 1979.

———. *Summa Theologiae*. Translated by Laurence Shapcote. Edited by John Mortensen and Enrique Alarcón. 8 vols. Lander, WY: Aquinas Institute for the Study of Sacred Doctrine, 2012.

Arbour, Benjamin H., ed. *Philosophical Essays against Open Theism*. Routledge Studies in the Philosophy of Religion. New York: Routledge, 2019.

Arbour, Benjamin H., and John R. Gilhooly. "Transgenderism, Human Ontology, and the Metaphysics of Properties." Evangelical Philosophical Society, 2019. https://

291

www.epsociety.org/userfiles/Arbour%20and%20Gilhooly_Transgenderism%20 (Final2019-1).pdf.

Arcadi, James M. "Kryptic or Cryptic? The Divine Preconscious Model of the Incarnation as a Concrete-Nature Christology." *Neue Zeitschrift für systematische Theologie und Religionsphilosophie* 58, no. 2 (June 2016): 229–43.

Augustine. *City of God*. In *City of God; Christian Doctrine*, 1–511. Vol. 2 of *Nicene and Post-Nicene Fathers*, series 1. Edited by Philip Schaff. Grand Rapids: Eerdmans, 1994.

———. *On the Holy Trinity*. In *On the Holy Trinity; Doctrinal Treatises; Moral Treatises*, 1–228. Vol. 3 of *Nicene and Post-Nicene Fathers*, series 1. Edited by Philip Schaff. Grand Rapids: Eerdmans, 1994.

Averbeck, Richard. "The Lost World of Adam and Eve: A Review Essay." *Themelios* 40, no. 2 (2015): 226–39.

Baillie, James. *Problems in Personal Identity*. Paragon Issues in Philosophy. New York: Paragon House, 1993.

Baker, Lynne Rudder. *Naturalism and the First-Person Perspective*. Oxford: Oxford University Press, 2013.

Balthasar, Hans Urs von. "Eschatology in Outline." In *Spirit and Institution*, translated by Edward T. Oakes, 423–68. Vol. 4 of *Explorations in Theology*. San Francisco: Ignatius, 1995.

———. *Theo-drama: Theological Dramatic Theory*. Translated by Graham Harrison. San Francisco: Ignatius, 1988.

Barr, James. *The Semantics of Biblical Language*. London: Oxford University Press, 1961.

Barry, William. "Arianism." *The Catholic Encyclopedia*. Vol. 1. New York: Robert Appleton, 1907. http://www.newadvent.org/cathen/01707c.htm.

Bauckham, Richard J. "Vision of God." In *New Dictionary of Theology*, edited by Ferguson and Wright, 711. Downers Grove, IL: InterVarsity, 2005.

Bavinck, Herman. *Reformed Dogmatics*. Edited by John Bolt. Translated by John Vriend. 4 vols. Grand Rapids: Baker Academic, 2010.

Beale, G. K. *The Temple and the Church's Mission: A Biblical Theology of the Dwelling Place of God*. New Studies in Biblical Theology. Downers Grove, IL: IVP Academic, 2004.

———. *We Become What We Worship: A Biblical Theology of Idolatry*. Downers Grove, IL: IVP Academic, 2008.

Bebbington, David. *Evangelicalism in Modern Britain: A History from the 1730s to the 1980s*. London: Unwin Hyman, 1989.

Berkhof, Louis. *Systematic Theology*. Grand Rapids: Eerdmans, 1938.

Billings, J. Todd. *Calvin, Participation, and the Gift: The Activity of Believers in Union with Christ*. Changing Paradigms in Historical and Systematic Theology. Oxford: Oxford University Press, 2007.

Blackwell, Ben C. *Christosis: Engaging Paul's Soteriology with His Patristic Interpreters*. Grand Rapids: Eerdmans, 2016.

Blackwell, Ben C., and Kris A. Miller. "Theosis and Theological Anthropology." Chapter 23 in Farris and Taliaferro, *The Ashgate Research Companion to Theological Anthropology*.

Blocher, Henri. *In the Beginning: The Opening Chapters of Genesis*. Translated by David G. Preston. Downers Grove, IL: InterVarsity, 1984.

Bloom, Paul. *Descartes' Baby: How the Science of Child Development Explains What Makes Us Human*. New York: Basic Books, 2005.

Boersma, Hans. *Heavenly Participation: The Weaving of a Sacramental Tapestry*. Grand Rapids: Eerdmans, 2011.

———. "Putting On Clothes: Body, Sex, and Gender in Gregory of Nyssa." *Crux* 54, no. 2 (Summer 2018): 27–34.

———. *Scripture as Real Presence: Sacramental Exegesis in the Early Church*. Grand Rapids: Baker Academic, 2017.

———. *Seeing God: The Beatific Vision in Christian Tradition*. Grand Rapids: Eerdmans, 2018.

———. *Violence, Hospitality, and the Cross: Reappropriating the Atonement Tradition*. Grand Rapids: Baker Academic, 2006.

Bray, Gerald. "The Significance of God's Image in Man." *Tyndale Bulletin* 42, no. 2 (November 1991): 195–225.

Brockman, John, ed. *Possible Minds: 25 Ways of Looking at AI*. New York: Penguin, 2019.

Brower, Jeffrey E. *Aquinas's Ontology of the Material World: Change, Hylomorphism, and Material Objects*. Oxford: Oxford University Press, 2014.

Brown, Christopher M. "St. Thomas, the Interim State of the Saints in Heaven, and Some Contemporary Philosophical Perspectives." Paper presented at the Interim State Workshop, Calvin College, Grand Rapids, July 15–19, 2015.

Brown, Warren S., Nancey Murphy, and H. Newton Malony, eds. *Whatever Happened to the Soul? Scientific and Theological Portraits of Human Nature*. Theology and the Sciences. Minneapolis: Fortress, 1998.

Brown, Warren S., and Brad D. Strawn. *The Physical Nature of Christian Life: Neuroscience, Psychology, and the Church*. Cambridge: Cambridge University Press, 2012.

Brownson, James V. *Bible, Gender, Sexuality: Reframing the Church's Debate on Same-Sex Relationships*. Grand Rapids: Eerdmans, 2013.

Budziszewski, J. *The Line through the Heart: Natural Law as Fact, Theory, and Sign of Contradiction*. Wilmington, DE: ISI Books, 2009.

———. *What We Can't Not Know: A Guide*. Dallas: Spence, 2003.

Burnell, Peter. *The Augustinian Person*. Washington, DC: Catholic University of America Press, 2005.

Bynum, Caroline. "Why All the Fuss about the Body? A Medievalist's Perspective." *Critical Inquiry* 22 (1995): 1–33.

Calvin, John. *Institutes of the Christian Religion*. Edited by John T. McNeil. Translated by Ford Lewis Battles. Library of Christian Classics 20–21. Philadelphia: Westminster, 1960.

———. "Lessons from the Death of Uzzah." In *Sermons on 2 Samuel: Chapters 1–13*, translated by Douglas Kelley, 244–61. Edinburgh: The Banner of Truth Trust, 1992.

Canlis, Julie. *Calvin's Ladder: A Spiritual Theology of Ascent and Ascension*. Grand Rapids: Eerdmans, 2010.

Carson, D. A. *The Difficult Doctrine of the Love of God*. Wheaton: Crossway, 2000.

———. *Divine Sovereignty and Human Responsibility: Biblical Perspectives in Tension*. Atlanta: John Knox, 1981.

———. *How Long, O Lord? Reflections on Suffering and Evil*. 2nd ed. Grand Rapids: Baker Academic, 2006.

Carter, J. Kameron. *Race: A Theological Account*. Oxford: Oxford University Press, 2008.

Chan, J. H. W. "A Cartesian Approach to the Incarnation." Chapter 27 in Farris and Taliaferro, *The Ashgate Research Companion to Theological Anthropology*.

Chapman, G. Clarke. "On Being Human: Moltmann's Anthropology of Hope." *Asbury Theological Journal* 55, no. 1 (Spring 2000): 69–84.

Chapman, John. "Eutychianism." *The Catholic Encyclopedia*. Vol. 5. New York: Robert Appleton, 1909. http://www.newadvent.org/cathen/05633a.htm.

Charles, J. Daryl. *Retrieving the Natural Law: A Return to Moral First Things*. Grand Rapids: Eerdmans, 2008.

Chisholm, Roderick M. *Person and Object: A Metaphysical Study*. La Salle, IL: Open Court, 1979.

———. "The Problem of the Criterion." Chapter 5 in *The Foundations of Knowing*. Brighton: Harvester, 1982.

Clark, Kelly James. *God and the Brain: The Rationality of Belief*. Grand Rapids: Eerdmans, 2019.

Clarke, Randolph, and Justin Capes. "Incompatibilist (Nondeterministic) Theories of Free Will." *Stanford Encyclopedia of Philosophy*. Edited by Edward N. Zalta. Spring 2017 ed. https://plato.stanford.edu/archives/spr2017/entries/incompatibilism-theories/.

Coakley, Sarah. "The Eschatological Body: Gender, Transformation, and God." *Modern Theology* 16, no. 1 (January 2000): 61–73.

Cohen-Bendahan, Celina C. C., Cornelieke van de Beek, and Sheri A. Berenbaum. "Prenatal Sex Hormone Effects on Child and Adult Sex-Typed Behavior: Methods and Findings." *Neuroscience & Biobehavioral Review* 29, no. 2 (April 2005): 353–84.

Collins, C. John. *Did Adam and Eve Really Exist? Who They Were and Why You Should Care.* Wheaton: Crossway, 2011.

Collins, Nate. *All but Invisible: Exploring Identity Questions at the Intersection of Faith, Gender, and Sexuality.* Grand Rapids: Zondervan, 2017.

Cooper, John W. "Biblical Anthropology and the Body-Soul Problem." In Corcoran, *Soul, Body, and Survival*, 218–28.

———. *Body, Soul, and Life Everlasting: Biblical Anthropology and the Monism-Dualism Debate.* Grand Rapids: Eerdmans, 2000.

Copan, Paul. "Original Sin and Christian Philosophy." *Philosophia Christi* 5, no. 2 (2003): 519–41.

Corcoran, Kevin J. *Rethinking Human Nature: A Christian Materialist Alternative to the Soul.* Grand Rapids: Baker Academic, 2006.

———, ed. *Soul, Body, and Survival: Essays on the Metaphysics of Human Persons.* Ithaca, NY: Cornell University Press, 2001.

Cortez, Marc. *Christological Anthropology in Historical Perspective: Ancient and Contemporary Approaches to Theological Anthropology.* Grand Rapids: Zondervan, 2016.

———. *Embodied Souls, Ensouled Bodies: An Exercise in Christological Anthropology and Its Significance for the Mind/Body Debate.* New York: Bloomsbury T&T Clark, 2008.

———. "Idealism and the Resurrection." Chapter 7 in Farris and Hamilton, *Idealism and Christian Theology*.

———. *Resourcing Theological Anthropology: A Constructive Account of Humanity in the Light of Christ.* Grand Rapids: Zondervan, 2017.

———. *Theological Anthropology: A Guide for the Perplexed.* New York: Bloomsbury T&T Clark, 2010.

Cortez, Marc, Joshua R. Farris, and S. Mark Hamilton, eds. *Being Saved: Explorations in Human Salvation.* London: SCM, 2018.

Cosden, Darrell. *The Heavenly Good of Earthly Work.* Peabody, MA: Hendrickson, 2006.

———. *The Theology of Work: Work and the New Creation.* Carlisle: Paternoster, 2004.

Crisp, Oliver. *An American Augustinian: Sin and Salvation in the Dogmatic Theology of William G. T. Shedd.* Eugene, OR: Wipf & Stock, 2007.

———. "A Christological Model of the *Imago Dei*." Chapter 17 in Farris and Taliaferro, *The Ashgate Research Companion to Theological Anthropology*.

———. *Divinity and Humanity: The Incarnation Reconsidered.* Current Issues in Theology. Cambridge: Cambridge University Press, 2007.

———. *God Incarnate: Explorations in Christology.* New York: T&T Clark, 2009.

———. *Jonathan Edwards and the Metaphysics of Sin*. Burlington, VT: Ashgate, 2005.

———. "Original Sin and Atonement." Chapter 19 in Flint and Rea, *The Oxford Handbook of Philosophical Theology*.

Crisp, Oliver D., and Fred Sanders. *Locating Atonement: Explorations in Constructive Dogmatics*. Grand Rapids: Zondervan, 2015.

Cullmann, Oscar. *Immortality of the Soul or Resurrection of the Dead? The New Testament Witness*. London: Epworth, 1958.

Culver, Robert Duncan. *Systematic Theology: Historical and Biblical*. Fearn: Mentor, 2002.

Cushing, Simon, ed. *Heaven and Philosophy*. Lanham, MD: Lexington Books, 2018.

Daley, Brian E. *The Hope of the Early Church: A Handbook of Patristic Eschatology*. Cambridge: Cambridge University Press, 1991.

Dalferth, Ingolf U. *Creatures of Possibility: The Theological Basis of Human Freedom*. Translated by Jo Bennett. Grand Rapids: Baker Academic, 2016.

Date, Christopher M., Gregory G. Stump, and Joshua W. Anderson. *Rethinking Hell: Readings in Evangelical Conditionalism*. Eugene, OR: Cascade Books, 2014.

Davis, Stephen T. "Eschatology and Resurrection." Chapter 21 in *The Oxford Handbook of Eschatology*, edited by Jerry L. Walls. Oxford: Oxford University Press, 2008.

———. "Redemption, the Resurrected Body, and Human Nature." Chapter 22 in Farris and Taliaferro, *The Ashgate Research Companion to Theological Anthropology*.

———. *Risen Indeed: Making Sense of the Resurrection*. Grand Rapids: Eerdmans, 1993.

Deane-Drummond, Celia. "Are Animals Moral? Taking Soundings through Vice, Virtue, Conscience and *Imago Dei*." Chapter 10 in *Creaturely Theology: On God, Humans and Other Animals*, edited by Celia Deane-Drummond and David Clough. London: SCM, 2009.

DeFranza, Megan K. *Sex Difference in Christian Theology: Male, Female, and Intersex in the Image of God*. Grand Rapids: Eerdmans, 2015.

DeGrazia, David. *Human Identity and Bioethics*. Cambridge: Cambridge University Press, 2005.

Dembski, William. *Intelligent Design: The Bridge between Science and Theology*. Downers Grove, IL: InterVarsity, 1999.

Dempster, Stephen G. *Dominion and Dynasty: A Theology of the Hebrew Bible*. Downers Grove, IL: InterVarsity, 2003.

Descartes, René. *Discourse on Method and Meditations on First Philosophy*. Translated by Donald A. Cress. Indianapolis: Hackett, 1980.

de Waal, Frans. *The Bonobo and the Atheist: In Search of Humanism among the Primates*. New York: Norton, 2013.

Dumbrell, William J. *Covenant and Creation: A Theology of the Old Testament Covenants*. Carlisle: Paternoster, 1984.

Eagleton, Terry. *The Illusions of Postmodernism*. Oxford: Blackwell, 1996.

Edwards, Jonathan. "The Great Christian Doctrine of Original Sin Defended." In vol. 1 of *The Works of Jonathan Edwards*, 146–233. Peabody, MA: Hendrickson, 1998.

———. *Original Sin*. Vol. 3 of *The Works of Jonathan Edwards*. Edited by Clyde A. Holbrook. New Haven: Yale University Press, 1970.

———. *Sermons*. Vol. 2 of *The Works of Jonathan Edwards*. Edited by Edward Hickman. Philadelphia: The Banner of Truth Trust, 1995.

———. *Works of Jonathan Edwards Online*. 73 vols. New Haven: Yale University Press, 2018. http://edwards.yale.edu.

Edwards, Paul, ed. *Immortality*. Amherst, NY: Prometheus Books, 1997.

Enns, Peter. *The Evolution of Adam: What the Bible Does and Doesn't Say about Human Origins*. Grand Rapids: Brazos, 2012.

Episcopal Church. "The Celebration and Blessing of a Marriage 2." New York: Church Publishing, 2015.

———. "The Witnessing and Blessing of a Marriage." New York: Church Publishing, 2015.

Ereshefsky, Marc. "Species." *Stanford Encyclopedia of Philosophy*. Edited by Edward N. Zalta. Fall 2017 ed. https://plato.stanford.edu/archives/fall2017/entries/species/.

Farley, Edward. *Good and Evil: Interpreting a Human Condition*. Minneapolis: Fortress, 1990.

Farris, Joshua R. "Bodily-Constituted Persons, Soulish Persons, and the *Imago Dei*." *Philosophy and Theology* 28, no. 2 (2016): 455–68.

———. "Christianity." Chapter 7 in Nagasawa and Matheson, *The Palgrave Handbook of the Afterlife*.

———. "Considering Souls of the Past for Today: Soul Origins, Anthropology, and Contemporary Theology." *Neue Zeitschrift für systematische Theologie und Religionsphilosophie* 57, no. 3 (September 2015): 368–98.

———. "Discovering God and Soul: A Reappraisal of and Appreciation for Cartesian Natural Theology." *Philosophia Christi* 16, no. 1 (2014): 37–57.

———. "Emergent Creationism: Another Option in the Origin of the Soul Debate." *Religious Studies* 50 (2014): 321–39. Modified and republished in Farris, *The Soul of Theological Anthropology*.

———. "Originating Souls and Original Sin: An Initial Exploration of Dualism, Anthropology, and Sins Transmission." *Neue Zeitschrift für systematische Theologie und Religionsphilosophie* 58, no. 1 (March 2016): 39–56.

———. "Pure or Compound Dualism? Considering Afresh the Prospects of Pure Substance Dualism." *Argument* 3, no. 1 (2013): 151–59.

———. "The Soul-Concept: Meaningfully Embrace or Meaningfully Disregard." *Annales Philosophici* 5 (2012): 64–67.

———. *The Soul of Theological Anthropology: A Cartesian Exploration.* Routledge New Critical Thinking in Religion, Theology and Biblical Studies. New York: Routledge, 2017.

———. "Substance Dualism and Theological Anthropology: A Theological Argument for a Simple View of Persons." *Philosophy and Theology* 27, no. 1 (2015): 107–26.

———. "A Substantive (Soul) Model of the *Imago Dei*: A Rich Property View." Chapter 13 in Farris and Taliaferro, *The Ashgate Research Companion to Theological Anthropology.*

Farris, Joshua R., and James Arcadi. "Introduction to the Topical Issue 'Analytic Perspectives on Method and Authority in Theology.'" *Open Theology* 3, no. 1 (2017): 630–32.

Farris, Joshua R., and Ryan Brandt. "Ensouling the Beatific Vision: Motivating the Reformed Impulse." *Perichoresis* 15, no. 1 (May 2017): 67–85.

———. "A Theology of Seeing, Experiencing, and Vision: An Editorial Introduction." *Perichoresis* 17, no. 2 (Spring 2019): 3–18.

Farris, Joshua R., and S. Mark Hamilton, eds. *Idealism and Christian Theology.* Idealism and Christianity. New York: Bloomsbury Academic, 2016.

———. "The Logic of Reparative Substitution: Contemporary Restitution Models of Atonement, Divine Justice, and Somatic Death." *Irish Theological Quarterly* 83, no. 1 (2018): 62–77.

———. "Reparative Substitution and the 'Efficacy Objection': Toward a Modified Satisfaction Theory of Atonement." *Perichoresis* 15, no. 3 (2017): 97–110. Republished in Cortez, Farris, and Hamilton, *Being Saved: Explorations in Human Salvation.*

Farris, Joshua R., and Charles Taliaferro, eds. *The Ashgate Research Companion to Theological Anthropology.* New York: Routledge, 2016.

Farrow, Douglas. *Theological Negotiations: Proposals in Soteriology and Anthropology.* Grand Rapids: Baker Academic, 2019.

Fenwick, John. *Anglican Ecclesiology and the Gospel.* Newport Beach, CA: Anglican House, 2016.

Feser, Edward. *Aristotle's Revenge: The Metaphysical Foundations of Physical and Biological Science.* Neunkirchen-Seelscheid: Editiones Scholisticae, 2019.

———. *Neo-scholastic Essays.* South Bend, IN: St. Augustine's Press, 2015.

Finnis, John. *Natural Law and Natural Rights.* 2nd ed. Clarendon Law Series. Oxford: Oxford University Press, 2011.

Flint, Thomas, and Michael Rea, eds. *The Oxford Handbook of Philosophical Theology.* Oxford: Oxford University Press, 2009.

Foster, John. *The Immaterial Self: A Defence of the Cartesian Dualist Conception of the Mind*. International Library of Philosophy. London: Routledge, 1991.

Fredriksen, Paula. *Sin: The Early History of an Idea*. Princeton: Princeton University Press, 2012.

Fudge, Edward William. *The Fire That Consumes: A Biblical and Historical Study of the Doctrine of Final Punishment*. 3rd ed. Eugene, OR: Wipf & Stock, 2011.

Gagnon, Robert. *The Bible and Homosexual Practice: Texts and Hermeneutics*. Nashville: Abingdon, 2001.

Garr, W. Randall. *In His Own Image and Likeness: Humanity, Divinity, and Monotheism*. Culture and History of the Ancient Near East 15. Leiden: Brill, 2003.

Gasser, Georg, ed. *Personal Identity and Resurrection: How Do We Survive Our Death?* Burlington, VT: Ashgate, 2010.

Geach, Peter. "Immortality." Chapter 23 in P. Edwards, *Immortality*.

Geffen, David. "The Genetics of Sex Differences in Brain and Behavior." *Frontiers in Neuroendocrinology* 32, no. 2 (October 2010): 227–46.

Gibb, Sophie, E. J. Lowe, and R. D. Ingthorsson, eds. *Mental Causation and Ontology*. Oxford: Oxford University Press, 2013.

Girgis, Sherif, Ryan T. Anderson, and Robert P. George. *What Is Marriage? Man and Woman: A Defense*. New York: Encounter Books, 2012.

Glasgow, Joshua. *A Theory of Race*. New York: Routledge, 2009.

Göcke, Benedikt Paul, ed. *After Physicalism*. Notre Dame, IN: University of Notre Dame Press, 2012.

———. "Christian Cyborgs: A Plea for Moderate Transhumanism." *Faith and Philosophy* 34, no. 3 (2017): 343–64.

Goetz, Stewart. *Freedom, Teleology, and Evil*. Continuum Studies in Philosophy of Religion. New York: Continuum, 2011.

———. "Modal Dualism: A Critique." In Corcoran, *Soul, Body, and Survival*, 89–104.

Goetz, Stewart, and Charles Taliaferro. *A Brief History of the Soul*. Brief Histories of Philosophy. Malden, MA: Wiley-Blackwell, 2011.

Graves, Mark. *Mind, Brain and the Elusive Soul: Human Systems of Cognitive Science and Religion*. Ashgate Science and Religion Series. Burlington, VT: Ashgate, 2008.

Green, Joel B. *Body, Soul, and Human Life: The Nature of Humanity in the Bible*. Grand Rapids: Baker Academic, 2008.

———. "Eschatology and the Nature of Humans: A Reconsideration of Pertinent Biblical Evidence." *Science and Christian Belief* 14, no. 1 (April 2002): 33–50.

Gregory of Nyssa. "On the Making of Man." In *Gregory of Nyssa: Dogmatic Treatises*, 387–427. Vol. 5 of *Nicene and Post-Nicene Fathers*, series 2. Edited by Philip Schaff and Henry Wace. Grand Rapids: Eerdmans, 1996.

———. *On the Soul and the Resurrection*. Translated by Catharine P. Roth. Popular Patristics. Crestwood, NY: St. Vladimir's Seminary Press, 2002.

Grenz, Stanley. *The Social God and the Relational Self: A Trinitarian Theology of the* Imago Dei. Louisville: Westminster John Knox, 2001.

Groothuis, Douglas. *Christian Apologetics: A Comprehensive Case for the Biblical Faith.* Downers Grove, IL: IVP Academic, 2011.

Habets, Myk. *Theosis in the Theology of Thomas Torrance.* Ashgate New Critical Thinking in Religion, Theology and Biblical Studies. Burlington, VT: Ashgate, 2009.

Habets, Myk, and Peter K. McGhee. "TGIF! A Theology of Workers and Their Work." *Evangelical Review of Theology* 40, no. 4 (October 2016): 32–47.

Haldane, John, and Patrick Lee. "Aquinas on Human Ensoulment, Abortion and the Value of Life." *Philosophy* 78 (2003): 255–78.

Halteman, Matthew C. "Ontotheology." *Routledge Encyclopedia of Philosophy*, 1998. https://www.rep.routledge.com/articles/thematic/ontotheology/v-1.

Hamilton, S. Mark. "On the Corruption of the Body: A Theological Argument for Metaphysical Idealism." Chapter 6 in Farris and Hamilton, *Idealism and Christian Theology.*

Harari, Yuval Noah. *Homo Deus: A Brief History of Tomorrow.* New York: Harper Perennial, 2017.

Harent, Stéphane. "Original Sin." *The Catholic Encyclopedia*. Vol. 11. New York: Robert Appleton, 1911. http://www.newadvent.org/cathen/11312a.htm.

Harris, Murray. "Resurrection and Immortality: Eight Theses." *Themelios* 1, no. 2 (Spring 1976): 50–55.

Harrison, Nonna Verna. *God's Many-Splendored Image: Theological Anthropology for Christian Formation.* Grand Rapids: Baker Academic, 2010.

———. "Male and Female in Cappadocian Theology." *Journal of Theological Studies* 41, no. 2 (October 1990): 441–71.

Harrison, William H. "Loving the Creation, Loving the Creator: Dorothy L. Sayers's Theology of Work." *Anglican Theological Review* 86, no. 2 (2000): 239–57.

Harrower, Scott. "A Trinitarian Doctrine of Christian Vocation." *Crucible* 5, no. 2 (November 2013): 1–12.

Hart, David Bentley. *The Beauty of the Infinite: The Aesthetics of Christian Truth.* Grand Rapids: Eerdmans, 2004.

Hasker, William. *The Emergent Self.* Ithaca, NY: Cornell University Press, 1999.

———. "Why Emergence?" Chapter 12 in Farris and Taliaferro, *The Ashgate Research Companion to Theological Anthropology.*

Hasker, William, and Charles Taliaferro. "Afterlife." *Stanford Encyclopedia of Philosophy.* Edited by Edward N. Zalta. Winter 2014 ed. http://plato.stanford.edu/archives/win2014/entries/afterlife/.

Hawley, Katherine. "Temporal Parts." *Stanford Encyclopedia of Philosophy.* Edited by Edward N. Zalta. Spring 2018 ed. https://plato.stanford.edu/archives/spr2018/entries/temporal-parts/.

Heine, Ronald E. *Classical Christian Doctrine: Introducing the Essentials of the Ancient Faith*. Grand Rapids: Baker Academic, 2013.

Helm, Paul. *Calvin at the Centre*. Oxford: Oxford University Press, 2010.

———. *Human Nature from Calvin to Edwards*. Grand Rapids: Reformation Heritage Books, 2018.

———. *John Calvin's Ideas*. Oxford: Oxford University Press, 2004.

Hentschel, Jason. "Thomas Aquinas, 2 Corinthians 5, and the Christian Hope for Life after Death." *Journal of Theological Interpretation* 8, no. 1 (2014): 63–80.

Hick, John. *Death and Eternal Life*. London: Collins, 1976.

———. "The Recreation of the Psycho-physical Person." Chapter 24 in P. Edwards, *Immortality*.

Hicks, John Mark, and Greg Taylor. *Down in the River to Pray: Revisioning Baptism as God's Transforming Work*. Abilene, TX: Leafwood, 2010.

Hill, Jonathan. Introduction to *The Metaphysics of the Incarnation*, edited by Anna Marmodoro and Jonathan Hill, 1–19. Oxford: Oxford University Press, 2011.

Hodge, Charles. *Systematic Theology*. 3 vols. Grand Rapids: Eerdmans, 2003.

Hoekema, Anthony A. *Created in God's Image*. Grand Rapids: Eerdmans, 1994.

Hoffmeier, James K., and Janet Siefert. "What Are Human Beings?" In *Can We Believe in Creation and Evolution?* Forthcoming.

Horton, Michael. "Atonement and Ascension." Chapter 12 in Crisp and Sanders, *Locating Atonement: Explorations in Constructive Dogmatics*.

———. *The Christian Faith: A Systematic Theology for Pilgrims on the Way*. Grand Rapids: Zondervan, 2011.

———. *Lord and Servant: A Covenant Christology*. Louisville: Westminster John Knox, 2005.

———. *Pilgrim Theology: Core Doctrines for Christian Disciples*. Grand Rapids: Zondervan, 2011.

Huxley, Julian. *Evolutionary Humanism*. Buffalo, NY: Prometheus Books, 1992.

James, Michael. "Race." *The Stanford Encyclopedia of Philosophy*. Spring 2017 ed. Edited by Edward N. Zalta. https://plato.stanford.edu/archives/spr2017/entries/race/.

Jeeves, Malcolm. *The Emergence of Personhood: A Quantum Leap?* Grand Rapids: Eerdmans, 2015.

———, ed. *Rethinking Human Nature: A Multidisciplinary Approach*. Grand Rapids: Eerdmans, 2011.

Jeeves, Malcolm, and Warren S. Brown. *Neuroscience, Psychology, and Religion*. West Conshohocken, PA: Templeton Foundation Press, 2009.

Jennings, James. *The Christian Imagination: Theology and the Origins of Race*. New Haven: Yale University Press, 2011.

Jensen, David H. *Responsive Labor: A Theology of Work*. Louisville: Westminster John Knox, 2006.

Jenson, Robert W. *Systematic Theology*. 2 vols. Oxford: Oxford University Press, 1997–99.

Jewett, Paul K. *Who We Are: Our Dignity as Human; A Neo-evangelical Theology*. Edited and completed by Marguerite Shuster. Grand Rapids: Eerdmans, 1996.

John Paul II. *Man and Woman He Created Them: A Theology of the Body*. Boston: Pauline Books & Media, 2006.

Johnson, Raynor. "Preexistence, Reincarnation and Karma." Chapter 18 in P. Edwards, *Immortality*.

Johnston, Mark. *Surviving Death*. Princeton: Princeton University Press, 2010.

Kapic, Kelly M. *Embodied Hope: A Theological Meditation on Pain and Suffering*. Downers Grove, IL: IVP Academic, 2017.

Kapic, Kelly M., and Bruce L. McCormack, eds. *Mapping Modern Theology: A Thematic and Historical Introduction*. Grand Rapids: Baker Academic, 2012.

Keathley, Kenneth, J. B. Stump, and Joe Aguirre, eds. *Old-Earth or Evolutionary Creation? Discussing Origins with Reasons to Believe and BioLogos*. Downers Grove, IL: IVP Academic, 2017.

Kehr, Marguerite Witmer. "The Doctrine of the Self in St. Augustine and in Descartes." *Philosophical Review* 25, no. 4 (July 1916): 587–61.

Kelly, J. N. D. *Early Christian Doctrines*. Rev. ed. New York: HarperCollins, 1978.

Kelsey, David. *Eccentric Existence: A Theological Anthropology*. Louisville: Westminster John Knox, 2009.

Kemp, Kenneth W. "Science, Theology, and Monogenesis." *American Catholic Philosophical Quarterly* 85 (2011): 217–36.

Kilner, John F. *Dignity and Destiny: Humanity in the Image of God*. Grand Rapids: Eerdmans, 2015.

Kim, Jaegwon. *Physicalism, or Something Near Enough*. Princeton Monographs in Philosophy. Princeton: Princeton University Press, 2005.

King, Martin Luther, Jr. "The American Dream." Sermon delivered at Ebenezer Baptist Church, Atlanta, July 4, 1965. https://kinginstitute.stanford.edu/king-papers/documents/american-dream-sermon-delivered-ebenezer-baptist-church.

Koons, Robert C., and George Bealer, eds. *The Waning of Materialism*. Oxford: Oxford University Press, 2010.

Kraut, Richard. "Plato." *Stanford Encyclopedia of Philosophy*. Edited by Edward N. Zalta. Spring 2015 ed. https://plato.stanford.edu/archives/spr2015/entries/plato/.

Küng, Hans. *Eternal Life?* Translated by Edward Quinn. Garden City, NY: Doubleday, 1984.

Kwan, Kai-man. *The Rainbow of Experiences, Critical Trust, and God: A Defense of Holistic Empiricism*. Continuum Studies in Philosophy of Religion. New York: Continuum, 2011.

Lacoste, Jean-Yves. *Experience and the Absolute: Disputed Questions on the Humanity of Man*. Translated by Mark Raftery-Skehan. Perspectives in Continental Philosophy 40. New York: Fordham University Press, 2004.

Lavazza, Andrea, and Howard Robinson, eds. *Contemporary Dualism: A Defense*. Routledge Studies in Contemporary Philosophy 54. New York: Routledge, 2014.

Lee, Patrick, and Robert P. George. *Body-Self Dualism in Contemporary Ethics and Politics*. Cambridge: Cambridge University Press, 2008.

———. *Conjugal Union: What Marriage Is and Why It Matters*. Cambridge: Cambridge University Press, 2014.

Leftow, Brian. "Souls Dipped in Dust." In Corcoran, *Soul, Body, and Survival*, 120–38.

Leibniz, G. W. *Discourse on Metaphysics and the Monadology*. Translated by George R. Montgomery. Mineola, NY: Dover Publications, 2005.

Leith, John H. *Creeds of the Churches: A Reader in Christian Doctrine, from the Bible to the Present*. 3rd ed. Atlanta: John Knox, 1982.

Levenson, John D. *Creation and the Persistence of Evil: The Jewish Drama of Divine Omnipotence*. San Francisco: Harper & Row, 1988.

Levering, Matthew. *Engaging the Doctrine of Creation: Cosmos, Creatures, and the Wise and Good Creator*. Grand Rapids: Baker Academic, 2017.

———. *Jesus and the Demise of Death: Resurrection, Afterlife, and the Fate of the Christian*. Waco: Baylor University Press, 2012.

Lilley, Christopher, and Daniel J. Pedersen, eds. *Human Origins and the Image of God: Essays in Honor of J. Wentzel van Huyssteen*. Grand Rapids: Eerdmans, 2017.

Locke, John. *An Essay Concerning Human Understanding*. Edited by Roger Woolhouse. London: Penguin, 1997.

Loftin, R. Keith, and Trey Dimsdale, eds. *Work: Theological Foundations and Practical Implications*. London: SCM, 2018.

Loftin, R. Keith, and Joshua R. Farris, eds. *Christian Physicalism? Philosophical Theological Criticisms*. Lanham, MD: Lexington Books, 2018.

Loke, Andrew. "On the Coherence of the Incarnation: The Divine Preconscious Model." *Neue Zeitschrift für systematische Theologie und Religionsphilosophie* 51, no. 1 (March 2009): 50–63.

———. "On the Divine Preconscious Model of the Incarnation and Concrete-Nature Christology: A Reply to James Arcadi." *Neue Zeitschrift für systematische Theologie und Religionsphilosophie* 59, no. 1 (March 2017): 26–33.

Lombard, Peter. *The Sentences, Book 1: The Mystery of the Trinity*. Translated by Giulio Silano. Mediaeval Sources in Translation 42. Toronto: Pontifical Institute of Mediaeval Studies, 2007.

Loose, Jonathan J. "Christian Materialism and Christian Ethics: Moral Debt and an Ethic of Life." Chapter 18 in Loftin and Farris, *Christian Physicalism? Philosophical Theological Criticisms*.

Loose, Jonathan J., Angus Menuge, and J. P. Moreland, eds. *The Blackwell Companion to Substance Dualism*. New York: Blackwell, 2019.

Louth, Andrew, ed. *Genesis 1–11*. Ancient Christian Commentary on Scripture 1. Downers Grove, IL: InterVarsity, 2001.

Lowe, E. J. "Identity, Composition, and the Simplicity of the Self." In Corcoran, *Soul, Body, and Survival*, 139–58.

———. "In Defence of the Simplicity Argument." *Australasian Journal of Philosophy* 78, no. 1 (March 2000): 105–12.

———. *Personal Agency: The Metaphysics of Mind and Action*. New York: Oxford University Press, 2010.

Lund, David H. *Making Sense of It All: An Introduction to Philosophical Inquiry*. 2nd ed. Upper Saddle River, NJ: Prentice Hall, 2003.

Macleod, Donald. "Original Sin in Reformed Theology." Chapter 6 in Madueme and Reeves, *Adam, the Fall, and Original Sin: Theological, Biblical, and Scientific Perspectives*.

Madden, James D. *Mind, Matter, and Nature: A Thomistic Proposal for the Philosophy of Mind*. Washington, DC: Catholic University of America Press, 2013.

Madigan, Timothy J. "Evolutionary Humanism Revisited: The Continuing Relevance of Julian Huxley." *Religious Humanism* 33, no. 1 (1999). UU Humanist Association. http://huumanists.org/publications/journal/evolutionary-humanism-revisited -continuing-relevance-julian-huxley.

Madueme, Hans, and Michael Reeves, eds. *Adam, the Fall, and Original Sin: Theological, Biblical, and Scientific Perspectives*. Grand Rapids: Baker Academic, 2014.

Mahon, Peter. *Posthumanism: A Guide for the Perplexed*. New York: Bloomsbury Academic, 2017.

Mallon, Ron. "A Field Guide to Social Construction." *Philosophy Compass* 2, no. 1 (2007): 93–108.

———. "Passing, Traveling and Reality: Social Constructionism and the Metaphysics of Race." *Noûs* 38, no. 4 (December 2004): 644–73.

———. "'Race': Normative, Not Metaphysical or Semantic," *Ethics* 116, no. 3 (April 2006): 525–51.

Marion, Jean-Luc. *The Reason of the Gift*. Translated by Stephen E. Lewis. Richard Lectures. Charlottesville: University of Virginia Press, 2011.

Marsen, Sky. "Playing by the Rules—or Not? Constructions of Identity in a Posthuman Future." Chapter 5 in *H+/-: Transhumanism and Its Critics*, edited by Gregory R. Hansell and William Grassie. Philadelphia: Metanexus Institute, 2011.

Martin, Raymond, and John Barresi, eds. *Personal Identity*. Blackwell Readings in Philosophy 11. Malden, MA: Blackwell, 2003.

Maston, Jason. "Christ or Adam: The Ground for Understanding Humanity." *Journal of Theological Interpretation* 1, no. 2 (Fall 2017): 277–93.

Maston, Jason, and Benjamin E. Reynolds, eds. *Anthropology and New Testament Theology*. New York: Bloomsbury T&T Clark, 2018.

Mayer, Lawrence S., and Paul R. McHugh. "Part 3: Gender Identity." In "Sexuality and Gender: Findings from the Biological, Psychological, and Social Sciences," special report, *The New Atlantis* 50 (Fall 2016): 86–113.

McCall, Thomas. *Against God and Nature: The Doctrine of Sin*. Foundations of Evangelical Theology. Wheaton: Crossway, 2019.

———. *An Invitation to Analytic Christian Theology*. Downers Grove, IL: IVP Academic, 2015.

McConville, J. Gordon. *Being Human in God's World: An Old Testament Theology of Humanity*. Grand Rapids: Baker Academic, 2016.

McDonald, Suzanne. "Beholding the Glory of God in the Face of Jesus Christ: John Owen and the 'Reforming' of the Beatific Vision." Chapter 8 in *The Ashgate Research Companion to John Owen's Theology*, edited by Kelly M. Kapic and Mark Jones. Burlington, VT: Ashgate, 2012.

McFarland, David. *Guilty Robots, Happy Dogs: The Question of Alien Minds*. Oxford: Oxford University Press, 2008.

McFarland, Ian A. *Difference and Identity: A Theological Anthropology*. Cleveland: Pilgrim, 2001.

McFadyen, Alistair I. *The Call to Personhood: A Christian Theory of the Individual in Social Relationships*. Cambridge: Cambridge University Press, 1990.

McGinnis, Andrew M. *The Son of God beyond the Flesh: A Historical and Theological Study of the Extra Calvinisticum*. T&T Clark Studies in Systematic Theology. London: Bloomsbury, 2014.

McGrath, Alister. *The Big Question: Why We Can't Stop Talking about Science, Faith and God*. New York: St. Martin's, 2015.

McNabb, Tyler Dalton. *Religious Epistemology*. Elements in the Philosophy of Religion. Cambridge: Cambridge University Press, 2019.

Meilaender, Gilbert. *Should We Live Forever? The Ethical Ambiguities of Aging*. Grand Rapids: Eerdmans, 2013.

Menn, Stephen. *Descartes and Augustine*. Cambridge: Cambridge University Press, 1998.

Menuge, Angus. "Christian Physicalism and Our Knowledge of God." Chapter 4 in Loftin and Farris, *Christian Physicalism? Philosophical Theological Criticisms*.

Merricks, Trenton. *Objects and Persons*. New York: Oxford University Press, 2001.

Metz, Thaddeus. *God, Soul and the Meaning of Life*. Elements in the Philosophy of Religion. Cambridge: Cambridge University Press, 2019.

Middleton, J. Richard. "Death, Immortality, and the Curse: Interpreting Genesis 2–3 in the Context of the Biblical Worldview." Paper presented at the Dabar Conference, Henry Center, Trinity Evangelical Divinity School, June 16, 2018.

————. *The Liberating Image: The* Imago Dei *in Genesis 1.* Grand Rapids: Brazos, 2005.

————. *A New Heaven and a New Earth: Reclaiming Biblical Eschatology.* Grand Rapids: Baker Academic, 2014.

Miley, John. *Systematic Theology.* 2 vols. New York: Eaton & Mains, 1892.

Mitchell, C. Ben, Robert D. Orr, and Susan A. Salladay, eds. *Aging, Death, and the Quest for Immortality.* Grand Rapids: Eerdmans, 2004.

Moltmann, Jürgen. "Man and the Son of Man." Chapter 11 in *No Man Is Alien: Essays on the Unity of Mankind,* edited by J. Robert Nelson. Leiden: Brill, 1971.

————. *Man: Christian Anthropology in the Conflicts of the Present.* Translated by John Sturdy. Philadelphia: Fortress, 1974.

————. *Theology of Hope: On the Grounds and the Implications of a Christian Eschatology.* New York: Harper & Row, 1967.

Moo, Douglas J. *The Epistle to the Romans.* New International Commentary on the New Testament. Grand Rapids: Eerdmans, 1996.

————. "'The Type of the One to Come': Adam in Paul's Theology." Paper presented at the Dabar Conference, Henry Center, Trinity Evangelical Divinity School, June 14, 2018.

Moreland, J. P. *Consciousness and the Existence of God: A Theistic Argument.* Routledge Studies in the Philosophy of Religion. New York: Routledge, 2008.

————. *The Recalcitrant* Imago Dei: *Human Persons and the Failure of Naturalism.* Veritas Series. London: SCM, 2009.

————. *The Soul: How We Know It's Real and Why It Matters.* Chicago: Moody, 2014.

Moreland, J. P., and William Lane Craig. *Philosophical Foundations for a Christian Worldview.* 2nd ed. Downers Grove, IL: IVP Academic, 2018.

Moreland, J. P., and Scott B. Rae. *Body and Soul: Human Nature and the Crisis in Ethics.* Downers Grove, IL: InterVarsity, 2000.

Moreland, J. P., et al., eds. *Theistic Evolution: A Scientific, Philosophical, and Theological Critique.* Wheaton: Crossway, 2017.

Moritz, Joshua M. "Evolutionary Biology and Theological Anthropology." Chapter 3 in Farris and Taliaferro, *The Ashgate Research Companion to Theological Anthropology.*

Morris, Thomas V. *The Logic of God Incarnate.* Eugene, OR: Wipf & Stock, 2001.

————. *Our Idea of God: An Introduction to Philosophical Theology.* Contours of Christian Philosophy. Vancouver: Regent College Publishing, 1997.

Mosser, Carl. "The Metaphysics of Union with God." Unpublished paper.

————. "Recovering the Reformation's Ecumenical Vision of Redemption." In "A Theology of Seeing, Experiencing, and Vision," edited by Joshua R. Farris and Ryan Brandt, special issue no. 2, *Perichoresis* 18 (forthcoming).

Mouw, Richard J., and Douglas A. Sweeney. *The Suffering and Victorious Christ: Toward a More Compassionate Christology*. Grand Rapids: Baker Academic, 2013.

Murphy, Nancey. *Bodies and Souls, or Spirited Bodies?* Current Issues in Theology. Cambridge: Cambridge University Press, 2006.

Murphy, Nancey C., and Warren S. Brown. *Did My Neurons Make Me Do It? Philosophical and Neurobiological Perspectives on Moral Responsibility and Free Will.* New York: Oxford University Press, 2007.

Murphy, Nancey, and Christopher C. Knight, eds. *Human Identity at the Intersection of Science, Technology and Religion*. Ashgate Science and Religion Series. New York: Routledge, 2016.

Murray, Michael, ed. *Reason for the Hope Within*. Grand Rapids: Eerdmans, 1998.

Nagasawa, Yujin, and Benjamin Matheson, eds. *The Palgrave Handbook of the Afterlife*. Palgrave Frontiers in Philosophy of Religion. London: Palgrave Macmillan, 2017.

Nelson, Derek R. *Sin: A Guide for the Perplexed*. London: T&T Clark, 2011.

Nelson, Paul, and John Mark Reynolds. *A Case for Young-Earth Creationism*. Grand Rapids: Zondervan, 2012.

Nichols, Ryan, and Gideon Yaffe. "Thomas Reid." *Stanford Encyclopedia of Philosophy*. Edited by Edward N. Zalta. Winter 2016 ed. https://plato.stanford.edu/archives/win2016/entries/reid/.

Nichols, Terence. *Death and Afterlife: A Theological Introduction*. Grand Rapids: Brazos, 2010.

Niederbacher, Bruno. "Anthropological Hylomorphism." Chapter 9 in Farris and Taliaferro, *The Ashgate Research Companion to Theological Anthropology*.

Nozick, Robert. *Anarchy, State, and Utopia*. New York: Basic Books, 1974.

O'Callaghan, Paul. "Luther and 'Sola Gratia': The Rapport between Grace, Human Freedom, Good Words and the Moral Life." *Scripta Theologica* 49 (2017): 193–212.

O'Connor, Timothy. *Persons and Causes: The Metaphysics of Free Will*. Oxford: Oxford University Press, 2000.

Oden, Thomas C. *Classic Christianity: A Systematic Theology*. San Francisco: HarperSanFrancisco, 1992.

Olson, Eric T. *The Human Animal: Personal Identity without Psychology*. Philosophy of Mind Series. New York: Oxford University Press, 1997.

———. "Immanent Causation and Life after Death." Chapter 3 in Gasser, *Personal Identity and Resurrection*.

O'Neil, Tyler. "What Does the Bible Say about Trans-gender Identity?" *The Christian Post*, September 26, 2013. http://www.christianpost.com/news/what-does-the-bible-say-about-trans-gender-identity-105311/.

Owen, John. *The Works of John Owen*. Edited by W. H. Goold. 24 vols. London: Johnstone & Hunter, 1850–55.

Pagels, Elaine. *Adam, Eve, and the Serpent*. New York: Vintage Books, 1989.

———. *The Gnostic Gospels*. Reprint edition. New York: Vintage Books, 1989.

Parker, David. "Original Sin: A Study in Evangelical Theology." *Evangelical Quarterly* 61, no. 1 (1989): 51–69.

Peoples, Glenn Andrew. "The Mortal God: Materialism and Christology." Chapter 25 in Farris and Taliaferro, *The Ashgate Research Companion to Theological Anthropology*.

Perkins, William. *A Reformed Catholicke*. Works of William Perkins 1. London: John Legatt, 1626.

Perry, John. *A Dialogue on Personal Identity and Immortality*. Indianapolis: Hackett, 1978.

———, ed. *Personal Identity*. 2nd ed. Berkeley: University of California Press, 2008.

Peterson, Jordan. "Three Forms of Meaning and the Management of Complexity." Chapter 2 in *The Psychology of Meaning*, edited by Keith D. Markman, Travis Proulx, and Matthew J. Lindberg. Washington, DC: American Psychological Association, 2013.

Peterson, Robert A., and Michael D. Williams. *Why I Am Not an Arminian*. Downers Grove, IL: IVP Academic, 2004.

Peterson, Ryan S. *The* Imago Dei *as Human Identity: A Theological Interpretation*. Winona Lake, IN: Eisenbrauns, 2016.

———. "Theological Predication, Doctrinal Location, and Method in Analytic Theology." In "Analytic Theological Method and Authority," special issue, *Open Theology* 3 (2017): 458–70.

Pierce, Ronald W., and Rebecca Merrill Groothuis, eds. *Discovering Biblical Equality: Complementarity without Hierarchy*. Downers Grove, IL: InterVarsity, 2004.

Pihlström, Sami. *Pragmatism and Philosophical Anthropology: Understanding Our Human Life in a Human World*. American University Studies, Series V, Philosophy 186. New York: Peter Lang, 1998.

Pinker, Steven. *The Blank Slate: The Modern Denial of Human Nature*. New York: Penguin, 2003.

Piper, John, and Wayne Grudem. *Recovering Biblical Manhood and Womanhood: A Response to Evangelical Feminism*. Wheaton: Crossway, 2012.

Plantinga, Alvin. "Against Materialism." Chapter 19 in *Providence, Scripture, and Resurrection*, edited by Michael Rea. Vol. 2 of *Oxford Readings in Philosophical Theology*. Oxford: Oxford University Press, 2009.

———. *Knowledge and Christian Belief*. Grand Rapids: Eerdmans, 2015.

———. "On Heresy, Mind, and Truth." *Faith and Philosophy* 16, no. 2 (April 1999): 182–93.

Pruss, Alexander R. *One Body: An Essay in Christian Sexual Ethics*. Notre Dame, IN: University of Notre Dame Press, 2012.

Putz, Oliver. "Moral Apes, Human Uniqueness, and the Image of God." *Zygon* 44, no. 3 (2009): 613–24.

Rahner, Karl. *Hominisation: The Evolutionary Origin of Man as a Theological Problem*. Translated by W. T. O'Hara. New York: Herder & Herder, 1965.

———. "Theological Reflexions on Monogenism." In *God, Christ, Mary and Grace*, translated by Cornelius Ernst, 229–96. Vol. 1 of *Theological Investigations*. London: Darton, Longman & Todd, 1961.

Ratzinger, Joseph (Benedict XVI). *Eschatology: Death and Eternal Life*. Translated by Michael Waldstein. 2nd ed. Washington, DC: Catholic University of America Press, 1988.

Rea, Michael C. "The Metaphysics of Original Sin." Chapter 14 in van Inwagen and Zimmerman, *Persons: Human and Divine*.

———. "Realism in Theology and Metaphysics." Chapter 14 in *Belief and Metaphysics*, edited by Conor Cunningham and Peter M. Candler Jr. Veritas. London: SCM, 2007.

Reeves, Michael, and Hans Madueme. "Threads in a Seamless Garment: Original Sin in Systematic Theology." Chapter 10 in Madueme and Reeves, *Adam, the Fall, and Original Sin: Theological, Biblical, and Scientific Perspectives*.

Reid, Thomas. "Of Mr. Locke's Account of Our Personal Identity." Chapter 7 in Perry, *Personal Identity*.

Richards, Jay Wesley. "Be Fruitful and Multiply: Work and Anthropology." Chapter 7 in Loftin and Dimsdale, *Work: Theological Foundations and Practical Implications*.

Roberts, Christopher C. *Creation and Covenant: The Significance of Sexual Difference in the Moral Theology of Marriage*. New York: T&T Clark, 2007.

Rogers, Jack. *Jesus, the Bible, and Homosexuality: Explode the Myths, Heal the Church*. Louisville: Westminster John Knox, 2009.

Rorty, Richard. *Philosophy and the Mirror of Nature*. Princeton: Princeton University Press, 1979.

Rosemann, Philipp W. *Peter Lombard*. Great Medieval Thinkers. Oxford: Oxford University Press, 2004.

Rosner, Brian S. *Known by God: A Biblical Theology of Personal Identity*. Grand Rapids: Zondervan, 2017.

Sanders, Fred. *The Deep Things of God: How the Trinity Changes Everything*. Wheaton: Crossway, 2010.

Sartre, Jean-Paul. *No Exit, and Three Other Plays*. Translated by Stuart Gilbert. New York: Vintage International, 1989.

Savulescu, Julian, and Nick Bostrom, eds. *Human Enhancement*. Oxford: Oxford University Press, 2011.

Sayers, Dorothy. *The Mind of the Maker*. San Francisco: Harper & Row, 1979.

Schwarz, Hans. *The Human Being: A Theological Anthropology*. Grand Rapids: Eerdmans, 2013.

Schwöbel, Christoph, and Colin E. Gunton, eds. *Persons, Divine and Human: King's College Essays in Theological Anthropology*. Edinburgh: T&T Clark, 1991.

Scroggs, Robin. *The Last Adam: A Study in Pauline Anthropology*. Philadelphia: Fortress, 1966.

Shaw, Ed. *Same-Sex Attraction and the Church: The Surprising Plausibility of the Celibate Life*. Downers Grove, IL: InterVarsity, 2015.

Shedd, William, G. T. *Dogmatic Theology*. Edited by Alan W. Gomes. 3rd ed. Phillipsburg, NJ: P&R, 2003.

Sherlock, Charles. *The Doctrine of Humanity*. Contours of Christian Theology. Downers Grove, IL: InterVarsity, 1996.

Shoemaker, David. *Personal Identity and Ethics: A Brief Introduction*. Peterborough, ON: Broadview, 2009.

Song, Robert. *Covenant and Calling: Towards a Theology of Same-Sex Relationships*. London: SCM, 2014.

Sowell, Thomas. *Black Rednecks and White Liberals*. San Francisco: Encounter Books, 2005.

Spencer, Andrew J. "The Inherent Value of Work." *Journal of Biblical and Theological Studies* 2, no. 1 (2017): 52–65.

Spiegel, James S. "Moral Heresy." *Philosophia Christi* 15, no. 2 (Winter 2013): 401–13.

Sprinkle, Preston, ed. *Two Views on Homosexuality, the Bible, and the Church*. Grand Rapids: Zondervan, 2016.

Stamps, R. Lucas. "Atonement in Gethsemane: The Necessity of Dyothelitism for the Atonement." Chapter 6 in Crisp and Sanders, *Locating Atonement: Explorations in Constructive Dogmatics*.

Stanglin, Keith D., and Thomas H. McCall. *Jacob Arminius: Theologian of Grace*. Oxford: Oxford University Press, 2012.

Staniloae, Dumitru. *The Experience of God: Orthodox Dogmatic Theology*. Vol. 2, *The World: Creation and Deification*. Bucharest: SVC Press, 2002.

Steiner, Richard C. *Disembodied Souls: The Nefesh in Israel and Kindred Spirits in the Ancient Near East, with an Appendix on the Katumawa Inscription*. Society of Biblical Literature Ancient Near East Monographs 11. Atlanta: SBL Press, 2015.

Steinhart, Eric. "Digital Afterlives." Chapter 13 in Nagasawa and Matheson, *The Palgrave Handbook of the Afterlife*.

Steward, Helen. *A Metaphysics for Freedom.* New York: Oxford University Press, 2012.

Strobel, Kyle. "Jonathan Edwards and the Polemics of *Theosis.*" *Harvard Theological Review* 105, no. 3 (July 2012): 259–79.

———. "Jonathan Edwards' Reformed Doctrine of the Beatific Vision." Chapter 11 in *Jonathan Edwards and Scotland*, edited by Kenneth Minkema, Adrian Cornelis Neele, and Kelly Van Andel. Edinburgh: Dunedin Academic Press, 2011.

Stubenberg, Leopold. "Neutral Monism." *Stanford Encyclopedia of Philosophy.* Edited by Edward N. Zalta. Winter 2017 ed. https://plato.stanford.edu/archives/win 2017/entries/neutral-monism/.

Stump, Eleonore. *Aquinas.* Arguments of the Philosophers. New York: Routledge, 2003.

———. "Orthodoxy and Heresy." *Faith and Philosophy* 16 (1999): 147–63.

Sutton, Ray R. *Signed, Sealed and Delivered: A Study of Holy Baptism.* Houston: Classical Anglican Press, 2001.

Swamidass, Joshua S. "The Overlooked Science of Genealogical Ancestry." *Perspectives on Science and Christian Faith* 70, no. 1 (March 2018): 19–35.

Swinburne, Richard. *The Christian God.* Oxford: Clarendon, 1994.

———. *The Evolution of the Soul.* Rev. ed. Oxford: Clarendon, 1997.

———, ed. *Free Will and Modern Science.* British Academy Original Paperbacks. Oxford: Oxford University Press, 2011.

———. *Mind, Brain, and Free Will.* Oxford: Oxford University Press, 2013.

———. "Personal Identity: The Dualist Theory." Chapter 37 in *Metaphysics: The Big Questions*, edited by Peter van Inwagen and Dean W. Zimmerman. Oxford: Blackwell, 1998.

———. *Responsibility and Atonement.* Oxford: Oxford University Press, 1989.

———. *Revelation: From Metaphor to Analogy.* 2nd ed. Oxford: Oxford University Press, 2007.

———. "A Theodicy of Heaven and Hell." In *The Existence and Nature of God*, edited by Alfred Freddoso, 37–54. University of Notre Dame Studies in the Philosophy of Religion 3. Notre Dame, IN: University of Notre Dame Press, 1983.

Talbott, Thomas. "The Doctrine of Everlasting Punishment." *Faith and Philosophy* 7, no. 1 (2000): 19–43.

Taliaferro, Charles. *Consciousness and the Mind of God.* Cambridge: Cambridge University Press, 2004.

———. "Human Nature, Personal Identity, and Eschatology." Chapter 31 in Walls, *The Oxford Handbook of Eschatology.*

———. "The Soul of the Matter." Chapter 1 in *The Soul Hypothesis: Investigations into the Existence of the Soul*, edited by Mark C. Baker and Stewart Goetz. London: Continuum, 2011.

Taliaferro, Charles, and Jil Evans. *The Image in Mind: Theism, Naturalism, and the Imagination.* Continuum Studies in Philosophy of Religion. New York: Continuum, 2011.

Tallis, Raymond. *Aping Mankind: Neuromania, Darwinists and the Misrepresentation of Humanity.* London: Routledge, 2011.

Tanner, Kathryn. *Christ the Key.* Current Issues in Theology. Cambridge: Cambridge University Press, 2010.

———. *Jesus, Humanity and the Trinity: A Brief Systematic Theology.* Minneapolis: Fortress, 2001.

———. *Theories of Culture: A New Agenda for Theology.* Minneapolis: Fortress, 1997.

Taylor, John. *The Scripture-Doctrine of Original Sin Proposed to Free and Candid Examination.* London: J. Waugh, 1740.

Tennant, F. R. *The Origin and Propagation of Sin.* Cambridge: Cambridge University Press, 1902.

Thiselton, Anthony. *The First Epistle to the Corinthians.* New International Greek Testament Commentary. Grand Rapids: Eerdmans, 2000.

Timpe, Kevin, and Audra Jenson. "Free Will and the Stages of Theological Anthropology." Chapter 18 in Farris and Taliaferro, *The Ashgate Research Companion to Theological Anthropology.*

Torrance, T. F. *The Christian Doctrine of God: One Being Three Persons.* Edinburgh: T&T Clark, 1996.

Toth, L. "Gender." In *New Dictionary of Theology: Historical and Systematic,* edited by Martin Davie et al., 358–59. Downers Grove, IL: InterVarsity, 2016.

Tucker, Chris. "Phenomenal Conservatism and Evidentialism in Religious Epistemology." Chapter 4 in *Evidence and Religious Belief,* edited by Kelly James Clark and Raymond J. VanArragon. Oxford: Oxford University Press, 2011.

Turner, James T., Jr. "How to Lose the Intermediate State without Losing Your Soul." Chapter 14 in Loftin and Farris, *Christian Physicalism? Philosophical Theological Criticisms.*

———. "Temple Theology, Holistic Eschatology, and the Imago Dei: An Analytic Prolegomenon." *TheoLogica* 2, no. 1 (2018): 95–114.

Turretin, Francis. *Institutes of Elenctic Theology.* Translated by George Musgrave Giger. Edited by James T. Dennison. 3 vols. Phillipsburg, NJ: P&R, 1997.

Tushnet, Eve. *Gay and Catholic: Accepting My Sexuality, Finding Community, Living My Faith.* Notre Dame, IN: Ave Maria Press, 2014.

Udry, J. Richard. "Biological Limits of Gender Construction." *American Sociological Review* 65, no. 3 (June 2000): 443–57.

United Church of Christ. *Book of Worship: United Church of Christ.* Cleveland, OH: United Church Press, 2012.

van der Kooi, Cornelis, and Gijsbert van den Brink. *Christian Dogmatics: An Introduction*. Translated by Reinder Bruinsma and James D. Bratt. Grand Rapids: Eerdmans, 2017.

VanDrunen, David. *Divine Covenants and Moral Order: A Biblical Theology of Natural Law*. Grand Rapids: Eerdmans, 2014.

Vanhoozer, Kevin J. "A Drama-of-Redemption Model." Chapter 3 in *Four Views on Moving beyond the Bible to Theology*, edited by Gary T. Meadors. Grand Rapids: Zondervan, 2009.

van Huyssteen, J. Wentzel. *Alone in the World? Human Uniqueness in Science and Theology*. Grand Rapids: Eerdmans, 2006.

van Inwagen, Peter. *Material Beings*. Ithaca, NY: Cornell University Press, 1990.

van Inwagen, Peter, and Dean Zimmerman, eds. *Persons: Human and Divine*. Oxford: Oxford University Press, 2006.

Velde, Dolf te, ed. *Synopsis of a Purer Theology*. Vol. 1, *Disputations 1–23*. Translated by Reimer A. Faber. Leiden: Brill, 2015.

Vidu, Adonis. *Atonement, Law, and Justice: The Cross in Historical and Cultural Contexts*. Grand Rapids: Baker Academic, 2014.

Vines, Matthew. *God and the Gay Christian: The Biblical Case in Support of Same-Sex Relationships*. New York: Convergent Books, 2014.

Visala, Aku. "Theological Anthropology and the Cognitive Sciences." Chapter 4 in Farris and Taliaferro, *The Ashgate Research Companion to Theological Anthropology*.

Volf, Miroslav. "Work as Cooperation with God." Chapter 7 in Loftin and Dimsdale, *Work: Theological Foundations and Practical Implications*.

———. *Work in the Spirit: Toward a Theology of Work*. Eugene, OR: Wipf & Stock, 2001.

Vorster, Nico. *The Brightest Mirror of God's Works: John Calvin's Theological Anthropology*. Eugene, OR: Pickwick, 2019.

Wainwright, William. "Jonathan Edwards." *Stanford Encyclopedia of Philosophy*. Edited by Edward N. Zalta. Winter 2016 ed. https://plato.stanford.edu/archives/win2016/entries/edwards/.

Wallace, Peter J. "The Defense of the Forgotten Center: Charles Hodge and the Enigma of Emancipation in Antebellum America." *Journal of Presbyterian History* 75, no. 3 (Fall 1997): 165–77.

Walls, Jerry L. *Heaven, Hell, and Purgatory: Rethinking Things That Matter Most*. Grand Rapids: Brazos, 2015.

———. *Heaven: The Logic of Eternal Joy*. Oxford: Oxford University Press, 2002.

———. "A Hell of a Choice: Reply to Talbott." *Religious Studies* 40 (2004): 203–16.

———. "A Hell of a Dilemma: Rejoinder to Talbott." *Religious Studies* 40 (2004): 225–27.

———. *Hell: The Logic of Damnation*. Notre Dame, IN: University of Notre Dame Press, 1992.

———, ed. *The Oxford Handbook of Eschatology*. Oxford Handbooks in Religion and Theology. Oxford: Oxford University Press, 2008.

———. "A Philosophical Critique of Talbott's Universalism." Chapter 6 in *Universal Salvation? The Current Debate*, edited by Robin A. Parry and Christopher H. Partridge. Grand Rapids: Eerdmans, 2003.

———. *Purgatory: The Logic of Total Transformation*. Oxford: Oxford University Press, 2011.

Walls, Jerry L., Jeremy Neill, and David Baggett, eds. *Venus and Virtue: Celebrating Sex and Seeking Sanctification*. Eugene, OR: Cascade Books, 2017.

Walton, John H. *Genesis 1 as Ancient Cosmology*. Winona Lake, IN: Eisenbrauns, 2011.

———. *The Lost World of Adam and Eve: Genesis 2–3 and the Human Origins Debate*. Downers Grove, IL: IVP Academic, 2015.

Ware, Timothy. *The Orthodox Church*. New York: Penguin, 1993.

Warfield, B. B. *The Significance of the Westminster Standards as a Creed*. New York: Charles Scribner's Sons, 1898.

Webb, Stephen H. *Jesus Christ, Eternal God: Heavenly Flesh and the Metaphysics of Matter*. Oxford: Oxford University Press, 2011.

Webster, John. *Confessing God: Essays in Christian Dogmatics II*. 2nd ed. London: Bloomsbury T&T Clark, 2016.

Wilhelm, Joseph. "The Nicene Creed." *The Catholic Encyclopedia*. Vol. 11. New York: Robert Appleton, 1911. http://www.newadvent.org/cathen/11049a.htm.

Williams, N. P. *The Ideas of the Fall and of Original Sin: A Historical and Critical Study*. London: Longmans, Green, 1927.

Witherington, Ben, III. *Conflict and Community in Corinth: A Socio-rhetorical Commentary on 1 and 2 Corinthians*. Grand Rapids: Eerdmans, 1995.

Witsius, Herman. *Conciliatory or Irenical Animadversions on the Controversies Agitated in Britain*. Translated by Thomas Bell. Glasgow: W. Lang, 1807.

Woznicki, Christopher. "Atonement and Anthropology: T. F. Torrance's Doctrine of Atonement as a Test Case." Evangelical Philosophy Society, 2018. https://www.epsociety.org/userfiles/CW_Atonement%20and%20Anthropology%20[final].pdf.

Wright, N. T. *Jesus and the Victory of God*. Christian Origins and the Question of God 2. Minneapolis: Fortress, 1996.

———. *The Resurrection of the Son of God*. Christian Origins and the Question of God 3. Minneapolis: Fortress, 2003.

———. *Surprised by Hope: Rethinking Heaven, the Resurrection, and the Mission of the Church*. San Francisco: HarperOne, 2008.

Wyma, Keith D. "Innocent Sinfulness, Guilty Sin: Original Sin and Divine Justice." In *Christian Faith and the Problem of Evil*, edited by Peter van Inwagen, 263–76. Grand Rapids: Eerdmans, 2004.

Young, Frances M. *From Nicaea to Chalcedon: A Guide to the Literature and Its Background*. 2nd ed. Grand Rapids: Baker Academic, 2010.

Zack, Naomi. *The Ethics and Mores of Race: Equality after the History of Philosophy*. Lanham, MD: Rowman & Littlefield, 2011.

———. *Philosophy of Science and Race*. New York: Routledge, 2002.

———. *Race and Mixed Race*. Philadelphia: Temple University Press, 1993.

———. *White Privilege and Black Rights: The Injustice of U.S. Police Racial Profiling and Homicide*. Lanham, MD: Rowman & Littlefield, 2015.

Ziegler, Philip G., ed. *Eternal God, Eternal Life: Theological Investigations into the Concept of Immortality*. New York: Bloomsbury T&T Clark, 2017.

Suggested Readings

Apart from theological anthropology in general in systematic theologies, see below for a fairly important representative list on the various topics within the study of theological anthropology. Many of these resources constitute the background of the present study but have not necessarily been cited because they are not directly relevant or quoted herein. The list is useful for researchers desiring to chase down various topics. Included are several philosophical sources that serve as important background for engaging in analytic theological anthropology.

Classical Readings in Theological Anthropology

Cortez, Marc, and Michael P. Jensen, eds. *T&T Clark Reader in Theological Anthropology*. New York: Bloomsbury Academic, 2017.

McFarland, Ian A., ed. *Creation and Humanity: The Sources of Christian Theology*. Louisville: Westminster John Knox, 2009.

Philosophy of Mind

Armstrong, David M. *The Mind-Body Problem: An Opinionated Introduction*. Boulder, CO: Westview, 1999.

Augustine. *On the Trinity, Books 8–15*. Edited by Gareth B. Matthews. Translated by Stephen McKenna. Cambridge Texts in the History of Philosophy. Cambridge: Cambridge University Press, 2002.

Baker, Lynne Rudder. *Naturalism and the First-Person Perspective*. Oxford: Oxford University Press, 2013.

———. *Persons and Bodies: A Constitution View*. Cambridge: Cambridge University Press, 2000.

Baker, Mark C., and Stewart Goetz, eds. *The Soul Hypothesis: Investigations into the Existence of the Soul*. London: Continuum, 2011.

Brower, Jeffrey E. *Aquinas's Ontology of the Material World: Change, Hylomorphism, and Material Objects*. Oxford: Oxford University Press, 2014.

Descartes, René. *Meditations on First Philosophy: With Selections from the Objections and Replies*. Edited by John Cottingham. Cambridge Texts in the History of Philosophy. Cambridge: Cambridge University Press, 1996.

Foster, John. *The Immaterial Self: A Defence of the Cartesian Dualist Conception of the Mind*. International Library of Philosophy. London: Routledge, 1991.

Göcke, Benedikt Paul, ed. *After Physicalism*. Notre Dame, IN: University of Notre Dame Press, 2012.

Goetz, Stewart, and Charles Taliaferro. *A Brief History of the Soul*. Brief Histories of Philosophy. Malden, MA: Wiley-Blackwell, 2011.

Hart, W. D. *The Engines of the Soul*. Cambridge Studies in Philosophy. Cambridge: Cambridge University Press, 1988.

Hasker, William. *The Emergent Self*. Ithaca, NY: Cornell University Press, 1999.

Lowe, E. J. *An Introduction to the Philosophy of Mind*. Cambridge: Cambridge University Press, 2000.

Lycan, William. "Giving Dualism Its Due." *Australasian Journal of Philosophy* 87, no. 4 (2009): 551–63.

Moreland, J. P., and Scott B. Rae, *Body and Soul: Human Nature and the Crisis in Ethics*. Downers Grove, IL: InterVarsity, 2000.

Olson, Eric T. *The Human Animal: Personal Identity without Psychology*. Philosophy of Mind Series. New York: Oxford University Press, 1997.

Petrus, Klaus, ed. *On Human Persons*. Metaphysical Research 1. Frankfurt: Ontos, 2003.

Popper, Karl, and John C. Eccles. *The Self and Its Brain: An Argument for Interactionism*. New York: Routledge & Kegan Paul, 1983.

Ryle, Gilbert. *The Concept of Mind*. New York: Barnes & Noble, 1949.

Searle, John R. *Mind: A Brief Introduction*. Fundamentals of Philosophy. Oxford: Oxford University Press, 2004.

Swinburne, Richard. *Mind, Brain, and Free Will*. Oxford: Oxford University Press, 2013.

van Inwagen, Peter. *Material Beings*. Ithaca, NY: Cornell University Press, 1990.

Theological Anthropology

Cortez, Marc. *Theological Anthropology: A Guide for the Perplexed*. New York: Bloomsbury T&T Clark, 2010.

Farris, Joshua R., and Charles Taliaferro, eds. *The Ashgate Research Companion to Theological Anthropology*. New York: Routledge, 2016.

Hoekema, Anthony A. *Created in God's Image*. Grand Rapids: Eerdmans, 1994.

Jewett, Robert. *Paul's Anthropological Terms: A Study of Their Use in Conflict Settings*. Arbeiten zur Geschichte des antiken Judentums und des Urchristentums 10. Leiden: Brill, 1971.

Lints, Richard, Michael S. Horton, and Mark R. Talbot, eds. *Personal Identity in Theological Perspective*. Grand Rapids: Eerdmans, 2006.

Robinson, H. Wheeler. *The Christian Doctrine of Man*. Edinburgh: T&T Clark, 1911.

Ross, Susan A. *Anthropology: Seeking Light and Beauty*. Engaging Theology: Catholic Perspectives. Collegeville, MN: Liturgical Press, 2012.

Human Constitution

Aquinas, Thomas. *On Being and Essence*. Translated by Armand Maurer. Rev. ed. Mediaeval Sources in Translation 1. Toronto: Pontifical Institute of Mediaeval Studies, 1968.

Aune, David E. "Anthropological Duality in the Eschatology of 2 Cor. 4:16–5:10." Chapter 10 in *Paul beyond the Judaism/Hellenism Divide*, edited by Troels Engberg-Pedersen. Louisville: Westminster John Knox, 2001.

Brown, Warren S., Nancey Murphy, and H. Newton Malony, eds. *Whatever Happened to the Soul? Scientific and Theological Portraits of Human Nature*. Theology and the Sciences. Minneapolis: Fortress, 1998.

Cooper, John. *Body, Soul, and Life Everlasting: Biblical Anthropology and the Monism-Dualism Debate*. Grand Rapids: Eerdmans, 2000.

Corcoran, Kevin. *Rethinking Human Nature: A Christian Materialist Alternative to the Soul*. Grand Rapids: Baker Academic, 2006.

Farris, Joshua R. *The Soul of Theological Anthropology: A Cartesian Exploration*. Routledge New Critical Thinking in Religion, Theology and Biblical Studies. New York: Routledge, 2017.

———. "Substance Dualism and Theological Anthropology: A Theological Argument for a Simple View of Persons." *Philosophy and Theology* 27, no. 1 (2015): 107–26.

Green, Joel B. *Body, Soul, and Human Life: The Nature of Humanity in the Bible*. Grand Rapids: Baker Academic, 2008.

———, ed. *What about the Soul? Neuroscience and Christian Anthropology*. Nashville: Abingdon, 2004.

Green, Joel B., and Stuart L. Palmer, eds. *In Search of the Soul: Four Views on the Mind-Body Problem*. Downers Grove, IL: InterVarsity, 2005.

Gundry, Robert H. *Sōma in Biblical Theology: With Emphasis on Pauline Anthropology*. Society for New Testament Studies Monograph Series 29. Cambridge: Cambridge University Press, 1976.

Jacobs, Nathan A. "Are Created Spirits Composed of Matter and Form? A Defense of Pneumatic Hylomorphism." *Philosophia Christi* 14, no. 1 (2012): 79–108.

Jeeves, Malcolm. *Human Nature: Reflections on the Integration of Psychology and Christianity*. Philadelphia: Templeton Foundation Press, 2006.

Lee, Patrick, and Robert P. George. *Body-Self Dualism in Contemporary Ethics and Politics*. Cambridge: Cambridge University Press, 2008.

Murphy, Nancey. *Bodies and Souls, or Spirited Bodies?* Current Issues in Theology. Cambridge: Cambridge University Press, 2006.

Ward, Keith. *In Defence of the Soul*. Oxford: Oneworld, 1998.

Divine and Human Agency

Farris, Joshua R. "Discovering God and Soul: A Reappraisal of and Appreciation for Cartesian Natural Theology." *Philosophia Christi* 16, no. 1 (2014): 37–57.

Grenz, Stanley J. *The Social God and the Relational Self: A Trinitarian Theology of the* Imago Dei. Louisville: Westminster John Knox, 2001.

Moreland, J. P. *Consciousness and the Existence of God: A Theistic Argument*. Routledge Studies in the Philosophy of Religion. New York: Routledge, 2008.

———. *The Recalcitrant* Imago Dei: *Human Persons and the Failure of Naturalism*. Veritas Series. London: SCM, 2009.

Morris, Thomas V. *Our Idea of God: An Introduction to Philosophical Theology*. Contours of Christian Philosophy. Vancouver: Regent College Publishing, 1997.

Schwöbel, Christoph, and Colin E. Gunton, eds. *Persons, Divine and Human: King's College Essays in Theological Anthropology*. Edinburgh: T&T Clark, 1991.

Vanhoozer, Kevin J. *Remythologizing Theology: Divine Action, Passion, and Authorship*. Cambridge Studies in Christian Doctrine 18. Cambridge: Cambridge University Press, 2010.

Free Will

Burrell, David B. *Freedom and Creation in Three Traditions*. Notre Dame, IN: University of Notre Dame Press, 1993.

McCall, Thomas. "Analytic Theology and Christian Scripture." Chapter 2 in *An Invitation to Analytic Christian Theology*. Downers Grove, IL: IVP Academic, 2015.

Timpe, Kevin. *Free Will and Philosophical Theology*. Bloomsbury Studies in the Philosophy of Religion. London: Bloomsbury, 2015.

Timpe, Kevin, and Daniel Speak, eds. *Free Will and Theism: Connections, Contingencies, and Concerns*. Oxford: Oxford University Press, 2016.

Imago Dei

Farris, Joshua R. "An Immaterial Substance View: *Imago Dei* in Creation and Redemption." *Heythrop Journal* 58, no. 1 (January 2017): 108–23.

Harrison, Nonna Verna, *God's Many-Splendored Image: Theological Anthropology for Christian Formation*. Grand Rapids: Baker Academic, 2010.

Hoekema, Anthony A. *Created in God's Image*. Grand Rapids: Eerdmans, 1994.

Kilner, John F. *Dignity and Destiny: Humanity in the Image of God*. Grand Rapids: Eerdmans, 2015.

Mouw, Richard. "The Imago Dei and Philosophical Anthropology." *Christian Scholar's Review* 41, no. 3 (Spring 2012): 253–66.

Peterson, Ryan S. *The* Imago Dei *as Human Identity: A Theological Interpretation*. Winona Lake, IN: Eisenbrauns, 2016.

Adam

Barrett, Matthew, and Ardel B. Caneday, eds. *Four Views on the Historical Adam*. Grand Rapids: Zondervan, 2013.

Madueme, Hans, and Michael Reeves, eds. *Adam, the Fall, and Original Sin: Theological, Biblical, and Scientific Perspectives*. Grand Rapids: Baker Academic, 2014.

Walton, John H. *The Lost World of Adam and Eve: Genesis 2–3 and the Human Origins Debate*. Downers Grove, IL: IVP Academic, 2015.

Natural and Social Sciences

Baker, Mark C., and Stewart Goetz, eds. *The Soul Hypothesis: Investigations into the Existence of the Soul*. London: Continuum, 2011.

Brown, Warren S., Nancey Murphy, and H. Newton Malony, eds. *Whatever Happened to the Soul? Scientific and Theological Portraits of Human Nature*. Theology and the Sciences. Minneapolis: Fortress, 1998.

Churchland, Paul. *Matter and Consciousness: A Contemporary Introduction to the Philosophy of Mind*. Cambridge, MA: MIT Press, 1984.

Green, Joel B., ed. *What about the Soul? Neuroscience and Christian Anthropology*. Nashville: Abingdon, 2004.

Lemons, J. Derrick, ed. *Theologically Engaged Anthropology*. Oxford: Oxford University Press, 2018.

Welker, Michael, ed. *The Depth of the Human Person: A Multidisciplinary Approach*. Grand Rapids: Eerdmans, 2014.

Human Origins

Argyle, A. W. "The Christian Doctrine of the Origin of the Soul." *Scottish Journal of Theology* 18, no. 3 (1965): 273–93.

Augustine. *Confessions*. Translated by Henry Chadwick. World's Classics. Oxford: Oxford University Press, 1992.

Burnell, Peter. *The Augustinian Person*. Washington, DC: Catholic University of America Press, 2005.

Farris, Joshua R. "Considering Souls of the Past for Today: Soul Origins, Anthropology, and Contemporary Theology." *Neue Zeitschrift für systematische Theologie und Religionsphilosophie* 57, no. 3 (September 2015): 368–98.

————. "Creational Problems for Soul-Emergence from Matter." *Neue Zeitschrift für systematische Theologie und Religionsphilosophie* 60, no. 3 (September 2018): 406–27.

————. "Emergent Creationism: Another Option in the Origin of the Soul Debate." *Religious Studies* 50 (2014): 321–39.

————. "Safe House Souls: Bodily Charged Souls—Responding to Hasker's 'Souls, Beastly and Human.'" *Neue Zeitschrift für systematische Theologie und Religionsphilosophie* 58, no. 4 (December 2016): 549–73.

Himma, Kenneth Einar. "Explaining Why This Body Gives Rise to Me qua Subject Instead of Someone Else: An Argument for Classical Substance Dualism." *Religious Studies* 47 (2011): 431–48.

Jones, David Albert. *The Soul of the Embryo: An Enquiry into the Status of the Human Embryo in the Christian Tradition*. New York: Continuum, 2006.

O'Connell, Robert J. *The Origin of the Soul in St. Augustine's Later Works*. New York: Fordham University Press, 1987.

Swinburne, Richard. *The Evolution of the Soul*. Rev. ed. Oxford: Clarendon, 1997.

Tertullian. *A Treatise on the Soul*. In *Latin Christianity: Its Founder, Tertullian: I. Apologetic; II. Anti-Marcion; III. Ethical*, 181–235. Vol. 3 of *Ante-Nicene Fathers*. Edited by Philip Schaff. 1885. Reprint, Grand Rapids: Eerdmans, 1981.

Yates, John C. "The Origin of the Soul: New Light on an Old Conception." *Evangelical Quarterly* 61, no. 1 (1989): 121–40.

Sin

Cortez, Marc, Joshua R. Farris, and S. Mark Hamilton, eds. *Being Saved: Explorations in Human Salvation*. London: SCM, 2018.

Farris, Joshua R. "Originating Souls and Original Sin: An Initial Exploration of Dualism, Anthropology, and Sins Transmission." *Neue Zeitschrift für systematische Theologie und Religionsphilosophie* 58, no. 1 (May 2016): 39–56.

McCall, Thomas H. *Against God and Nature: The Doctrine of Sin*. Foundations of Evangelical Theology. Wheaton: Crossway, 2019.

Odo of Tournai. *On Original Sin; and, A Disputation with the Jew, Leo, concerning the Advent of Christ, the Son of God: Two Theological Treatises*. Translated by Irven M. Resnick. Middle Ages Series. Philadelphia: University of Pennsylvania Press, 1994.

Williams, N. P. *The Ideas of the Fall and of Original Sin: A Historical and Critical Study*. London: Longmans, Green, 1927.

Gender, Sexuality, and Marriage

Coakley, Sarah. *God, Sexuality, and the Self: An Essay "On the Trinity."* Cambridge: Cambridge University Press, 2013.

Johnson, Elizabeth A. *She Who Is: The Mystery of God in Feminist Theological Discourse*. New York: Crossroad, 2002.

McFague, Sallie. *Models of God: Theology for an Ecological, Nuclear Age*. Minneapolis: Fortress, 1987.

Scott, Kieran, and Michael Warren, eds. *Perspectives on Marriage: A Reader*. 3rd ed. Oxford: Oxford University Press, 2007.

Thatcher, Adrian. *The Oxford Handbook of Theology, Sexuality, and Gender*. Oxford: Oxford University Press, 2015.

Complementarianism and Egalitarianism

Lee-Barnewall, Michelle. *Neither Complementarian nor Egalitarian: A Kingdom Corrective to the Evangelical Gender Debate*. Grand Rapids: Baker Academic, 2016.

Pierce, Ronald W., and Rebecca Merrill Groothuis, eds. *Discovering Biblical Equality: Complementarity without Hierarchy*. Downers Grove, IL: InterVarsity, 2004.

Piper, John, and Wayne Grudem. *Recovering Biblical Manhood and Womanhood: A Response to Evangelical Feminism*. Wheaton: Crossway, 2012.

Body Theology

Alison, Gregg. "Toward a Theology of Human Embodiment." *Southern Baptist Journal of Theology* 13, no. 2 (2009): 4–17.

John Paul II. *Man and Woman He Created Them: A Theology of the Body*. Boston: Pauline Books & Media, 2006.

Nelson, James B. *Body Theology*. Louisville: Westminster John Knox, 1992.

Ethnicity and Race

Carter, J. Kameron. *Race: A Theological Account*. Oxford: Oxford University Press, 2008.

Cone, James. *A Black Theology of Liberation*. Maryknoll, NY: Orbis, 2010.

Hays, J. Daniel. *From Every People and Nation: A Biblical Theology of Race*. Downers Grove, IL: InterVarsity, 2003.

Jennings, Willie James. *The Christian Imagination: Theology and the Origins of Race*. New Haven: Yale University Press, 2011.

Sowell, Thomas. *Black Rednecks and White Liberals*. San Francisco: Encounter Books, 2005.

Disability

Brock, Brian, and John Swinton, eds. *Disability in the Christian Tradition: A Reader*. Grand Rapids: Eerdmans, 2012.

Reynolds, Thomas E. *Vulnerable Communion: A Theology of Disability and Hospitality*. Grand Rapids: Brazos, 2008.

Yong, Amos. *The Bible, Disability, and the Church: A New Vision of the People of God*. Grand Rapids: Eerdmans, 2011.

Christological Anthropology

Cortez, Marc. *Christological Anthropology in Historical Perspective: Ancient and Contemporary Approaches to Theological Anthropology*. Grand Rapids: Zondervan, 2016.

———. *Embodied Souls, Ensouled Bodies: An Exercise in Christological Anthropology and Its Significance for the Mind/Body Debate*. New York: Bloomsbury T&T Clark, 2008.

Tanner, Kathryn. *Christ the Key*. Current Issues in Theology. Cambridge: Cambridge University Press, 2010.

Death

Alcorn, Randy. *Heaven*. Wheaton: Tyndale House, 2004.

Anderson, Ray S. *Theology, Death and Dying*. Eugene, OR: Wipf & Stock, 2012.

Davies, Douglas J. *The Theology of Death*. London: T&T Clark, 2008.

Ratzinger, Joseph (Benedict XVI). *Eschatology: Death and Eternal Life*. Translated by Michael Waldstein. 2nd ed. Washington, DC: Catholic University of America Press, 1988.

Reichenbach, Bruce R. *Is Man the Phoenix? A Study of Immortality*. Grand Rapids: Eerdmans, 1977.

Toner, Patrick. "Personhood and Death in St. Thomas Aquinas." *History of Philosophy Quarterly* 26, no. 2 (2009): 121–38.

Walls, Jerry L. *Heaven: The Logic of Eternal Joy*. Oxford: Oxford University Press, 2002.

———. *Purgatory: The Logic of Total Transformation*. Oxford: Oxford University Press, 2011.

The Intermediate State

Edwards, Paul, ed. *Immortality*. Amherst, NY: Prometheus Books, 1997.

Johnston, Mark. *Surviving Death*. Princeton: Princeton University Press, 2010.

Yates, Stephen. *Between Death and Resurrection: A Critical Response to Recent Catholic Debate concerning the Intermediate State*. London: Bloomsbury Academic, 2017.

Resurrection Studies

Bynum, Caroline Walker. *The Resurrection of the Body in Western Christianity, 200–1336*. New York: Columbia University Press, 1995.

Corcoran, Kevin J. "Constitution, Resurrection, and Relationality." Chapter 11 in Gasser, *Personal Identity and Resurrection*.

Cullmann, Oscar. *Immortality of the Soul or Resurrection of the Dead? The New Testament Witness*. London: Epworth, 1958.

Dahl, M. E. *The Resurrection of the Body: A Study of I Corinthians 15*. Studies in Biblical Theology 36. London: SCM, 1962.

Eberl, Jason T. "The Metaphysics of Resurrection: Issues of Identity in Thomas Aquinas." *Proceedings of the American Catholic Philosophical Association* 74 (January 2000): 215–30.

Gasser, Georg, ed. *Personal Identity and Resurrection: How Do We Survive Our Death?* Burlington, VT: Ashgate, 2010.

Gregory of Nyssa. "On the Making of Man." In *Gregory of Nyssa: Dogmatic Treatises*, 387–427. Vol. 5 of *Nicene and Post-Nicene Fathers*, series 2. Edited by Philip Schaff and Henry Wace. Grand Rapids: Eerdmans, 1996.

———. *On the Soul and the Resurrection*. Translated by Catharine P. Roth. Popular Patristics. Crestwood, NY: St. Vladimir's Seminary Press, 2002.

Hoekema, Anthony A. "Heaven: Not Just an Eternal Day Off." *Christianity Today*, June 1, 2003. https://www.christianitytoday.com/ct/2003/juneweb-only/6-2-54.0.html.

Levering, Matthew. *Jesus and the Demise of Death: Resurrection, Afterlife, and the Fate of the Christian*. Waco: Baylor University Press, 2012.

McGrath, Alister. *A Brief History of Heaven*. Malden, MA: Blackwell, 2003.

Merricks, Trenton. "How to Live Forever without Saving Your Soul." In *Soul, Body, and Survival: Essays on the Metaphysics of Human Persons*, edited by Kevin Corcoran, 183–200. Ithaca, NY: Cornell University Press, 2006.

Plantinga, Alvin. "Against Materialism." Chapter 19 in *Providence, Scripture, and Resurrection*, edited by Michael Rea. Vol. 2 of *Oxford Readings in Philosophical Theology*. Oxford: Oxford University Press, 2009.

———. "Materialism and Christian Belief." Chapter 4 in *Persons: Human and Divine*, edited by Peter van Inwagen and Dean Zimmerman. Oxford: Oxford University Press, 2006.

van Dyke, Christina. "Human Identity, Immanent Causal Relations, and the Principle of Non-repeatability: Thomas Aquinas on the Bodily Resurrection." *Religious Studies* 43 (2007): 373–94.

Wright, N. T. "Mind, Spirit, Soul and Body: All for One and One for All—Reflections on Paul's Anthropology in His Complex Contexts." Chapter 28 in *Pauline Perspectives: Essays on Paul, 1978–2013*. Minneapolis: Fortress, 2013.

———. *The Resurrection of the Son of God*. Christian Origins and the Question of God 3. Minneapolis: Fortress, 2003.

———. *Surprised by Hope: Rethinking Heaven, the Resurrection, and the Mission of the Church*. San Francisco: HarperOne, 2008.

Beatific Vision / Theosis

Canlis, Julie. *Calvin's Ladder: A Spiritual Theology of Ascent and Ascension*. Grand Rapids: Eerdmans, 2010.

Kapic, Kelly M., ed. *Sanctification: Explorations in Theology and Practice*. Downers Grove, IL: IVP Academic, 2014.

Lossky, Vladimir. *The Vision of God*. Translated by Asheleigh Moorhouse. Crestwood, NY: St. Vladimir's Seminary Press, 1983.

Strobel, Kyle. "Jonathan Edwards and the Polemics of *Theosis*." *Harvard Theological Review* 105, no. 3 (July 2012): 259–79.

———. "Jonathan Edwards's Reformed Doctrine of Theosis." *Harvard Theological Review* 109, no. 3 (July 2016): 371–99.

Transhumanism

Estes, Douglas. *Braving the Future: Christian Faith in a World of Limitless Tech*. Harrisonburg, VA: Herald, 2018.

Garreau, Joel. *Radical Evolution: The Promise and Peril of Enhancing Our Minds, Our Bodies—and What It Means to Be Human*. New York: Broadway Books, 2006.

Hansell Gregory R., and William Grassie, eds. *H+/-: Transhumanism and Its Critics*. Philadelphia: Metanexus Institute, 2011.

Herzfeld, Noreen L. *In Our Image: Artificial Intelligence and the Human Spirit*. Minneapolis: Fortress, 2002.

Kaku, Michio. *The Future of the Mind: The Scientific Quest to Understand, Enhance, and Empower the Mind*. New York: Doubleday, 2014.

Mahon, Peter. *Posthumanism: A Guide for the Perplexed*. New York: Bloomsbury Academic, 2017.

More, Max, and Natasha Vita-More. *The Transhumanist Reader: Classical and Contemporary Essays on the Science, Technology, and Philosophy of the Human Future*. Chichester: Wiley-Blackwell, 2013.

Savulescu, Julian, and Nick Bostrom, eds. *Human Enhancement*. Oxford: Oxford University Press, 2011.

Young, Simon. *Designer Evolution: A Transhumanist Manifesto*. Amherst, NY: Prometheus Books, 2005.

Vocation

Edgar, William. *Created and Creating: A Biblical Theology of Culture*. Downers Grove, IL: IVP Academic, 2017.

Loftin, R. Keith, and Trey Dimsdale, eds. *Work: Theological Foundations and Practical Implications*. London: SCM, 2018.

Author Index

Scripture Index

Old Testament

Genesis

1 82
1–2 xx, 146, 224
1:26 79, 80, 82
1:26–27 61
1:26–28 80, 81, 88, 129, 189, 197, 212, 213, 214
1:26–31 61
1:27 80
1:28 82, 132, 214, 215
2 20, 45
2:2 51
2:7 20, 21n2, 61, 189, 241
2:16–17 118
2:19–20a 81n7
2:20b–24 211
2:22 61
2:23 215
2:24 214, 215, 216
3 xx, 92
3:6 xx, 136
3:17–18 146
3:19 245n37
4:6–7 118
5 82, 106, 107, 189
5:1–3 80, 81, 82, 92, 105
5:2 205
6 92, 137, 138
6:5–7 137
9 106, 107
9:6 82, 92, 105, 129, 177, 189, 197
25:21 203
28:12–13 xx
50:20 113

Exodus

23:25–26 203
33 xx
33:18 256
33:20 256
33:22 256
33:23 257

Leviticus

11:44–45 176
18:22 218, 219n19

Numbers

6:24–26 45

Deuteronomy

6:4 190
6:25 176
11:26–28 119
23:17–18 219

Joshua

24:15 119

1 Samuel

28 25

Job

4:19 95
14:1–2 46

Psalms

8 83, 89, 106
8:4 xiii, 19, 20

8:5 20
8:6 20
27:13 231
42:11 23
51:5 135, 136
82:6–7 278
84:11 113
89:17 113
90:17 113
104:5 188
104:24 113
139:16 113

Ecclesiastes

12:7 20, 95, 189, 245, 245n37

Isaiah

6:1 xx
42:5 21
42:16 203
55:6–7 119

Jeremiah

29:11 1

Ezekiel

13 25

Daniel

7:9 xx

Micah

4:6–7 203

333

Subject Index